CRIME AND CRIMINAL JUSTICE IN A
DECLINING ECONOMY

Crime and Criminal Justice in a Declining Economy

Edited by
Kevin N. Wright
State University of New York at Binghamton

 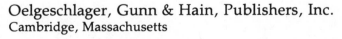

Oelgeschlager, Gunn & Hain, Publishers, Inc.
Cambridge, Massachusetts

International Standard Book Number: 0-89946-046-1

Library of Congress Catalog Card Number: 80-26623

Printed in West Germany

Library of Congress Cataloging in Publication Data
Main entry under title:

Crime and criminal justice in a declining economy.

   Includes bibliographical references and index.
   1. Crime and criminals—United States—Addresses, essays, lectures.   2. Criminal justice, Administration of—United States—Addresses, essays, lectures.
3. United States—Economic conditions—1971–
I. Wright, Kevin N.
HV6789.C683   364′.973   80-26623
ISBN 0-89946-046-1

To Karen, April, and Will

Contents

Preface

For many of the contributors to this volume and for myself, this project began during the spring of 1979. Public awareness of the seriousness of the nation's economic situation was rapidly growing at that time. People were facing double-digit inflation for the first time, interest rates were beginning to shoot up, and the likelihood of recession seemed imminent. The media was replete with analyses of the economic status and future of the nation. We even began to hear murmurs of *depression*. For me as a criminologist and criminal justice policy analyst, the situation raised questions about the effects the economic situation might have on crime and criminal justice. For that reason, I contacted several colleagues who I thought might have an interest in the problem and organized a session to address the topic at the annual meetings of the American Society of Criminology. Early drafts of four papers in this volume were presented at that session.

Since that spring, the number of individuals involved in the project as reflected in this work has grown. As a group, we watched the economy slip into recession during the early part of 1980 and tested our ideas concerning the effects of the economy on crime and criminal justice against what could be observed during that time.

As I write this preface, many governmental officials and a few economic experts are claiming that the end of the recession is near and that the economy is on the mend. Some claim that the 1980s will see the restabilization of the economy and new growth. (One cannot help but wonder if these predictions might be related to the 1980 presidential elections.) Despite the predictions, high inflation still threatens most Americans' buying power. American industry is faced with the weighty problem of obtaining low-cost fuel or acquiring more efficient machines. The futurist Peter Schwartz may have accurately depicted our economic future in a recent interview in *Quest* magazine. He argues that there is a basis for much optimism concerning our economic future; however, he foresees significant economic changes and he believes that the possibility of cataclysmic change such as depression is not entirely remote because the system is presently so unstable.

The essays included in this volume are intended to serve two purposes. First, they provide important empirical and theoretical contributions to our understanding of the etiology of crime and the role that economic factors play in the production of the phenomenon. The selections probably represent the most up-to-date and complete work in this area. Second, each essay develops a scenario of the future of crime and criminal justice in a declining economy. It is hoped that criminal justice policymakers will consider the conjectures and will anticipate predicted problems.

This work would not have been possible without the help and patience of several individuals. Colleagues and administrators in the Center for Social Analysis, School of General Studies, and Department of Political Science at the State University of New York at Binghamton provided me with the time and resources to complete this work. Finally, and most importantly, the contributors were a pleasure to work with and are responsible for any contribution that this volume may make.

K.N.W.
October 14, 1980

Introduction

Concern for the U.S. economy deepened throughout the latter part of the 1970s. Initial forecasts predicted an upcoming general recession; yet by 1979, many economists stated that the occurrence of a depression during the 1980s was both possible and probable. Downturns in the economy, of course, are not unusual. During the past 125 years of monitoring by the National Bureau of Economic Research, the economy has fluctuated in a rollercoaster fashion. Periods of economic expansion have been followed by periods of contraction. The year 1975, following a two-year recession, marked the beginning of an expansion in business which lasted until mid-1980, when the economy once again entered a general recession. This downturn marked the twenty-ninth down-phase since the National Bureau of Economic Research began its monitoring.[1]

The difference between reactions to the economy today and the typical responses to the cyclical trends is the current overall pessimism. Throughout the history of economic analysis, there have been those who have predicted impending disaster; however, today pessimism has extended beyond those few doomsday forecasters such as Howard Ruff[2] to an extensive group of experts. Economists have fairly consistently predicted, and the American people generally believe, that the economy will undergo significant and pervasive change in the near future.

The nature and extent of the probable economic downturn is uncertain. The following description by Kaufmann is, however, a common portrayal of the future status of the economy: "The 1980s will arrive in the United States accompanied by such burdensome economic baggage as rapid price increases and escalating interest rates, slow growth and slackening innovation, capital shortages, and a further erosion of already low productivity. These conditions will be exacerbated by severe labor shortages in certain areas that will push inflation upward while holding growth down."[3] There are various explanations for the state of the economy; a dominant theme, succinctly expressed by Levine, is that "the once mighty U.S. economy, following years of neglect and overuse, is aging and tired."[4]

The possibility of a worse economic situation in the near future raises concerns in a number of areas. Most obviously, economic adversity poses a threat to the economic standard of living currently sustained by many Americans. At worst, it could mean unemployment for some families; for other families, a significant reduction in buying power might result in a less "comfortable" lifestyle.

Another area in which the possibility of economic adversity raises concern involves the problem of crime. This concern can be expressed in terms of a number of unanswered questions: will the rate of crime increase as the economy worsens? If so, at what rate will it increase? Will certain categories of crime, such as property offenses in contrast to personal offenses, be more adversely affected? What will the general reaction of the public be to any change in the incidence of crime? Will the agencies of the criminal justice system be able to respond to these changes? Will they be able to contain them or not? We must answer these and other questions concerning the relationship of economic adversity and criminality if potential problems are to be anticipated and appropriate strategies for their resolution are to be developed. The answers are vital if social control is to be maintained during a time of crisis and upheaval.

There are at least four economic factors which could have a significant impact on crime and the criminal justice system. Levels of productivity, which have been described as the best single indication of vitality within the economy, might influence the production of criminality and the provision of resources to control such behavior. Rising productivity is responsible for gains in the standard of living. However, the last decade has seen a slackening off in productivity levels. During the period from 1947 to 1966, indicators of productivity growth averaged 3.2 percent, but between 1966 and 1973 growth dropped to 2.1 percent, and since that time it has been less than 1.0 percent. These changes suggest stagnation within the economy.[5] If the rate of growth remains at this low level, the individual family could be faced with increased economic hardship. Furthermore, since governmental efforts would probably be directed toward technological improvements that would spur productivity, criminal justice agencies could find necessary resources increasingly difficult to obtain.

Two additional economic factors, unemployment and inflation, could similarly affect crime and criminal justice effectiveness. The rate of unemployment has continued to vary with fluctuations of the economy, yet has recently begun to rise across the nation and in some parts of the country has risen above 20 percent. Typically, governmental resources are shifted to address the problem. Sustained high inflation, by reducing buying power, exacerbates the economic status of individuals as well as governmental agencies. The recent extremely high levels have had significantly adverse effects. Each of these factors—low productivity, unemployment, and inflation—may, therefore, produce economic hardship for the individual and make resource acquisition more difficult within the criminal justice system.

Reduced state revenues, a final economic factor, could also in time have considerable ramifications on the ability of the system to deliver criminal justice services. Reduced taxation and reduced government spending have become common themes for politicians. The most dramatic illustration of this trend was the approval of Proposition 13 in California, although less dramatic and less publicized cuts have been made in almost every state and local budget across the nation. Such changes place criminal justice agencies in a situation of greater competition for scarce resources. When the money available overall is reduced from one year to the next, it may well mean that agencies will have to reduce services and/or personnel. In the final analysis, the ability of the system to control crime could be reduced.

The potentiality of these four economic problems serves as a basis for the conjectures advanced in this volume. Empirical research has not established a direct, universal, and strong relationship among the factors which would allow a simple predictive function to be used. However, the relationship between economic adversity, expressed in some combination of the four factors, and either criminality or criminal justice service delivery have been utilized in the process of forecasting.

In focusing on the relationship between criminality and economic conditions, Vold reached the following conclusion:

> In the objective data reviewed, assumptions involving either *positive* or
> *negative* relationships with economic conditions may be supported with
> some show of statistical significance. The obvious inference is that the
> general relations of economic conditions and criminality are so indefi-
> nite that no clear or definite conclusions can be drawn. Hence, there is a
> general tendency to accept the position that economic conditions repre-
> sent only one of a large number of environmental circumstances. As

such, this then becomes one factor in the "multiple factor" approach to the causation of crime.[6]

In a similar vein, Radzinowicz concluded that the interconnection between economic conditions and crime were as follows:

> First, it may sometimes be possible to identify a clear link between an increase in crimes characteristic of a particular class and the direct effect upon that class of economic change.

> [Second], as regards the correlation between the economic curve and the curve of crime, it would be futile to expect an exact parallelism. More often the correlation expresses itself in the fact that the two curves move in the same direction and close to each other in time, but they do not display a similar intensity of change.

> [Third], it would not be true to assume that crimes committed as the result of a deterioration in economic conditions are, in general, genuine "crimes of want" . . . ., but on the whole the relationship between deteriorations in the economic situation and the rise in crime is much more complicated than that. It may imply a failure in adaptation to change conditions, an acquired rigidity in habits which have grown during better times, a sudden shock, a weakening of social ties, or simply a latent disposition reinforced by economic pressure.[8]

The conclusions of Vold and Radzinowicz imply that the covariance between the economy and crime depends on the nature of economic change, the type of crime, and various additional social and political factors which may interact in the production functions. A direct and simultaneous effect should never be expected.

The relationship between changes in the criminal justice system and economic adversity is one in which there is virtually no basis for comparison. The criminal justice system, composed of a diversity of levels, agencies, and organizations, developed during the post–World War II period of economic expansion. Its expansion has not been hindered to any significant extent by economic burdens. Throughout this developmental period, the governmental resource base has likewise continued to expand, making it possible for the system to grow or at least maintain its size and services from year to year. Present budgetary cutbacks are, therefore, a new obstacle for the system.

Given these constraints and limitations, the models presented in this volume have had to be complex and incorporate a diversity of variables. They incorporate second- and third-order interactions. And finally, as do all conjectures, they contain a certain amount of uncertainty and must be regarded as probability statements.

The book is divided into four parts. Part I examines the possible changes in the incidence of crime which might be expected during an economic decline. Each selection proceeds from a different set of assumptions concerning forthcoming economic problems and utilizes a different theoretical or empirical basis in the development of its conjecture. Consequently, a somewhat different portrait of the future is derived in each of the selections.

Parts II and III focus on the changes which might occur in the criminal justice system during a time of economic adversity. Adaptive endeavors which have been initiated in response to economic crisis are reviewed in Part II. In particular, the two selections examine an actual response by the criminal justice system in California to the fiscal problems generated by Proposition 13. Each selection in Part III focuses on a specific component of the justice system and analyzes the changes which might occur in the organizational structure or functions during economic decline.

A traditional, structured economic model which assesses the relationship among the economy, crime, and the criminal justice activity is presented in Part IV. Analyses are made in terms of the net costs of crime and the factors that can increase or decrease those costs.

NOTES

1. Alfred L. Malabre, "The Outlook: Review of Current Trends in Busineks and Finance," *Wall Street Journal,* January 8, 1979, p. 1.
2. Howard J. Ruff, *How to Prosper During the Coming Bad Years* (New York: Times Books, 1979).
3. Felix Kaufmann, "The Jobs That Nobody Wants: Economic Challenges of the 1980s," *The Futurist* (August 1979): 269–274.
4. Richard Levine, "The Outlook: Review of Current Funds in Business and Finance," *Wall Street Journal,* June 25, 1979, p. 1.
5. William Bowen, "Better Prospects for Our Ailing Productivity," *Fortune* 100 (December 3, 1979): 68–86.
6. George B. Vold, *Theoretical Criminology,* 2nd ed. (New York: Oxford Univeristy Press, 1979), p. 179.
7. The numbering sequence has been reordered with some points deleted.
8. Leon Radzinowicz, "Economic Pressures," in Leon Radzinowicz and Marvin E. Wolfgang (eds.), *Crime and Justice: The Criminal in Society,* 2nd ed., Vol. 1 (New York: Basic Books Inc., 1977), pp. 555–556.

The Future of Crime in America

The selections in Part I concern the basic question of the book—the possible effects which a declining economy might have on crime and criminal justice. Each essay develops a scenario based on its particular theoretical perspective and on certain assumptions concerning the present and future state of the economy. Since each was developed from different perspectives, conjectures about effects and future consequences are somewhat different. Readers must evaluate each selection and reach their own conclusions concerning the validity of each scenario.

In the opening essay, by Michael Hughes and Timothy Carter, three major sociological theories of crime causation—Marxian criminology, anomie theory, and labeling theory—are utilized to predict the effects of a declining economy on crime. By elaborating certain aspects of each theory in a manner which is consistent with its basic tenets, and by making certain assumptions about the contingent conditions of economic decline, the authors are successful in specifying the direction of expected change, the intensity of change, and the categories of crime which will be affected. All three theories predict precipitant increases in crime during economic crisis; however, the conditions and circumstances of the predicted changes vary from theoretical perspective to perspective. An increase in all categories of criminal activity would be predicted by Marxian criminology. If cultural expectations do not fluctuate, then anomie theory would also predict increases in certain types of crime, because a decline in opportunities results from economic adversity. According to labeling theory, intensification of enforcement should be expected during an economic crisis. That outcome would, however, lead to secondary deviance at a later time which would produce more crime. The authors are careful to point out that the set of predictions generated under each theoretical framework is dependent on the validity of the theory. The future can thus be used as a means to falsify each theoretical stance.

Jeffrey Reiman and Sue Headlee, noting the inability of the Keynesian economic model to accommodate and explain simultaneously high levels of inflation and unemployment, argue that the Marxian analysis is appropriate for the assessment of current economic situations. From this perspective, they extend David Gordon's radical model to consider the effects which an economic decline might have on criminality and the criminal justice system. The prediction is that crime will rise during economic adversity since the pressures of a capitalist system which produce criminality under normal conditions will be exacerabated during a crisis. Heightened competition will produce increases in street crime as well as white collar crime. Reiman and Headlee argue that intensified enforcement will occur at all levels. Enforcement of white collar and corporate crime laws will serve as an issue in the competitive struggle among corporations; likewise, criminal justice policy will reflect a harsher attitude toward the criminal.

In the third chapter, Peter Meyer predicts that crime at all levels—street, white collar, and corporate—will increase in an economy which experiences extended "stagflation," or concurrent stagnation and inflation. The expected criminality, however, will be oriented toward survival. Individuals subsisting marginally may turn to criminality in order to survive during economic hardship. Similarly, corporations may engage in illegal activities in order to survive the heightened competition which would result from economic adversity. Meyer argues that both forms of economically produced criminality, individual and business, can claim a moral distinction between their motives and those of the traditional perpetrator of crime. In such a situation, further social tensions and conflicts will result between business, claiming that its acts are "justifiable" for the preservation of private property and free enterprise, and impoverished individuals claiming a survival justification for an attack on private property and free enterprise.

According to Meyer, the combination of stagflation with a growing "Proposition 13 mentality" will limit public funds and place criminal justice agencies in greater competition for resources. He argues that the criminal justice system will therefore align itself with a politically powerful sponsor to ensure its survival. It is predicted that criminal justice will intensify its efforts to suppress individual criminality which might threaten the economically privileged and the distribution of private property.

In reviewing current theoretical and empirical assessments concerning the relationship of the economy and crime, Kevin Wright suggests that there is no direct and universal relationship, but that under certain conditions, changes in the economy may produce corresponding changes in the incidence of certain crimes. He argues that a specific idea concerning expected economic trends is necessary for predicting precipient changes in criminality. The popular economic scenario depicting reindustrialization is suggested as a probable future recourse to current economic problems. Wright predicts that three significant changes in criminality and criminal justice will result if reindustrialization is pursued. First, corporate crime and enforcement of that crime will increase as economic adversity intensifies competition. Correspondingly, pressure will be exerted to decriminalize many actions which are currently considered to be illegal. The second precipitant effect of reindustrialization will be the widening of the socioeconomic gap between haves and have-nots, a heightening of the sense of relative deprivation, and greater amounts of criminality. Wright also predicts that reindustrialization will intensify competition for resources among governmental agencies, thus possibly reducing fiscal support for criminal justice. The expected response of the system is the fostering of public fear of crime to justify its present budgetary levels and possible growth. It is also expected that criminal justice will be called on to control larger portions of the population who have in the past been serviced by other social agencies.

The final chapter in Part I, by Sharon Long and Ann Witte, provides the most extensive review to date of research into the relationship between economic factors and crime. The authors examine the findings of studies concerned with the effects of economic variables on the overall crime rate, violent crime, property crime, the seven major FBI index crimes, and juvenile delinquency. Their survey offers only weak support for deterministic models which relate such economic factors as high unemployment, low income, and high returns to illegal activity directly to criminality. The literature does suggest that there is a relationship between economic factors and crime, but it is a complex relationship. The effect of economic fluctuations influences different categories of crime in different ways. Long and Witte predict that continued and sustained high unemployment and inflation will produce increases in property crime, growing markets for stolen goods, and greater amounts of tax evasion.

Chapter 1

A Declining Economy and Sociological Theories of Crime: Predictions and Explications

*Michael Hughes and Timothy J. Carter**

INTRODUCTION

Jack Gibbs pointed out recently in an article entitled "The Elites Can Do Without Us,"[1] sociologists should be doing more than explaining things to one another and arguing with one another about the implications of their findings. If this is all we do, the "elites" (and everyone else for that matter) can certainly do without us, and eventually probably will. There are less expensive ways to provide scientific legitimacy for political ideology than to fund social research and maintain sociology, political science, and criminal justice departments. Theories must be made relevant to the real life experiences of citizens in such a way that effective social policies can be created and implemented. Of course, if we have scientific commitments, creating applicable theories is not all we should do but if we are going to be able to justify our existence, it is at least the bare minimum. This is a

*Department of Sociology, Virginia Polytechnic Institute and State University

dictum often heard (one could hear almost nothing else in the late sixties), but seldom followed.

This is obvious when one takes the most prominent theories of criminal behavior and tries to predict what will happen to crime rates in a declining economy. Social theories are supposed to explain and to predict. Successful or accurate predictions make us more confident about theories, and unsuccessful, inaccurate predictions make us feel less confident about them. Although there is plenty of theoretical substance to criminology when considered as attempts at explanation, we lack the theoretical focus in the dominant perspectives which would enable us, using economic variables, to make clear predictions which could be used to make judgments about the relative merits of theories so that we would know which could be used as guides to social policy in various economic circumstances, including a declining economy.

One reason for this is that many of the theoretical differences in the area of criminology, and in deviance generally, stem from deep ideological divisions between the various theoretical camps. Theories remain vague in the service of ideological wars, since the more vaguely a theory is stated, the more likely it can withstand empirical scrutiny due to the difficulty of deriving testable propositions from it. Another, less sinister reason is that criminological theories tend to be derived from the more general theories of deviance—theories which were developed to account for the existence of a wide variety of deviant behaviors and which employ a very diverse set of explanatory variables not always specifically including economic phenomena.

If we want to make policy-relevant statements about what variation in crime rates to expect in a declining economy, we could do two things. We could ignore deviance theory entirely and extrapolate, using econometric techniques, from models derived empirically from crime and economic data. Or we could try to clarify various deviance theories, making certain assumptions relevant to a declining economy, such that predictions could be derived and tested which would allow us to choose among various theoretical perspectives. The first alternative is not acceptable for two reasons. As the review in Vold makes clear,[2] the evidence linking economic phenomena to criminal behavior is so inconsistent and ambiguous that it makes it impossible to make any general statement of regularities; thus we could not make any extrapolations with any confidence. Furthermore, even if we could make such extrapolations, we would have no way of knowing what social contingencies are responsible for the regularities we observe, and thus would have no way of knowing what sort of social changes or social policy implementations would have effects on the relationship.

The purpose of this paper is to take three of the most influential perspectives in criminology today: Marxist criminology, anomie theory, and labeling theory, to elaborate each one briefly, and then to make some specific predictions about what one would expect in a declining economy were the theory true. Our predictions specify the direction of the relationships expected, the duration of the effects, and the particular crimes which should be affected. In some cases, it has been necessary to make certain assumptions about contingent conditions which are expected to occur along with a declining economy and which may facilitate or retard the growth in crime. This is important because it is recognized in most theoretical perspectives that crime and the reaction to it occur in a complex environment of institutions and emerging social structures.

There are two ways these predictions can be used. First, by specifying what to expect from each perspective if one were to collect crime data and economic data, over time, we can then examine these relations using time series analysis. This sort of thing has been tried before, but not, to our knowledge, in the context of evaluating specific theoretical predictions while at the same time looking separately at different kinds of crimes. This last point is quite important as it is clearly the case that different types of crimes may be differentially motivated, and be affected by different kinds of changes in the environment.[3] Second, since as this is being written the United States is in what some might call an economic decline, we can use these predictions as guides to examine the social and economic processes related to crime in the same way one might microscopically examine some social processes in case analyses. In this case, where the economy is in decline, we have the opportunity to observe carefully, and with a number of theoretical perspectives to guide us, what happens and how various institutions respond and are affected by criminal phenomena.

The outcomes of such research programs will probably not allow us to refute certain theories and support others, although such outcomes would be welcome. Rather, we expect that certain aspects of the various theories will come into doubt, and that others will appear more acceptable. In such an enterprise we should then be able to find ways of synthesizing theories where possible; where this is not possible, we should know whether this is because some theories yield accurate predictions and others do not, or whether, in spite of the fact that two or more theories yield accurate predictions, they are irreconcilable with one another because of ideological reasons.

Marxian Criminology

Marxian criminology is not an "objective" criminology bound by the goals, procedures, and rules of evidence of positivist science. Marxian criminologists have not directly concerned themselves with generating testable hypotheses or developing a system of related propositions about the causes and consequences of crime. Consequently, we must extrapolate from Marxian theory and Marxian criminology a testable proposition concerning the effect of a declining capitalist economy on crime. We begin with Marxian theory.

Crime and/or criminality are not objects of Marxist theory; rather, as Hirst notes, "The objects of Marxist theory are specified by its own concepts: the mode of production, the class struggle, the state, ideology, etc."[4] Therefore, the relevance of Marxian theory for an analysis of crime resides in the implications of these theoretical "objects."

According to this theory, the fabric of all social life is man's basic need and capacity to produce. Thus, it is the mode of production—including the means of production (technology and natural resources) and the social relations of production (forms of ownership and/or control of the means of production)—that give society its historically specific form. Where the ownership or the means of production is private, as in capitalism, a fundamental class division between the bourgeoisie, who own and control the major means of production, and the proletariat, who must sell their labor, predominates all sociocultural life. Crime is a social form that corresponds with a given mode of production, and therefore, an understanding of crime in capitalist society begins with an analysis of class.

The motivation for criminal behavior results from a fundamental contradiction in the capitalist social relations of production. This contradiction has been summarized by Chambliss, who notes, ". . . the structure of capitalism creates both the desire to consume and—for a large mass of people—an inability to earn the money necessary to purchase the items they have been taught to want."[5] Crime thus represents a rational and predictable response to the motivation to consume in the absence of legitimate opportunities (work), or to supplement legitimate means that are insufficient to meet perceived consumption needs. From this thesis, we can begin to address the question of what impact a declining economy will have on crime rates.

America's present declining economy is marked by increasing inflation and recession. Inflation coupled with an unequal increase in wages results in reduced purchasing power for the consumer. Recession, defined as a continuous decline in productivity, results in an increase in unemployment which, of course, translates into a drastic reduction in purchasing power for an increasing population of unemployed workers. Yet, survival and a sense of self worth depend upon the ability to work and consume. It can therefore be expected that increasing numbers of persons will turn to alternative means for work and consumption, including crime, assuming that the motivation for work and consumption is not also reduced. Because all crime in capitalist societies are functionally equivalent in that they ". . . represent perfectly rational responses to the structure of institutions upon which capitalist societies are based,"[6] increases in a variety of crimes—including unorganized street crimes, white-collar crime, and corporate crime—can be expected in light of a declining capitalist economy.

Unorganized street crimes are comprised of crimes against the person (murder, rape, assault and robbery) and crimes against property (burglary, larceny and auto theft). With an increasing number of working-class people facing unemployment, underemployment and low-paying jobs, street crimes, and particularly crimes of theft such as burglary, robbery, larceny, and auto theft, represent a rational alternative means of making money or securing valued property. An increase in violent crimes against the person can also be expected. As Gordon suggests, the use of violence represents a rational response to the bias of law enforcement.[7] Because law enforcement concentrates on the criminal activities of the lower class, lower-class criminals are more dependent upon violence to avoid apprehension and conviction. In this sense, violence is a rational response to the higher risks of detection and punishment that result from selective law enforcement. As more crimes are committed and law enforcement becomes more coercive, violence can be expected to increase.

Occupational crime, "offenses committed by individuals for themselves in the course of their occupations" and "offenses by employees against their employers,"[8] occurs for the same reasons as street crime—to maintain or improve one's purchasing power relative to that of others. In a situation where inflation rises in the absence of an equivalent increase in earnings, an increase in occupational crime is predictable.

Corporate crime also can be expected to increase under the strains of a declining economy. Decreasing productivity, decreasing markets, and increased foreign competition will only perpetuate already high corporate violations of the law. It becomes more costly to abide by government safety regulations and environmental standards, especially in light of the increasing profit demands of stockholders who themselves are trying to maintain their purchasing power relative to inflation.

In sum, criminal behavior is viewed in Marxian criminology as an inevitable social reality *motivated* by the innate contradictions of a capitalist mode of production and *shaped* by the class structure of capitalist society. A declining economy characterized by the "dynamic duo" of inflation and recession intensifies the contradiction of consumption and production and heightens class antagonisms, the result of which should be apparent by increasing crime rates.

All members of the working class, employed or unemployed, white or blue collar, are subject to the contradiction of consumption and production which motivates criminal behavior. All varieties of crime are expected to increase. However, marginality of occupation and income remains a significant factor for determining which fractions of the working class will be subject to control by the criminal justice system. Official statistics, themselves the product of selective crime control, will primarily reflect the increasing criminality of an unstable working class comprised of a growing body of unemployed and underemployed workers—Marx's "reserve army."

With the decline of capitalist economy, the surplus population of unemployed and underemployed workers increases in size. This reserve army of workers functions to facilitate capitalist expansion and maintain a low wage structure as long as those workers remain in reserve for employment. However, if the reserve army continues to expand, an increasing number of workers will drop out of the reserve army and into the ranks of the permanently unemployed. Because such a shift is detrimental to the capitalist political economy, the state is faced with the problem of regulating surplus labor. This problem is met by increased activity within formal systems of social control to maintain order, increasing in turn the criminalization of the surplus population.

Our predictions of the impact of a declining economy on crime from a Marxian perspective are as follows:

1. A declining economy is directly related to an increase in criminal activity.

In capitalist societies, the motivation for criminal activity results from the contradiction between consumption and production. This contradiction is intensified by a declining economy and affects both the capitalist and working class. The type of crime, whether corporate, occupational, or street crimes, is shaped by class position rather than a motivation for crime. An increase in criminal activity is expected regardless of one's class position.

2. Official indices of crime will reflect a disproportionate increase in the rate of unorganized street crimes.

This disproportionate increase in the rate of unorganized street crimes results not from a declining economy per se but rather from selective repression by the criminal justice system. Beyond the function of regulating the surplus population, the increased criminalization of marginal portions of the working class functions to maintain the myth that street crimes pose the "real" crime problem and that a "dangerous class" of persons are responsible for crime.

The repressive class bias of crime control that is intensified in periods of economic decline will also lead to an increase in the violent crime rate. Among those groups who have become the target of crime control, threat of force and violence become increasingly necessary to avoid apprehension and conviction. Thus, our final prediction is:

3. During periods of economic decline, both violent crimes against person and crimes against property will increase.

Labeling Theory

Labeling theory, according to its critics[9] as well as its proponents,[10] does not propose to explain primary deviance.[11] It has been criticized[12] for making unsubstantiable claims—that apprehension of persons by social control agents leads to an inevitable change in status leading such persons in turn to embark upon careers of stabilized secondary deviance. Labeling theorists themselves argue that they are concerned with the process of interaction between persons who have committed various acts and agents of social control.[13] The process is seen as one in which certain acts become defined as deviant through rule creation and sanction application. Labeling theorists also are concerned with the way which an individual's roles, status, and self-definition are contingent upon the amount of deviance engaged in, the social visibility of the individual, the amount of exposure to societal reaction, and the strength of societal reaction.[14] Labeling theorists are interested, furthermore, in the ways in which changes in status, role, and self-definition facilitate the emergence and stabilization of secondary deviance—deviance, that is, which is largely the result of being placed in a deviant role.[15]

Since labeling theory is primarily interested in the interaction between individuals and social control agents and in the consequences of various contingencies in that interaction, there are no direct predictions which can be made on the basis of the theory to show how a declining economy should affect crime. If, however, we can assume

that a declining economy will have effects on the structure and functioning of social control institutions, then labeling theory may be relevant to our discussion. This is because labeling theory is essentially a
theory of institutions and only secondarily a theory of behavior, as
shown in two statements defending labeling theory from its critics.
Arguing for the distinctiveness of labeling theory, Kitsuse closes out
his discussion with this comment: "Its distinctiveness leads away from
these social psychological issues to a consideration of how deviants
come to be differentiated by imputations made about them by others,
how these imputations activate systems of social control activities and
become legitimated as institutional responses to deviance."[16]

Schur, in an accompanying comment, mentions two main concerns
of labeling theory. The reaction orientation's aim ". . . is . . . to focus on
the processes through which social *meanings* come to be attached to
types of behavior (and to individuals), and the consequences of such
attachment. The central focus then is on *characterization of behavior
rather* than on behavior itself."[17] He says later ". . . a reactions perspective is centrally concerned with *rule creation*, at various levels."[18]

As Becker argues, these are essentially collective behaviors, with
the "deviant" interacting with the social groupings which create and
apply the rules to the offenders.[19] These activities typically occur in
the context of social control institutions which have some sort of legitimacy and the authority to create and enforce rules. This is true of
formal social control agencies including mental hospitals, the courts,
the criminal justice system (the police, the courts, correctional facilities, and the like), and probation and parole institutions, as well as
the informal social control exercised by the family which at various
times may find itself defining certain behaviors as mental illness,[20]
drug addiction,[21] or alcoholism.[22] Thus, if labeling theory is a theory
about rule creation, the ways meanings are attached to behaviors, and
how social control activities are made legitimate in a wide variety of
situations, then it makes sense that it is a theory about the social institutions through which these functions are carried out. The literature cited above and the classical statements of labeling theory clearly
do not imply the alternative—that labeling theory is a theory about
how certain individuals deal with others who engage in undesirable
behaviors, or that it is a theory of how societies temporarily mobilize
and resist random threats, disbanding after each incident. The social
processes discussed by labeling theorists occur as part of definite, continuous, and organized social arrangements. While informal, family,
and community-centered reactions to deviance should not be de-em-
phasized, the most obvious and significant reactions (and those most
frequently written about) are those of the formally organized systems

of social control embodied in the criminal justice system, state and county mental hospitals, and so on.

If we can show that a declining economy has an effect on the behavior of the criminal justice system, then we can show that labeling theory has something to tell us about the effect of a declining economy on crime.

Two additional points will help us in our discussion of labeling theory. First, since some of the most important societal reactions discussed by labeling theorists occur as part of formal institutions and are carried out through organized bureaucratic means, then the actions of social control institutions follow in part the same patterns we would expect in any complex organization. For example, we should see particular social control organizations as being imbedded in an environment of other organizations and institutions which constitute an external polity and economy.[23] This involves crucial contingencies which must be taken into account as the institution functions normally in the society. We should view social control institutions as negotiating with important elements in their environments for the resources necessary to their existence and for the continued legitimacy of their operation. Clearly contingent on these negotiations are the particular structures of social control, power relationships among participants in social control institutions, and distribution of material resources among the various activities of the particular social control organizations.

Secondly, let us incorporate Quinney's first three propositions from his theory in *The Social Reality of Crime:*

Proposition 1 (Definition of crime): Crime is a definition of human conduct that is created by authorized agents in a politically organized society.

Proposition 2 (Formulation of criminal definitions): Criminal definitions describe behaviors that conflict with the interests of the segments of society that have the power to shape public policy.

Proposition 3 (Application of criminal definitions): Criminal definitions are applied by the segments of society that have the power to shape the enforcement and administration of criminal law.[24]

The only difference between these propositions and some of the more general statements in labeling theory is that these deal specifically with crime and suggest that differing amounts of power of various segments in the society are important contingencies in the creation of rules (formulation of criminal definitions) and the application of sanctions. These corollaries to labeling theory are consistent with the work of persons more directly identified with the labeling movement, such as Scheff and Rushing, who argue that the status of persons—that is, their status resources or personal power—is related to their ability to resist the sanctions typically applied to persons who engage in residual deviance, and Schur who argues that status resources are related to an enhanced ability to choose the desired outcome of an encounter with social control agencies—an ability, that is, to reject labels, accept labels, and put labels on others.[25]

These additions to labeling theory have several implications. First, locating labeling activity in an organizational context makes it possible to understand labeling activities as outcomes of particular social processes in tangible social situations, not simply as the function of abstract disembodied institutions of social control. Since this gives us a general idea of where and how these activities are being carried out, it helps us make predictions about what should happen in a declining economy.

Second, the assumption that it is persons with power who contribute most heavily to the processes of social definition of crime and the application of sanctions for its commission gives us some idea of the direction in which the criminal justice system may proceed under certain conditions.

Third, an organizational perspective on labeling theory views the particular way in which labeling or deviance-defining activities are carried out as being directly contingent on the social structures of the organizations which are involved in social control. There is nothing immutable, in other words, about a particular labeling process. Social structures may change and thereby eliminate or change societal reactions to particular forms of so-called deviance. The predictions or consequences of labeling which we explicate in regard to its consequences on crime in a declining economy are valid deductions only if there are no profound changes in the way the criminal justice functions over the time of the decline. For example, the predictions one might have made under Scheff's version of labeling theory[26] concerning the impact of mental health institutions on the rates of persons being labeled mentally ill and on mental illness behavior in general are quite different than those one might make today in the midst of the deinstitutionalization movement.[27]

Since labeling theory makes two sorts of assertions about deviance, we could make two sorts of predictions using labeling theory about crime in a declining economy. Labeling makes assertions about the *process* of labeling certain actions and certain persons as deviant. Thus, labeling theory would predict something about the identification and processing of persons as criminals in the short run. Also, since labeling theory is concerned with the consequences of labeling for the stabilization of secondary deviance in the form of careers, then the theory would predict something about deviance in the long run.

If we assume that the criminal justice system, as suggested above, is organizationally based and subject to pressures both from its own internal imperatives to fulfill its mission (much as Becker describes the motives behind the Treasury Department's Bureau of Narcotics movement to make marijuana a heinous drug[28]) and from segments of society who are strong enough to shape public policy, then as the economy declines, we should expect a greater degree of activity on the part of the criminal justice system. This should occur for two reasons. First, as the economy declines and unemployment increases, common sense indicates that the criminal justice system should anticipate an increase in criminal activity. Second, as the economy declines, persons in the society who have a great deal to lose if there is a general, broad-based increase in property crime and who are the persons Quinney describes as having the power to shape public policy[29] will put pressure on the criminal justice system to stem an increase in crime. These two factors may manifest themselves as increased appropriations or lobbying for increased appropriations for law enforcement, changes in the budgeting procedures within the criminal justice system (such as shuffling money around so that there is more for enforcement and less for things like community service) and in changes in the way enforcement is carried out (increased patrols in "crime" areas, increased surveillance of persons suspected of committing crimes, and so forth), or all three.

As the criminal justice system is mobilized and engages in more crime control activities, then, independent of the actual rates of criminal activity in the community, there should be an increase in the official rates of crime. There will be an increase in the number of persons arrested and processed. If there is a modest increase in the actual level of criminal activity in a declining economy due to unemployment and/or other factors, this should likewise produce a reaction in the criminal justice system and be related to increased activity, out of proportion to the true increase in crime and leading to more persons being arrested than would otherwise be. Thus, in the short run, labeling theory would predict with a declining economy an increase in crime rates independent of the true level of criminal activity. This increase should be particularly evident for crimes which have traditionally low clearance rates and where police departments can actually improve their performances. There should be no increase with crimes such as homicide and manslaughter which have very high clearance rates.

In the long run, there should also be increases in rates of criminal activity due to a declining economy. These increases should not result directly from economic pressure but rather from the increase in activity of the criminal justice system. As more persons are processed by the police departments and the courts, there is an increased probability that persons will embark on criminal careers as described by Becker.[30] Thus, as a declining economy mobilizes the criminal justice system to process more persons than it would otherwise, independent of the true level of criminal activity, it produces an elevated level of criminal activity at a later time, as a result of stabilized secondary deviance. This will be readily observable in official crime statistics only if the energy and resources expended by the criminal justice system remains constant over time. A decline in effectiveness of the criminal justice system and an increase in actual criminal activity will not appear as a change in crime rates across time. The increase in actual crime over time should be most pronounced for property crimes, but if it could be established that becoming a career criminal increases the probability that one will commit crimes against persons, then we would expect an increase in violent crimes as well as property crimes.

To summarize, since labeling theory does not have anything to say about primary deviance, the only way we can postulate any effects of a declining crime rate on crime by way of labeling theory is to suggest that in a declining economy there will be a greater societal reaction against crime. An increase in societal reaction will produce an increase in official rates and an increase in persons processed regardless of the true level of criminal activity. This increase in the number of persons processed increases the probability that career deviance will be created. If labeling theory is correct, there should be correlation between declining economic indicators at time 1 and crime rates for certain (probably property) crimes at time 1—a correlation which should disappear when we control for increased activity of the criminal justice system (increased police per capita, increased spending for police, jails, prisons, and so forth). There should also be a lagged positive correlation between a declining economy at time 1 and criminal activity at time 2 which disappears when police activity at time 1 is introduced as a control. There should remain a strong positive correlation between police activity at time 1 and criminal activity at time 2.

Anomie Theory

According to anomie theory, deviant behavior is more likely in social structural arrangements in which the desires or goals of persons are out of alignment with their abilities to satisfy, or the likelihood of their satisfying, these desires. Durkheim's classical view of this stresses the importance of social constraint and regulation to hold desires in check,[31] while Merton's reformulation stresses the importance of access to institutionalized means for attaining culturally approved goals.[32] Whether we look to Durkheim's or Merton's version of this theory, we get the same prediction concerning the impact of a declining economy on crime. In a declining economy, the mechanisms of social constraint break down and the crime rate escalates accordingly.

Durkheim argued that a basic ingredient of feelings of well-being for all animals was that their needs be satisfied. This is relatively nonproblematic for lower animals since, due to their lack of ability to reflect on their lives, their needs are determined entirely by material conditions. The human case is a different story, however: ". . . For beyond indispensable minimum which satisfies nature when instinctive, a more awakened reflection suggests better conditions, seemingly desirable ends craving fulfillment."[33] Durkheim further maintains that nothing in the organic makeup of human beings sets a limit to their desires. "[Needs and desires] are thus unlimited so far as they depend on the individual alone. Irrespective of any external regulatory force, our capacity for feeling is in itself an insatiable and bottomless abyss."[34] Under such conditions, human life is torturous, tenuous, and continuously restless. Durkheim's solution, or the solution he sees implemented in society, is that "passions . . . must be limited."[35] Passions are limitable only through means which people can recognize as just. "Either directly and as a whole, or through the agency of one of its organs, society alone can play this moderating role; for it is the only moral power superior to the individual, the authority of which he accepts."[36]

Society controls passions and desires through a moral consciousness which produces conceptions about what kinds of rewards are due various categories of persons and which sets up relatively precise rules whereby rewards are made available to members of the society. There is what we would call a normative consensus (Durkheim refers to "public opinion") which legitimates these reward levels and distribution rules such that persons conform to the authority of society through "respect, not fear."[37] It is the strength of this normative consensus, essentially, which prevents passions and desires from getting out of control, and which prevents persons from becoming excessively confused and tormented and thus from committing suicide.

Man's characteristic privilege is that the bond he accepts is not physical but moral: that is, social. He is governed not by a material environment brutally imposed on him, but by a conscience superior to his own, the superiority of which he feels. Because the greater, better part of this existence transcends the body, he escapes the body's yoke, but is subject to that of society.

But when society is disturbed by some painful crisis or by beneficent but abrupt transitions, it is momentarily incapable of exercising this influence; thence come the sudden rises in the curve of suicides which we have pointed out above.[38]

During what Durkheim calls "economic disasters," or downturns in the economy, the balance between needs and satisfaction is lost because many persons lose the ability to earn an income. Since it takes some time for persons to become resocialized to new expectations, they go through a period of grave suffering. Durkheim also argues that imbalances between perceived needs and satisfactions occur during booms in the economy and there is an abrupt growth of power and wealth.

Appetites, not being controlled by a public opinion become disoriented, no longer recognize the limits proper to them. Besides, they are at the same time seized by a sort of natural erethism simply by the greater intensity of public life. With increased prosperity, desires increase. At the very moment when traditional rules have lost their authority, the richer prize offered these appetites stimulates them, and makes them more exigent and impatient of control. The state of deregulation or anomy is thus further heightened by passions being less disciplined, precisely when they need more disciplining.[39]

The key element in Durkheim's argument is the balance between perceived needs and gratifications. Anything which disrupts this balance will lead to confusion, suffering, and disorderly behavior. A declining economy affects the balance since it makes it more difficult for persons to gratify their legitimate, normatively defined and legitimated, perceived needs. A booming economy affects the balance by suggesting to persons the possibility that the need patterns defined and legitimated in the society may be too modest, and that it may be possible for one to expect much more. As restraint on perceived need is lifted, one's expectations for gratification increase and can get out of control.

Although it is clear that Durkheim's dependent variable is suicide, it is now widely agreed that the general weakening of restraint is also related to a variety of deviant behaviors including mental disorder, alchohol and drug abuse, juvenile delinquency, and crime.[40] If we accept this extension of Durkheim's theory to other deviant phenomena, then anomie is directly relevant to a discussion of the effect of a declining economy on crime. The deduction is very simple. As the economy declines, unemployment increases and firms go out of business. The ability of persons to generate material rewards for themselves declines, revealing a significant gap between their expectations or desires and reality. In such a situation, we would expect increases in crime as part of an attempt to realign reality and expectation. We would expect an increase in property crimes. However, since anomie is a general weakening of constraint which produces much suffering, confusion, and restlessness, we would also expect an increase in irrational crimes such as assault and homicide.

Crime rates should also be affected by positive changes in the economy. That is, when the economy is growing and the stability of expectations is undermined, then we should also see an increase in both property crimes and irrational personal crimes, because expectations are growing out of proportion to the ability of the society to provide, or the ability of persons to achieve satisfaction. The optimal situation, with the lowest rates of crime, would be during extended periods in which economic changes were very slight, with no abrupt changes in either direction.

Merton's theory of anomie also has implications for crime in a declining economy, but they are not so clear cut as those of Durkheim. Merton, like Durkheim, saw anomie as resulting from an imbalance between expectations and achievement; however, he emphasizes the fact that the means for achievement are likely to be institutionalized in the social structure of the society, that the goals (or expectations) are generated by the culture and defined on a continuum of legitimacy. Access to the institutionalized means for achieving culturally approved goals is likely to be differentially distributed in the society, certain broad categories of persons having more access, others less. Merton is thus more interested in explaining variations in deviance across societies than across time. Persons who lack access to institutionalized means for achieving the goals they have been socialized to believe are legitimate and desirable have a high probability of engaging in "innovative" behavior to achieve these goals. If these innovative behaviors violate the norms of the society, then this is deviance. If we are speaking of financial, economic, or social status goals which can be attained with money, then this particular form of anomie would be related to increased crime rates for categories of persons who lack access to institutionalized means.

If we assume that the definition of appproved goals is relatively stable, then in a declining economy, when access to legitimate means is limited, this form of anomie theory would predict an increase in the crime rate. This would be true only of property crimes since the kind of deviance expected is determined by the goal or desire which is frustrated. If, however, for whatever reason, goal definition changes with changing economic circumstances—for example, the expectations of persons in the society decline during a depression—then one would expect no change in the rate of crime according to Merton's version of anomie theory.

Richard Cloward, in a reformulation of Merton's theory, has added the notion of illegitimate opportunity structure.[41] Goals may be attained either through legitimate or illegitimate means. If criminal behavior is increased for any reason because of a declining economy, then we would expect this would increase the probability that illegitimate opportunity structures would arise. For example, if prostitution increases in frequency and prevalence, this increases the probability that persons will attempt to organize it. As the organization becomes larger and stronger, the probability increases that other kinds of crimes will be perpetrated such as drugs, gambling, fencing stolen goods, and so forth. The more these structures pervade the society, the more access people have to illegitimate means, and the more crime there should be. Thus, the building of an opportunity structure for crime should accelerate the increase in crime, independent of the initial impetus for increase in crime. This should be most evident for money-making property crimes, less so for petty theft, and much less so for homicides which should hardly be affected at all.

In summary, Durkheim's classical anomie theory predicts an increase in all forms of crime with a decline in the economy. It predicts a similar increase in crime within a growing economy, since economic changes in either direction lead to a weakening in mechanisms of constraint. Merton's theory of anomie predicts an increase in the property crime rate in a declining economy but in the absence of a corresponding decline in expectations or desires. Cloward's anomie theory predicts an exponential increase in property crime rates in a declining economy if there is an initial increase due to legitimate opportunities being blocked and if, as the crime rate increases, this provides an impetus for the development of illegitimate opportunity structures.

Conclusions

This discussion of what we would predict if certain theories were true leads us to two different sets of conclusions, one set having to do with the predictions, the other with the theories themselves and how it is we are able to make predictions at all.

Marxian criminology predicts an increase in criminal activity in a declining economy, for all classes of potential offenders and for all kinds of crimes. As criminal behavior is simply an alternative form of production which may be tapped when the capitalist economy is in decline, rich and poor, capitalists and workers, all have an increased probability of engaging in crime. Official statistics, however, will reflect mainly the offenses of the poor. There is no reason to believe that there will be an increase in prosecutions for corporate and white-collar crime. This, of course, reflects the more powerful positions perpetrators of these crimes have in society. Finally, due to the repressive nature of the state in capitalist economies, in a declining economy we would expect an increase in violent state reaction to crime, a corresponding violent reaction among those committing crimes, and a concomitant rise in violence in the society due to the general rise in alienation as the economy increasingly fails to provide the citizens with the opportunity to engage in meaningful production. We would therefore expect increased assaults, homicides, and robberies, in addition to the property crimes suggested above.

Anomie theory predicts an increase for all crimes with abrupt changes in the economy, either up or down. This is because of a general lessening of social control when expectations and realization are not in balance. Merton's anomie theory typically predicts increased deviance with declines in opportunitites within a declining economy. However, his predictions are contingent on two corollaries: that when the economy declines, expectations (belief in culturally approved goals) do not shrink with the shrinking opportunities; and that in an expanding economy, culturally approved goals or expectations do not increase out of proportion to the ability of even the increased opportunity base (that is, the expanding economy) to satisfy them. For Merton's theory to predict the same thing as Durkheim's, culturally approved goals must remain the same during economic decline and expand during economic growth.

Labeling theory's predictions are all contingent on the reaction of social control institutions to the threat of crime in a declining economy, with the assumption that an increase in arrest rates will lead to an increase in subsequent crime because of the increased probability of persons embarking on criminal careers. Thus, in a declining economy, we will see an increase in arrest rates as the criminal justice system reacts to the fears of the more powerful persons in the society. This increase will be independent of the real increase (if any) in crime. Since processing leads to secondary deviance, then arrests should lead to more crime in the future—an effect which is due to the increase in police behavior, which in turn is due to the perceived threat of crime in a declining economy.

We do not expect any of these sets of predictions to lead to confirmation of one perspective over another. We expect some predictions to be accurate, and others not. However, some predictions are crucial for some perspectives. For example, if the lagged effect of a declining economy at time 1 on crime rate at time 2 is not explained away by the introduction of police expenditures at time 1 as a control, then labeling theory is in trouble. If police expenditures at time 1 lead to a decline in the crime rate at time 2, this too is very damning evidence against labeling theory.

If there is an increase in white-collar and corporate crime, as reflected in the official crime rates, which either keeps pace with or exceeds the increase in street crime or other property crime, then this calls into question the Marxian theories which assume that crimes of capitalists go unpunished while those of the oppressed classes are prosecuted with vigor.

If the absolute value of abrupt economic changes is not related to increases in all crimes, personal as well as property, then the classical anomie theory is called into question since abrupt changes in the economy in either direction supposedly undermine the moral order.

There are clearly many other possible outcomes, but it is not our place to try to anticipate all of them. We believe that researchers ought to look at empirical data of all kinds—official crime rates, victimization data, and data on the operation of official institutions of social control. We should look at those data which exist and those which are coming into being now, as the economy changes, and attempt to make theoretical sense out of what is called crime and the institutional response to it. The only way we can do that with the minimum of ideological disruption is to make predictions in advance and to make our decisions about which parts of theories to accept based on empirical outcomes, keeping a keen eye, meanwhile, on both the deficiencies and strengths of our data.

The second set of conclusions has to do with the nature of the economic approach to crime generally. In order for us to make the dominant perspectives in the sociology of crime relevant to an understanding of what will happen to crime in a declining economy, it is necessary for us to make assumptions about contingent conditions and the structure and functioning of noneconomic institutions in the society.

Both the traditional economic analysis of the relationship between economic factors and crime and traditonal theories of crime generally tend to focus so heavily on one or another single variable or process that we must make *ad hoc* additions to the traditional perspectives to make them valuable for predicting what will happen as the economy declines.

This could, possibly, reflect reality. The economy may be irrelevant to criminal behavior. However, given the strong common sense appeal of such a relationship and the fact that while the empirical evidence does not unequivocally support such a relationship—the evidence is at least inconsistent—we are not quite ready to accept such a conclusion. Instead, the theories we develop in future should, as Vold indicates, integrate both economic and social structural factors more closely:

> The lessening of the significance of economic factors to that of making an undetermined contribution to a whole brings to the fore the theoretical orientation of interdependence and interrelationship that is so fundamental to sociological theories. In any serious sociological sense, influence is a two-way street. If economic conditions contribute to the structure and functioning of various social arrangements, including crime, it is equally true that the social and institutional structure affects the nature of economic affairs. Economic conditions are then no longer "determining" factors, and the theoretical orientation changes.[42]

Theorists of crime should make consideration of economic phenomena central to their arguments, whether positive or negative, and researchers should make consideration of economic variables explicit in research designs until we are able to subtly interweave economic variables into our theories, or determine, finally, that they are of no importance.

NOTES

1. Jack P. Gibbs, "The Elites Can Do Without Us," *The American Sociologist* 14 (May 1979): 79–85.
2. George B. Vold, *Theoretical Criminology*, 2nd edition prepared by Thomas J. Bernard (New York: Oxford University Press, 1979).
3. Michael Geerken and Walter R. Gove, "Social Control, Deterrence, and Perspectives on Social Order," *Social Forces* 56 (1977): 408–23.
4. Paul Q. Hirst, "Marx and Engels on Law, Crime, and Morality," in Ian Taylor, P. Walton, and J. Young (eds.), *Critical Criminology* (Boston: Routledge and Kegan Paul, 1975), p. 204.
5. William J. Chambliss, "Toward a Political Economy of Crime," *Theory and Society* (Summer 1975): 151.
6. David M. Gordon, "Capitalism, Class, and Crime in America," *Crime and Delinquency* (April 1973): 176.

7. Ibid.
8. Marshall B. Clinard and Richard Quinney, *Criminal Behavior Systems: A Typology*, 2nd edition (New York: Holt, Rinehart and Winston, 1973), p. 188.
9. Jack P. Gibbs, "Conceptions of Deviant Behavior: the Old and the New," *Pacific Sociological Review* 9 (Spring 1966): 9–14; Ronald L. Akers, "Problems in the Sociology of Deviance: Social Definitions and Behavior," *Social Forces* 46 (June 1968): 455–465; Walter R. Gove, "Societal Reaction as an Explanation of Mental Illness: an Evaluation," *American Sociological Review* 35 (October 1970): 873–884; Walter R. Gove, "Labelling and Mental Illness: a Critique," in Walter R. Gove (ed.), *The Labelling of Deviance: Evaluating a Perspective* (New York: Sage/Halsted, 1975).
10. Howard S. Becker, *Outsiders: Studies in the Sociology of Deviance*, 2nd edition (New York: Macmillan, 1973); Thomas Scheff, *On Being Mentally Ill: A Sociological Theory* (Chicago: Aldine, 1966).
11. Edwin M. Lemert, *Social Pathology* (New York: McGraw-Hill, 1951).
12. Gove, "Societal Reaction"; Gove, "Labelling and Mental Illness"; Lee N. Robins, "Alcoholism and Labelling Theory," in Walter R. Gove (ed.), *The Labelling of Deviance: Evaluating a Perspective* (New York: Sage/Halsted, 1975); Charles R. Tittle, "Labelling and Crime: An Empirical Evaluation," in Walter R. Gove (ed.), *The Labelling of Deviance: Evaluating a Perspective* (New York: Sage/Halsted, 1975); Travis Hirschi, "Labelling Theory and Juvenile Delinquency: An Assessment of the Evidence," in Walter R. Gove (ed.), *The Labelling of Deviance: Evaluating a Perspective* (New York: Sage/Halsted, 1975).
13. Becker, *Outsiders*.
14. John I. Kitsuse, "The 'New Conception of Deviance' and Its Critics," in Walter R. Gove (ed.), *The Labelling of Deviance: Evaluating a Perspective* (New York: Sage/Halsted, 1975).
15. Becker, *Outsiders*.
16. Kitsuse, "The 'New Conception of Deviance,' " p. 282.
17. Edwin M. Schur, "Comments," in Walter R. Gove (ed.), *The Labelling of Deviance: Evaluating a Perspective* (New York: Sage/Halsted, 1975), p. 287. Emphasis in the original.
18. Ibid. p. 291. Emphasis in the original.
19. Becker, *Outsiders*.
20. Marion Yarrow, Charlotte Schwartz, Harriet Murphy, and Leila Deasy, "The Psychological Meaning of Mental Illness in the Family," *Journal of Social Issues* 11, 4 (1955): 12–24.
21. William E. McAuliffe, "Beyond Secondary Deviance: Negative Labelling and Its Effects on the Heroin Addict," in Walter R. Gove (ed.), *The Labelling of Deviance: Evaluating a Perspective* (New York: Sage/Halsted, 1975).
22. Ann Sundgren, "Sex Differences in the Adjustment to an Alcoholic Spouse," Ph.D. dissertation, University of Washington, 1978.
23. Mayer N. Zald, "Political Economy: Framework for Comparative Analysis," in Mayer N. Zald (ed.), *Power in Organizations* (Nashville, Tenn.: Vanderbilt University Press, 1970).
24. Richard Quinney, *The Social Reality of Crime* (New York: Little, Brown, 1970), pp. 15–24
25. Scheff, *On Being Mentally Ill*; William A. Rushing, "Individual Resources, Societal Reaction and Hospital Commitment," *American Journal of Sociology* 77(1971): 511–526; William A. Rushing, "Status Resources, Societal Reactions and Type of Mental Hospital Admission," *American Sociological Review* 43 (August 1978): 521–533; William A. Rushing and Jack Esco, "Status Resources and Behavioral

Deviance as Contingencies of Societal Reaction," *Social Forces* 56 (September 1977): 132–147; Schur, "Comments"; Edwin M. Schur, *Interpreting Deviance: A Sociological Introduction* (New York: Harper and Row, 1979).
26. Scheff, *On Being Mentally Ill.*
27. J. Morrissey, "Keeping Patients Out: Organization and Policy Implications of Emergent State Hospital Deinstitutionalization Practices," paper presented at the annual meeting of the Southern Sociological Society, Atlanta, 1979; Walter R. Gove, "Labelling Theory's Explanation of Mental Illness: A Critical Review," *Archives of General Psychiatry* (forthcoming, 1980).
28. Becker, *Outsiders,* p. 138.
29. Quinney, *The Social Reality of Crime.*
30. Becker, *Outsiders.*
31. Emile Durkheim, *Suicide,* translated by John A. Spaulding and George Simpson (New York: Free Press, 1951).
32. Robert K. Merton, "Social Structure and Anomie" and "Continuities in the Theory of Social Structure and Anomie," *Social Theory and Social Structure,* 2nd edition (New York: Free Press, 1957).
33. Durkheim, *Suicide,* p. 247.
34. Ibid., p. 247.
35. Ibid., p. 248.
36. Ibid., p. 249.
37. Ibid., p. 252.
38. Ibid., p. 252.
39. Ibid., p. 253.
40. Sebastian De Grazia, *The Political Community: A Study of Anomie* (Chicago: University of Chicago Press, 1948); Marshall B. Clinard (ed.), *Anomie and Deviant Behavior* (New York: MacMillan, 1964).
41. Richard A. Cloward, "Illegitimate Means, Anomie, and Deviant Behavior," *American Sociological Review* 24 (April 1959): 164–76.
42. Vold, *Theoretical Criminology,* p. 179.

Chapter 2

Crime and Crisis

Jeffrey H. Reiman* and Sue Headlee**

In this chapter we explore the significance of the current declining economy for crime and criminal justice in the following fashion. First, recognizing that the Keynesian model of a trade-off between inflation and unemployment does not help in an economic situation characterized by inflation and unemployment working in tandem, we sketch out a Marxian analysis of the current economic crisis. Second, we suggest what such an analysis would lead us to expect about the incidence of crime. Here we take off from David Gordon's seminal article, "Capitalism, Class, and Crime in America,"[1] arguing that the pressures toward crime that Gordon saw at work at all levels in normally functioning capitalism are exacerbated at all levels of capitalism in crisis. Third, we explore the implications of this analysis for moral judgments about crime in the economic crisis. We argue that there is continuity between much of what is called crime at the bottom of the society and what is done under color of law, at the top of society, to cope with the crisis. Finally, we suggest that the Marxian analysis

This chapter was originally presented at the American Society of Criminology Conference in Philadelphia, November 1979.
*School of Justice, The American University
**Department of Economics, The American University

of the crisis enables us to understand current developments in criminal justice policy, in particular, the so-called justice model.

After a short respite, crime is once more on the rise. Police chiefs and mayors who were briefly able to claim credit for a declining crime rate must now be content with congratulating themselves when the acceleration of the crime rate slows. Some have also recognized that there must be a connection between this increase in crime and the decrease in the American standard of living produced by the one-two punch of double-digit inflation and persistent unemployment.[2] We will not try to prove this connection.[3] It appears obvious to those who are prepared to ascribe a significant causal role to economics in the etiology of crime, and a mere correlation to those who are not. We confess to viewing the connection as obvious.

Unemployment and inflation hit hardest the very groups who appear most prevalent in crime statistics—the poor, the black, the young, the inner-city dweller. Unemployment among inner-city youth hovers around 50 percent. And inflation, since it is most rampant in necessities like food and fuel, hits hardest those who must devote all or most of their income to purchasing the necessities of life. To affirm that such realities produce crime does not require one to deny the obvious fact that not all poor or unemployed folks resort to crime. Since social causation rarely takes the form of iron laws in which causes invariably produce their consequences, it is sufficient to affirm that increases in the severity of the struggle for the necessities of life increase with the pressures which incline individuals toward criminal solutions to their problems. Whether crime results in individual cases will be a function of the strength of pressures operating in the other direction.

On the other hand, to deny that increases in unemployment are criminogenic is to suggest that the fact that the same groups figure in both unemployment and crime statistics implies that some third thing causes the poor to have trouble holding jobs and resisting criminal temptations. This third thing is either some form of social disorganization or some kind of character defect. Since social disorganization itself has economic causes (unless one assumes, for example, that blacks left the rural South during most of the first half of this century out of wanderlust, and huddled in Northern slums out of togetherness), this is just another form of economic causation. The attribution of crime and unemployment to character defect is either historically naive (it ignores the fact that many groups now within the mainstream passed through an earlier period of poverty, crime and unemployment) or blatantly ideological. It amounts to asserting an identity between the present social order and the moral order: Whether it is prison or poverty, everyone is getting what they deserve.[4] For these reasons we take it that economic hardships like unemployment and inflation are criminogenic in the qualified sense described above. Rather than belabor the point, we turn now to a sketch of a Marxian analysis of the economic crisis which, though brief, may give us greater insight into the relation between crime and the crisis.

Marx was by no means the first economist to notice the problems endemic to capitalism.[5] Indeed, the fluctuations of business and trade cycles—the alternations of prosperity and austerity, of boom and depression, growth and recession—have convinced many that there is an inherent instability in the very structure of the capitalist mode of production. The coexistence of poverty and need alongside unprecedented productive capacity, underutilized in the form of idle plants and overstocked inventories, has also convinced many that the instability of capitalism reflects its profound irrationality as a mode of satisfying the world's needs. It is, however, a mistake to assume that the Marxian view of capitalism tending inherently to crisis is equivalent to the claim that capitalism will inevitably break down and be replaced by a more rational and less unstable system. As we shall see, while crises destabilize capitalism and increase its vulnerability and thus the possibility of its downfall and replacement, crises are also part of the mechanism by which capitalism rights itself, corrects its organizational defects, and gets ready for the next period of growth.[6]

The heart of the Marxian analysis of capitalism is the claim that the profits that capitalists plow back to expand production have their sole source in the labor of productive workers. For Marx, only labor has the capacity to produce something of greater value than itself. Labor is thus the secret ingredient in the capitalist cauldron that results in an output greater than the sum of its inputs and which can serve as the basis for initiating the process anew on greater scale. The other so-called factors of production like capital itself, whether in the form of money or machines, only have productive efficacy insofar as they are the incarnations of previous, in Marx's terms, *dead* labor and insofar as they are activated by present *living* labor.

For Marx, the *value* of something is equivalent to the average amount of socially necessary labor that produces it.[7] Everything produced for sale in capitalism has value, including the worker's labor power. Its value is the amount of labor socially necessary to produce and maintain a laborer at the generally accepted standard of living.[8] The worker sells his labor power, his ability to work, to the capitalist in return for wages which represent (or in other words, which give the worker a claim upon the product of) the labor necessary to produce this standard of living. Once purchased, this labor power has the capacity to produce more in value than its own value.[9] If it did not, the worker would produce no more than the value of his wage; the capitalist would have no incentive to hire him. The capitalist's incentive lies in the surplus of the value produced by labor power over the value of that labor power. This surplus value, as Marx called it, is the material basis of profit.

Competition between capitalists places them under a harsh discipline that requires them to decrease the cost of inputs by replacing machines with increasingly productive ones and by expanding to take advantage of economies of scale. This has two consequences that are crucial to an understanding of crises. First of all, it makes all capitalists dependent on credit. The amount of surplus realized in any one cycle of production or in any one firm is generally insufficient for large-scale expansion or technological innovation. Thus it is necessary that surplus value be pooled and extended to individual capitalists in return for the promise of a share in future profits. This is the credit system, and it sets the stage for conflict between financial capital and industrial capital over the division of the surplus value produced. Interest is the share of surplus value that goes to finance capital; the remainder, the profits of enterprise, go to industrial capital.

The second consequence of the need of capital to expand and increase productivity is what Marx called, "The Law of the Tendency of the Rate of Profit to Fall."[10] This follows directly from the labor theory of value. The value of a commodity is equivalent to the average socially necessary labor—dead and living, past and present—that goes into producing it. The amount of this value that the capitalist can realize as profit is the surplus value produced by living labor over the costs of the worker's wage and the costs of dead labor in the form of machines. To increase productivity by adopting newer technology means that more products are produced in the same time by the same amount of living labor. And this means that, all other things being equal, the percentage of living labor "embodied" in each product declines. If profit has its basis in surplus value, and surplus value has its basis in the proportion of living labor in the product, and if this declines as a percentage of the value produced, then the rate of profit (the amount of profit relative to the cost of inputs) declines.[11]

Marx did note a number of influences that counteract this tendency. For example, the same increases in productivity decrease the cost of producing the wage-goods that the worker receives, and thus have the effect of increasing the relative amount of surplus value each worker produces. For this and related reasons, there is nothing inevitable about a decline in profit. It is a *tendency,* and by no means always the tendency that predominates. Nevertheless, it points to one major source of the inherent instability of capitalism which can result in crisis when counteracting influences are not sufficiently strong.

Crisis results when the decline in produced surplus value does not leave enough profit over to continue production. The effects of this are common enough: idled plants, laid-off workers, and unsold goods. Furthermore, the slowing down of accumulation makes industrialists all the more dependent on credit, and the bankers all the more insistent that debts be paid off promptly, before firms close down or collapse. The result is a credit crunch that exacerbates the crisis, since firms that previously could pay their debts by extending credit further cannot now do so and therefore go under.[12] But it is precisely at this point that the crisis contributes to its own correction. Not all firms fail in the face of declining surplus value. The most efficient are still able to expand production to profitable levels. The less efficient go under, and are bought up in turn (at depreciated value) by the surviving, efficient firms, enabling ever greater economies of scale. Indeed, the crisis is resolved for the time being when inefficient firms are weeded out and capitalist production is restructured on a scale and level of technology that enables profitable investment, and therefore growth, once again.

This process in itself, though it explains recession—that is, a slowing of production and unemployment—does not explain inflation. All of the above occurs with money holding or, in the case of depreciated machines or overstocked goods, increasing its purchasing power. To understand inflation, one must recall as well that the crisis happens in neither a human vacuum nor a political vacuum.

Marx held that capitalism has need of a pool of unemployed workers available to be brought into production when and where capitalists see opportunity for profitable investment. Marx called this the "industrial reserve army." It functions as well to hold wages down since there always appear to be others willing to work for less. During crisis, as plants shut down, the ranks of this industrial reserve army are swelled. One unwanted consequence is that the increase in the number and visibility of the poor and jobless increases the possibility of unrest and even organized challenges to the capitalist system. We have witnessed, during the half-century since the Great Depression, a vast increase in the level of government intervention in the economy aimed at softening these natural tendencies of capitalism. Much of this has taken the form of guaranteeing loans to faltering businesses and of increasing the amount of money in the economy by increasing the government's own indebtedness. This means that the government has supplied some of the money necessary to enable inefficient firms to continue in business in face of declining surplus. The government does this by increasing the money supply, giving tax credits, granting loans or guaranteeing loans made in the private sector. The effect is inflation: the reality of declining surplus confronting an increasing supply of money means the value of the money must decline. But inflation is a two-edged sword. It works alongside the swelling industrial reserve army to lower the real wages of workers. But it also destabilizes the system further, giving rise to speculation which in turn further fuels the inflation.

In our own period, we can see many of these phenomena reaching critical proportions. The recession of 1974–1975—the worst since the 1930s and already referred to in a standard economic textbook as *The Great Recession*[13]—brought with it inflation at 12 percent. At present, inflation is worse than in the 1974–1975 period; the GNP is declining and unemployment is rising. Under such conditions, it is no surprise that the Carter administration has reneged on its campaign promises and cut social services while adopting the traditionally Republican policy of trying to cool inflation by tightening the money supply and credit.[14] In addition to making life harder for those at the bottom of society, this will also have the effect of forcing more and more inefficient firms out of business. At the same time new depreciation allowances are under consideration that would ease the way for those firms capable of making the shift to more productive technology. Although government policy is affected by many pressures in addition to those exercised by giant corporations, the general drift of this government's policy is toward encouraging a restructuring of capitalism under the domination of the most efficient firms. In our estimation, this explains the supine attitude the Carter administration has taken to the oil companies as these giants raise their prices far beyond the increase in their costs[15] and use their increased surplus to buy up the producers of other forms of energy. Since the money to pay higher gasoline and fuel oil prices must come from somewhere, and need not go into the production of new sources of oil and gasoline, one must view the government's policy as one of allowing a redistribution of the declining surplus into the coffers of the oil majors and in order to be used to buy up huge hunks of the rest of the economy. This money comes not simply out of the hands of consumers, but also out of the companies who either must pay them higher wages to cover the increase or who would have received the dollars that now are spent on higher fuel costs.

The restructuring of capital is proceeding at an accelerating pace. The past months have witnessed a marked upsurge in major take overs and mergers, particularly in energy, electronics, and transportation. At the same time, less efficient companies, like Chrysler, find themselves threatened with collapse. The outcome of the crisis is not predictable. Much depends on the balance of forces between capital and labor, and within capital, between finance capital and industrial capital, and within industrial capital, between the small number of large firms and the large number of small ones. It is possible that the mergers, take overs, and collapses will lead to reorganizing American capital at a higher level of productivity. The combination of increased unemployment, decreased social services, and inflation may depress real wages and thus contribute to more profitable production. In short, it is fully possible that the crisis will rectify itself and lead to a new period of growth.

What is crucial for our purposes is to see that the reality of the crisis is not the vision portrayed in the media. In the press and on TV, we are treated to the spectacle of different politicians offering their recommendations for dealing with the troubled economy as if it were a natural catastrophe or a disagreeable monster. But the crisis is not an event "out there" which is happening to our society; rather, it is a struggle in our society to gather up the declining surplus to survive for another round. This struggle takes the form of rising fuel costs, depreciation allowances, interest rates, inflation, and the rest. Each wrests a portion of the declining value away from some persons (or corporations or sectors or fractions of capital) and gives it to others. If it is true that a capitalist society is a society whose members are locked in a fierce survival struggle over the division of a declining surplus, then the implications are clear: what we call ordinary crime is but the form this struggle takes at the bottom of our society. Of course, the conditions of life at the bottom of our society are not that different in or out of crises. What changes with inflation and unemployment, is the number of people who are at the bottom or fear they may end up there. What changes is the population of the industrial reserve army, particularly that part of the industrial reserve army hovering between employment and unemployment.

Ordinary crime is by and large the form that class struggle takes in the industrial reserve army. The conditions which swell the ranks of the industrial reserve army will increase the incidence of ordinary crime. The nature of this crime reflects the material conditions of the industrial reserve army. Furthest from the socializing and politicizing impact of advanced large-scale factory production, the acts of members of the industrial reserve army are both antisocial and without political consciousness. That the victims of ordinary crimes are often also members of the industrial reserve army reflects the antisocial and unpolitical nature of their reality, as well as the fact that at the bottom of society the struggle for survival takes the form of competition for scarce jobs and resources with people who are also at the bottom. In other words, not only are they deprived of the socializing and politicizing effect of large-scale industry, their actual reality is one of antagonistic relations with people in the same situation. It is for this reason that the industrial reserve army has often been fertile ground for recruiting goons or scabs or brown- or blackshirts to fight against those who have called for a better shake for the working class and the poor.

If this were all there was to say, the above hypothesis would amount to no more than a Marxian translation of the claim that unemployment and inflation are criminogenic. However, the real cutting edge of the hypothesis, based on the analysis that preceded it, is that the crimes of the poor are continuous with acts done at all levels of society under the pressures generated by the crisis. By this, we refer not merely to the so-called white collar crimes or crimes of the rich. The claim is much broader. Under capitalism, competition for scarce resources is a general imperative. In a crisis, the resources become scarcer, the stakes higher, the number of possible winners fewer, the imperative to compete all the more strident. In a crisis, then, at all levels of society, people are grabbing for the declining surplus. The question of whether they do it in a lawful or an unlawful manner is really a question of whether they have the power—the organization, finances, alliances, and so forth—to use the law and its institutions to do their grabbing, or to protect what they already have.

Thus, no simple prediction follows for the incidence of corporate crime. White collar crime of the plebeian sort, like employee pilfering and small-scale embezzling, can be expected to expand. These are actions by people just a few steps removed from the industrial reserve army; the forces which swell its ranks cannot help but make their existence shakier. As crisis heightens the need and the temptation to step over the frontier from sharp to shady business practices, one also ought to expect an increase of corporate crime at the higher levels. But since the crisis intensifies the struggle on all sides, one can expect at these levels an increased mobilization against corporate crime—in the private sector in the form of increased security measures, and in the public sector in the form of increased enforcement of corporate crime statutes. We have of late heard some murmurs of increased prosecution of white collar criminals. Of course, since the rich have nearly infinite understanding for the peculations of their fellows, we should not expect to see this become very harsh. And because the largest corporations have access to the law and the lawmakers, the largest grabs are likely to be within the law, or the law will be stretched out to reach them. Thus, windfall profits as well as depreciation allowances and other tax gifts to the well off will work a "lawful" redistribution of income from some folks' pockets to others. Thus, the oil companies will be railed at but allowed to double the price of oil and gasoline even after all the excuses have been shown to be false, such as the higher price of crude, the Iranian shut-off, and so on.[16] Oil will be "lawfully" decontrolled and as a consequence, upwards of thirty billion additional dollars will be "lawfully" taken from some people's pockets and placed into the already overflowing coffers of the oil companies, while the windfall profits tax is "lawfully" gutted and the requirement that these profits go into the development of new oil sources will be "lawfully" ignored.

In "Capitalism, Class, and Crime in America," David Gordon argues

> that nearly all crimes in capitalist societies represent perfectly *rational* responses to the structure of institutions upon which capitalist societies are based. Crimes of many different varieties constitute functionally similar responses to the organization of capitalist institutions, for those crimes help provide a means of survival in a society within which survival is never assured. Three different kinds of crime in the United States provide the most important examples of this functionally similar rationality among different kinds of crime, ghetto crime, organized crime, and corporate (or "white-collar") crime.[17]

Gordon's argument, in short, is that capitalism needs inequality, insecurity, and competition to drive people to higher and higher levels of productivity. These same features make it rational for individuals to pursue illegal means to survival when legal means won't do: "Driven by fear of economic insecurity and by a competitive desire to gain some of the goods unequally distributed throughout the society, many individuals will eventually become 'criminals.' "[18]

Our analysis takes this argument two steps further. First of all, we wish to emphasize what should be obvious: if normally functioning capitalism generates pressures and incentives toward criminal behavior, capitalism in crisis intensifies the pressures and increases the incentives. Our second point is less evident but of wider significance. Not only is crime a rational response to economic insecurity in a competitive society; it is but one form that competition takes as economic insecurity grows. This in turn means more than simply that crisis pushes individuals at all levels of society to move downward on the spectrum of competitive activities, starting from legitimate forms, then passing the legal frontier into criminal forms. Rather, the location of the legal frontier is itself part of the competitive struggle. Gordon's analysis does not question the legitimacy of the distinction between criminal and noncriminal forms of competitive struggle; he argues that capitalism makes it *rational* to engage in the noncriminal forms. Our analysis asserts that the distinction between criminal and noncriminal forms of competition is itself a product of the competitive struggle. Thus, we are confronted with a range of forms of competition ranging from tax loopholes and price gouging down to shoplifting and burglary—all of which are morally on the same plane. That is, they are all forms of taking property away from people and placing it in new hands. For those who think that the forms of taking property characteristic of the so-called ordinary crimes are morally distinct from actions like tax loopholes and price gouging because the former are violent and the latter not, we have two responses. Since the vast majority of ordinary crimes are property crimes, our overall point is made if the continuity between corporate competition and ordinary property crimes is accepted. However, there is evidence in abundance to prove that the effects of corporate actions are not merely "economic." They result in death, disease, and the whole panorama of suffering and social disintegration that flows from insecurity and unemployment.[19] In short, the notion that only the crimes of the poor are violent is a piece of ideology, dubious in the extreme.

Capitalist society is organized so that the accumulation of value is necessarily at someone else's expense. Greater profits require outdoing competitors and holding down wages. In periods of growth, there is enough around so that accumulation can proceed without major dislocation, except at the very bottom of society. The pressures of competition lead, as we saw above, to shrinking the surplus produced, which leads in turn to driving competitors out of business or taking them over and laying off workers until real wages are low enough and production profitable enough to start up again. In times of crisis, the competition to accumulate values at the expense of others heats up as the available value decreases. With this, the expense to others increases. In this struggle, people resort to the means available to them to grab what they think they need to survive. If the means available include not only legal means but the means of *making* things legal, their grabs will be legal. If not, they will be criminal. From this perspective, then, the moral distinction between criminal and noncriminal forms of competition falls away, leaving virtually all of the forms on the same moral plane. The maintenance of such a moral distinction comes to look increasingly like an ideological cover serving to enhance the efficacy of the law as a weapon in the competitive struggle.

We can speculate on the sort of criminal justice policy this analysis would lead us to expect during a period of crisis. First of all, with declining surplus, we can expect a decline in money for social programs to rehabilitate offenders or provide alternatives to those on the road to criminal careers. This is consistent with the general drying up of resources for social services. In addition, however, the analysis above suggests the need to shore up the public's belief in the moral distinction between lawful forms of competition and criminal forms. In other words, as the crisis forces businesses to engage in even more blatant forms of competitive grabbing, the belief in the moral distinction between these and ordinary crimes is threatened. Were this public belief to be seriously weakened, the legitimacy of the economic system would be seriously undermined. Hence, as competition intensifies throughout the system, we should expect increasing efforts to brand the ordinary criminal forms of competition with moral condemnation. We should not be surprised to see the criminal portrayed as evil and directly responsible for his crime, and the state's role in responding to the criminal portrayed as one of straightforward punishment, with no frills for the bleeding heart liberals who think the state also owes the criminal some remediation of the conditions that led him to crime. In short, one should expect a kind of fundamentalist revival in criminal justice: a return to basics, doing simple justice, holding individuals responsible for their evil deeds, and punishing the wicked—no more and no less. On the basis of this analysis, then, what is currently called "the justice model" is precisely what one would expect during the crisis.[20] Conventional analysis regards the shift to the "justice model" as a response to the failures of rehabilitation and as a result of a shift in the public's mood. Since the general way in which criminal justice responds to its failures is by doing more of the same, and since shifts in the public's mood are not like changes in the weather but have social causes, this conventional explanation is rather lame. We submit that the analysis we have sketched out in this paper provides a much more fruitful path to an understanding of the source and function of the so-called justice model.

NOTES

1. David M. Gordon, "Capitalism, Class and Crime in America," *Crime and Delinquency* (April 1973), pp. 163–185.
2. "For April, May and June [1979], crimes against persons—homicide, rape, robbery and assault—increased 6 percent [in the District of Columbia]. Crimes against property—burglary, larceny, and theft—jumped 9 percent.
   " 'The whole economic situation has a bearing on the crime trend,' [D.C. Police Chief Burtell M.] Jefferson said. He blamed unemployment and inflation for the increase." "District Crime Up Again but Rate of Increase Slowing," *Washington Post,* September 15, 1979, p. C1.

3. For such proof, see, for example, Harvey Brenner, *Paper No. 5: Estimating the Social Costs of National Economic Policy: Implications for Mental and Physical Health and Criminal Aggression*, a study prepared for the use of the Joint Economic Committee of the Congress of the United States, October 26, 1976 (Washington, D.C.: U.S. Government Printing Office, 1976).
4. For an analysis of the ideological role played by the American criminal justice system, see Jeffrey H. Reiman, *The Rich Get Richer and the Poor Get Prison: Ideology, Class, and Criminal Justice* (New York: John Wiley & Sons, 1979), esp. pp. 138–169.
5. Ricardo thought that capitalism tended naturally toward stagnation and other classical political economists fretted over the tendency of the profit rate to fall.
6. Our presentation of the Marxian theory of the crises of capitalism follows that of Ben Fine and Laurence Harris, *Rereading Capital* (New York: Columbia University Press, 1979), pp. 76–89, and John Weeks, *Capital and Exploitation* (Princeton, N.J.: Princeton University Press, forthcoming).
7. Karl Marx, *Capital: A Critique of Political Economy* (New York: International Publishers, 1967), p. 189.
8. Ibid., p. 171.
9. Ibid., p. 193.
10. This is the title of Part III of Volume III of *Capital*.
11. As long as capital accumulation is progressing smoothly, the fall in the rate of profit is offset by the increasing amount of capital advanced which results in an absolute increase in the total surplus value (and thus profit) even though it is declining relatively as a fraction of the total product.
12. For example, the Franklin National Bank of New York (twentieth largest in the U.S.) in 1974, the American National Bank of Houston in 1979.
13. William J. Baumol and Alan S. Blinder, *Economics: Principles and Policy* (New York: Harcourt Brace Jovanovich, 1979), p. 80. Marxist theorist Ernest Mandel calls it "The Second Slump," the first being the Great Depression of the 1930s.
14. On October 6, 1979, the Federal Reserve Board instituted a sharply restrictive monetary policy. See *Newsweek*, October 22, 1979, pp. 36–47.
15. "[I]ncreases in the price of crude oil by the OPEC (cartel) nations can account for less than one-half of the price increase so far this year in refined petroleum products." *Washington Post*, November 7, 1979, p. A1.
16. "Even as imports increased steadily in the first half of 1979, oil companies cut gasoline supplies to service stations by as much as 15 percent. The resulting tight market led to a 50 percent increase in the price of gasoline.
   "The records show that just after Iran stopped oil production on Dec. 26, the U.S. companies sharply increased their crude oil imports from other nations, including Saudi Arabia, Kuwait, Nigeria, Algeria and Venezuela. . . .
   "Indeed, just as Iran concluded its first full month of shutdown in January, Exxon was setting its record for a single month's imports—26.6 million barrels." *Washington Post*, August 29, 1979, p. A22.
17. Gordon, "Capitalism, Class and Crime," p. 174.
18. Ibid.
19. I have documented the extent of this violence in *The Rich Get Richer and the Poor Get Prison*, pp. 44–87.
20. For a conventional defense of "the justice model," see John Conrad, "Corrections and Simple Justice," *Journal of Criminal Law and Criminology*, 54 (1973).

Chapter 3

"Survival" in Economic Downturns: Some Implications for the Criminal Justice System

*Peter B. Meyer**

This chapter is addressed to the problems of "economic down-turns," "survival" in such conditions, and the problems such survival needs impose on the justice system. The definitions of economic down-turn and of this kind of survival are not likely to be familiar to people from different disciplines or professions, and even less familiar to people from divergent socioeconomic groups. We thus begin with a discussion of definitions and meanings.

A number of different actors—or potential survivor units—are of interest to us; for each, we need to define both the nature of an economic downturn and survival. The distinct actors include 1. individuals, that is, human persons, 2. businesses, which might be thought of as corporate persons, and 3. organizations which comprise part of the criminal justice system, such as correctional agencies or institutions. Since these units' perceptions of economic trends and pressures are, in part, functions of real economic measures and conditions, let us examine the so-called objective conditions associated with economic declines.

A version of this chapter was originally presented at the American Society of Criminology Conference in Philadelphia, November 1979.

*Program in Administration of Justice, The Pennsylvania State University.

ECONOMIC DOWNTURNS

An economic downturn has traditionally been defined by a decline in employment levels in the economy as a whole. There are two major gradations of such downturns—recessions and depressions; no depression has hit since that of the 1930s. However, we developed a new national measure of economic decline, "stagnation," in the postwar years to identify periods in which the economy as a whole failed to *grow*. Economic expansion was expected to occur. To a large degree, we still expect expansion in real terms and see static conditions as a form of downturn, since our real growth lies below that which we wanted.

In the past decade, the conception of an economic downturn, reversal, or adverse trend has come to include not merely a drop in employment or in growth of output, but also a rise in the rate of inflation. We have incurred sufficiently drastic price increases that we now recognize as a downturn those situations in which real purchasing power and thus real standards of living fall because inflation is pushing prices up faster than earning power. The term "stagflation" has been employed to designate those periods in which growth has been minimal in real terms, but inflation has accelerated and depressed real buying power.

Traditional recessions, stagnation, and stagflation may all be considered in terms of their impact on the three actors we designated above. Their effects will differ with the extent of another form of economic downturn which has manifested itself in one sector of the U.S. economy and which is of particular concern to those associated with the supply of publicly supported goods and services in this society. This has to do with the willingness of individuals and businesses to support the public sector in general, and is manifest most specifically in state and local actions rejecting or rolling back tax increases. The trend may be labeled PTM, the "Proposition Thirteen Mentality."

PTM emerges from the transformation of the pattern of economic downturns we experienced in the 1970s. Public support for government spending has historically been strong during wars and crises such as major recessions and even stagnation periods, and people griped only minimally about their taxes. The view was, "the nation is in trouble, and we must help." At these times, those with incomes let themselves be taxed to support others without earnings or in order to support a war effort. In either case, the taxpapers were not adversely affected—in income terms—by the crisis. With stagflation, those with incomes high enough to pay taxes to the government are themselves adversely affected by the downturn. In a recession, the taxpayers are those who still have jobs, or businesses, or professions, and they are reasonably certain their taxes will help those in real need, a need which they do not feel. In an inflationary period, everyone suffers a decline in the buying power of their dollars, and even those who are paying taxes will suffer some loss of income. At the same time as they suffer an income loss due to rising prices, however, these people are asked to increase their tax payments. This imposition appears excessive, and a tax revolt results. The response of these taxpayers is not irrational, as is often alleged, or even a reflection of a particular political sentiment—a conservative view of government and its role. In fact, the tax revolt represents a logical response to an economic pinch in which people find themselves, often with little warning, and out of which they see no easy route. (I do not mean to allege that restraints on government revenue collection of the Proposition 13 variety are necessarily logical responses in themselves. A logical concern and worry, when translated into a political demand, often results in an illogical, or even damaging, government action. This issue, however, lies beyond the purview of this paper).

REACTIONS TO ECONOMIC DOWNTURNS

We turn now to how individuals, firms, and the criminal justice system perceive and react to economic downturns. As we proceed, we will find it simpler to distinguish the different perceptions than to identify the responses. For example, our discussion of individual and firm responses to downturns inevitably includes the corrections system and other components of the criminal justice system as we consider the incentives and pressures to which potential criminals respond in conditions of economic downturns.

Economic Downturns and Individuals

Consider the following hypothetical case: a thief charged with armed robbery of a grocery store is having a jury trial. His attorney is summarizing for the defense:

> ... and so, you see, Mr. Smith is *not* a criminal; he is a hardworking member of our society, not having missed a day of work at the Jones and Nagouchi Widget Factory in the twenty years he worked there. Mr. Smith took home his pay and he did not waste it. You have seen the figures: last winter Mr. Smith maintained a 60° temperature in

his home, but paying the fuel oil bill in addition to his mortgage and other fixed costs took all his money. He ran out of borrowing power, as we all can do, and there he was with a wife and two kids—and no food!

Mr. Smith is no welfare cheater or beggar—he was not eligible for assistance because he earned a good wage, and that income made him ineligible for assistance in paying for the enormous fuel bills we have shown you here in court. Was Mr. Smith supposed to let his family become undernourished or starve? Who is the *real* criminal here: Mr. Smith, an honest working man who in desperation held up a grocery store—for food, not money—or the oil companies and the government which have pushed Mr. Smith and the rest of us into this desperate corner?

Would the jury convict? In a nonjury trial, would the judge, who might have to convict, impose a prison sentence? The hypothetical defense summary I have offered here points to *motivation* as a major issue in the guilt or degree of culpability of a person engaged in criminal acts. The question is not simply criminal intent, because Mr. Smith knowingly held up a grocery store; it is also the objective which the proceeds of the crime are to serve. Armed robbery for food is different from armed robbery for drugs, or so it would appear to most people in this society.

The issue of motivation does not allow for desperation as the measure of acceptable motive, since the drug addict may be as desperate for drugs as the starving person is for food. Even so, the issue becomes clouded when the good moral character of the perpetrator of the act is not clearcut. The summary above might be applied to an unemployed worker receiving unemployment compensation which is inadequate to cover his costs. The case would be weaker in that instance, especially since the attorney would have to demonstrate that the defendant had been trying to find work. Similarly, we might apply the summary to a perfectly honest recipient of public assistance, since, to take Pennsylvania as a real case in point, assistance payment levels have not been raised in several years, despite inflation. The success of the desperation-of-the-honest-citizen defense would probably be still lower in this case than for the unemployed worker.

In a stagflation-type economic downturn, then, the justice system might find itself under great pressure to distinguish pure from unacceptable motivations for intentionally criminal acts. This pressure on the judicial arm of the system translates into problems for all the other branches:

1. Police would be expected to judge motives as part of the discretion they exercise in deciding whether to arrest for a certain overt act, while at the same time they are likely to come under ever-increasing pressure to preserve private property rights, and protect businesspeople who are also feeling the economic downturn.

2. Public defenders will be required for an increasing number of cases, if the economic desperation of people who have no criminal record drives them to criminality. Their very desperation reflects a situation in which they have no resources with which to hire attorneys. Criteria for establishing priorities for such cases may become critical if these demands for services are not met by increased public sector funds—a condition which is very likely in stagflation-type downturns. We may face a type of judicial "triage," reserving defense services only for the "deserving" defendents and letting the rest float through the system with minimal assistance or support from attorneys.

3. The correctional establishment will be under pressure to design sanctions which are appropriate to the new types of criminals which the downturn generates. Should they be incarcerated? (In which case, how will their families eat?) What are the appropriate forms of probation or parole supervision, and how would the corrections system provide them? Would correctional officers in probation and parole departments have to get even more intimately involved in the income maintenance system? It is likely that they would—with the possible result being the triage effects suggested above for defense attorneys: we would provide assistance to those who, without assistance, might commit crimes rather than go away quietly. Such assistance provision would make sense from the criminal justice system perspective, since it would cost less than processing a new crime committed in desperation, but the tendency of the welfare establishment has been to favor the "deserving poor," and criminals are *not* more deserving than law-abiding poor people. The conflict of orientations and goals is bound to worsen in this area.

This discussion of a particular criminal act and its defense has served to illustrate how the effects of an economic downturn on individuals may make itself felt on other organizations and institutions. We can now be more specific in identifying the effects of recent economic downturns on people, and some of the system responses to criminal actions in these downturns. We consider first the characteristics of the new bank robber of the late 1970s, as profiled in the *New York Times;* we then turn to data on incarceration tendencies developed by the Congressional Research Service.

New York City has been experiencing a major surge in bank robberies, hitting six per working day in August 1979, and apparently doubling the number of such robberies in the early 1970s.[1] There have been charges that the problem is attributable to a decline in bank security measures, but one specialist in bank security responded that, ". . . what's happening in New York is the result of big city problems such as unemployment. . . ."[2] What may happen as the problem attributed to big cities becomes more widespread in an economic downturn is an expansion, both in geographic location and in total recorded events, of the types of incidents now described as "big city problems."

The characteristics of bank robbers have also changed, according to the New York police:

> Only a decade ago, the police profile of the average bank robber was that of an experienced, professional criminal who usually worked with a heavily armed team on a few well-planned holdups.
>
> Today, the experts say, the average bank robber is in his 20s, unemployed, a petty criminal who normally works alone. About half the time he is an unarmed note passer who decides impulsively which bank to rob. The average loot is less than $1000, and eventually most of the robbers are arrested.[3]

Bank robbery, a federal offense, has thus changed in character, yet the offense remains the same on the books. The judicial and correctional treatment of the perpetrators may not have shifted appropriately.

In fact, there is startling evidence about patterns of incarceration which suggests that, while the danger and impact level of the crime of bank robbery has declined, the likelihood of incarceration for a convicted perpetrator has increased as the economic downturn has become more severe. The Congressional Research Service of the Library of Congress presented a study in 1974, at the request of the Subcommittee on Penitentiaries of the Senate Judiciary Committee, which attempted long-range predictions of prison populations.[4] The study examined prison admissions and populations during the period 1960–1972 and extrapolated from that experience for the 1973–1980 period. Attempting to project admissions to Federal penitentiaries, the authors had to confront a common dilemma:

> The pattern of fluctuations of admissions from 1960 to 1972 was quite irregular. There was neither an increasing nor a decreasing trend. . . .
> Thus, it was obvious that we could not make a straight-line projection based on our data; neither were we successful in correlating with our prison admissions any of the following: total U.S. population (or some

population subset); birth rate; crime rate; or any other measure which seemed to bear an *a priori* relationship to admissions.[5]

Needing some measure which had been projected into the future and which correlated with prison admissions in order to project the admissions themselves, the authors continued their search until they came to the annual U.S. unemployment rate. They discovered that: "The unemployment rate has a striking similarity to the pattern of admissions. The simple correlation between new admissions and the unemployment rate for the period 1960 to 1972 was 0.906—meaning that the unemployment rates could describe 82% of the year-to-year variation in new admissions to prisons. . . . The relationship was found to have a one-year lag. . . ."[6]

To the extent that this correlation has held since 1972, we find that the probability of any convicted federally charged person going to prison has risen with the unemployment rate, and our "modern" bank robbers are more likely to go to prison than their more violent forebearers were during periods of high employment. Pursuing a logical explanation for the statistical relationship, the authors of the CRS report identify a number of possible reasons for this pattern, citing marginal workers shifting to crime as one possible cause (belied by their own data on crime rates), and concluding that, "an offender would be more likely to be confined to prison in a time of high unemployment—when job opportunities and, therefore, rehabilitation prospects would appear low."[7] The one-year lag in response to the shift in unemployment seems to reflect the need for judicial personnel to react to changes in job prospects.

The economic downturn which affects people and their criminal activity levels, therefore, may have a compounded effect on the corrections establishment. To the extent that people are convicted of crimes, more of them will be likely to go to prison. (The state prison admission data correlation with unemployment was 0.859, almost as high as the coefficient for the Federal prisons.[8]) Thus, the economic downturn which raises unemployment rates is also likely to pinch the resources of the corrections establishment by demanding more expensive incarceration, rather than less expensive probation.

Economic Downturns and Businesses

Little has been written in a systematic way about businesses as violators of law, especially criminal law. Even the analysis and examination of white-collar criminality moves in cycles, possibly in response to economic downturns, but the study of corporate criminality has been marked by virtual absence from discussions of the criminal justice system.

The significance of white-collar crime was well described by Hermann Mannheim over thirty years ago:

> For the U.S., it is estimated that the total losses from conventional robbery, burglary, thievery, pocket-picking, and the like, amount to something between fifty and four hundred million dollars a year, whereas the damage inflicted on the American public by two types of fraud, i.e., bogus bankruptcies and the sale of worthless stocks and bonds, is estimated at about one billion dollars per year.[9]

All white-collar criminality obviously presented a larger total "bill," despite the presence of the Securities and Exchange Commission and, as of 1948, roughly one dozen different fraud agencies in the Federal government. Nineteen-forty-eight was a period of economic boom, yet white-collar crime was massive. During an economic downturn, the volume of such criminality may be expected to expand almost exponentially, although the problems of discovery and reporting of such offenses make it difficult to provide statistical evidence of such a trend.

The contention that such activity expands exponentially is based upon simple logic: the only entities whose actual survival gets threatened significantly in an economic downturn are businesses, which can fail or go bankrupt under adverse conditions. There is thus tremendous pressure to cheat or cut costs to increase sales in whatever manner is possible. Moreover, in the U.S., we have found that, ". . . it is virtually impossible to see a person as both a respectable entrepreneur and a criminal," so criminal justice system sanctions on white-collar criminals, even when they have been caught, have been very light.[10] John Watkins has noted that businessmen's criminal actions are seen as *mala prohibita*, not *mala in se*, and that, "the values held by an industrial elite have belittled the hazards of white-collar criminality and correspondingly the condemnation sanctions available. . . ."[11]

The bottom line, as the accountants tabulating business profits are likely to comment, is that white-collar criminality, is not punished in any sense. A case is brought either before administrative authorities (in the regulatory proceedings for civil charges) or before a criminal court judge (although we have been loath to employ the authority to impose criminal charges in most business law violations). A consent decree, typically with a cease and desist order designed to stop the activity which was illegal, is the normal outcome of the regulatory proceeding, while *nolo contendere* pleas and suspended sentences characterize the rare criminal treatment. No real incarceration or control sanction is imposed, the avoidance of a trial minimizes status losses, and the nature of the sanctions is such that no economic loss is suffered for the discovery of the crime, since fines can be passed on to customers in higher prices. (The 1970s have seen the development of consent decrees which actually ask the perpetrators to repay the funds they have acquired by fraudulent means, but this is a new development in the imposition of sanctions; the only recourse available previously for the victim was personal civil suit against the perpetrator. The complainant had to prove wrongdoing in such cases, since no violation of law was admitted in court by the perpetrator.)

Recent years have seen much more widespread news coverage and other discussions of corporate criminality. This new pattern has not focused primarily on the white-collar type of economic crimes perpetrated by corporate and other business entities, but rather has dealt with so-called pure business crimes—activities private individuals can rarely engage in by themselves. We have seen businesses charged not merely with labor relations violations (as was J.P. Stevens, alleged to have violated the National Labor Relations Act over 1400 times), but also with pollution of air and water, endangerment of workers and others in dangerous workplaces, and by engaging in shoddy waste disposal practices. Environmental law has brought the corporation and its actions in violation of law out of the shadows and into the limelight. The more we examine corporate actions, however, starting with environmental activities, the more we discover that their manner of dealing with government regulators, with communities in which they have plants or other places of business, and with workers involves actions which are questionable from a criminal law perspective.

Despite the publicity, there is little evidence that white-collar, and especially corporate business criminality is being deterred, or that the criminal justice system is responding to the need to control private economic power. Watkins explains this phenomenon by noting simply that, "The criminal label is antithetical to all our assumptions of what an American businessman represents."[12] This is a nonanswer to the dilemma posed by this criminal activity. We need to understand *why* we cannot reconcile criminality and business activity in order to understand how the business response to economic downturns affects the criminal justice system. Warren Gramm has provided the kernel of an explanation in a discussion of the use of "higher law" to undermine common law on behalf of some special interest group:

> The advanced private market system—mature industrial capitalism—
> has within it elements that are destructive of the rule of law on which
> liberal capitalism historically was grounded . . .
>
> . . . unlawful activity is rationalized by recourse to a higher principle . . .
> a higher law . . . For capitalism . . . such higher law is the protection of
> individual freedom.
>
> Institutionalization of the higher law, that is, the systematic avoiding,
> evading and disobeying of the common law . . . [is] . . . manifested in the
> preferred treatment of the corporate person.
>
> The liberal rule of law has broken down under the unstated yet overrid-
> ing end of protecting private property and preserving capitalism.

The urgency of the need to protect private property and businesses
rises with the severity of economic downturns. Consequently, the
higher law rationalization for business and white-collar illegalities
will be called upon more and more. However, since this higher law is
the principle of individual freedom, citation of this "right" will affect
nonbusiness criminality as well. The perpetrator of street crimes can,
by extension of the individual freedom logic cited by businesses, ra-
tionalize his or her actions, regardless of indirect consequences for
others. Since the pressure for economic rewards increases in an economic downturn, the broader the acceptance of the business rationalization, the greater the crime problem—and the more pervasive and
extensive the breakdown in the liberal rule of law. In such a setting,
the idea of corrections has little meaning, except in so far as a strongly
retributive and punitive system may deter criminality. Of course, this
contribution can emerge only if the sanctions are, in fact, imposed. We
have seen that sanctions are not likely to be imposed on white-collar
and corporate criminals; the example of the defense attorney pleading
purity of motive in crimes perpetrated for economic survival, not material gain or other less legitimate ends, suggests that the sanctions
may not be imposed on individuals convicted of street crimes either, at
least not when economic duress is sufficiently severe.

Downturns and the Criminal Justice System

We have established that major economic downturns, especially those
of a stagflation type, produce the following effects:

1. A major increase in individual criminality, born in part out of
   desperation, and likely to be more acceptable to society as a
   whole than routine, traditional criminality;

2. A concurrent decrease in willingness to support government spending, especially as inflated by uncontrolled price increases;
3. An ever-widening net of white-collar and business crimes, with attendant rationales which tend to undermine the rule of law;
4. Greater reliance on the principle of individual freedom as a goal to be served, resulting in a conflict between preservation of private property through adherence to this principle and an attack on private property by impoverished individuals, claiming the individual freedom rationale for their acts; and
5. A heightening of social tensions and conflicts between social classes as a result, coinciding with an apparent decline in the deterrent and social control capacities of the criminal justice system as a whole, especially that of corrections.

What are the imperatives facing criminal justice institutions and agencies concerned with their own survival in such downturns?

The key to survival for any government agency is the sponsorship or protection of a powerful political interest group. The more severe the pressure on an agency or program, the more desperate its need for such political protection. The reduced capacity for social control, which may be expected to emerge in future economic downturns as it has in the past, will impose severe pressures on the criminal justice system. The declining real dollar value of the public fisc, which results from the stagflation condition and the rational taxpayer response to this kind of downturn, will exacerbate the interagency conflict over allocation of limited public funds. We must expect that the criminal justice system will look to serve a powerful political sponsor.

The contradiction and conflict identified above as the fourth stagflation effect will be resolved by the justice system in favor of a sponsor, if the system can find such a source of support. The support required by the system may be expected to emerge from the corporate business sector, in pursuit of the preservation of its privileges and private property. We can return to Warren Gramm for an assessment of the implications of the "adoption" of the criminal justice system by the corporate interests acting in government: "Authoritarianism stems from the intimate, symbiotic relationship between economic and political interests and power. Pluralists . . . ignore the fundamental dualism of . . . oligopolistic firms on the one side and small firms, workers, and consumers on the other."[14]

An increase in authoritarianism seems to be the least dangerous result to emerge from the survival pressures associated with the new types of economic downturns we must now confront.

Returning to the last downturn which produced major institutional change, we can cite the warning of an avid observer of the institutional shifts which emerged during the Depression as another frame of reference and a basis for judgment. Henry Simons saw in the reforms of the Roosevelt years the emergence of "private monopolies with the blessing of regulation and support of law" which would eventually prove to be "malignant cancers in the system."[15] A cancer will eventually kill the system which carries it; oil companies and other multinational corporations have been charged with laying the foundations of our current economic malaise, which some speculate might be a terminal illness.

Simon's vision might be all too accurate. The real challenge to the criminal justice system, in responding to the pressures brought on by the economic downturns we now experience, is to find the homeowner in the hypothetical case developed above "not guilty, since he did not act freely but while under coercion," and to find the oil company guilty of the coercion, if not effective extortion. Can the system rise to this challenge? I doubt it. Yet, it must; the alternative is Simon's final prediction: the emergence of a fascist police state.

NOTES

1. Selwyn Raab, "Profile of Today's Bank Robber: A Jobless Petty Criminal in 20's," *New York Times* (August 23, 1979), pp. Al and B7.
2. Richard Rescoria, of the Bank Administrator's Institute, quoted in Raab, "Profile," p. B7.
3. Raab, "Profile," p. Al.
4. William H. Robinson, Phyllis Smith, Jean Wolf, "Prison Population and Costs—Illustrative Projections to 1980," *Congressional Reference Service Report No. 74–95 ED*, Library of Congress, Washington, D.C., April 24, 1974, multilithe.
5. Ibid., pp. 18–19.
6. Ibid., p. 19.
7. Ibid., p. 20.
8. Ibid., p. 31.
9. Hermann Mannheim, *Criminal Justice and Social Reconstruction* (1948), p. 119, cited in John H. Watkins; "White-Collar Crime, Legal Sanctions and Social Control," *Crime and Delinquency* XXIII:3 (July 1977): 297.
10. Watkins, "White-Collar Crime," p. 291.
11. Ibid., p. 301.
12. Ibid., p. 298.
13. Warren S. Gramm, "Industrial Capitalism and the Breakdown in the Liberal Rule of Law," *Journal of Economic Issues* VII:4 (December 1973): 577, 578, 579, 595.
14. Ibid., p. 597.
15. Henry S. Simons, "The Requisites of Free Competition," *American Economic Review* XXVI, Supplement (March 1936): 74–75.

Chapter 4

Economic Adversity, Reindustrialization, and Criminality

*Kevin N. Wright**

THEORETICAL CRIMINOLOGY AND ECONOMIC ADVERSITY: COUNTERVAILING PREDICTIONS

A consideration of the changes in the incidence of crime which might occur during an economic decline raises an old research question about economic determinism as a causal explanation of criminality. If there is a causal relationship between economic factors and influences and crime, then we should expect a corresponding change in the incidence of crime during any economic fluctuation. Vold has summarized the basic assumptions concerning economic determinism and criminality as follows:

There is, of course, good historical basis for the ideology of economic influence on human arrangements. The production, distribution, consumption and exchange of goods and services everywhere occupy a major part of the activities of most human beings. This is the simple but far-reaching fact behind the idea that economic factors influence the nature and form of all social relations... Since in theories of economic in-

*School of General Studies and Department of Political Science, State University of New York at Binghamton

fluence, it is assumed that social arrangements generally are profoundly affected by (determined in the view of extremists) the existing system of economics, it follows that the problems and maladjustments of society, such as crime, are also the product of and affected by the existing economy.[1]

It is obvious that the effects of the economy on our lives is pervasive; many would even contend that in some manner the economy affects every aspect of our lives. For this reason, several, if not most, of the theories of crime causation incorporate various economic variables. Products of economic adversity such as unemployment and familial disruption have been found to be related to criminality. It is, therefore, certainly reasonable to expect that the probability of the crime rate remaining unchanged would be quite low.

Radzinowicz has shown that there are at least three ways of thinking about the relationship of economic factors and criminality. Crime has been viewed as embedded in the capitalist system, in relation to economic insecurity, and in relation to affluence.[2] The first of the ideas, which is based on the Marxian paradigm, takes a firmer stand than the latter two on the strength of economic determinism in that economic conditions are considered to *determine,* or control, all aspects of social relations and social institutions.[3] Crime is considered to be a direct result of the inevitable competition and insecurity of the capitalist system and is, therefore, viewed as a method of coping with these economic contingencies.[4] It is expected or predicted that crime would virtually disappear when the capitalist system is replaced with a classless, egalitarian society, because such a change would eliminate the economic conditions which produce criminality.[5] On the other hand, during economic adversity within the capitalist system, economic insecurity and competition would be heightened and crime would be expected to increase.[6]

The second line of inquiry as outlined by Radzinowicz concerning the relationship of criminality to economic factors focuses on "the extent to which economic factors—much more narrowly defined—can be regarded as among the many contributory causes of certain types of crime."[7] Clearly, this perspective does not take the uncompromisingly deterministic Marxist viewpoint, yet contains strong elements of a production function. Intuitively, it is easy to imagine that economic adversity could create situations which would drive some individuals to commit crimes. An unemployed and impoverished person might steal in order to survive. It is also easy to imagine middle- and upper-class people committing various property and white-collar offenses during an economic downturn, in order to maintain their past standard of living. In both of these cases, criminal behavior would serve a utilitarian purpose and would represent one method of adapting to economic adversities.

Economic adversity and disaster have been shown to disrupt the stability and structure of the social system. In such situations, social bonds may be broken and the cultural system which contributes to social control may be modified or destroyed. Old cultural rules and social standards may no longer be appropriate for controlling the behavior of societal members. The end result of economic change may be a high degree of social disorganization and anomie. The increased incidence of criminal behavior has often been described by criminologists as an inevitable symptom or product of social disorder. Accordingly, the entire community, during severe economic depression, might experience rates of street crime as high as those normally experienced in slum areas.[8]

A final reason why acceleration of the crime rate might be experienced during an economic decline is found in the effects of such a situation on the individual. Economic strain often increases individual tension and anxiety, which for certain personality types could lead to personal violence. Most theories concerned with stress indicate that different people cope in different ways. One method involves the displacement of frustration and anger by striking out at others. In this manner, not only economic and property, but personal offenses as well might increase during an economic decline.

While the ideas just outlined may be intuitively appealing and logical, empirical investigation has shown the relationship between economic conditions and criminality to be quite complex. Radzinowicz's own research indicated that at times a clear link can be identified between an increase in a particular type of crime and a particular type of economic change. However, as Radzinowicz notes, it is "futile to expect an exact parallelism" between crime and economic conditions. "More often the correlation expresses itself in the fact that the two curves move in the same direction and close to each other in time; but they do not display a similar intensity of change." It seems that certain crimes are more sensitive to economic fluctuations than others. There is also a period of lag-time involved in the causal relationship—a length of time which passes before economic change begins to effect the incidence of crime. Furthermore, Radzinowicz found that periods of affluence have a less dramatic influence in reducing crime than do periods of adversity in increasing it.[9]

Current research on the relationship between unemployment and criminality has also indicated the complexity of the causal relationship which exists between the two variables. Analyses of aggregate data have identified a slight but significant relationship between unemployment and crime such that a small to moderate increase in crime should occur corresponding to higher unemployment. Studies of individual data have indicated that the type of individual involved is also an important variable in the production function. Unemployment increases chances for the incidence of some types of crime but reduces the probability for some other types. This research indicates, furthermore, that the quality of employment and the work experience may also be important factors in the production of criminality.[10]

The final line of inquiry into the relationship between the economy and criminality has argued that crime is produced in the midst of affluence. Radzinowicz describes this diverse group of theories as follows:

> In more limited terms these explanations may be related directly to the driving forces of a prosperous society, to its competitive spirit and emphasis on material achievement. Or they may be related to the discrepancies in such societies, the comparative frustration of those who cannot get to the top. Or they may be related to the outright failures of affluent societies, the gaps in welfare, the pockets of sheer poverty that survive almost untouched by general progress ... Traces of the Marxist interpretation merge into theories about the impact of poverty in a wealthy society and emerge in such concepts as anomie.[11]

Radzinowicz points out that according to these theories crime is an element of economic expansion, a response to economic frustration, and a product of economic dereliction.[12]

It is interesting to note that the theories falling within this category produce seemingly conflicting predictions about the effects of economic adversity on the incidence of crime. One well established theory which considers crime in relation to affluence can be conceptualized in terms of "relative deprivation." Relative poverty rather than absolute poverty is theorized to produce criminality. Thus, when the poor are exposed to affluent life styles or live in close proximity to the wealthy, poverty crime is more likely to occur.[13] Insofar as economic adversity in the forms of recession and inflation may widen the gap between the poor and the wealthy during economic adversity, and those services which ameliorate the effects of poverty may be substantially reduced, an increase in crime would be predicted.

On the other hand, various criminologists have suggested that American values and the American way of life may actually produce criminal behavior. Tannenbaum, for example, suggested that it is only logical that a society produces or generates a particular behavior, since the society provides an environment for the development and persistence of that behavior.[14] Similarly, Taft suggested that certain societies embody a culture which can be linked to the production of high crime rates.[15] Values such as materialism, individualism, extravagant consumption, and status striving contribute to the high rate of crime experienced in the United States. In contrast, a society which emphasizes self-control and integrity above economic and social success may have significantly lower rates of crime. Two recent comparative studies have found the presence of particularly effective, yet different, informal controls in Japan[16] and Switzerland[17] provides for relatively low rates of crime. Bayley, in concluding his report, described the significance of these findings:

> [T]he levels of criminal behavior that Americans find so disturbing may be the inevitable consequence of aspects of national life that Americans prize—individualism, mobility, privacy, autonomy, suspicion of authority, and separation between public and private roles, between government and community. The United States may have relatively high levels of criminality because it is inhabited by Americans.[18]

The significance to our discussion of the widely held sentiment of criminologists that the American way of life produces crime lies in the possibility that economic change could precipitate a change in the American culture in such a way as to reduce crime. An economic decline would probably reduce mobility, travel, and recreation outside of the neighborhood. This reduction in turn might contribute to the revitalization of community life and the neighborhood and the reestablishment of complimentary informal social controls. Similarly, economic change and its consequences might also promote significant changes in the family which would in turn reduce crime. Reduced, inflation-adjusted income may force many families to spend greater amounts of leisure time in the home. Economic strain might also enhance cohesion with the familial group. These two changes would strengthen the effectiveness of the primary group in affecting social control.

A shift from a consumption ethic to a survival ethic would probably accompany severe economic adversity and would possibly serve to reduce the incidence of crime. The acceptability and tolerance of economic crimes would probably drop. The "Robinhood" rationalization would lose some of its meaning in a severely depressed economy. During times of opulence, material goods, because they are possessed in such quantity, may not be respected by either their owner or the thief. The material possessions necessary for survival, however, may be accorded a special recognition and value. The incidence of property crime could, therefore, be drastically reduced during severe economic adversity.

Based on the two examples just given, it is quite possible that different economic situations can have very different effects on different kinds of crime. For this reason, simultaneous increases and decreases in various categories of crime during an economic downturn may not be contradictory but simply the product of the economic effect on different situations. To date, neither the theoretical models nor the empirical research that includes economic factors provide a clear picture of the relationship between the economy and crime. In fact, it seems fairly certain that the various theories and studies have considered different economic factors or different sets of interactions which incorporate economic factors in the formulation of their causal propositions. Both Vold and Radzinowicz have concluded that the relationship between economic factors and criminality is quite complex in that additional factors and variables play important roles in the production of criminality. Radzinowicz summarizes these thoughts as follows:

> Economic factors are still a major factor in the etiology of crime. They are so by their direct impact and by their indirect influences over many other social circumstances and moral attitudes. But in our complex society their effect can be redirected, or reshaped, by the intervention of other circumstances and forces—the whole representing an interconnected complex which cannot be easily disentangled.[19]

Radzinowicz's summary leads us to conclude that any prediction concerning the effects of economic adversity on crime will be fraught with a high degree of uncertainty. In order to begin to predict the outcome of the effects of the economy on crime, it is necessary to have a fairly explicit description of the nature of the economic change and any accompanying social and political changes. Specific attention to the complexity of the economic situation and the corresponding social and political factors, would, therefore, be an appropriate place to begin such an analysis.

THE STATUS OF THE AMERICAN ECONOMY

The extent and nature of economic adversity which will be experienced in the U.S. in the near future can be analyzed only by reviewing the current status of the economy and the factors that influence it. It has been shown that fluctuations in the economy are cyclical in nature, with upswings followed by downturns, and so forth. The fact that the economy is entering a declining phase, therefore, does not necessarily indicate that severe problems exist or that significant changes are imminent. However, experts today fairly consistently predict that rising economic problems are both extensive and complex and that significant and pervasive change is highly probable.

As Levine has succinctly described, "the once mighty U.S. economy, following years of neglect and overuse, is aging and tired."[20]

Many of the problems faced by the U.S. economy result from the faulty assumption that fossil fuel energy sources would be indefinitely available and inexpensive. Owing to recent developments in this area, the industrial base is in many areas antiquated, and transportation systems are insufficient and are growing increasingly expensive to operate. There is a pressing need to modernize machinery and technology so that industry may operate in a more efficient way. It is also imperative that new energy sources be developed. But problems of the economy go beyond the energy crisis. Within the industrial base, that has such a need for substantial renovation, there is a lack of innovation and low productivity. These problems are exacerbated by high interest rates, slow growth, and capital shortages. These conditions create a situation within the economy which has been described as stagnation. During such a period, high rates of unemployment can be expected. Individuals and families, as well as businesses, can expect to experience high rates of inflation along with high interest rates. There is, therefore, a basic need to rebuild the U.S. industrial base—a need, as currently described, to *reindustrialize*.

The fact that the U.S. economy is faced with the substantial task of reindustrialization may also be part of its cyclical nature. In addition to its short phase cycle of upswings and downturns, there may also be a longer phase including periods of significant adversity. The Russian economist Nikolai Kondratieff was the first to observe this 45- to 60-year cycle; contemporary and conservative econometricians such as Jay W. Forrester have now made similar observations.[21] Imbalances such as overcapacity and excessive debt seem to develop within the economic system over time; depressions seem to rectify the problems and return stability and growth to the system. The American economic system, in other words, seems to foster a situation in which unavoidable imbalances are created by short-term exploitation at the expense of long-term stability.

The noted sociologist Amitai Etzioni suggested recently that American society has reached a crossroad at which it must make the "fundamental choice between a society that stresses 'quality of life' objectives such as a cleaner environment and more leisure and a society dedicated to the task of 'reindustrialization.'" Etzioni, like others, argues that the country's industrial base has been neglected and abused in recent years and is now ill prepared to meet future demands and levels of consumption. The nation's industrial machine is in need of modernization. It is argued that the industrial base must be rebuilt or else Americans will suffer a lower standard of living. Reindustrialization will be extremely expensive, however, costing billions of dollars each year—an expenditure which, as Etzioni suggests, will preclude the simultaneous promotion of quality of life. The nation simply cannot afford to pursue both sets of objectives. In the final analysis, Etzioni states, the United States will probably select reindustrialization since "it is our most recent tradition and what we do best."[22] His assessment of the current dilemma, and his prediction that the option of reindustrialization will be selected, are both probably accurate. However, his rationale—that reindustrialization will be pursued because it is "what we do best" and what we have always done—is inaccurate.

Nations and societies, as collective bodies, do not make decisions or take action. Interest groups and political influentials make decisions and dictate action to be taken. If the decision to reindustrialize is made, it will be because those within the national interest structure who favor it have sufficient power to see that such an objective is pursued.

The current political climate would in many ways seem to be gravitating toward such a trend. Force behind conservative and ultraconservative ideologies and politics is intensifying. The extension of tax benefits and incentives to corporations (with the exception of the windfall tax bill) is receiving greater attention. Industries and utilities are lobbying for reduced federal regulation, particularly in the area of environmental protection, in order that cheaper forms of energy can be utilized and developed. The reduction of government spending is a topic which is receiving considerable discussion and action.

In an article considering the similarities between the present social situation and the pre-1930 depression, Stoken advances a most interesting thesis. He notes that at the peak of an economic upswing, people tend to be carefree, liberal, and even hedonistic; however, as a *crunch* approaches, people tend to revert to a more conservative lifestyle. Stoken discusses how such a trend is evidenced today. The style of dress and music, the ways in which leisure time is spent, politics, and values all seem to be directed toward a more conservative orientation.[23] The nation may well be readying itself for, or at least drifting toward, a period of restabilization.

ECONOMIC FLUCTUATIONS AND SOCIAL CHANGE

The future economic picture discussed in the preceding section is one of stagnation. Short-term exploitation has brought about an imbalance in which high inflation and unemployment will be experienced along with sustained limited growth and recession. Without significant efforts to modernize the industrial base, continued industrial and economic growth could be precluded. I am arguing in this chapter that reindustrialization will be an important if not the paramount priority within the U.S. in coming years. In this section, I analyze the effects such a trend will have on specific social changes and, in particular, on crime and criminal justice. At least three significant changes are probable.

Corporate Competition and Domination

Based upon the assumptions that the industrial base needs to be modernized and that reindustrialization will be a priority of the future, we should expect that competition for survival among corporations will be heightened. Survival of the individual enterprise will depend upon the ability to redevelop by modernizing technology, seeking low-cost energy or energy-conserving equipment and machinery, and developing new products, new markets, and new ways of doing things without overextending and overtaxing the enterprise in the short-term. In short, corporations will be forced to give added attention to long-term survival while trying to survive the short-term adversity. Obviously, the stronger corporations will be more competitive and better able to adapt and survive. This situation will create two changes that are important to the discussion at hand.

First, during a period of economic adversity and heightened competition, greater demands for *legalized* corporate crime will probably arise. Corporations will lobby for the redefinition of acts which have in the past been considered illegal. For example, the complaint is frequently voiced that governmental regulation stifles growth and the development of new technologies. A concise, yet somewhat emotional, summary of these voices has been written by John Tirman:

> [T]he true guardians of the Right, the relative anonymous corporate
> managers, were waging what appears increasingly to be a religious
> war—the crusade against government regulation. The call to arms can
> be heard, as usual, in the business media. The *Wall Street Journal,* no
> surprise, never misses a chance to excoriate an offending agency. *Time,*
> *Newsweek,* the *New York Post,* the *Los Angeles Times,* the *Washington*
> *Post*—all have recently railed against the multiple sins and wickedness
> of "excessive regulation" ... Government regulation has been blamed
> for the misfortunes of the steel industry, the energy crisis, skyrocketing
> food costs and a chronic housing shortage. The cost of regulation, say its
> foes, has reached $100 billion a year—5% of GNP—and is rising
> rapidly.[24]

It is often claimed that environmental protection standards must be tempered if corporations are to remain competitive and able to develop new and less dangerous means of providing energy. Similarly, employee protection regulations are cited as a cause of unemployment due to the added bureaucratic and economic burdens placed on companies. Recent studies have indicated trends toward deregulation resulting from the effects of pressure exerted by businesses.[25]

The exploitation of communities by corporations is yet another example of legal corporate crime which will probably increase during intensified economic adversity and competition. Meyer has identified three forms of economic coercion that is perpetrated by corporations on communities:

(a) *Requiring a Payoff or Kickback:* A corporation, indifferent as to whether to expand its existing plant in a community or build a new plant elsewhere, informs the local government of the community in which it operates that, in the absence of tax advantages for its new construction, it will move elsewhere (and cause substantial local unemployment).

(b) *Influence Peddling:* A corporation with a manufacturing plant in a community informs the local authorities that, should the municipality enforce environmental regulations as regards sewage discharges, it will advise other manufacturers that the community is a poor location with inadequate services.

(c) *Affecting Reputation:* A commercial bank involved in floating municipal bonds informs a locality entering the bond market that, unless it deposits its funds in a stipulated local bank, its bond rating will be lowered.[26]

As the effects of economic adversity are felt and competition intensifies, the likelihood of this form of exploitation would be correspondingly heightened. The same economic factors would be affecting the community simultaneously, making it a more viable candidate for victimization.

A final example of legal corporate crime that can be expected to increase in the future is monopolization. As competition intensifies and weaker competitors are forced out of the market, an obvious tendency toward monopoly will arise. The government will be forced to recognize and regulate, to a certain extent, monopolies in industries such as communications, transportation, and business machines.

The push to legalize corporate crime can be understood as an attempt to deregulate corporate activities and to grant greater freedoms to industry. During an economic upswing, industry can financially tolerate government regulation; but during economic adversity, the need to streamline production, to retrench, and to emphasize redevelopment reduces such tolerance. For this reason, greater demands can be expected to follow. The social and political conservatism which accompanies a significant economic downswing, as outlined in the preceding section, provides an appropriate climate for such change. It seems highly probable, therefore, that an increase in legal corporate crime will be experienced during the coming years.

A second important change that will result from intensified corporate competition will affect the enforcement of laws regarding white-collar and corporate crime. It can be argued, and has been elsewhere in this volume, that white-collar crime such as employee theft, embezzlement, and tax evasion, and corporate crime such as price fixing, consumer fraud, and stock manipulations, will increase as a result of the insecurities produced by economic adversity. However, irrespective of any probable increase, there is presently sufficient incidence of such activity to make it an important issue in a highly competitive environment. The demand for more intensive enforcement of laws regarding white-collar crime might serve as a means of cutting costs and retrenchment for an individual corporation. The growing popularity of such consulting firms as Kroll Associates, Unitel Inc., and Intertel, which specialize in white-collar investigation, supports this possibility.[27] Similarly, the demand for enforcement laws regarding corporate crime might be an effective method of hindering or eliminating a competitor. A stable and financially solvent corporation can stand the scrutiny of increased enforcement and the financial losses associated with detection and punishment better than less stable competitors. For this reason, the strong and more powerful corporations within the market are likely to push for more stringent enforcement of laws against white-collar and corporate crime. The corresponding conservative climate associated with significant economic downturns will again support such a change. Promotion of enforcement will not only cut costs and hurt competitors but will also improve the corporation's public image.

Exacerbation of the Socioeconomic Gap

The direct influence of any upcoming economic adversity on street criminality will probably be marginal. As indicated by the theoretical and empirical evidence discussed in the first section of this chapter, and the in-depth review of research presented by Long and Witte in Chapter 5, the influence of economic fluctuations on criminality has not been found to be substantial. Continued high inflation and growing unemployment might increase property crimes slightly, but such potential gains would possibly be offset by increased cohesion and reduced disorganization within the family and community. However, this factor does not preclude the possibility of the secondary effects of economic adversity producing important changes in crime and criminal justice.

Various economists have argued that capitalist society produces and requires a surplus labor force. This segment of the population is composed of two groups: one which fluctuates between employment and unemployment and can be called into the work force when needed, and one which for various reasons is unemployable and not needed within the work force.[28] Economic adversity in the form of continued high inflation and growing unemployment might further clarify and widen the socioeconomic gap between this segment and the rest of the population. Those who move in and out of the work force will be unable to find employment during economic adversity and industrial retrenchment, and the marginal economic situation of the unemployable will be further exacerbated by high inflation. As this gap between "haves" and "have-nots" becomes more pronounced, a stronger sense of relative deprivation might be fostered within the surplus population. Relative deprivation, as outlined in the first section of this chapter, has been regarded by many theorists as a significant factor in the production of criminality. If the economic situation in any way exaggerates this sense of relative deprivation, then crime should increase. In this sense, precipitating crime could be, and has been, regarded as a form of political crime—that is, as a cognizant or incognizant reaction to the inequities of the economic system. Such an increase, however, would not be predicted by the empirical research to date, since that research examines only the covariance of such economic factors as unemployment and criminality and falls short of considering the secondary effects of economic adversity that are much more difficult to study.

During the next few years, the economic situation of the surplus population could be further complicated by the reduction of social and economic programs designed to maintain or control the poor.[29] If, as noted in the second section above and as described by Etzioni, the attention of the nation is focused on reindustrialization, leaving severely limited resources available for quality of life factors, then it is likely the plight of the poor would be neglected. Trends in this direction are already indicated. Tax reduction is a topic often discussed throughout the nation which could drastically affect the funds that are available for assistance programs. Proposition 13 in California, which was muted by the failure of a recent referendum, provided a dramatic example of this type of activity. Less comprehensive calls for reductions and actual limits are being considered in several other states. There is also a growing conservative attitude toward public assistance, and the reduction of welfare rolls is often advocated. If these trends affect the economic situation of the surplus population, then it follows that there could be a further increase in criminality.

A final issue related to economic adversity, the exacerbation of the socioeconomic gap, and criminality concerns racism. It has been observed that overt racism is more pronounced during times of economic hardship. This phenomenon is thought to occur because the social status of those in marginal economic situations is less well defined and therefore more threatened during times of economic change. Typical manifestations of overt racism include covert and violent activity on the part of white racists and a corresponding backlash from the black population.[30] The current revival of the Ku Klux Klan in the South clearly indicates that white racist activity is on the rise. The recent riot in Miami also indicates the possibility of a strong black reaction to growing racism. It should, therefore, be expected that during any forthcoming continued economic downswing that race-related violence would increase.

Criminal Justice Adaptation

A final area in which significant changes can be expected in reaction to economic adversity is in the criminal justice system itself. As the political, economic, and social environment changes, criminal justice will be forced to modify its activities and operations and to adapt to a new set of values and circumstances. Since these changes will be of a second order, in that they involve probable reactions to probable changes in other areas, it is difficult to predict their outcome with a high degree of certainty. However, several possibilities can be considered.

One of the most likely circumstances which will face the criminal justice system is enhanced and intensified competition for scarce resources. There are three basic reasons why this situation will arise. First, a focus on reindustrialization will potentially divert attention and fiscal support away from crime and from programs for its control. In this manner, crime may simply be regarded as an unavoidable by-product of the economic process, and insofar as it does not hinder reindustrialization, it will not receive significant attention. Second, tax cuts may reduce the financial support available for justice programs. Finally, inflation alone, irrespective of any budgetary reductions, can reduce the buying power of criminal justice agencies if their budgetary increases do not keep pace with the rate of inflation. Any of these three factors would place criminal justice in greater competition with other public agencies and programs for the limited amount of resources available for their support.

At least three things could happen to criminal justice in a more competitive fiscal environment. First, financial resources could be cut in one way or another which would result in the system being unable to maintain past levels of performance. In such a situation, the agencies of the system would be forced to retrench, possibly by cutting personnel and programs, while attempting not to seriously limit overall

service delivery. If the crime rate should accelerate during a time
when criminal justice resources are reduced, then the overall ability of
the system to control crime could be limited even further.

A second possibility is that in the process of competing for resources,
criminal justice might justify its continued status or growth. Pepensky has suggested one way in which such a justification could be advanced in his discussion of police-produced crime rates. He argues
quite persuasively that crime statistics are manipulated either to
show the public that the police are effective or make the public more
afraid of crime. If additional resources are desired, the rates are
shown to increase; however, if proof that existing programs are working is needed, the rates decrease.[31] In a competitive market, criminal
justice might play on public fear of crime by indicating that rates are
increasing and thus be able to justify expansion of the system.[32]

Justification of a continued or an expanded resource base might also
be forthcoming if a conservative public or conservative political influentials, in particular, view the criminal justice system as a more
viable medium for controlling the surplus population than other forms
of public assistance and maintenance. Individuals who are not needed
in the reindustrialization effort could be controlled if they interfere
with the process. Quinney has outlined this function as follows:

> The criminal justice system serves more explicitly to control that which
> cannot be remedied by available employment within the economy or by
> social services for the surplus population. The police, the courts, and the
> penal agencies—the entire criminal justice system—expands to cope as
> a last resort with the problems of surplus population.[33]

If public assistance programs are reduced in the future, criminal justice may end up as the last resort for controlling "unnecessary" segments of the population. This possibility obviously takes on a higher
probability of occurrence in a more conservative social and political
climate.

A final method by which criminal justice could cope with intensified
competition for resources would be to expand its boundaries. In doing
so, the system would assume new functions and address the problems
of a new set of clients. Consistent with the discussions above, greater
efforts to enforce laws regarding white-collar and corporate crime
could be exerted. The system would need additional resources, of
course, in order to assume these new functions. Duffee, in Chapter 10,
has provided an additional example of such activity that is possible
within the corrections field. He argues that corrections may begin to
process new types of deviates in order to justify its continued growth.
It should be noted that the pursuit of boundary expansion is entirely
consistent with the move toward an expanded role in the control of the

surplus population. The system needs only to redefine the conditions and circumstances in which individuals will be classified as deviant.

Given the size, diversity, and fragmentation of the criminal justice system, all three of the adaptive orientations just presented might be incorporated into various segments of the system. However, there is a high probability that whatever changes in the system do occur will be consistent with the dominant trends within society and its economic system. If the nation reindustrializes at the expense of quality of life, criminal justice may become a primary, if not *the* primary, institution for controlling the cultural conflict which ensues—that is, unrest in the surplus population. In order to accomplish such a task, the system will necessarily have to increase its size, improve efficiency, and become more repressive. The growing conservatism within the nation would support this orientation.

Signs of increasing repression are clearly evident in the American society. Procedural safeguards associated with search and seizure, arrest, and trial are being questioned. Greater numbers of first offenders are incarcerated today than ever before, and the length of sentences is tending to increase. In several states, mandatory incarceration for certain offenses has been incorporated into the statutes, and the death penalty has been reactivated. There has, in general, been a renewed interest in punishment, deterrence, and retribution. Books such as Wilson's *Thinking About Crime* and van den Haag's *Punishing Criminals* have enjoyed wide popularity. It would thus seem that in promoting reindustrialization, the American public is relinquishing substantial amounts of individual freedom.

CONCLUSIONS

In considering the effects of a declining economy on criminality, it has been necessary to make first- and second-order conjectures. As indicated in the first-order prediction, significant changes in the American economy are highly probable in the near future. On the basis of current theoretical and empirical analyses, I also predicted that this change would occur in the form of reindustrialization, as a response to the stagnation within the economy. Having depicted the economic scenario as such, it then became possible to consider the second-order changes in crime and criminal justice which might occur. At least three significant changes that are probable in a period of economic decline and reindustrialization were identified: enhanced corporate competition and domination, exacerbation of the socioeconomic gap, and precipitant criminal justice adaptation.

Unfortunately, each of these predicted changes will tend to confirm Etzioni's prediction that quality of life issues will suffer during reindustrialization. Corporate efforts to reduce government regulation will enhance such societal problems as pollution and employee protection. Corporate exploitation of communities will increase the economic hardships for the community as a whole and for individual taxpayers as they attempt to finance the variety of local services that will benefit corporations as well as themselves. Monopolization could potentially reduce the quality of goods and the variety and diversity of products, and drive the cost of goods upward. It must, therefore, be concluded that increased corporate competition and domination will essentially direct attention and resources away from quality of life issues toward the reindustrialization effort.

Economic adversity itself will have a dire effect on the quality of life of the poor. Continued high inflation and increased unemployment will increase the number of individuals who are actually living in poverty and worsen the plight of those who currently fall within the poverty level. Any reduction in the benefits and services provided to the poor would further decay their economic situation. Increases in crime and racism would also erode the already dismal quality of life within poor neighborhoods.

On a somewhat more abstract level, the expansion of the criminal justice system would also represent a reduction in the quality of life. Since the criminal justice system is the only agency which has a recognized and "legitimate" right to use force, its growth would provide for the increased use of the ultimate form of control within society. Such a trend, when compared to other forms of formal and informal control, is objectionable from a humanitarian perspective and raises serious questions about the ability of society to provide for the needs of its members. In the final analysis, the growth of the criminal justice and the expansion of its controlling activities cannot be regarded as favorably influencing the quality of life.

The research problem which was outlined in the introductory section of this chapter was posed in the form of a simple causal statement: Is there a relationship between economic fluctuations and criminality? The answer cannot be a simple yes or no. Empirical research on the relationship has not found a consistent covariation; it has found that certain economic factors and certain forms of criminality vary in similar ways under certain conditions. This made it necessary to consider the forms of economic adversity that might be expected in the future. The scenario which seems likely is that the economy will experience continued stagnation. Reindustrialization, in turn, will be the overall strategy employed to reverse the poor economic situation. Under such conditions, three changes in criminality and criminal justice are likely to occur, and the causal relationship between these changes and economic conditions is, therefore, quite complex. The proposition that if the economic situation declines then criminality will increase may not always be accurate nor extremely significant; however, the reaction to economic adversity may have an important influence on criminality and criminal justice. As I suggest in this chapter, such changes may be undesirable and may reduce the quality of life within the nation. The secondary relationships between economic factors and criminality may be more important and more significant than the direct ones.

NOTES

1. George B. Vold, *Theoretical Criminology,* 2nd ed. (New York: Oxford University Press, 1979), pp. 162 and 163.
2. Leon Radzinowicz, "Economic Pressures," in Leon Radzinowicz and Marvin E. Wolfgang (eds.), *Crime and Justice,* 2nd ed. (New York: Basic Books, 1977), pp. 542–565.
3. Vold, *Theoretical Criminology,* p. 163.
4. David M. Gordon, "Class and the Economics of Crime," in David M. Gordon, *Problems in Political Economy: An Urban Perspective* (Lexington, Mass.: D. C. Heath and Company, 1977), pp. 378–387.
5. Radzinowicz, "Economic Pressures," p. 551.
6. See Jeffrey A. Reiman and Sue Headlee, Chapter 2 in this volume.
7. Radzinowicz, "Economic Pressures," p. 551.
8. See Clifford R. Shaw and Henry D. McKay, *Juvenile Delinquency and Urban Areas,* Rev. Ed. (Chicago: University of Chicago Press, 1969) and James F. Short (ed.), *Delinquency, Crime and Society* (Chicago: University of Chicago Press, 1976).
9. Radzinowicz, "Economic Pressures," pp. 555–557.
10. See Sharon Kay Long and Ann Dryden Witte, Chapter 5 in this volume, for a review of this research.
11. Radzinowicz, "Economic Pressures," p. 558.
12. Ibid., pp. 558–561.
13. C. Ronald Chester, "Perceived Relative Deprivation as a Cause of Property Crime," *Crime and Delinquency* 17 (January 1976) pp. 17–30.
14. Frank Tannenbaum, *Crime and the Community* (New York: McGraw-Hill, 1951).
15. Donald R. Taft and Ralph W. England, Jr., *Criminology,* 4th ed. (New York: Macmillan, 1964).
16. David H. Bayley, "Learning About Crime—The Japanese Experience," *The Public Interest* 44 (1976): 55–68.
17. Marshall B. Clinard, *Cities with Little Crime* (New York: Cambridge University Press, 1978).
18. Bayley, "Learning About Crime," p. 68.
19. Radzinowicz, "Economic Pressures," p. 565. See also Vold, *Theoretical Criminology,* p. 179.
20. Richard L. Levine, "The Outlook: Review of Current Trends in Business and Finance," *Wall Street Journal* (June 25, 1979) p. 1.
21. Edward Cornish, "The Great Depression of the 1980s: Could It Really Happen?" *The Futurist* (August 1979): 267–274.
22. Levine, "The Outlook." See also Amitai Etzioni, "Work in the American Future: Reindustrialization or Quality of Life," in Clark Kerr and Jerome M. Rosow (eds.), *Work in America* (New York: D. Van Nostrand, 1978) pp. 27–34.

23. Dick Stoken, "What the Long-Term Cycle Tells Us About the 1980s: The Kondratieff Cycle and Its Effects on Social Psychology," *The Futurist* (February 1980) pp. 14–19.

24. John Turman, "Business Wars on the Regulators," *Nation* 227 (December 30, 1978) pp. 730–731.

25. For discussions of recent trends in deregulation, see Patricia M. Scherschel, "Trouble for Regulators Has Only Begun," *U.S. News and World Report* (June 2, 1980) p. 59; *U.S. News and World Report*, "Troubled OSHA Faces Further Loss of Power" (February 11, 1980) pp. 79–80; *U.S. News and World Report,* "Hard Times Come to Environmentalists" (March 20, 1980) pp. 49–50; and *Saturday Review,* "A Special Section: Overregulation" (January 20, 1979).

26. Peter B. Meyer, "Communities as Victims of Corporate Crimes," presented at the Second International Symposium on Victimology, Boston, Massachusetts (September, 1976).

27. See Timothy D. Schellhardt, "It Takes an Expert to Catch a Thief in Executive Suite: Investigative Firms Pinpoint High-Level Wrongdoing, Using Specialized Sleuths," *Wall Street Journal* (October 16, 1978) p. 1.

28. See James O'Connor, *The Fiscal Crisis of the State* (New York: St. Martin's Press, 1973) pp. 158–162.

29. It was argued that public assistance functions to control the poor in order to maintain the political stability of the system. See Francis Fox Piven and Richard A. Cloward, *Regulating the Poor: The Functions of Public Welfare* (New York: Pantheon Books, 1971); and Joe R. Feagin, *Subordinating the Poor: Welfare and American Beliefs* (Englewood Cliffs, New Jersey: Prentice-Hall, 1975).

30. Pierre L. van den Bengle, *Race and Ethnicity* (New York: Basic Books, 1970) p. 30.

31. Harold E. Pepensky, *Crime Control Strategies* (New York: Oxford University Press, 1980) pp. 94–102.

32. Several examples of this strategy which have been used in the expansion of criminal justice activities and organizations in the past are discussed in Max Towenthal, "The Beginning of a Crime-Control Bureaucracy"; Author Millspaugh, "The Politics of Drug-Control: Its Early History"; Alfred Lindsmith, "The Drug-Control Bureaucracy Creates the Drug Problem"; and Donald T. Dickerson, "Criminalizing Marijuana: The Crusade Continues." In Isidore Silver (ed.), *The Crime-Control Establishment* (Englewood Cliffs, New Jersey: Prentice-Hall, 1974) pp. 1–85.

33. Richard Quinney, *Class, State and Crime* (New York: Longman, 1977) p. 109.

Chapter 5

Current Economic Trends: Implications for Crime and Criminal Justice

Sharon K. Long and Ann D. Witte*

The response of policy makers, law enforcement officials and the general public to recent periods of economic recession has included a heightened concern with the potential effects of a declining economy on the level of criminal activities. There has been increasing speculation about the magnitude of these effects, and at times even their direction, in the face of a continuing recession—especially one which in recent years has been accompanied by high rates of inflation. Current economic forecasts (Council of Economic Advisors, Chase Econometrics, Data Resources, Inc. and Wharton Econometric Forecasting Associates, [73]) project a decline in growth for 1980 that ranges from 0.4 percent (Council of Economic Advisors) to 2.9 percent (Chase). This decline is expected to be reversed, at least partially, by the fourth quarter of 1981. The forecasts predict continued double-digit inflation of 12 to 14 percent throughout 1980, slowing to approximately 10 percent in 1981. This is to be accompanied by high levels of unemployment in 1980 and 1981. In general, the expected trend for the economy is high inflation, declining productivity, and very little real growth.

*Department of Economics, University of North Carolina

If, as has been conjectured, a worsening economy will lead to increases in criminal activity, then it is important that policy makers become aware of the probable nature of these changes. In addition, shifts in the nature of crime and criminal populations may require adjustments in all phases of the criminal justice system.

In this chapter, we first briefly discuss the theoretical bases for models of criminal behavior. The following section surveys previous work examining the relationship between economic factors and crime. The third section discusses the implications of current economic trends for crime rates and criminal justice. The final section contains our summary and conclusions.

THEORETICAL APPROACHES TO MODELING CRIMINAL BEHAVIOR

We begin with a brief survey of theoretical approaches to the modeling of crime, because we are convinced that it is only with adequate models of criminal behavior that we can sort out economic factors from other effects on criminal behavior. For example, only models can tell us for what other factors it is necessary to adjust before we can attribute a change in crime rate to a change in the level of unemployment. We will consider the models used by economists as well as empirical models used by sociologists and criminologists.

At present, there are two basic variants of the economic model of crime. The first, which has relied most heavily on Becker's seminal work, has been developed by Issac Ehrlich ([26], [27], [29]). The second has been developed by Block and Lind [11], [12], and Block and Heineke [10].

Ehrlich considers an individual who maximizes his expected utility, which is a function of wealth, including the monetary equivalent of nonpecuniary returns, and time in consumption activity. The individual's choice is to allocate a fixed amount of time—total time available minus a fixed amount of time spent in consumption activities—between legal and illegal income-generating activities. The following are assumed to hold: legal and illegal income-generating activities are perfect substitutes; returns in each activity are monotonically related to the time spent in the activity with no cross effects; legal returns occur with certainty,[1] and illegal returns are conditional upon whether an individual is apprehended and punished; offenders have a determinant subjective probability of apprehension and punishment, which depends on the amount of time spent in illegal activity; and the punishment is evaluated in monetary terms. Under these assumptions, Ehrlich derives the following comparative static results: a relative increase in legal wages (illegal returns) will reduce (increase) the incentive to participate in illegal activity, assuming absolute risk aversion; an increase in either the probability of apprehension and conviction or the punishment if convicted reduces the incentive to participate in illegitimate activities; the deterrent effect of a 1 percent increase in the marginal or average penalty per offense will exceed or fall short of that of a similar increase in the probability of apprehension and punishment if the offender is a risk avoider or a risk preferrer, respectively.

Block and Lind have called into question a number of Ehrlich's assumptions and comparative static results. First, they show that a monetary equivalent for a prison term may fail to exist [11]. Second, they find that risk preference is not a necessary condition for a greater relative deterrent effect for increased probability of punishment over severity of punishment [12].

The major attack on Ehrlich's model and results, however, has come more recently in a paper by Block and Heineke [10]. They show that if the time allocated to legal and illegal activity is introduced explicitly into the utility function, no comparative static results are forthcoming under traditional preference restrictions.[2] This is true because increasing (decreasing) the relative return to an activity will cause a wealth as well as a substitution effect. Restrictions that allow the wealth effects to be signed are necessary if unambiguous results are to be forthcoming. Specifically, they show that Ehrlich's comparative static results are forthcoming only if psychic or ethical costs emanating from time allocation decisions are independent of wealth.[3] The authors conclude: "Hence in the area of law enforcement as in taxation policy, policy recommendations do not follow from theory but rather require empirical determination of relative magnitudes" [10].

The theoretical bases of crime models established by sociologists and criminologists are less formally developed and thus more difficult to test empirically. Most tests of these theories have seen crime as caused largely by economic and demographic factors which condition the individual's environment and alternatives. These "ecological" theories have been heavily influenced by Merton's [58] theory of anomie. According to researchers pursuing this tradition, criminal patterns are transmitted socially through certain structural conditions producing higher probabilities of deviance.[4] In general, these studies assume that objective personal economic gains and losses have little relevance in explaining criminal behavior; consequently, these variables have little influence in most sociological or criminological empirical analyses.

PREVIOUS STUDIES EXAMINING THE RELATIONSHIP BETWEEN ECONOMIC FACTORS AND CRIME

In analyses of the relationship between the level of criminal activity and economic factors, the primary emphasis has been on some measure of the level of employment and of the level and/or distribution of income in the population studied. This work has considered the effect of these economic factors on the overall crime rate, on general crime types such as property crimes and violent crimes, and on the level of specific offense—burglary, robbery, larceny, auto theft, assault, rape, murder, and so on. The effect of economic factors on the level of crime for specific populations, such as juveniles ([33], [34], [35], [81], [93]) and ex-offenders ([66], [96], [99]) has received additional attention. To facilitate the evaluation of these studies, we have summarized the findings for the effects of economic factors on the overall crime rate, violent crimes, and property crimes in Tables 5–1, 5–2, and 5–3, respectively. Tables 5–4 through 5–10 deal with the relationship of the economic factors to the seven major crimes included in the FBI's crime index: robbery, burglary, larceny, auto theft, assault, rape and homicide. Table 5–11 is a summary of the work dealing with juvenile delinquency.

Surveying this rather extensive literature, one is struck by the fact that most research dealing with the relationship between economic factors and crime has used data for jurisdictions such as cities, states, nations, rather than data for individuals. Yet the theory and intuition which lead us to believe that economic factors are related to crime is based on beliefs about the way individuals behave. According to Becker's [6] model of criminal activity based on rational individual choice, "a person commits an offense if the expected utility to him exceeds the utility he could get by using his time and other resources at other activities." ([6], p. 176) This model has been refined and extended since 1968, but has remained a model of individual choice.

Researchers have not used aggregate data by choice, but rather have been forced to use it because of the lack of appropriate data for individuals. This use of aggregate data can provide reliable insights about individual behavior only if certain restrictive distributional[5] or sociological[6] assumptions hold. In practice, the assumptions seldom hold which could allow individual crime functions to be generalized into aggregate crime functions for the community. Thus, in discussing the conclusions to be drawn from economic models of crime, we will distinguish between those using aggregate data and those which use individual data.

Table 5–1. Summary of the Literature on the Effect of Economic Factors on All Crime (t-ratios in parentheses)

Model: Dependent Variable	Deterrent Variables	Education	Employment	Income	Population	Family	Race	Neighborhood	Other	F	R²	N	Functional Form of Model	Estimation Technique	Theoretical Base	Sample
Quinney (1966): all offenses known to the police per 100,000 population[a] (data: UCR)											—	50	linear	product moment correlation	ecological	50 states of the U.S. 1959–1961; cross-sectional
(1) Rural		.30	−.36 .43 .01 .05	.19	−.24 .48		.00	−.22								
(2) Urban		.29	−.48 .16 .25	.26	−.51 .67		.02	−.08								
(3) SMSA		.16	−.20 .09 −.38 −.11 .05	.09	−.27 .63		.15	−.07								
Gylys (1970: all offenses per 100,000 population[b] (data: FBI, Census)	.0451	.0059	.0207	.1804 .1536	.0641 .0010	.0849	.0057	.0730 .0761	1059		.4750	57	linear	OLS—to derive partial coefficients of determination	no explicit theory	57 largest central cities (population equal to or greater than 250,000) in 1968, 1960; cross-sectional
McPheters and Stronge (1976): total crime rates per 1,000 persons[c] (data: UCR)	−.39 (−2.88)	2.40 (2.96)			.85 (1.92)		−.05 (−.06)	4.86 (3.20) 2.92 (2.44) .57 (1.54)	.88 (14.32)	65.97	.935	43	linear lagged value of dependent variable	OLS on principal components	wealth maximization	43 largest U.S. central cities, 1970; cross-sectional
Brenner (1975): total imprisonment in state prisons rate per 10,000 population[d] (data: Bureau of Prisons, LEA and Census)			1.52 (5.60)		1.31 (4.27)				.57 (3.07) −2.55 (2.38) 180.9 (2.93)	23.9	.90	34	linear (lag 0–2)	OLS	no explicit theory	United States, 1935–73 (minus 1942–45); time series
Morris and Tweeten (1971): total crime rate per 100,000 population[e] (data: UCR)	22.95 (22.95)			−.01 (.333)	.03 (3.0) −26.74 (2.309) 40.14 (1.438)		23.26 (4.938)		−452.34 (4.006) 1,253.74 (10.741) −244.52 (1.829)		.67	754	linear	recursive least squares	wealth maximization	U.S. cities, 1967–1968; cross-sectional
Phillips and Votey (1975): crime rate per capita[f]	(1)−.701 (−5.05) −.051 (−.85)	−.376 (−2.22)						.126 (3.89)				50	log-linear	2SLS	cost minimization of crime to community	California counties, 1966; cross-sectional

73

Table 5-1. (continued)

Phillips and Votey (continued)

Model: Dependent Variable	Deterrent Variables	Education	Employment	Income	Population	Family	Race	Neighborhood	Other	F	R²	N	Functional Form of Model	Estimation Technique	Theoretical Base	Sample
(data: Crime and Delinquency in California, 1966)	(2)–553 (–5.57) 10.32 (.10)		.115 (3.29)	.032 (1.49)	.013 (.61) .010 (.250)	.031 (.87)					.60	50	log-linear	OLS on principle components		
Forst (1976): number of index crimes per 100,000 population^a (data: UCR)	–2595.19 (–.14) –.018 (–.64)		610.39	.155 (1.51) 1.643 (1.93)	3173 (3.42) 2539.10 (2.17) 27399.23 (1.45) 3202.26 (.65)	7675.48 (2.13)	–1445.41 (–1.51)		4.783 (.37)		–	51	linear	2SLS	wealth maximization	50 states and the District of Columbia, 1970; cross-sectional
Pogue (1975): number of index crimes per 100,000 population^b (data: FBI)	–.959 (–2.597)	.726 (1.209)	–.059 (–.349) .004 (.066)	.175 (.341) .703 (3.370)	1.023 (1.464) 1.509 (.816) .015 (.218)	–.761 (–1.307) .195 (2.571) .461 (1.598)	–.433 (–1.823)				.425	66	log-linear	2SLS	ecological	SMSAs, 1968; cross-sectional
Ehrlich (1973, 1974): all offenses known to the police per 100,000 (state) population^d (data: UCR)	–.991 (–5.898) –1.123 (–4.483)			1.292 (2.609) 1.775 (4.183)			.265 (5.069)				–	47	linear	2SLS	time allocation	47 states, 1960; cross-sectional
Allison (1972): crime rate^f		455.3 (1.912)	846.3 (3.782)		155.4 (1.563) –208.9 (–2.760)			–26.00 (–1.722)	–14.71 (–1.074)		.78	–	linear	step-wise regression	no explicit theory	Chicago and communities within a forty mile radius which had a 1960 population of 25,000 or more, 1960; cross-sectional
Peterson et al. (1980): individual's total crime offense rate of average number of crimes per year^g (data: self report)					–.143 ( )				.275 ( ) .103 ( ) .229 ( ) –.080 ( ) .160 ( )		.342	624	linear	step-wise multiple regression	no explicit theory	624 male felons in 5 California state prisons, 1976; cross-sectional

74

Table 5–1. (continued)

Model: Dependent Variable	Deterrent Variables	Education	Employment	Income	Population	Family	Race	Neighborhood	Other	F	R²	N	Functional Form of Model	Estimation Technique	Theoretical Base	Sample
Carr-Hill and Stern (1973): log of the number of indictable offenses per capita[m] (data: Supplementary Statistics Relating to Crime and Criminal Proceedings)	(1) -.26 (.81) -.17 (1.72) (2) -.66 (2.55)			(1) .45 (2.63) -.06 (.30)		.44 (.71) .44 (2.94) -.28 (3.41) / .31 (1.97)		.16 (2.70) .18 (3.65)		17.769[a] 8.834[a]	— —	66 64	log-linear	FIML	wealth maximization	Urban police districts in England and Wales (1) 1966, (2) 1961; cross-sectional
Witte and Schmidt (1977): total time sentenced during a follow-up period after release from incarceration[e] (data: individual interview and police records)	(1) 28.9001 (.59) -2.0499 (-.58)	.07630 (.09)				1.6820 (.44)	-13.8990 (-3.22)		-1.8500 (-1.86) -16.8197 (-2.01) -.4208 (-2.02) .05016 (2.74) -2552 (-.06) 6.0431 (.80) -19.9663 (-4.19) 5.5513 (.89) -.00998 (-.06)		—	582	linear	maximum likelihood truncated lognormal distribution	no explicit model	[e] 641 men imprisoned in North Carolina in 1969 or 1971; cross-sectional
	(2)						-14.3138 (-3.41)		-1.1487 (-2.34) -16.6306 (-5.47) -.4918 (-3.70) .05120 (3.22)		.105[p]	582				
Witte (1980): (1) number of arrests per month free[e] (data: individual interview and police records)	-.0006 (-1.663) -.0801 (-2.469)[r]		-.0388 (-1.208)	-.0004 (-.093) -.0251 (-1.337)			-.0155 (-.496) -.0771 (-2.656)		-.0643 (-.998) .0024 (.679) .0164 (1.851) -.0858 (-.927) .0160 (5.093) -.0104 (-1.116) .0292 (.982) .0000 (.459) .1182 (1.991)	88.361[a]	—	641	linear	maximum likelihood tobit	time allocation	641 men imprisoned in North Carolina in 1969 or 1971; cross-sectional
(2) number of convictions per month free[r] (data: individual interview and police files)	-.0004 (-1.338) -.0572 (-2.09)[r]		-.0075 (-1.224)	-.0000 (-1.224) -.0189 (-1.197)			-.0267 (-1.014) -.0802 (-3.281)		-.0319 (-.588) .0024 (1.131) .0153 (2.063) -.0784 (-.995) .0164 (4.311) -.0118 (-1.496) .0435 (1.731) .0000 (-.784) .1101 (2.216)	76.466[a]	—	641				

[a]The variables used by Quinney are as follows: education is median years of schooling; employment is percent employed in manufacturing, a measure of occupational diversity, percent females in the labor force, and percent white collar males; income is median family income; population is percent aged 50 and over, and percent change in residence; race is percent nonwhite; neighborhood is percent owner-occupied housing.

[b]The independent variables used by Gylys are as follows: the deterrent variable is per capita police expenditures; education is median years of schooling; employment is percent of labor force unemployed; income is percent of families with $3000 or less and median income; population is median age of population, population density, and population size; family is percent of broken homes; race is percent of population nonwhite; neighborhood is percent of owner occupied homes, percent of deteriorating homes, and population per housing unit; other is median temperature

[c]The principal components used by McPheters and Stronge are as follows: the deterrent variable is police expenditures; education is a component measuring education; race is a measure of minority presence; population is a measure of youth presence; neighborhood is a measure of central city decay, a measure of central city affluence, and a measure of housing quality; other is the lagged value of crime.

[d]Brenner uses the following independent variables: employment is the total unemployment rate for ages 16 and up; income is linear and logarithmic time trends; population is the proportion of males aged 15–29; other is inflation as measured by the percent change in the consumer price index, and a linear and a logarithmic time trend; not shown is a dummy constant to correct for data problems.

[e]Morris and Tweeten use the following independent variables: the deterrent variable is number of police per capita; income is median income; population is population density, median age, and percent males; race is percent nonwhite; other is three binary variables taking the value 1 if the city is in the Northeast, South, or West, respectively, and 0 otherwise. Not shown are a series of variables for city size and for size-police interactions. The results are derived from a two-equation simultaneous system, with the other dependent variable being police number per capita.

[f]Phillips and Votey derive the results for (1) using a four-equation, jointly determined model, with the other dependent variables being the likelihood of conviction, the demand for labor, and the supply of labor. The variables used in the regression are as follow: the deterrent variables are the likelihood of conviction, a measure of felony sentences, and the fraction of the sentences which were probation with jail; neighborhood is an index of socioeconomic causal factors.

The variables used in (2) are as follows: the deterrent variable is the likelihood of conviction; employment is a socioeconomic index of frustrated economic ambition; income is a socioeconomic index of poverty; population is an urban, a disadvantaged youth, and a migration socioeconomic index.

gThe independent variables used by Forst are as follows: deterrent variables are the number of imprisonments divided by number of offenses, the number of prisoners divided by number of imprisonments during year, and expenditures on correction system per prisoner; employment is proportion of adult population that is unemployed or not in the labor force; income is median family income, and the difference between median family income and national poverty level weighted by proportion of families below poverty level; population is net migrants divided by number of residents, proportion of residents living in places defined by the Census Bureau as "urban," proportion of residents between 18 and 20 years of age, and proportion of male residents; family is proportion of households that are not husband-wife households; race is proportion of residents who are nonwhite; other is average temperature (°F). These results are derived from a five-equation model, with the other dependent variables being the estimated probability of apprehension and imprisonment, expenditure on correction system per prisoner, expenditure on police per state resident, and expenditure on correction system per state resident.

hThe following independent variables are used by Pogue: the deterrent variable is the proportion of this particular crime category that is cleared by arrest; education is the median years of school completed of the SMSA population; employment is the percentage unemployed, and the 1968 unemployment rate divided by the 1967 rate; income is per capita income in dollars per year, and percentage of households with incomes below $3000 per year; population is percentage of population aged 12 to 17, percentage aged 18 to 24, percentage male, total population in thousands, population density in thousands per square mile, and the 1968 population divided by the 1960 population; race is percent of population that is white. The second stage of the 2SLS estimates relationships between police expenditures and clearance ratios. Pogue also runs regressions for the 1962–1967 period.

iThe independent variables used by Ehrlich are as follows: the deterrent variables are the number of offenders imprisoned per offenses known, average time served by offenders in state prisons; income is median income of families, percentage of families below one-half of median income; race is percentage of nonwhites in the population. The second equation model is a production function of law-enforcement activity.

jAllison's independent variables are as follows: education is the mean number of years of education completed by males 25 years old and older in the community; employment is the percent of male civilian members of the work force over 14 years of age which are employed; population is the percentage of the community's population which is fifteen through 24 years of age, and the difference between the percent of females and males in the population of the community; neighborhood is expenditure for parks and recreation per 1000 persons in the community; other is the distance in miles between the community and core of the city. Allison included in his regression, but did not report variables for police protection, population density, community income and race.

77

[k]The independent variables used by Peterson et al. are as follows: race is a binary variable taking the value 1 if the individual is black and 0 otherwise; other is a measure of the individual's tendency to identify himself in terms of one or more criminal activities, a juvenile crime scale, a measure of composite criminal attitudes, a binary variable taking the value 1 if the individual is a drug user and 0 otherwise, and a social stability scale.

[l]The values shown are beta coefficients or coefficients on standardized variables. The coefficients for each characteristic are signifcant by t-tests with $p > .05$.

[m]Carr-Hill and Stern use the following independent variables: (1) The deterrent variables are the proportion of crimes cleared up; the number of policemen per capita, the proportion of convicted given custodial treatment, and total police expenditure per officer; population is proportion of males aged 15 to 24, and proportion of population that is working class; neighborhood is the total rateable value per area. (2) The deterrent variables are the proportion of crimes "cleared up," and the proportion of convicted given custodial treatment; population is proportion of males aged 15 to 24; neighborhood is total rateable value per area.

These results are derived from a three equation, jointly determined model, with the other dependent variables being the proportion of crime "cleared up," and the number of policemen per capita.

[n]This is the likelihood ratio test, which is $-2 \log(\lambda)$, where $\log(\lambda)$ is the difference between the log of the maximized value of the likelihood function with only a constant term as an independent variable and the log of the maximized value of the likelihood function with the independent variables in the regression under consideration. This statistic is distributed χ_k^2, where k is the number of explanatory variables (excluding the constant) in the regression under consideration. The statistic tests the joint significance of the independent variables and is equivalent to the F test in least squares regression.

[o]Witte and Schmidt use the following independent variables: (1) The deterrent variables are a binary variable equal to 1 if the individual's release from the sample sentence was under supervision (e.g. parole) and 0 otherwise, and a binary variable equal to one if the individual had been on the North Carolina work release program prior to release and 0 if he had not; education is number of school years completed; family is a binary variable equal to 1 if the individual was married and 0 otherwise; race is a binary variable equal to 1 for whites and 0 for nonwhites; other is the number of rule violations during the prison sentence preceding release, the number of convictions prior to the one leading to the sample prison sentence, age in months at release, a binary variable equal to 1 if individual's record indicates a diagnosis of alcoholism or a serious problem with alcohol and equal to 0 otherwise, a binary variable equal to 1 if the individual's record indicates use of hard drugs and equal to zero otherwise, two binary variables taking the value 1 if the sample imprisonment was for a crime against property or a crime against a person, respectively, and 0 otherwise, a binary variable equal to 1 if the sample imprisonment was for a felony and 0 if for a misdemeanor, and the length in months of the sample imprisonment. 2. is a reduced specification where race is a binary variable taking the value 1 if the individual is white and 0 otherwise;

other is the number of rule violations during the prison sentence preceding release, the number of convictions prior to the one leading to the sample prison sentence, age (in months) at arrest, and a dummy variable taking the value 0, 1 and 2, with 1 corresponding to an individual who is either an alcoholic or a user of hard drugs, 2 corresponding to an individual who is both, and 0 corresponding to one who is neither.

^{p}The results have the same level of joint significance as would the corresponding linear regression (with log of the dependent variable) with an R^2 as shown.

^{q}Witte uses the following independent variables: the deterrent variables are the individual's historical average sentence length received (in months) prior to release in 1969–1971, and a binary variable equal to 1 if an individual was supervised (e.g., on parole) when released and 0 otherwise; employment is the number of months until first job after release; income is accumulated work release funds (in $100) received after release, and hourly wage after release; family is a binary variable equal to 1 if an individual was married and 0 otherwise; race is a binary variable equal to 1 for nonwhites and 0 for whites; other is the number of convictions divided by number of arrests prior to release from 1969–1971 imprisonment, number of convictions resulting in imprisonment divided by total number of convictions prior to release from 1969–1971 imprisonment, age (years) at release, age (years) at release squared, age at first arrest, number of arrests before incarceration in 1969 or 1971 (in (1)) number of convictions before incarceration in 1971 (in (2)), a binary variable equal to 1 if an individual's history indicates a serious alcohol problem and 0 otherwise, a binary variable equal to 1 if an individual's history indicates drug use and 0 otherwise, and the number of rule violations during 1969–1971 prison term.

^{r}The numbers in parentheses are "asymptotic t ratios," the ratio of the coefficient to the asymptotic standard error.

Table 5–2. Summary of the Literature on the Effect of Economic Factors on Violent Crime (t-ratios in parentheses)

Model: Dependent Variable	Deterrent Variables	Education	Employment	Income	Population	Family	Race	Neighborhood	Other	R²	N	Functional Form of Model	Estimation Technique	Theoretical Base	Sample
Pressman and Carol (1976): Crimes against persons rate[c] (data: Department of Commerce)			−.05		.09 .21		.66 ( )[b]			.70[c] ( )[b]	—	linear	partial correlation	ecological	SMSAs of all population sizes, 1965; cross-sectional
Glaser and Rice (1959): arrests of males for crimes against persons[d] (data: FBI) (1) all ages (1a)(1b)(1c) (2) 20 and under (2a)(2b)(2c) (3) 21 through 24 (3a)(3b)(3c)			.56[f] .03 .63[g] — −.39[g] −.79[g] .60[g] .16 .61[g]							— — —	26 26 26	linear	correlation	ecological	(a) Boston, (b) Chicago, (c) Cincinnati, 1930–1956; time-series
Brown et al. (1979): offenses against the person[a] (data: magistrates' court and court of quarter sessions)			.05[i] .01	.01				−.05 .01		—	15	linear	Spearman-Rho rank order correlation	ecological	15 electoral wards of a Northern urban town in Britain, 1969; cross-sectional
Land and Felson (1976): reported national violent crime rate per 100,000 (mid year) population[f] (data: Social Indicators)	.79 (11.61) −41.84 (1.73) .09 (6.64)		−.43 (.42)		−3.26 (1.07)				−.08 (.08)	.9996	25	linear	OLS	ecological	United States, 1947–1972; time series
Fleisher (1966): U.S. violence crimes per 1,000 population ages 24 and under[k] (data: UCR)			−2.1 (−.3)	.000011 (.05) 4.6×10⁻⁴ (.1)	−1.2 (−.8)	26.2 (3.4)	1.9 (1.5)		.01 (.03)	.42	101	linear	OLS	wealth maximization	101 U.S. cities with population greater than 25,000, 1960; cross-sectional
Morris and Tweeten (1971): violent crime rate per 100,000 population[l] (data: UCR)	1.78 (9.889)		−.003 (.050)		.008 (4.00) 10.92 (2.171) .70 (.335)		10.46 (12.306)		−109.65 (5.388) 55.26 (2.628) −45.65 (1.894)	.57	754	linear	recursive least squares	wealth maximization	U.S. cities, 1967–1968; cross-sectional
Bartel (1979): female personal[m] crime arrests per capita[m] (data: FBI) (1)	.557 (1.26) −.029 (−.09) .699 (1.72)		4.627 (1.28) −1.533 (−.74) .488 (.57) .033 (.03)	1.668 (.72) 3.363 (1.35)	2.348 (.31)	−.806 (−.48) 3.174 (.97) −3.696 (−.68) 2.118 (1.23) −4.921 (−.85)	.309 (1.73)			.83	33	log-linear	weighted OLS	time allocation	33 states, 1970; cross-sectional
(2)	.474 (1.33) −.161 (−.57) −.474 (1.44)		7.782 (2.69) −2.611 (−1.67) .769 (.99) −.405 (.57)	.105 (.05) 3.981 (1.97)	3.167 (1.88)	−.798 (−.26)	.402 (2.95)			.83	33	log-linear	weighted 2SLS		33 states, 1970; cross-sectional

Table 5-2. (continued)

Model: Dependent Variable	Deterrent Variables	Education	Employment	Income	Population	Family	Race	Neighborhood	Other	R²	N	Functional Form of Model	Estimation Technique	Theoretical Base	Sample
Bartel (continued)															
male personal crime arrests per capita (data: FBI) (3)	−.349 (−1.25) −.388 (−1.97) .632 (2.34)		.494 (.17) −.296 (−.06) .390 (.66) −.495 (−.56)	2.452 (1.69) 1.926 (1.08)	−5.123 (−1.68)	.457 (.17) −3.894 (−2.31) 1.926 (1.08)	.205 (1.72)			.83	33	log-linear	weighted OLS		47 states, 1960; cross-sectional
(4)	.314 (.31) −.217 (−.50) .592 (1.77)		.991 (.59) −.056 (−.01) .471 (.74) −.260 (−.23)	4.303 (1.82) 4.727 (1.82)	−1.698 (−.77)	4.432 (1.22)	.221 (1.46)			.73	33	log-linear	weighted 2SLS		
Ehrlich (1973, 1974): crimes against persons known to the police to have occurred per 100,000 (state) population (data: UCR)	−.803 (−6.603) −.495 (−3.407)			.328 (.570) .587 (1.098)			.376 (4.833)			—	47	linear	2SLS	time allocation	47 states, 1960; cross-sectional
Swimmer (1974a): violent crime rate (data: FBI)	−.030 (−1.01) −.0079 (−.57)	−.0069 (−.31)	−.033 (−.53)	−.044 (−2.46) −.015 (.56)	.122 (3.89)	−.0014 (−3.26)	.032 (3.32)	−.176 (−.51)		—	119	log-linear	2SLS	wealth maximization	All cities with 100,000 or more residents, 1960; cross-sectional
Peterson et al. (1980): individual's violent crime offense rate of average number of violent crimes per year (data: self report)								−.151 ( )r	.198 ( ) .134 ( ) .146 ( ) .145 ( ) .154 ( ) .121 ( ) .110 ( ) .098 ( ) −.098 ( )	.276	624	linear	stepwise multiple regression	no explicit theory	624 male felons in 5 California state prisons, 1976; cross-sectional
Greenwood and Wadycki (1976): per capita crimes against persons (data: Department of Justice)	1.68 (4.82) .54 (3.06)				−.02 (−.50)		.29 (6.86)		.14 (1.10)	.54	199	log-linear	3SLS	wealth maximization	199 SMA's, 1960; cross-sectional
Witte and Schmidt (1979): log of the ratio of the probability that the most serious conviction is a crime against a person to the probability of no conviction (data: police files and individual interview)	−.62679 (−1.44) −.07018 (−.22)	−.0724 (−.24)				.21191 (.58)	.25228 (.71)		−.56841 (−1.17) 1.2374 (3.46) 1.1374 (2.35) .62719 (1.30) .10936 (2.24) −.24148 (−.79) −.73733 (−3.10) .44181 (3.60) .20786 (1.66)	—	596	linear	maximum likelihood logit	time allocation	641 men imprisoned in North Carolina in 1969 or 1971; cross-sectional

81

[a] The variables used by Pressman and Carol are as follows: income is median family income; population is number of people per square mile, and net migration; race is percent of population nonwhite.

[b] t-test level of significance: .01.

[c] This is the multiple correlation coefficient.

[d] Glaser and Rice estimate correlation coefficients relating arrests of males for crimes against persons to percent of male labor force unemployed.

[e] Significance of difference from r = 0: .05.

[f] Significance of difference from r = 0: .01.

[g] Significance of difference from r = 0: .001.

[h] The variables used by Brown, McCulloch, and Hiscox are as follows: employment is able-bodied unemployed and disabled unemployed; income is persons receiving social security payments; neighborhood is owner-occupied housing, and rented council houses. Houses with fewer than 0.5 persons per room, Irish immigrants, and overcrowding were not found to be correlated with offenses against the person.

[i] The values shown are level of significance (p value).

[j] Land and Felson use the following independent variables: the deterrent variables are lagged reported violent crime, reported property crime, and the federal, state and local police expenditures in billions of year t dollars per 100,000 midyear population; employment is the annual average national civilian unemployment rate in year t; population is the percentage of the total population that is male, ages 15 to 24, in year t; other is the consumer price index for year t, expressed as a percentage of the 1967 (base) CPI.

[k] The following independent variables are used in the study by Fleisher: employment is the male civilian unemployment rate; income is the mean income of the second lowest quartile of families, and the mean income of the highest quartile of families; population is the proportion of population of five-year-olds that lived in another county in 1955 (1960); family is the proportion of females over 14 who are separated or divorced; race the proportion of the population that is nonwhite; other is a regional binary variable equal to one for southern cities, zero otherwise. Fleisher runs additional regressions using various stratifications of the data.

[l] Morris and Tweeten use the following independent variables: the deterrent variable is number of police per capita; income is median income; population is population density, median age, and percent males; race is percent nonwhite; other is three binary variables taking the value 1 if the city is in the Northeast, South, or West, respectively, and 0 otherwise. Not shown are a series of variables for city size and for size-police interactions. The results are derived from a two-equation simultaneous system, with the other dependent variable being police number per capita.

[m]The independent variables used by Bartel are as follows: (1) deterrent variables are the probability of apprehension and conviction for property crimes, average time served by offenders in the state prison for a personal crime before their first release, and probability of arrest; employment is percentage of single females aged 16 and over who are in the civilian labor force, the unemployment rate of females aged 35 to 39, and the unemployment rates of females aged 16 to 19; income is the state's median family income, and the percentage of families with incomes below one-half the state's median; population is the median age of the female population; family is the average number of children under 6 in female-headed families, the average number of children aged 6–17 in female-headed families, the average number of children under 6 in husband-wife families, the average number of children aged 6–17 in husband-wife families, and the percentage of females aged 16 and over who are married with spouse present; race is percentage of females who are nonwhite.

(2) The independent variables are as in (1), except as noted: family is percentage of females aged 16 and over who are married with spouse present.

(3) The independent variable are as in (1), except as noted: family is average number of children under 6 in husband-wife families, average number of children aged 6 to 17 in husband-wife families, and the percentage of females aged 16 and over who are married with spouse present.

(4) The independent variables are as in (2).

[n]Personal crimes include murder, nonnegligent manslaughter, and assault.

[o]The independent variables used by Ehrlich are as follows: the deterrent variables are the number of offenders imprisoned per offenses known, and average time served by offenders in state prisons; income is median income of families, and percentage of families below one-half of median income; race is percentage of nonwhites in the population. The second equation of the two equation model is a production function of law enforcement activity.

[p]The independent variables used by Swimmer are as follows: deterrent variables are total expenditure on police per capita, and average time served by convicted first offenders; education is percent of 14 to 17-year-olds in school; employment is unemployment rate; income is median income in $100s, and percentage of families with incomes less than $3000 or greater than $10,000; population is population in 100000's, and population squared; race is percent of population nonwhite; other is a binary variable for South-Non-South.

[q]Peterson, et al. use the following independent variables: race is a binary variable taking the value 1 if the individual is black and 0 otherwise; other is a juvenile crime scale, a measure of the individual's tendency to identify himself in terms of one or more criminal activities, a measure of temper motives, a binary variable taking the value 1 if the commitment offense was robbery and 0 otherwise, a measure of composite criminal attitudes, a binary variable taking the value 1 if the commitment offense was assault and 0 otherwise, a binary variable taking the value 1 if the commitment offense was homicide and 0 otherwise; a measure of perception that straight life is unpleasant, and age while committing crimes.

^{r}The values shown are beta coefficients or coefficients on standardized variables. The coefficients for each characteristic are significant by t-tests with $p > .05$.

^{s}The independent variables used by Greenwood and Wadycki are as follows: the deterrent variables are per capita local government expenditures for police protection, and per capita full-time equivalent employment in police protection; population is population per square mile; race is percent of population that is black; other is a binary variable taking the value 1 for observations south of a line drawn at the northern border of North Carolina, Tennessee, Oklahoma, etc., and the value 0 otherwise. These results are derived from a 3-equation, simultaneous equation model, with the other dependent variables being per capita local government expenditures for police protection and per capita full-time equivalent employment in police protection.

^{t}This is the value of an equivalent OLS R^2.

^{u}The independent variables used by Witte and Schmidt are as follows: the deterrent variables are a binary variable taking the value 1 for an individual with supervised release (e.g. parole) and 0 otherwise, and a binary variable taking the value 1 if the individual participated in prisoner work release program and 0 otherwise; education is number of years of school completed before sample incarceration; family is a binary variable taking the value 1 if married and 0 otherwise; race is a binary variable taking the value 1 for a felony and 0 otherwise, a white and 0 otherwise; other is a binary variable taking the value 1 if the sample incarceration was for a felony and 0 otherwise, a binary variable taking the value 1 for a serious alcohol problem or hard drug use and 0 otherwise, a binary variable taking the value 1 if the sample binary variable taking the value 1 for a crime against a person and 0 otherwise, a binary variable taking the value 1 if the sample incarceration is for a crime against property and 0 otherwise, the number of convictions before the sample sentence, age at first arrest, conviction is for a crime against property and 0 otherwise, length of individual's follow-up period, and number of prison rule violations during age at time of release from sample sentence, length of individual's follow-up period, and number of prison rule violations during sample sentence.

Table 5-3. Summary of the Literature on the Effect of Economic Factors on Property Crime (t-ratios in parentheses)

Model: Dependent Variable	Deterrent Variables	Education	Employment	Income	Population	Family	Race	Neighborhood	Other	R²	N.	Functional Form of Model	Estimation Technique	Theoretical Base	Sample
Glaser and Rice (1959): arrests of males for property crimes[a] (data: FBI)															
(1) all ages (1a)			.14							—	26	linear	correlation	ecological	(a) Boston, (b) Chicago, (c) Cincinnati, 1930–1956; time-series
(1b)			.50[b]												
(1c)			.77[b]												
(2) 20 and under (2a)			–.01							—	26				
(2b)			.28												
(2c)			.62[c]												
(3) 21 through 24 (3a)			.53[c]							—	26				
(3b)			.87[b]												
Pressman and Carol (1976): property crime rate[d] (data: Department of Justice, Department of Commerce)	.19				.09		.43			.59[f]	( )[e]	linear	partial correlation	ecological	SMSAs of all population sizes, 1965; cross-sectional
					.35		( )[e]			( )[e]					
Brown et al. (1972): offenses against property with violence[g] (data: magistrates' court and court of quarter sessions)								–.05[h]		—	15	linear	Spearman-Rho rank order correlation	ecological	15 electoral wards of a Northern urban town in Britain, 1969; cross-sectional
								.01							
Land and Felson (1976): reported national property crime rate per 100,000 (mid year) population (data: Social Indicators)	1.27 (5.66)	–1196.50 (4.14)	14.87 (1.02)	2492.46 (2.16)	39.19 (1.17)				25.81 (2.81)	.9988	25	linear	OLS	ecological	United States, 1947–1972; time series
Fleisher (1966b, 1963): property arrest divided by the population for:[j] (1) under 21 (data: FBI)			.39 (2.3)		.78 (2.3)					.56	60	linear	OLS of first difference	ecological	Boston, Chicago and Cincinnati, 1936/37–1955/56; pooled cross-sectional time series
			16		–.15 (–1.2)					.60	60				
(2) 21–24 (data: FBI)			16.0 (.3)	–.00094 (–.6)	8.2 (.6)					.60	60				
			1.9	–.00016 (–.4)											
(3) U.S. property crimes per 1,000 population (data: UCR)				.101 (.347)	.189 (1.453)	279 (4.6)	6.9 (.3)		–5.9 (–2.4)	.48	101	linear	OLS		101 U.S. cities with population greater than 25,000, 1960; cross-sectional
				.383 (.240)											
Sjoquist (1973): property crimes reported to FBI by local police per 1,000 (community) population[k] (data: FBI)	–.356 (–3.608)	.820 (1.546)	.347 (2.794)	.101 (.347)	.189 (1.453)		.130 (2.964)			.638	53	log-linear	OLS	wealth maximization	53 municipalities with populations (1960) 25,000 to 200,000 1960; cross-sectional
	–.204 (–1.051)			.383 (.240)	.001 (.006)										
Morris and Tweeten (1971): 20.51 (20.959) property crime rate per 100,000 population[l] (data: UCR)	20.51 (20.959)		–.04 (1.333)	–.04 (1.333)	.02 (2.00)		12.71 (2.765)		–408.16 (3.701)	.62	754	linear	recursive least squares	wealth maximization	U.S. cities, 1967–1968; cross-sectional
					–21.74 (1.922)				–293.21 (2.245)						
					24.51 (.899)				1,153.39 (10.117)						

Table 5–3. (continued)

Model: Dependent Variable	Deterrent Variables	Education	Employment	Income	Population	Family	Race	Neighborhood	Other	R²	N	Functional Form of Model	Estimation Technique	Theoretical Base	Sample
Bartel (1979): (1) female property crime arrests per capita[m] (data: FBI)	−.331 (−2.52) −.097 (−.73) −.390 (2.00)		4.242 (2.92) −.883 (−1.15) .505 (1.30) −.829 (−1.95)	−.822 (−.72) .512 (.48)	−5.677 (−1.71)	.271 (.35) .781 (.53) −4.901 (−2.18) .218 (.32) 4.430 (1.70)	.068 (.88)			.94	33	log-linear	weighted OLS	time allocation	33 states, 1970; cross-sectional
(2)	−.811 (−2.31) −.394 (−1.41) .329 (1.20)		5.083 (2.37) −.178 (−.17) .862 (1.31) −.418 (−.69)	−3.311 (−1.26) −.076 (−.04)	1.290 (.82)	20.238 (3.24)	.336 (2.18)			.79	33	log-linear	weighted 2SLS		
male property crime arrests per capita (data: FBI) (3)	−.365 (−2.92) −.233 (−1.94) .783 (5.22)		−1.268 (−.92) 5.939 (1.55) .185 (.56) −.119 (−.27)	2.491 (2.72) 1.937 (1.79)	−2.366 (−1.27) −.702 (−.45) −1.114 (−1.00)	4.842 (2.02)	.055 (.69)			.88	33	log-linear	weighted OLS		
(4)	−1.211 (−2.41) −.681 (−2.10) .831 (2.93)		−1.796 (−1.55) 13.231 (1.87) .280 (.46) −.271 (−.31)	−.732 (−.30) 1.431 (.69)	1.478 (.61)	14.234 (2.49)	.310 (1.58)			.44	33	log-linear	weighted 2SLS		
Swimmer (1974a): property crime rate[e] (data: FBI)	.0068 (.49) −.010 (−.06)	−.012 (−.96)	.027 (.90)	−.0041 (−.51) .044 (3.58)	.037 (2.57) −.0004 (−2.28)		.0028 (.53)		−1.30 (−.81)	—	119	log-linear	2SLS	wealth maximization	All cities with 100,000 or more residents, 1960; cross-sectional
Thaler (1975): (1) number of arrests for property crimes per population[a]		−.0021 (.65)	−.0021 (1.55)	.52×10⁻³ (1.78)	−.00091 (2.34) .024 (7.82) .0010 (1.04)	−.0023 (2.77) .28 (4.21)	.00019 (.97)	−.00060 (2.19)		.86	89	linear	2SLS	wealth maximization	Rochester, New York census tracts, 1970; cross-sectional
(2) property offense rate per population (data: Rochester PD)	2.56 (13.5) .22 (1.91) −.00064 (.165)							.00059 (1.31)		.92	89		2SLS		

86

Table 5-3. (continued)

Model: Dependent Variable	Deterrent Variable	Education	Employment	Income	Population	Family	Race	Neighborhood	Other	F	R²	N	Functional Form of Model	Estimation Technique	Theoretical Base	Sample
Ehrlich (1973, 1974): crimes against property known to the police to have occurred per 100,000 (states) population[a] (data: UCR)	-.796 (-6.140) -.915 (4.297)			1.883 (4.246) 2.132 (5.356)			.243 (4.805)				—	47	linear	2SLS	time allocation	47 states, 1960; cross-sectional
Peterson, et al. (1980): individual's property crime offense rate of average number of property crimes per year[a] (data: self report)				.076 ( )[r]			.130 ( )		.237 ( ) .299 ( ) -.151 ( ) -.124 ( ) .109 ( ) .104 ( ) .158 ( )		.431	624	linear	stepwise multiple regression	no explicit theory	624 male felons in 5 California state prisons, 1976; cross-sectional
Greenwood and Wadycki (1976): per capita crimes against property[a] (data: Department of Justice)	1.30 (5.04) 0.23 (1.97)				-.03 (-1.27)		.001 (.04) .24 (1.61)		.22 (2.81)		.34[1]	199	log-linear	3SLS	wealth maximization	199 SMSA's, 1960; cross-sectional
Weiler et al. (1978): binary for individual arrested for property crime during the quarter[a] (data: California Department of Corrections, Bureau of Criminal Statistics)		.03114 (.92126) .01315 (2.00291)	-1.51671 (-2.32309)				.28159 (2.13557)		-0.01577 (-2.01514)	4313.47[a]	[a]	3227	linear	logit	time allocation	Sample of individuals who had been arrested at least once for a felony in Los Angeles County, 1953(2)–1975(3); time series
Witte and Schmidt (1979): log of the ratio of the probability that the most serious conviction is a crime against property to the probability of no conviction[a] (data: police files and individual interview)	-.38794 (-1.09) -.02278 (-.08)	-.04562 (-.77)				-.36561 (-1.16)	.36795 (1.30)		-.82009 (-2.0) .79014 (2.65) -.85891 (-1.72) -.18451 (-.77) -.56926 (-2.92) .35791 (.98) .34459 (3.41) -.10068 (2.28) .23384 (2.33)		—	596	linear	maximum likelihood logit	maximum time allocation	641 men imprisoned in North Carolina in 1969 or 1971; cross-sectional

[a]Glaser and Rice estimate correlation coefficients relating arrests of males for property crimes to percent of male labor force unemployed.

[b]Significance of difference from $r = 0$: .01.

[c]Significance of difference from $r = 0$: .001.

[d]The variables used by Pressman and Carol are as follows: income is median family income; population is number of people per square mile, and net migration; race is percent of population nonwhite.

[e]t-test level of significance: .01.

[f]This is the multiple correlation coefficient.

[g]The variables used by Brown, McCulloch, and Hiscox are as follows: neighborhood is owner-occupied houses, and houses with fewer than 0.5 persons per room. Rented council houses, able-bodied unemployed, disabled unemployed, persons receiving social security payments, Irish immigrants, and overcrowding were not found to be correlated with property offenses.

[h]The values shown are level of significance (p value).

[i]The independent variables used by Land and Felson are as follows: the deterrent variables are lagged reported property crime, and the federal, state and local police expenditures in billions of year t dollars per 100,000 midyear population; employment is the annual average national civilian unemployment rate in year t; income is the actual dollar value of GNP in billions of year t dollars per 100,000 midyear population; population is the percentage of the total population that is male, ages 15–24, in year t; other is the consumer price index for year t, expressed as a percentage of the 1967 (base) CPI.

[j]Fleisher uses the following independent variables: (1), (2) employment is male civilian unemployment rate; population is the number of armed forces personnel in the United States. Fleisher also runs a regression on a log-linear model of property arrest rates and a regression on the Boston data alone. (3) In his cross-sectional analysis Fleisher uses the following variables: employment is the male civilian unemployment rate; income is the mean income of the second lowest quartile of families, and the mean income of the highest quartile of families; population is the proportion of the population of five-year-olds that lived in another county in 1955 (1960); family is proportion of females over 14 who are separated or divorced; race is the proportion of the population that is nonwhite; other is a regional binary variable equal to 1 for Southern cities, zero otherwise. Fleisher runs a number of other regressions with different variables and stratifications of the data.

[k]Sjoquist uses the following independent variables: the deterrent variables are the probability of arrest for a property crime, and the average sentence served by inmates released from State and Federal Institutes who had been charged with a property crime (statewide); education is mean school years completed by residents of the community in 1960; employment is the labor force unemployment rate in 1968; income is yearly income in $1000 (countywide), yearly sales per retail establishment in $1000, and percent of families in the community with incomes below $3000 in 1959; population is community population in 1000s, and persons per square mile; race is percent of city population which was nonwhite in 1960. Sjoquist runs a number of other regressions using different variables.

[l]Morris and Tweeten use the following independent variables: the deterrent variable is number of police per capita; income is median income; population is population density, median age, and percent males; race is percent nonwhite; other is three binary variables taking the value 1 if the city is in the Northeast, South or West, respectively, and 0 otherwise. Not shown are a series of variables for city size and for size-police interactions. The results are derived from a two-equation simultaneous system, with the other dependent variable being police number per capita.

[m]The independent variables used by Bartel are as follows: (1) the deterrent variables are the probability of apprehension and conviction for property crimes, average time served by offenders in the state prison for a property crime before their first release, and probability of arrest; employment is percentage of single females aged 16 and over who are in the civilian labor force, percentage of married spouse present females aged 16 and over who are in the civilian labor force, the unemployment rate of females aged 35 to 39, and the unemployment rate of females aged 16 to 19; income is the state's median family income, and percentage of families with incomes below one-half the state's median; population is the median age of the female population; family is the average number of children under 6 in female-headed families, the average number of children aged 6–17 in female-headed families, the average number of children under 6 in husband-wife families, the average number of children aged 6–17 in husband-wife families, and the percentage of females aged 16 and over who are married with spouse present; race is percentage of females who are nonwhite.

(2) The independent variables are as in (1), except as noted: family is percentage of females aged 16 and over who are married with spouse present.

(3) The independent variables are as in (1) except as noted: family is percentage of females aged 16 and over who are married with spouse present, average number of children under 6 in husband-wife families, and average number of children aged 6 to 17 in husband-wife families.

(4) The independent variables are as in (2).

[n]Swimmer used the following independent variables: deterrent variables are total expenditure on police per capita, and average time served by convicted first offenders; education is percent of 14- to 17-year-olds in school; employment is unemployment rate; income is median income in $100s, and percentage of families with incomes less than $3000 or greater than $10,000; population is population in 100,000s, and population squared; race is percent of population nonwhite; other is a binary variable for South–Non-South.

[o]The independent variables used by Thaler are as follows: (1) education is median school years completed; employment is percent unemployed; income is median income; population is population density, percentage males 15–24, and percentage male married; family is percent families with both husband and wife, and number of unrelated individuals per population; race is percent Negro; neighborhood is percent of houses greater than $20,000 in value. (2) the deterrent variables are arrest rate, police density, and arrest clearance rate; neighborhood is percent of houses greater than $20,000 in value; not shown is the variable for mean reported losses. The results are from a 3-equation model, with the other dependent variables being police presence per acre and the "clearance rate" for property crimes.

[p]The independent variables used by Ehrlich are as follows: the deterrent variables are the number of offenders imprisoned per offenses known, and average time served by offenders in state prisons; income is median income of families, and percentage of families below one-half of median income; race is percentage of nonwhites in the population. The second equation of the two equation model is a production function of law enforcement activity.

[q]Peterson et al. use the following independent variables: income is an index of economic distress motives; race is a binary variable taking the value 1 if the individual is white and 0 otherwise; other is a binary variable taking the value 1 if the individual is a drug user and 0 otherwise, a measure of the individual's tendency to identify himself in terms of one or more criminal activities, age of first serious crime, a measure of temper motives, a binary variable taking the value 1 if the commitment offense is theft or fraud and 0 otherwise, a binary variable taking the value 1 if the commitment offense is burglary and 0 otherwise, and a measure of composite criminal attitudes.

[r]The values shown are beta coefficients or coefficients on standardized variables. The coefficients for each characteristic are significant by t-tests with $p > .05$.

[s]The independent variables used by Greenwood and Wadycki are as follows: the deterrent variables are per capita local government expenditures for police protection, and per capita full-time equivalent employment in police protection; income is the percentage of families with 1959 income below $3,000 in 1960; population is population per square mile; race is percent of population that is Black; neighborhood is median value of owner occupied housing units; other is a binary variable taking the value 1 for observations south of a line drawn at the northern border of North Carolina, Tennessee, Oklahoma, etc., and the value 0 otherwise. These results are derived from a 3-equation, simultaneous equation model, with the other dependent variables being per capita local government expenditures for police protection and per capita full-time equivalent employment in police protection.

tThis is the value of an equivalent OLS R^2.

uThe dependent variables used by Weller et al. are as follows: education is highest grade in school recorded for each individual, and tested IQ of each individual; employment is the imputed value for employment generated by a logit regression on observed employment, where employed equals 1 if the individual earned a positive amount during the quarter by working in a job covered by Social Security, and 0 otherwise; race is a binary variable equal to 1 if the individual is white and 2 if he is not; other is the individual's age in years. A variable for year is not shown. Also not shown are several logit equations to explain employment.

vThis is the likelihood ratio test, which is $-2 \log(\lambda)$, where $\log(\lambda)$ is the difference between the log of the maximized value of the likelihood function with only a constant term as an independent variable and the log of the maximized value of the likelihood function with the independent variables in the regression under consideration. This statistic is distributed x^2_k, where k is the number of explanatory variables (excluding the constant) in the regression under consideration. The statistic tests the joint significance of the independent variables and is equivalent to the F test in least squares regression.

wThe norm of the gradient for this equation is 2.348D–07.

xThe independent variables used by Witte and Schmidt are as follows: the deterrent variables are a binary variable taking the value 1 for an individual with supervised release (e.g. parole) and 0 otherwise, and a binary variable taking the value 1 if the individual participated in prisoner work release program and 0 otherwise; education is number of years of school completed before sample incarceration; family is a binary variable taking the value 1 if married and 0 otherwise; race is a binary variable taking the value 1 for white and 0 otherwise; other is a binary variable taking the value 1 if the sample incarceration was for a felony and 0 otherwise, a binary variable taking the value 1 for a serious alcohol problem or hard drug use and 0 otherwise, a binary variable taking the value 1 if the sample incarceration is for a crime against a person and 0 otherwise, a binary variable taking the value 1 if the sample conviction is for a crime against property and 0 otherwise, the number of convictions before the sample sentence, age at first arrest, age at time of release from sample sentence, length of individual's follow-up period, and number of prison rule violations during sample sentence.

Table 5-4. Summary of the Literature on the Effect of Economic Factors on Property Crime (t-ratios in parentheses)

Model: Dependent Variable	Deterrent Variables	Education	Employment	Income	Population	Family	Race	Neighborhood	Other	F	R²	N	Functional Form of Model	Estimation Technique	Theoretical Base	Sample
Quinney (1966): all robbery offenses known to the police per 100,000 population (data: UCR)[a] (1) Rural (2) Urban (3) SMSA		.06 .25 -.03	-.41 .25 -.16 -.12 -.49 .16 -.05 .19 -.09 -.02 -.18 .04	-.06 .22 .20	-.16 .35 -.40 .62 .04 .29		.03 -.09 .01	-.24 -.02 .04			—	50	linear	product moment correlation	ecological	50 states of the U.S., 1959–1961; cross-sectional
Pressman and Carol (1976): robbery offense rate[a] (data: Department of Justice, Department of Commerce)				.18 .02	.15 .25		.47 ( )[e]				.594 ( )[c]	95	linear	partial correlation	ecological	95 SMSAs with populations of 250,000 or more, 1965; cross-sectional
Schmid (1950): non-residential robbery offenses known to the police[a] (data: Seattle PD files)			-.194		-.340 -.306 .539		.055				.716[f]	93	linear	factor analysis (correlation)	ecological	93 census tracts in the city of Seattle, 1949–1951; cross-sectional
Schuessler and Slatin (1964): robbery rate of[g] (1) 1950 (2) 1960			.11			.05	-.22 .49		.77 -.05 -.70 .21		.651[f] -.771[f]	101 133	linear	factor analysis (partial correlation)	ecological	101 U.S. cities with population 100,000 and over, 1950; 113 U.S. cities with population 100,000 and over, 1950; cross-sectional
Gylys (1970): robbery offenses per 100,000 population[h] (data: FBI, Census)	.1247	.0093	.0215	.0707 .0571	.0389 .0172	.0059	.0000	.0625 .1168	.0519 .0011		.5077	57	linear	OLS - to derive partial coefficients of determination	no explicit theory	57 largest central cities (population equal to or greater than 250,000) in 1968, 1960; cross-sectional
Block (1972): robbery offenses known to the police per juvenile arrested for any offense[i] (data: Los Angeles PD)	-.097512 (1.80076)				.46967 (3.55649)				.000006 (.40000)		.65	14	linear	OLS	wealth maximization	Police districts in the city of Los Angeles, 1965; cross-sectional

Table 5–4. (continued)

Model: Dependent Variable	Deterrent Variables	Education	Employment	Income	Population	Family	Race	Neighborhood	Other	F	R²	N	Functional form of Model	Estimation Technique	Theoretical Base	Sample
Phillips et al. (1972): robbery arrest rate for males 18–19: proportion of offenses cleared by arrest (data: UCR) (1)			-8.37 (-1.91)							5.3	.47	15	linear	OLS	wealth maximization	U.S. urban areas, 1952–1967; time series
(2)			-35.92 (-4.50)							12.1	.67	15				
Hoch (1974): robbery offenses known to the police per 100,000 (SMSA) population [b] (data: UCR) (1)					53.906 (2.776) .274 (1.982) 26.645 (4.336) -4.897 (2.678) -3.428 (1.383)		1.964 (2.689) -1.248 (2.007) -2.142 (2.028) -.696 (1.921)	3.513 (3.396)	10.864 (1.819)		.556	136	linear	OLS	ecological	136 SMSAs, 1960.
(2)			6.409 (1.649)		14.007 (2.036)	103.450 (1.940)	8.074 (5.169) -7.834 (4.426) 8.408 (3.071) -2.952 (2.084)	-6.640 (2.058)	4.286 (2.648) 76.384 (2.541) 36.185 (1.762) 31.985 (2.377)		.784	137				137 SMSAs, 1970; cross-sectional
Danziger and Wheeler (1975a): number of robberies per 100,000 population [c] (data: UCR)	-.510 (2.59) -.805 (1.90)	-.220 (.751)	-.037 (.12)	-1.290 (1.05) 2.243 (1.98)	-.872 (1.76) .256 (2.01) .295 (1.92)		.312 (2.87)		-1.182 (5.75)		.758	57	log-linear	OLS	wealth maximization	57 large SMSAs, 1960–1961; cross-sectional
Danziger and Wheeler (1975b): robbery offenses known to the police per 100,000 population [m] (data: UCR)	-.011 (.124) -.805 (5.227)	-.742 (2.659)	-.056 (.889)	1.144 (3.375) 2.596 (2.630)	-.274 (.506)					118.3	.9845	21	log-linear	GLS (Cochrane-Orcutt Estimation)	wealth maximization	United States, 1949–1970; time series
Ehrlich (1979): urban robbery rate per 100,000 population [n] (data: UCR)	-.570 (-2.60) -.146 (-1.61)	-.887 (-7.20)		1.309 (1.69) .932 (1.25)	-.593 (-.68) .439 (.85)		.266 (2.54)				.9819	35	log-linear	GLS	wealth maximization	35 states, 1950; cross-sectional
Peterson et al. (1980): a binary variable taking the value 1 if the individual committed armed robbery and 0 otherwise [p] (data: self-report)				.088 [p] ( )					.345 ( ) .135 ( ) .205 ( )		.236	624	linear	stepwise multiple regression	no explicit theory	624 male felons in 5 California state prisons, 1976; cross-sectional

93

Table 5–4. (continued)

Model/Dependent Variable	Deterrent Variables	Education	Employment	Income	Population	Family	Race	Neighborhood	Other	F	R²	N	Functional Form of Model	Estimation Technique	Theoretical Base	Sample
Avio and Clark (1976): number of robbery offenses recorded by police per 1,000 population† (data: police statistics)	-.663 (3.413) -1.872 (4.580) -.229 (2.009)		.078 (.349) .164 (.128)	-.268 (.682)	-3.269 (2.216)		.260 (3.249)		.149 (2.660)		.973	24	log-linear	2SLS	time allocation	8 Canadian Provinces, 1970–1972; cross-sectional
Mathieson and Passell (1976): robbery offenses per capita* (data: NYC police department)	-2.95 (-4.08)			-1.30 (-1.36) .184 (.71) (-1.81) (-1.83)				.989 (1.29) 1.20 (1.91)			–	–	log-linear	2SLS	wealth maximization	New York City police precincts, 1971; cross-sectional
Pogue (1976): reported robbery offenses per 100,000 population* (data: FBI)	-1.403 (-1.898)	1.056 (.756)	.046 (.239) .061 (1.068)	-.021 (-.037) .727 (3.536)	1.223 (1.597) -1.734 (-2.406) 3.974 (1.729) .353 (2.048) .034 (.481) .663 (2.334)		-.353 (-1.259)				.469	66	log-linear	2SLS	ecological	SMSAs, 1968; cross-sectional
Swimmer (1974b): log of robbery offenses known to the police per 1,000 population† (data: FBI)	-.0392 (-1.29) -.0653 (-1.83) -.0260 (-1.29)		.0430 (.97)	-.00659 (-.51) .0523 (2.56)	.0878 (3.59) -9.74E-4 (-3.03)		.0290 (3.59)		-.514 (-1.88)		.426	119	log-linear	2SLS	wealth maximization	All cities with 100,000 or more residents in 1960; cross-sectional
Ehrlich (1973, 1974): robbery offenses known to the police per 100,000 population* (state) (data: UCR)	(1)-1.303 (-7.011)(-1.395) -.372 (2)-1.112 (-6.532) -.236 (-.750)			1.689 (1.969) 1.279 (1.660) 2.120 (2.548) 1.409 (1.853)			.334 (4.024) .346 (4.191)				–	47 47	linear linear	2SLS SUR	time allocation	47 states, 1960; cross-sectional

94

[a]The variables used by Quinney are as follows: education is median years of schooling; employment is percent employed in manufacturing, a measure of occupational diversity, percent females in the labor force, and percent white collar males; income is median family income; population is percent aged 50 and over, and percent change in residence; race is percent nonwhite; neighborhood is percent owner-occupied housing.

[b]Pressman and Carol use the following variables: income is percent of population with income over $10,000 and percent of population with income under $3,000; population is number of people per square mile, and net migration; race is percent of population nonwhite.

[c]t-test level of significance: .01.

[d]This is the multiple correlation coefficient.

[e]The variables (factors) used by Schmid are as follows: employment is a factor reflecting low social cohesion–low occupational status; population is a factor reflecting low family and economic status, a factor indicating high population mobility, and a factor showing low population mobility; family is a factor indicating low social cohesion–low family status; race is a factor reflecting the Negro population; not shown are an ambiguous factor and an atypical crime pattern factor. Schmid also analyzes a highway and car robbery variable.

[f]This is the h^2 of factor analysis, which is the proportion of the variation in the data accounted for by the factors.

[g]The variables (factors) used by Schuessler and Slatin are as follows: (1) education is a factor reflecting education; income is a factor reflecting economic characteristics; race is a factor dealing with minority; other is a factor reflecting the abstract theoretical anomie, and a factor of social conformity. (2) the factors are as above, except as noted: income is a factor dealing loosely with economic variables; family is a factor reflecting family characteristics.

[h]The independent variables used by Gylys are as follows: the deterrent variable is per capita police expenditures; education is median years of schooling; employment is percent of labor force unemployed; income is percent of families with $3000 or less and median income; population is median age of population, population density, and population size; family is percent of broken homes; race is percent of population nonwhite; neighborhood is percent of owner-occupied homes, percent of deteriorating homes, and population per housing unit; other is median temperature.

[i]The following independent variables are used in the study by Block: the deterrent variable is number of robbery offenses cleared by arrest; population is the proportion of the number of juveniles arrested who reside in the police district; other is the average value of a robbery.

jThe independent variables used by Phillips, Votey and Maxwell are as follows: (1) employment is the ratio of the male, white, civilian labor force to the total noninstitutional population; population is the ratio of white, civilian, noninstitutional population to the total noninstitutional population. (2) employment is the ratio of the male, nonwhite, civilian labor force to the total noninstitutional population; population is the ratio of nonwhite, civilian, noninstitutional population to the total noninstitutional population.

kHoch used the following independent variables: (1) population is the log of the SMSA population (in 1000), percent growth in the SMSA population, percent male primary individuals, percentage of population under 21 years of age, and percentage age 65 or over, (not shown are various SMSA size and percent black interaction terms); race is percent of SMSA population that is black, a binary variable, Confederacy, times percent black (where Confederacy takes the value 1 if the SMSA is in a state that was in the Confederacy during the Civil War, and 0 otherwise), percentage Japanese, and percent with parent foreign born; neighborhood is percent crowded housing; other is a binary variable taking the value 1 for SMSAs in the North Central U.S. and 0 otherwise. (2) employment is the percent unemployment in the current year; population is percent male primary individuals, (not shown are various SMSA size and percent black interaction terms); family is population per household; race is percent of SMSA population that is black, the binary variable Confederacy times percent black, percentage foreign born, and percentage with parent foreign born; neighborhood is percent crowded housing; other is average temperature (°F in July), the binary variable Confederacy, and two binary variables (West, North Central) taking the value 1 if the SMSA is in that region of the U.S., and 0 otherwise.

lDanziger and Wheeler use the following independent variables: the deterrent variables are the ratio of prisoners received from the courts to the total number of index crimes, and the average time served by felony prisoners at first release from state and federal institutions; education is the percent of population over 25 years of age with less than 8 years of schooling; employment is the average annual rate of unemployment for males aged 16 and over; income is a measure of the absolute income gap, and a measure of the relative income inequality; population is the percentage of the population between the ages of 15 and 24, the size of the SMSA, and the central city population per square mile; race is the percentage of the population nonwhite; other is a binary variable taking the value 1 if the SMSA is located in the Northeast region and 0 otherwise.

mThe independent variables used by Danziger and Wheeler are as follows: the deterrent variables are the ratio of persons charged and held for prosecution to the total number of robbery offenses known to the police, the ratio of persons found guilty to the number of those originally charged, and the ratio of prisoners (sentenced for robbery offenses) received from courts by state and federal institutions to the total number of convictions for that crime; employment is the average annual rate of unemployment for males aged 16 and over; income is a measure of the absolute income gap, and a measure of the relative inequality of income distribution; population is the percentage of the population between the ages of 15 and 24.

[n]Ehrlich uses the following independent variables: the deterrent variables are median time spent in state prisons by robbery offenders prior to first release, the ratio of prisoners received in state prisons to the estimated total number of robberies, and the conditional probability of execution given a robbery conviction; income is median income of families in year $t - 1$, and percentage of families with income below one-half of median income; population is the percent of population in age group 15–24, and percent of urban population in the total state population. The equation is weighted by the square root of the size of population in 100,000s in UCR samples reporting robbery rates in 1951.

[o]Peterson et al. use the following independent variables: income is an index of economic distress motives; other is a binary variable taking the value 1 if the individual's current offense is robbery and 0 otherwise, a juvenile crime scale, and a measure of the individual's tendency to identify himself in terms of one or more criminal activity.

[p]The values shown are beta coefficients or coefficients on standardized variables. The coefficients for each characteristic are significant by t-tests with $p > .05$.

[q]Avio and Clark use the following independent variables: the deterrent variables are the number of clearances divided by number of offenses, the number of convictions divided by the number of charges, and the weighted average of sentences handed down corrected for remissions and parole; employment is total unemployment rate, and total participation rate; income is percentage of families with incomes less than one-half the median family income; population is percentage of males aged 15 to 24 in the total male population; race is percentage of North American Indians in the population; other is the number of households with record players. These results are derived from a 3-equation model, with the other dependent variables being expenditures per capita by police on labor and capital, and the clearance rate for the crime.

[r]These are the results derived by Mathieson and Passell for a 3-equation model, with the other dependent variables being the number of arrests per reported crime, and the police manpower assigned to a precinct. The variables used in the regression are as follow: the deterrent variable is the number of arrests per reported crime; income is median family income in the precinct, percentage of families with incomes greater than $25,000, and median family income in adjacent precincts; neighborhood is a binary variable taking the value 1 for predominantly residential districts and the value 2 for predominantly business districts, and a binary variable taking the value 1 if there are no large parks or airports and the value 2 if there are large parks or airports.

[s]The following independent variables are used by Pogue: (1) the deterrent variable is the proportion of this particular crime category that is cleared by arrest; education is the median years of school completed by the SMSA population; employment is the percentage unemployed, and the 1968 unemployment rate divided by the 1967 rate; income is per capita income in dollars per year, and percentage of households with incomes below $3000 per year; population is percentage of population aged 12 to 17, percentage

aged 18 to 24, percentage male, total population in thousands, population density in thousands per square mile, and the 1968 population divided by the 1960 population; race is percent of population that is white. These results are derived from a 3-equation model, with the other dependent variables being police expenditure and clearance ratio. Pogue also runs regressions for the 1962–1967 period.

*Swimmer uses the following independent variables: deterrent variables are total expenditure on police per capita, and average time served by convicted first offenders; education is percent of 14- to 17-year-olds in school, employment is unemployment rate; income is median income in $100s, and percentage of families with incomes less than $3000 or greater than $10,000; population is population in 100,000s, and population squared; race is percent of population nonwhite; other is a binary variable for South–Non-South.

"The independent variables used by Ehrlich are as follows: the deterrent variables are the number of offenders imprisoned per offenses known, average time served by offenders in state prisons; income is median income of families, and percentage of families below one-half of median income; race is percentage of nonwhites in the population. The second equation of the two equation model is a production function of law enforcement activity.

"We are aware of another work by Hoover Institution dealing with the effect of economic factors on crime. However, we had difficulty with this study because of their failure to explain their estimation technique and their failure to define certain coefficients. We were therefore unable to include the results of this study in our tables.

Table 5-5. Summary of the Literature on the Effect of Economic Factors on Burglary (t-ratios in parentheses)

Model: Dependent Variable	Deterrent Variables	Education	Employment	Income	Population	Family	Race	Neighborhood	Other	F	R²	N	Functional Form of Model	Estimation Technique	Theoretical Base	Sample
Quinney (1966): all burglary offenses known to the police per 100,000 population[a] (data: UCR)											—	–50	linear	product moment correlation	ecological	50 states of the U.S., 1959–1961; cross-sectional
(1) Rural		.35	–.11 .28 .15 .20	.34	.06	.31	–.14	–.02								
(2) Urban		.10	–.42 .25 .09 .10	.03	–.37	.52 *	.18	.00								
(3) SMSA		.16	–.38 .09 –.12 .04	.00	–.27	.64	.20	.03								
Pressman and Carol (1976): burglary offense rate[b] (data: Department of Justice, Department of Commerce)				.15 –.10	.03 .44 ( )[e]		.47 ( )[e]				.68[e] ( )[e]	95	linear	partial correlation	ecological	95 SMSA's with population of 250,000 or more, 1965; cross-sectional
Schmid (1960): burglary offenses known to the police[c] (data: Seattle PD files)														factor analysis (correlation)	ecological	93 census tracts in the City of Seattle, 1949–1951; cross-sectional
(1) Residence Day			.305		.267	.275 .110 .802	–.170				.954[d]	93	linear			
(2) Residence Night			.238		.353	.349 .145 .735	–.158				.935[f]	93	linear			
Schuessler and Slatin (1964): burglary rate[e]														factor analysis (partial correlations)	ecological	101 U.S. cities with population 100,000 and over, 1950; 133 U.S. cities with population 100,000 and over, 1960; cross-sectional
(1) 1950		.16		.18			–.09		.78 –.08		.68[g]	101	linear			
(2) 1960				–.14		.11	.38		–.76 .05		.76[g]	133	linear			
Gylys (1970): burglary offenses per 100,000 population[i] (data: FBI, Census)	.0293	.0021	.0021	.2168 .1329	.0587 .0014	.1583	.0028 .0868 .0901 .1122		1560		.5718	57	linear	OLS-to-derive partial coefficients of determination	no explicit theory	57 largest central cities (population equal to or greater than 250,000 in 1968, 1960; cross-sectional
Block (1972): burglary offenses known to the police per juvenile who had been arrested for any offense in 1965[f] (data: Los Angeles PD)	–.72230 (4.57339)				1.28068 (4.71427)				.00017 (3.40000)		.78	14	linear	OLS	wealth maximization	Police districts in the City of Los Angeles, 1965; cross-sectional

Table 5-5. (continued)

Model: Dependent Variable	Deterrent Variables	Education	Employment	Income	Population	Family	Race	Neighborhood	Other	F	R^2	N	Functional Form of Model	Estimation Technique	Theoretical Base	Sample
Phillips et al. (1972): burglary arrest rate for males 18–19 + proportion of offenses cleared by police[a] (data: UCR)	(1) -54.61 (-3.93) (2) -178.51 (-8.37)				26.80 (4.78) 130.56 (4.07)					14.3 39.6	.71 .86	15 15	linear	OLS	wealth maximization	U.S. urban areas, 1952–1967; time series
Hoch (1974): burglary offenses known to the police per 100,000 (SMSA) population[f] (data: UCR)	(1) (2)		14.326 (1.764) 104.370 (5.485)		3.161 (3.476) 113.721 (2.045) 223.040 (2.197) 7.820 (3.665) 214.151 (3.032)	158.127 (2.036) -405.345 (1.938) 18.017 (1.764) -28.722 (2.907) 612.805 (1.809)	11.013 (2.926) -13.300 (2.676) 19.598 (2.867) -21.830 (2.418) -138.059 (1.848) 141.089 (2.168)	12.215 (1.609)	8.286 (1.769) 269.191 (2.947) 19.291 (2.724) 62.724 (2.570) 412.826		.524 .560	136 137	linear	OLS	ecological	136 SMSAs, 1960 137 SMSAs, 1970; cross-sectional
Danziger and Wheeler (1974a): number of burglaries per 100,000 population[m] (data: UCR)	-.480 (3.63) -.491 (1.76) -.210 (.62)		-.049 (.219)	-1.172 (1.37) 2.045 (2.58)	-.376 (1.08) -.034 (.32)	.047 (.52)	.148 (1.82)		-.721 (4.47)		.635	57	log-linear	OLS	wealth maximization	57 large SMSAs, 1960–1961; cross-sectional
Danziger and Wheeler (1975b): burglary offenses known to the police per 100,000 population[n] (data: UCR)	-.059 (.621) -.077 (.448) -.204 (2.372)		.060 (1.538)	1.949 (7.265) 0.059 (.097)	.430 (1.239)					371.1	.995	21	log-linear	GLS (Cochrane-Orcutt Estimation)	wealth maximization	United States, 1949–1970; time series
Peterson et al. (1980): a binary variable taking the value 1 if the individual committed burglary, and 0 otherwise[p] (data: self-report)				.106 ( )b			-.156 ( )		.190 ( ) .219 ( ) .106 ( ) .103 ( ) -.123 ( )		.262	624	linear	stepwise multiple regression	no explicit theory	624 male felons in 5 California state prisons, 1976; cross-sectional
Avio and Clark (1976): number of breaking and entering offenses recorded by police per 1,000 population[q] (data: police statistics)	-.661 (1.312) -.112 (-.127) .221 (2.053)		.400 (3.391)	.784 (1.855) .366 (.845)	-.328 (.415)		.152 (2.389)		.113 (4.770)		.976	24	log-linear	2SLS	time allocation	8 Canadian provinces, 1970–1972; cross-sectional

Table 5-5. (continued)

Model: Dependent Variable	Deterrent Variables	Education	Employment	Income	Population	Family	Race	Neighborhood	Other	F	R^2	N	Functional Form of Model	Estimation Technique	Theoretical Base	Sample
Swimmer (1974b): log of burglary offenses known to the police per 1,000 population[a] (data: FBI)	-.0246 -.341 (-1.25) (-2.24)	.00101 (.08)	.0154 (.52)	-.00838 .0361 (-1.08) (2.99)	.0214 -2.7E-4 (1.47) (-1.42)		.00618 (1.12)		.0380 (.23)		.284	119	log-linear	2SLS	wealth maximization	All cities with 100,000 or more residents in 1960; cross-sectional
Pogue (1976): reported burglary offenses per 100,000 population[b] (data: FBI)	-.892 (-3.179)	1.251 (2.002)	.046 .061 (.289) (1.068)	-.021 .727 (-.037) (3.536)	1.223 -1.734 3.974 .132 .034 .663 (1.597) (-2.406) (1.729) (1.720) (.481) (2.334)		-.353 (-1.259)				.461	66	log-linear	2SLS	ecological	SMSAs, 1968; cross-sectional
Ehrlich (1973, 1974): burglary offenses known to the police per 100,000 (state) population[f] (data: UCR)	(1) -.724 (-6.003) -1.127 (-4.799) (2) -.624 (-5.576) -0.996 (-4.260)			1.384 (2.839) 2.000 (4.689) 1.581 (3.313) 2.032 (4.766)			.250 (4.579) .230 (4.274)				– –	47 47	linear linear	2SLS SUR	time allocation	47 states, 1960; cross-sectional

[a]The variables used by Quinney are as follows: education is median years of schooling; employment is percent employed in manufacturing, a measure of occupational diversity, percent females in the labor force, and percent white collar males; income is median family income; population is percent aged 50 and over, and percent change in residence; race is percent nonwhite; neighborhood is percent owner-occupied housing.

[b]Pressman and Carol use the following variables: income is percent of population with income over $10,000 and percent of population with income under $3000; population is number of people per square mile, and net migration; race is percent of population nonwhite.

[c]t-test level of significance: .01.

[d]t-test level of significance: .05.

[e]This is the multiple correlation coefficient.

[f]The variables (factors) used by Schmid are as follows: employment is a factor reflecting low social cohesion–low occupational status; population is a factor reflecting low family and economic status, a factor indicating high population mobility, and a factor showing low population mobility; family is a factor indicating low social cohesion–low family status; race is a factor reflecting the Negro population; not shown are an ambiguous factor and an atypical crime pattern factor. Schmid also has a nonresidential burglary variable.

[g] This is the h^2 of factor analysis, which is the proportion of the variation in the data accounted for by the factors.

[h] The variables (factors) used by Schuessler and Slatin are as follows: (1) education is a factor reflecting education; income is a factor reflecting economic characteristics; race is a factor dealing with minority; other is a factor reflecting the abstract theoretical anomie, and a factor of social conformity. (2) the factors are as above, except as noted: income is a factor dealing loosely with economic variables; family is a factor reflecting family characteristics.

[i] The independent variables used by Gylys are as follows: the deterrent variable is per capita police expenditures; education is median years of schooling; employment is percent of labor force unemployed; income is percent of families with $3000 or less and median income; population in median age of population, population density, and population size; family is percent of broken homes; race is percent of population nonwhite; neighborhood is percent of owner occupied homes, percent of deteriorating homes, and population per housing unit; other is median temperature.

[j] The following independent variables are used in the study by Block: the deterrent variable is number of burglary offenses cleared by arrest; population is the proportion of the number of juveniles arrested who reside in the police district; other is average value of a burglary.

[k] The independent variables used by Phillips, Votey, and Maxwell are as follows: (1) employment is the ratio of the male, white, civilian labor force to the total noninstitutional population; population is the ratio of white, civilian, noninstitutional population to the total noninstitutional population. (2) employment is the ratio of the male, nonwhite, civilian labor force to the total noninstitutional population; population is the ratio of nonwhite, civilian, noninstitutional population to the total noninstitutional population.

[l] Hoch used the following independent variables: (1) employment is percent unemployed; population is percent growth in SMSA population, a binary variable taking the value 1 if the SMSA has a population of over 2.5 million and zero otherwise, percent male primary individuals, and percent of population under 21 years of age; family is population per household; race is percent of SMSA population that is black, and Confederacy times percentage black (where Confederacy is a binary variable taking the value 1 if the SMSA is in a state that was a part of the Confederacy during the Civil War, and 0 otherwise); neighborhood is percent of crowded housing; other is average temperature (°F in July) and the binary variable, Confederacy. (2) employment is percent unemployed in current year; population is the log of SMSA population (in 1000s), percent growth in SMSA population, a binary variable taking the value 1 for New York City SMSA and 0 otherwise, and percent male primary individuals; race is percentage of SMSA population that is black, the binary variable Confederacy times percent black, percent Japanese, and percent other nonwhite (i.e. not American Indian, Japanese, or black); other is average temperature (°F in July) and the binary variable Confederacy.

[m]Danziger and Wheeler use the following independent variables: the deterrent variables are the ratio of prisoners received from the courts to the total number of index crimes, and the average time served by felony prisoners at first release from state and federal institutions; education is the percent of population over 25 years of age with less than 8 years of schooling; employment is the average annual rate of unemployment for males aged 16 and over; income is a measure of the absolute income gap, and a measure of the relative income inequality; population is the percentage of the population between the ages of 15 and 24, the size of the SMSA, and the central city population per square mile; race is the percentage of the population nonwhite; other is a binary variable taking the value 1 if the SMSA is located in the Northeast region and 0 otherwise.

[n]The independent variables used by Danziger and Wheeler are as follows: deterrent variables are the ratio of persons charged and held for prosecution to the total number of burglary offenses known to the police, the ratio of persons found guilty to the number of those originally charged, and the ratio of prisoners (sentenced for burglary offenses) received from courts by state and federal institutions to the total number of convictions for that crime; employment is the average annual rate of unemployment for males aged 16 and older; income is a measure of the absolute income gap, and a measure of the relative inequality of income distribution; population is the percentage of the population between the ages of 15 and 24.

[o]The variables used by Peterson et al. are as follows: income is an index of economic distress motives; race is a binary variable taking the value 1 if the individual is black and 0 otherwise; other is a binary variable taking the value 1 if the individual's current commitment offense is burglary and 0 otherwise, a measure of the individual's tendency to identify himself in terms of one or more criminal activities, a measure of composite criminal attitudes, a juvenile crime scale, and age of first serious crime.

[p]The values shown are beta coefficients or coefficients on standardized variables. The coefficients for each characteristic are significant by t-tests with $p > .05$.

[q]Avio and Clark use the following independent variables: the deterrent variables are the number of clearances divided by number of offenses, the number of convictions divided by the number of charges, and the weighted average of sentences handed down corrected for remissions and parole; employment is total unemployment rate, and total participation rate; income is percentage of families with incomes less than one-half the median family income; population is percentage of males aged 15 to 24 in the total male population; race is percentage of North American Indians in the population; other is the number of households with record players. These results are derived from a 3-equation model, with the other dependent variables being expenditures per capita by police on labor and capital, and the clearance rate for the crime.

rThe independent variables used by Swimmer are as follows: deterrent variables are total expenditure on police per capita, and average time served by convicted first offenders; education is percent of 14- to 17-year-olds in school; employment is unemployment rate; income is median income in $100s, and percentage of families with incomes less than $3000 or greater than $10,000; population is population in 100,000s, and population squared; race is percent of population nonwhite; other is a binary variable for South–Non-South.

sThe following independent variables are used by Pogue: the deterrent variable is the proportion of this particular crime category that is cleared by arrest; education is the median years of school completed by the SMSA population; employment is the percentage unemployed, and the 1968 unemployment rate divided by the 1967 rate; income is per capita income in dollars per year, and percentage of households with incomes below $3000 per year; population is percentage of population aged 12 to 17, percentage of population aged 18 to 24, percentage male, total population in thousands, population density in thousands per square mile, and the 1968 population divided by the 1960 population; race is percent of population that is white. These results are derived from a 3-equation model, with the other dependent variables being police expenditure and clearance ratio. Pogue also runs regressions for the 1962–1967 period.

tThe independent variables used by Ehrlich are as follows: the deterrent variables are the number of offenders imprisoned per offenses known, and average time served by offenders in state prisons; income is median income of families, and percentage of families below one-half of median income; race is percentage of nonwhites in the population. The second equation of the two equation model is a production function of law enforcement activity.

uWe are aware of another work by Hoover Institution dealing with the effect of economic factors on crime. However, we had difficulty with this study because of their failure to explain their estimation technique and their failure to define certain coefficients. We were therefore unable to include the results of this study in our tables.

Table 5–6. Summary of Literature on the Effect of Economic Factors on Larceny (*t*-ratios in parentheses)

Model: Dependent Variable	Deterrent Variables	Education	Employment	Income	Population	Family	Race	Neighborhood	Other	F	R²	N	Functional Form of Model	Estimation Technique	Theoretical Base	Sample
Quinney (1966): all larceny offenses known to the police per 100,000 population[a] (data: UCR)											—	50	linear	product moment correlation	ecological	50 states of the U.S., 1959–1961; cross-sectional
(1) Rural		.40	−.47 −.06	.29 .21	−.19 .44		−.08	−.16								
(2) Urban		.50	−.45 .12	.07 .50	−.42 .63		−.20	−.06								
(3) SMSA		.22	−.38 −.07	.33 .17 .12 .02	−.17 .54		−.01	−.14								
Pressman and Carol (1976): larceny offense rate[a] (data: Department of Justice, Department of Commerce)				.12 −.02	−.03 .39 ( )[d]		.35				.55* ( )[c]	95	linear	partial correlation	ecological	95 SMSAs with populations of 230,000 or more, 1965; cross-sectional
Brown et al. (1972): larceny offenses[f] (data: magistrates' court and court of quarter sessions)		.01[f]	.01	.01			.01	−.05 .01			—	15	linear	Spearman-Rho rank order correlation	ecological	15 electoral wards of a Northern urban town in Britain, 1969; cross-sectional
Schuessler and Slatin (1964): grand larceny rate[a]														factor analysis (partial correlation)	ecological	
(1) 1950		.08		−.13			−.11		.67 −.12		.50[i]	101	linear			101 U.S. cities with population 100,000 and over, 1950;
(2) 1960				.04		−.06	.09		−.71 .02		.52[i]	133				133 U.S. cities with population 100,000 and over, 1960; cross-sectional
Schmid (1960): petty larceny offenses known to the police per 1,000 population[f] (data: Seattle PD files)			.391		−.050 −.187 −.070	.871	.062				.965[j]	93	linear	factor analysis correlation	ecological	93 census tracts in the City of Seattle, 1949–1951; cross-sectional
Gylys (1970): larceny offenses per 100,000 population[a] (data: UCR, Census)	.0262	.0000	.0032	.1266 .1504	.0085 .0031 .0311	.0036	.0551	.0123 .0538 .0179	.047		.4049	57	linear	OLS-to derive partial coefficients of determination	no explicit theory	57 largest central cities (population equal to or greater than 250,000) in 1968, 1960; cross-sectional

105

Table 5-6. (continued)

Model: Dependent Variable	Deterrent Variables	Education	Employment	Income	Population	Family	Race	Neighborhood	Other	F	R²	N	Functional Form of Model	Estimation Technique	Theoretical Base	Sample
Block (1972): larceny offenses known to the police per juvenile arrested for any offense in 1965[1] (data: Los Angeles PD)	-17.1902 (2.2552)								.06040 (4.62835)		.71	14	linear	OLS	wealth maximization	Police districts in the City of Los Angeles, 1965; cross-sectional
Phillips et al. (1972): larceny arrest rates for males 18-19 + proportion of offenses cleared by arrest[a] (data: UCR)	(1)		-95.22 (-4.16)		36.06 (3.90)					12.0	.67	15	linear	OLS	wealth maximization	U.S. urban areas, 1952-1967; time series
	(2)		-259.46 (-7.71)		256.29 (5.06)					38.1	.86	15				
Hoch (1974): larceny offenses known to the police per 100,000 (SMSA) population[a] (data: UCR)	(1)				1.257 (2.378) 61.293 (2.474)	273.987 (2.526)	7.289 (3.387) -5.015 (1.693) 79.694 (1.991)		93.664 (1.708) 120.231 (2.952) 36.193 (1.555)			.390	136	linear	OLS	ecological	136 SMSAs, 1960
	(2)		60.401 (3.113)		-29.220 (2.723) 576.654 (1.682) 162.069 (2.653)	7.079 (3.168) -40.140 (1.846)	21.105 (3.229) -16.673 (2.972) -115.499 (1.640) 123.551 (2.012) 35.868 (2.548) -16.075 (2.235)					.395	137				137 SMSAs, 1970; cross-sectional
Avio and Clark (1976): number of thefts recorded by police per 1,000 population[a] (data: police statistics)	-.636 (3.717) .120 (2.123)	-1.379 (3.967)	.168 (3.203) -.721 (1.894)	1.322 (8.467)	-.470 (1.062)		.057 (2.579)		.222 (8.180)		.992	24	log-linear	2SLS	time allocation	8 Canadian provinces, 1970-1972; cross-sectional
Swimmer (1974b): log of larceny offenses known to the police per 1,000 population[a] (data: FBI)	-.328 (-1.30) -.235 (-.72)	.00644 (.38)	.0161 (.40)	.00789 (.73) .0262 (1.58)	.0221 (1.09) -9.08E-5 (-.34)		1.66E-4 (.03)		.103 (.41)		.05	119	log-linear	2SLS	wealth maximization	All cities with 100,000 or more residents in 1960; cross-sectional

106

Table 5–6. (continued)

Model/Dependent Variable	Deterrent Variables	Education	Employment	Income	Population	Family	Race	Neighborhood	Other	F	R²	N	Functional Form of Model	Estimation Technique	Theoretical Base	Sample
Pogue (1976): reported grand larceny per 100,000 population[f] (data: FBI)	-.862 (-2.831)	.498 (.709)	.125 (.744)	.588 (1.043) .540 (2.525)	.348 (.458) .473 (.216) -.047 (-.623)	.159 (.250) .172 (2.186) .390 (1.401)	-.249 (-.915)				.459	66	log-linear	2SLS	ecological	SMSAs, 1968; cross-sectional
Ehrlich (1973, 1974): larceny offenses known to the police per 100,000 (state) population[e] (data: UCR)	(1) -.371 (-2.482) -.602 (-1.937)			2.229 (3.465) 1.792 (2.992)			.142 (2.019)				—	47	linear	2SLS	time allocation	47 states, 1960; cross-sectional
	(2) -.358 (-2.445) -.654 (-1.912)			2.241 (3.502) 1.785 (2.983)			.139 (1.980)				—	47	linear	SUR		

[a]The variables used by Quinney are as follows: education is median years of schooling; employment is percent employed in manufacturing, a measure of occupational diversity, percent females in the labor force, and percent white collar males; income is median family income; population is percent aged 50 and over, and percent change in residence; race is percent nonwhite; neighborhood is percent owner-occupied housing.

[b]Pressman and Carol use the following variables: income is percent of population with income over $10,000 and percent of population with income under $3000; population is number of people per square mile, and net migration; race is percent of population nonwhite.

[c]t-test level of significance: .01.

[d]t-test level of significance: .05.

[e]This value is the multiple correlation coefficient.

[f]The variables used by Brown, McCulloch, and Hiscox are as follows: employment is able-bodied unemployed, and disabled unemployed; income is persons receiving social security payments; race is Irish immigrants; neighborhood is owner-occupied houses, and rented council houses. Houses with fewer than 0.5 persons per room and overcrowding were not found to be correlated with larceny offenses.

gThe values shown are level of significance (p value).

hThe variables (factors) used by Schuessler and Slatin are as follows: (1) education is a factor reflecting education; income is a factor reflecting economic characteristics; race is a factor dealing with minority; other is a factor reflecting the abstract theoretical anomie, and a factor of social conformity. (2) the factors are as above, except as noted: income is a factor dealing loosely with economic variables; family is a factor reflecting family characteristics.

iThis is the h² of factor analysis, which is the proportion of the variation in the data accounted for by the factors.

jThe variables (factors) used by Schmid are as follows: employment is a factor reflecting low family and economic status, a factor indicating high population mobility, and a factor showing low population mobility; family is a factor indicating low social cohesion–low family status; race is a factor reflecting the Negro population; not shown are an ambiguous factor and an atypical crime pattern factor. Schmid analyzes three additional larceny measures: shoplifting, bicycle theft, and theft from automobile.

kThe independent variables used by Gylys are as follows: the deterrent variable is per capita police expenditures; education is median years of schooling; employment is percent of labor force unemployed; income is percent of families with $3000 or less and median income; population is median age of population, population density, and population size; family is percent of broken homes; race is percent of population nonwhite; neighborhood is percent of owner-occupied homes, percent of deteriorating homes, and population per housing unit; other is median temperature.

lThe following independent variables are used in the study by Block: the deterrent variable is number of larceny offenses cleared by arrest; other is average value of a larceny.

mThe independent variables used by Phillips, Votey, and Maxwell are as follows: (1) employment is the ratio of the male, white, civilian labor force to the total noninstitutional population; population is the ratio of white, civilian, noninstitutional population to the total noninstitutional population. (2) employment is the ratio of the male, nonwhite, civilian labor force to the total noninstitutional population; population is the ratio of nonwhite, civilian, noninstitutional population to the total noninstitutional population.

nHoch uses the following independent variables:: (1) population is percent growth in SMSA population, a binary variable taking the value 1 for New York City SMSA, and 0 otherwise, and percent male primary individuals; race is percent of SMSA population that is black, a binary variable, Confederacy, times percent black (where Confederacy takes the value 1 if the SMSA is in a state which was a part of the Confederacy during the Civil War, and is 0 otherwise), and percent American Indian; other is a series of binary variables (Confederacy, West, North Central) taking the value 1 if the SMSA is in that region and 0 otherwise. (2) employment is percentage unemployment in current year; population is city density in 1,000s, percent growth in SMSA population, a binary variable equal to 1 for the New York City SMSA and 0 otherwise, percent of population age 65 or over, and percent of female primary individuals; race is percent of SMSA population that is black, Confederacy times percent black, percent of population all other nonwhite (i.e. not black, Japanese, Indian), percent of population Japanese, population with parent foreign born.

[o]Avio and Clark use the following independent variables: the deterrent variables are the number of clearances divided by number of offenses, the number of convictions divided by the number of charges, and the weighted average of sentences handed down corrected for remissions and parole; employment is total unemployment rate, and total participation rate; income is percentage of families with incomes less than one-half the median family income; population is percentage of males aged 15 to 24 in the total male population; race is percentage of North American Indians in the population; other is the number of households with record players. These results are derived from a 3-equation model, with the other dependent variables being expenditures per capita by police on labor and capital, and the clearance rate for the crime.

[p]Swimmer uses the following independent variables: deterrent variables are total expenditure on police per capita, and average time served by convicted first offenders; education is percent of 14- to 17-year-olds in school; employment is unemployment rate; income is median income in $100s, and percentage of families with incomes less than $3000 or greater than $10,000; population is population in 100,000s, and population squared; race is percent of population nonwhite; other is a binary variable for South-Non-South.

[q]The following independent variables are used by Pogue: the deterrent variable is the proportion of this particular crime category that is cleared by arrest; education is the median years of school completed of the SMSA population; employment is the percentage unemployed, and the 1968 unemployment rate divided by the 1967 rate; income is per capita income in dollars per year, and percentage of households with incomes below $3000 per year; population is percentage of population aged 12 to 17, percentage aged 18 to 24, percentage male, total population in thousands, population density in thousands per square mile, and the 1968 population divided by the 1960 population; race is percent of population that is white. These results are derived from a 3-equation model, with the other dependent variables being police expenditure and clearance ratio. Pogue also runs regressions for the 1962–1967 period.

[r]The independent variables used by Ehrlich are as follows: the deterrent variables are the number of offenders imprisoned per offenses known, and average time served by offenders in state prisons; income is median income of families, percentage of families below one-half of median income; race is percentage of nonwhites in the population. The second equation of the two equation model is a production function of law enforcement activity. Ehrlich also runs a regression using the dependent variable larceny and auto theft offenses.

[s]We are aware of another work by Hoover Institution dealing with the effect of economic factors on crime. However, we had difficulty with this study because of their failure to explain their estimation technique and their failure to define certain coefficients. We were therefore unable to include the results of this study in our tables.

Table 5-7. Summary of the Literature on the Effect of Economic Factors on Auto Theft (t-ratios in parentheses)

Model: Dependent Variable	Deterrent Variables	Education	Employment	Income	Population	Family	Race	Neighborhood	Other	F	R^2	N	Functional Form of Model	Estimation Technique	Theoretical Base	Sample
Quinney (1966): all auto theft offenses known to the police per 100,000 population[a] (data: UCR)														product moment correlation	ecological	50 state of the U.S. 1959–1961; cross-sectional
(1) Rural		.20	−.41 .30 / −.10 .07	.13	−.44	.30	.03	−.18			—	50	linear			
(2) Urban		.48	−.54 .15 / .24 .44	.53	−.52	.72	−.19	−.13								
(3) SMSA		.23	−.35 .02 / −.03 .10	.27	−.31	.49	.05	−.22								
Pressman and Carol (1976): auto theft offenses rate[b] (data: Department of Justice, Department of Commerce)				.20 / .06	.40 / (.21)[d]		.35				.60[e] / ( )[c]	95	linear	partial correlation	ecological	95 SMSAs with population of 250,000 or more, 1965; cross-sectional
Schuessler and Slatin (1964): auto theft rate[b]													linear	factor analysis (partial correlation)	ecological	101 U.S. cities with population 100,000 and over, 1950; 133 U.S. cities with population 100,000 and over, 1960; cross-sectional
(1) 1950		.20		−.09		.01	.03		.82 .04		.72[a]	101				
(2) 1960				−.20			.19		−.65 .39		.65[a]	133				
Schmid (1960): auto theft offenses known to the police[b] (data: Seattle PD files)			−.220		.307 / −.135	.671	.279				.782[a]	93	linear	factor analysis	ecological	93 census tracts in the city of Seattle, 1949–1951; cross-sectional
Gylys (1970): auto theft offenses per 100,000 population[f] (data: FBI, Census)		.0006	.0034	.1593 / −.1746	.0079 / .0534	.0463 / .0976	.0788	.0367 .1183 / .0024	.1160		.4429	57	linear	OLS to derive partial coefficients of determination	no explicit theory	57 largest central cities (population equal to or greater than 250,000 in 1968, 1960; cross-sectional
Phillips et al. (1972): auto theft arrest rate for males 18-19 + proportion of offenses cleared by arrest (data: UCR)													linear	OLS	wealth maximization	U.S. urban areas, 1952–1967; time-series
(1)		−22.20 (−2.56)			14.33 (4.09)						.60	15				
(2)		−94.32 (−7.38)			69.16 (3.60)						.84	15				

110

Table 5-7. (continued)

Model: Dependent Variable	Deterrent Variables	Education	Employment	Income	Population	Family	Race	Neighborhood	Other	F	R²	N	Functional Form of Model	Estimation Technique	Theoretical Base	Sample
Hoch (1974): auto theft offenses known to the police per 100,000 (SMSA) population[b] (data: UCR) (1)					90.121 (4.332) -188.147 (2.495) -13.655 (2.964) .850 (2.256) 43.551 (2.719) -15.973 (2.653)	15.729 (2.9008)	105.790 (4.058)	11.308 (4.683)	27.482 (1.702)		.543	136	linear	OLS	ecological	136 SMSAs, 1960
(2)					220.937 (3.829) -12.992 (1.912) -14.378 (1.286) -26.853 (2.041)	43.348 (3.156)	16.109 (3.774) 12.279 (3.85) 24.123 (3.982)		8.245 (2.052) 74.047 (1.204) 78.491 (1.580)		.505	137				137 SMSAs, 1970; cross-sectional
Swimmer (1974b): log of auto theft offenses known to the police per 1,000 population[j] (data: FBI)	.0377 (1.68)	-.137 (-.82)	-.0259 (-1.79) .0245 (.71)	-.00741 (-.80) .044 (3.17)	.0311 (1.80) -4.81E-4 (-2.12)		-.00415 (-.71)		-.142 (-.73)		.272	119	log-linear	2SLS	wealth maximization	All cities with 100,000 or more residents in 1960; cross-sectional
Pogue (1976): number of auto thefts per 100,000 population[m] (data: FBI)	-.380 (-.962)	1.425 (1.436)	.101 (.371) -.021 (-.247)	-.238 (-.294) .068 (.205)	.841 (.759) -.563 (-.615) .184 (.062) .154 (1.213) .156 (1.420) -.279 (-.450)		-.282 (-.733)				.312	66	log-linear	2SLS	ecological	SMSAs, 1968; cross-sectional
Ehrlich (1973, 1974): auto theft offenses known to the police per 100,000 (state) population[n] (data: UCR) (1)	-.407 (-4.173) -.246 (-1.682)			2.608 (5.194) 2.057 (4.268)			.102 (1.842)				—	47	linear	2SLS	time allocation	47 states, 1960; cross-sectional
(2)	-.409 (-4.674) -.233 (-1.747)			2.590 (5.253) 2.054 (4.283)			.101 (1.832)				—	47	linear	SUR		

[a]The variables used by Quinney are as follows: education is median years of schooling; employment is percent employed in manufacturing, a measure of occupational diversity, percent females in the labor force, and percent white collar males; income is median family income; population is percent aged 50 and over, and percent change in residence; race is percent nonwhite; neighborhood is percent owner-occupied housing.

[b]Pressman and Carol use the following variables: income is percent of population with income over $10,000 and percent of population with income under $3000; population is number of people per square mile, and net migration; race is percent of population nonwhite.

[c]t-test level of significance: .01.

[d]t-test level of significance: .05.

[e]This value is the multiple correlation coefficient.

[f]The variables (factors) used by Schuessler and Slatin are as follows: (1) education is a factor reflecting education; income is a factor reflecting economic characteristics; race is a factor dealing with minority; other is a factor reflecting the abstract theoretical anomie, and a factor of social conformity. (2) the factors are as above, except as noted: income is a factor dealing loosely with economic variables; family is a factor reflecting family characteristics.

[g]This is the h^2 of factor analysis, which is the proportion of the variation in the data accounted for by the factors.

[h]The variables (factors) used by Schmid are as follows: employment is a factor reflecting low social cohesion–low occupational status; population is a factor reflecting low family and economic status, a factor indicating high population mobility, and a factor showing low population mobility; family is a factor indicating low social cohesion–low family status; race is a factor reflecting the Negro population; not shown are an ambiguous factor and an atypical crime pattern factor.

[i]The independent variables used by Gylys are as follows: the deterrent variable is per capita police expenditures; education is median years of schooling; employment is percent of labor force unemployed; income is percent of families with $3000 or less and median income; population is median age of population, population density, and population size; family is percent of broken·homes; race is percent of population nonwhite; neighborhood is percent of owner occupied homes, percent of deteriorating homes, and population per housing unit; other is median temperature.

[j]The independent variables used by Phillips, Votey and Maxwell are as follows: (1) employment is the ratio of the male, white, civilian labor force to the total noninstitutional population; population is the ratio of white, civilian, noninstitutional population to the total noninstitutional population. (2) employment is the ratio of the male, nonwhite, civilian labor force to the total noninstitutional population; population is the ratio of nonwhite, civilian, noninstitutional population to the total noninstitutional population.

112

kThe independent variables used by Hoch are as follows: (1) population is the log of the SMSA population in 1000s, percent growth in SMSA population, a binary variable taking the value 1 for the New York City SMSA and 0 otherwise, percentage male primary individuals, percent under 21 years of age, and age 65 or over; family is percentage head of household white female; race is percent American Indian; neighborhood is percent crowded housing; other is a binary variable taking the value 1 if the SMSA is the North Central Region of the U.S., and 0 otherwise. (2) population is the log of the SMSA population in 1000s, percent under 21 years of age, and age 65 or over; family is percentage head of household white female; race is percentage of SMSA population that is black, a binary variable, Confederacy, times percent black (where Confederacy takes the value 1 if the SMSA is in a state that was in the Confederacy during the Civil War, and 0 otherwise), and percent foreign born; other is temperature (°F in July), and two binary variables (West, North Central) taking the value 1 if the SMSA is in that region of the U.S., and 0 otherwise.

lSwimmer uses the following independent variables: deterrent variables are total expenditure on police per capita, and average time served by convicted first offenders; education is percent of 14- to 17-year-olds in school; employment is unemployment rate; income is median income in $100s, and percentage of families with incomes less than $3000 or greater than $10,000; population is population in 100,000s, and population squared; race is percent of population nonwhite; other is a binary variable for South–Non-South.

mThe following independent variables are used by Pogue: the deterrent variable is the proportion of this particular crime category that is cleared by arrest; education is the median years of school completed by the SMSA population; employment is the percentage unemployed, and the 1968 unemployment rate divided by the 1967 rate; income is per capita income in dollars per year, and percentage of households with incomes below $3000 per year; population is percentage of population aged 12 to 17, percentage of population aged 18 to 24, percentage male, total population in thousands, population density in thousands per square mile, and the 1968 population divided by the 1960 population; race is percent of population that is white. These results are derived from a 3-equation model, with the other dependent variables being police expenditure and clearance ratio. Pogue also runs regressions for the 1962–1967 period.

nEhrlich uses the following independent variables: the deterrent variables are the number of offenders imprisoned per offenses known, and average time served by offenders in state prisons; income is median income of families, and percentage of families below one-half of median income; race is percentage of nonwhites in the population. The second equation of the two equation model is a production function of law enforcement activity.

Table 5-8. Summary of the Literature on the Effect of Economic Factors on Assault (t-ratios in parentheses)

Model: Dependent Variable	Deterrent Variables	Education	Employment	Income	Population	Family	Race	Neighborhood	Other	F	R²	N	Functional Form of Model	Estimation Technique	Theoretical Base	Sample
Quinney (1966): all assault offenses known to the police per 100,000 population[a] (data: UCR)												50	linear	product moment correlation	ecological	50 states of the U.S., 1959–1961; cross-sectional
(1) Rural		−.45	−.03 .39 −.04 −.26	−.42	−.36 −.28		.45	−.39								
(2) Urban		−.33	.02 −.02	−.37	−.39 .19		.39	−.19								
(3) SMSA		−.28	.38 −.11 −.11 .11 −.12 −.01	−.34	−.26 .26		.40	−.03								
Pressman and Carol (1976): aggravated assault offense rate[b] (data: Department of Justice Department of Commerce)				−.09 .12	−.04 .22		.63 ( )[c]				.69[d] ( )[e]	95	linear	partial correlation	ecological	95 SMSAs with population of 250,000 or more, 1965, cross-sectional
Schuessler and Slatin (1964): Aggravated assault rate[f]		.26		.28 −.05		−.01	−.48 .69		.39 −.29 .19 .14		.57[f] .58[f]	101 133	linear	factor analysis (partial correlation)	ecological	101 cities with population 100,000 or more, 1950; 133 cities with population 100,000 or more, 1960; cross-sectional
(1) 1950																
(2) 1960																
Colys (1970): assault offenses per 100,000 population[g] (data: FBI, Census)	.0565	.0181	.0509	.0002 .0122	.0282 .0236	.0107 .0000	.0834	.0393 .0186 .0074	.0009		.4229	57	linear	OLS – to derive partial coefficients of determination	no explicit theory	57 largest central cities (population equal to or greater than 250,000) in 1968, 1960; cross-sectional
Hoch (1974): assault offenses known to the police per 100,000 (SMSA) population[h] (data: UCR) (1)			4.599 (3.194)		52.137 (3.044) 30.139 (3.690) −9.349 (4.352)		3.615 (4.303) −2.790 (2.597) −2.580 (1.914)		2.996 (3.326) 50.153 (2.541)		.62	136	linear	OLS	ecological	136 SMSAs, 1960
(2)			11.275 (2.159)		1.751 (4.028) 51.057 (3.471)		−6.056 (3.150) −4.671 (1.389) −3.038 (2.606)	6.468 (1.784)	3.707 (1.795) 129.632 (3.220)		.49	137				137 SMSAs, 1970; cross-sectional

Table 5–8. (continued)

Model: Dependent Variable	Deterrent Variables	Education	Employment	Income	Population	Family	Race	Neighborhood	Other	F	R²	N	Functional Form of Model	Estimation Technique	Theoretical Base	Sample
Danziger and Wheeler (1975a): number of aggravated assaults per 100,000 population/ (data: UCR)	-.077 (1.58) .148 (.342)	-.681 (1.45)	-.115 (.329)	-.716 (.54)	.217 (.404) .343 (2.48)		.531 (4.37)		-.417 (1.58)		—	57	log-linear	OLS	wealth maximization	57 large SMSAs, 1960-1961; cross-sectional
Danziger and Wheeler (1975b): assault offenses known to the police per 100,000 population/ (data: UCR)	-.146 (1.403) -.166 (1.596) -.455 (5.290)		-.066 (1.784)	1.094 (5.819) .319 (.591)	.435 (1.408)					195.3	.9906	21	log-linear	GLS-Cochrane Orcutt Estimation	wealth maximization	United States, 1949-1970; time series
Ehrlich (1979): urban assault rate per 100,000 population^k (data: UCR)	-.416 (-2.00) -.429 (-4.37) -.024 (-.22)		1.694 (2.42) .175 (.20)		-.173 (-.19) -.160 (-2.29)		.761 (6.89)				.9818	35	log-linear	GLS	wealth maximization	35 states, 1950; cross-sectional
Swimmer (1974b): log of assault offenses known to the police per 1,000 population^l (data: FBI)	-.00288 (-.09) -.199 (-2.11) -.0657 (-3.01)		.0279 (.56)	.00848 (.62) .0157 (.75)	.0599 (2.40) -6.09E-4 (-1.86)		.0366 (4.67)		.124 (.45)		.586	119	log-linear	2SLS	wealth maximization	All cities with 100,000 or more residents in 1960; cross-sectional
Pogue (1976): reported aggravated assaults per 100,000 population^m (data: FBI)	-1.807 (-.889)	-.722 (-.634)	-.363 (-1.005)	.366 (.378)	.426 (.334) -.531 (-3.51) .565 (.149) .232 (1.111) -.055 (-.434) .585 (.904)		-.781 (-1.526)				.412	66	log-linear	2SLS	ecological	SMSAs, 1968; cross-sectional
Ehrlich (1973, 1974): (1) assault offenses known to the police per 100,000 (state) population^n (data: UCR)	-.724 (-3.701) -.979 (-2.301)			1.650 (2.018) 1.707 (2.111)			.465 (3.655)				—	47	linear	2SLS	time allocation	47 states, 1960; cross-sectional
(2)	-.718 (-4.046) -.780 (-2.036)			1.404 (1.751) 1.494 (1.871)			.460 (3.801)				—	47	linear	SUR		

^aThe variables used by Quinney are as follows: education is median years of schooling; employment is percent employed in manufacturing, a measure of occupational diversity, percent females in the labor force, and percent white collar males; income is median family income; population is percent aged 50 and over, and percent change in residence; race is percent nonwhite; neighborhood is percent owner-occupied housing.

[b]Pressman and Carol use the following variables: income is percent of population with income over $10,000 and percent of population with income under $3000; population is number of people per square mile, and net migration; race is percent of population nonwhite.

[c]t-test level of significance: .01.

[d]This value is the multiple correlation coefficient.

[e]The variables (factors) used by Schuessler and Slatin are as follows: (1) education is a factor reflecting economic characteristics; race is a factor dealing with minority; other is a factor reflecting the abstract theoretical anome, and a factor of social conformity.

(2) the factors are as above, except as noted: income is a factor dealing loosely with economic variables; family is a factor reflecting family characteristics.

[f]This is the h² of factor analysis, which is the proportion of the variation in the data accounted for by the factors.

[g]The independent variables used by Gylys are as follows: the deterrent variable is per capita police expenditures; education is median years of schooling; employment is percent of labor force unemployed; income is percent of families with $3000 or less and median income; population is median age of population, population density, and population size; family is percent of broken homes; race is percent of population nonwhite; neighborhood is percent of owner-occupied homes, percent of deteriorating homes, and population per housing unit; other is median temperature.

[h]The independent variables used by Hoch are as follows: (1) employment is percent unemployed the preceding year; population is a binary variable taking the value 1 if the SMSA population is greater than 2.5 million, 0 otherwise; percentage of male primary individuals, percentage age 65 or over; race is black population as a percent of total SMSA population, Confederacy times percentage black (where Confederacy is a binary variable taking the value 1 for SMSAs in states which were a part of the Confederacy during the Civil War, and 0 otherwise), and percent of population Japanese; other is two location-climate variables for temperature (°F in July) and the binary variable for Confederacy.

(2) employment is percentage unemployed in current year; population is log of population times percent black, and percent primary individuals male; race is Confederacy times black, percent Japanese, and percent of population with foreign born parents; neighborhood is percent crowded housing; other is temperature (°F in July) and the binary variable Confederacy.

[i]Danziger and Wheeler use the following independent variables: the deterrent variables are the ratio of prisoners received from the courts to the total number of index crimes, and the average time served by felony prisoners at first release from state and federal institutions; education is the percent of population over 25 years of age with less than 8 years of schooling; employment is the average annual rate of unemployment for males aged 16 and over; income is a measure of the absolute income gap, and a measure of the relative income inequality; population is the percentage of the population between the ages of 15 and 24, the size of the SMSA, and the central city population per square mile; race is the percentage of the population nonwhite; other is a binary variable taking the value 1 if the SMSA is located in the Northeast region and 0 otherwise.

^{j}The independent variables used by Danziger and Wheeler are as follows: deterrent variables are the ratio of persons charged and held for prosecution to the total number of assault offenses known to the police, the ratio of persons found guilty to the number of those originally charged, and the ratio of prisoners (sentenced for assault offenses) received from courts by state and federal institutions to the total number of convictions for that crime; employment is the average annual rate of unemployment for males aged 16 and older; income is a measure of the absolute income gap, and a measure of the relative inequality of income distribution; population is the percentage of the population between the ages of 15 and 24.

^{k}Ehrlich uses the following independent variables: the deterrent variables are median time spent in state prisons by assault offenders prior to first release, the ratio of prisoners received in state prisons to be estimated total number of assaults, and the conditional probability of execution given a murder conviction; income is median income of families in year $t - 1$, and percentage of families with income below one-half of median income; population is the percent of population in age group 15–24, and percent of urban population in the total state population; race is percent nonwhites in the population. The equation is weighted by the square root of the size of population in 100,000s in UCR samples reporting assault rates in 1951.

^{l}Swimmer uses the following independent variables: deterrent variables: education is percent of 14- to 17-year-olds in school; income is average time served by convicted first offenders; education is percent of 14- to 17-year-olds in school; employment is unemployment rate; income is population in median income in $100s, and percentage of families with incomes less than $3000 or greater than $10,000; population is population in 100,000s, and population squared; race is percent of population nonwhite; other is a binary variable for South-Non-South.

^{m}The following independent variables are used by Pogue: (1) the deterrent variable is the proportion of this particular crime category that is cleared by arrest; education is the median years of school completed by the SMSA population; employmnt is the percentage unemployed, and the 1968 unemployment rate divided by the 1967 rate; income is per capita income in dollars per year, and percentage of households with incomes below $3000 per year; population is percentage of population aged 12 to 17, percentage aged 18 to 24, percentage of population aged 12 to 17, percentage of population aged 18 to 24, population density in thousands per square mile, and the 1968 population divided by the percentage male, total population in thousands, population density in thousands per square mile, and the 1968 population divided by the 1960 population; race is percent of population that is white. These results are derived from a 3-equation model, with the other dependent variables being police expenditure and clearance ratio. Pogue also runs regressions for the 1962–1967 period.

^{n}The independent variables used by Ehrlich are as follows: the deterrent variables are the number of offenders imprisoned per offenses known, and average time served by offenders in state prisons; income is median income of families, and percentage of families below one-half of median income; race is percentage of nonwhites in the population. The second equation of the two equation model is a production function of law enforcement activity.

117

Table 5–9. Summary of the Literature on the Effect of Economic Factors on Rape (*t*-ratios in parentheses)

Model: Dependent Variable	Deterrent Variables	Education	Employment	Income	Population	Family	Race	Neighborhood	Other	F	R^2	N	Functional Form of Model	Estimation Technique	Theoretical Base	Sample
Quinney (1966): all rape offenses known to the police per 100,000 population[a] (data: UCR)																
(1) Rural		-.12	-.25, -.21	.42, .00, -.19	.41		.19	-.15			—	50	linear	product moment correlation	ecological	50 states of the U.S., 1959–1961; cross-sectional
(2) Urban		.26	-.42, -.38	.04, .33, .40	.65		.09	-.27								
(3) SMSA		.11	-.23, -.20	.16, .16, .06	.45		-.02	.10								
Pressman and Carol (1976): rape offense rate[b] (data: Department of Justice, Department of Commerce)				-.03, .32	-.09, .20		.77				.86[d] ( )[c]	95	linear	partial correlation	ecological	95 SMSAs with population of 250,000 or more, 1965; cross-sectional
Gylys (1970): rape offenses per 100,000 population[e] (data: FBI, census)	.0948	.0308	.0062	.0310, .0470	.0285, .0362	.0097	.0263	.0172, .0366	.0080		.3200	57	linear	OLS-to derive partial coefficients of determination	no explicit theory	57 largest central cities (population equal to or greater than 250,000) in 1968, 1960; cross-sectional
Hoch (1974): rape offenses known to the police per 100,000 (SMSA) population[f] (data: UCR)																
(1)				.034 (1.934)	7.031 (4.324)		.367 (4.958), -.219 (3.294), 4.624 (3.336), -.308 (2.115)	.236 (2.266)	4.166 (3.393)		.468	136	linear	OLS	ecological	136 SMSAs, 1960
(2)				-.850 (3.498), 5.638 (3.099)	6.673 (2.619), -.940 (2.559)		.698 (4.002), -.371 (2.495), -.377 (1.825)		.471 (2.777), 7.881 (2.803)		.501	137				137 SMSAs, 1970; cross-sectional
Swimmer (1974b): log of rape offenses known to the police per 1,000 population[g] (data: FBI)	-.111 (-1.80), -.0151 (-.66)	.00260 (.63)	-.0880 (-.90)	-.0247 (-.94), -.00394 (-.10)	.190 (3.87), -.00211 (-3.30)		.0378 (.46)		-.431 (-.76)		.220	119	log-linear	2SLS	wealth maximization	All cities with 100,000 or more residents in 1960; cross-sectional
Pogue (1976): reported rape offenses per 100,000 population[h] (data: FBI)	-1.990 (-2.263)	-.310 (-.268)	-.229 (-.841), -.037 (-.383)	.483 (.498), .586 (1.475)	2.283 (1.788), -.204 (-.059), .016 (.138), 1.034 (1.039), .088 (.534), .286 (.641)		-.180 (-.391)				.492	66	log-linear	2SLS	ecological	SMSAs, 1968; cross-sectional

Table 5–9. (continued)

Model: Dependent Variable	Deterrent Variables	Education	Employment	Income	Population	Family	Race	Neighborhood	Other	F	R²	N	Functional Form of Model	Estimation Technique	Theoretical Base	Sample
Ehrlich (1973, 1974): rape offenses known to the police per 100,000 (state) population[1] (data: UCR)	(1) −.896 (−6.08) −.399 (−2.005) (2) −.930 (−6.640) −.436 (−2.318)			.409 (.605) .459 (.0743) .333 (.502) .425 (.692)			.072 (.922) .065 (.841)				−	47	linear	2SLS	time allocation	47 states, 1960; cross-sectional
										−	47	linear	SUR		

[a]The variables used by Quinney are as follows: education is median years of schooling; employment is percent employed in manufacturing, a measure of occupational diversity, percent females in the labor force, and percent white collar males; income is median family income; population is percent aged 50 and over, and percent change in residence; race is percent nonwhite; neighborhood is percent owner-occupied housing.

[b]Pressman and Carol use the following variables: income is percent of population with income over $10,000 and percent of population with income under $3000; population is number of people per square mile, and net migration; race is percent of population nonwhite.

[c]t-test level of significance: .01.

[d]The value shown is the multiple correlation coefficient.

[e]The independent variables used by Gylys are as follows: the deterrent variable is per capita police expenditures; education is median years of schooling; employment is percent of labor force unemployed; income is percent of families with $3000 or less and median income; population is median age of population, population density, and population size; family is percent of broken homes; race is percent of population nonwhite; neighborhood is percent of owner-occupied homes, percent of deteriorating homes, and population per housing unit; other is median temperature.

[f]Hoch's independent variables are as follows: (1) population is percent growth in SMSA population, a binary variable taking the value 1 for an SMSA with population over 2.5 million, and 0 otherwise; race is percent of SMSA population that is black, a binary variable Confederacy times percent black, (where Confederacy takes the value 1 if the SMSA is in a state which was a part of the Confederacy during the Civil War, and 0 otherwise), percent American Indian, and percent Japanese; neighborhood is percent crowded housing; other is a binary variable taking the value 1 if the SMSA is in the Western U.S., and 0 otherwise.

119

(2) population is city density in 1000s, log of SMSA Population in 1000s, percent male primary individuals, percent age 65 or over; race is percent of SMSA population that is black, Confederacy times percentage black, percent Japanese; other is temperature (°F in July), a binary variable taking the value 1 if the SMSA is in the Western U.S., and 0 otherwise.

^{g}The independent variables used by Swimmer are as follows: deterrent variables are total expenditure on police per capita, and average time served by convicted first offenders; education is percent of 14- to 17-year-olds in school; employment is unemployment rate; income is median income in $100s, and percentage of families with incomes less than $3000 or greater than $10,000; population is population in 100,000s, and population squared; race is percent of population nonwhite; other is a binary variable for South–Non-South.

^{h}The following independent variables are used by Pogue: the deterrent variable is the proportion of this particular crime category that is cleared by arrest; education is the median years of school completed by the SMSA population, employment is the percentage unemployed, and the 1968 unemployment rate divided by the 1967 rate; income is per capita income in dollars per year, and percentage of households with incomes below $3000 per year; population is percentage of population aged 12 to 17, percentage aged 18 to 24, percentage male, total population in thousands, population density in thousands per square mile, and the 1968 population divided by the 1960 population; race is percent of population that is white. These results are derived from a 3-equation model, with the other dependent variables being police expenditure and clearance ratio. Pogue also runs regressions for the 1962–1967 period.

^{i}The independent variables used by Ehrlich are as follows: the deterrent variables are the number of offenders imprisoned per offenses known, and average time served by offenders in state prisons; income is median income of families, and percentage of families below one-half of median income; race is percentage of nonwhites in the population. The second equation of the two equation model is a production function of law enforcement activity. Ehrlich also runs a regression using murder and rape as his dependent variable.

120

Table 5–10. Summary of the Literature on the Effect of Economic Factors on Homicide (t-ratios in parentheses)

Model/Dependent Variable	Deterrent Variables	Education	Employment	Income	Population	Family	Race	Neighborhood	Other	F	R²	N	Functional Form of Model	Estimation Technique	Theoretical Base	Sample
Quinney (1966): all homicide offenses known to the police per 100,000 population[a] (data: UCR) (1) Rural		−.44	−.04 −.07 .36 −.20	−.46	−.40 .32		.52	−.46			—	50	linear	product moment correlation	ecological	50 states of the U.S., 1959–1961; cross-sectional
(2) Urban		−.28	−.15 .41 .02 .00	−.34	−.39 .32		.42	−.20								
(3) SMSA		−.24	−.37 −.01 .25 −.02	−.62	−.43 .45		.54	−.04								
Pressman and Carol (1976): murder offense rate[d] (data: FBI, Census)				−.03 .32	−.09 .20		.77 ( )[e]				.86[d] ( )[e]	95	linear	partial correlation	ecological	95 SMSAs with populations of 250,000 or more, 1965; cross-sectional
Gylys (1970): homicide offenses per 100,000 population[g] (data: FBI, Census)	.0037	.0010	.0225	.1237 .0237	.0618 .0061	.0785	.1473	.1462 .0423 .0610	.0231		.6734	57	linear	OLS-to derive partial coefficients of determination	no explicit theory	57 largest central cities (population equal to or greater than 250,000) in 1968, 1960; cross-sectional
Hoch (1974): homicide offenses known to the police per 100,000 (SMSA) population[f] (data: UCR) (1)							.287 (5.857) −.160 (2.675) 2.541 (3.304) −.097 (1.773)		.095 (1.936) 2.504 (3.007) 2.471 (2.916) .935 (1.547)		.768	136	linear	OLS	ecological	136 SMSAs, 1960
(2)	−.796 (2.823)				−.141 (1.647) −.494 (2.209)		.519 (7.644) −.309 (3.995) −.322 (2.305)	.356 (2.244)	.153 (2.084) 4.059 (3.287) 2.719 (3.032)		.742	137				137 SMSAs, 1970; cross-sectional
Brenner (1976): homicide mortality rate for U.S. per 100,000 population[g] (data: Vital Statistics of the United States)			.10 (2.38)	.0016 (1.56)	.30 (3.16)				.11 (.92)	115.6	.99	33	2nd degree polynomial distributed lag equation (Lag 0–5)	PDL	no explicit theory	United States, 1940–1973; time series
Ehrlich (1979): urban homicide rate per 100,000 population[h] (data: UCR) (1)	−.292 (−2.35) −.673 (−4.70) −.339 (−3.48)			.436 (1.21)	−2.101 (−2.23) −.982 (−4.43)		.508 (7.26)				.9539	33	log-linear	GLS	wealth maximization	33 states, 1940
(2)	−.459 (−3.59) −.687 (−5.23) −.272 (−4.74)			1.226 (2.65) 1.206 (2.22)	.274 (.44) −.742 (−2.08)		.496 (7.13)				.9581	35				35 states, 1950; cross-sectional

Table 5–10. (continued)

Model: Dependent Variable	Deterrent Variables	Education	Employment	Income	Population	Family	Race	Neighborhood	Other	F	R^2	N	Functional Form of Model	Estimation Technique	Theoretical Base	Sample
Swimmer (1974b): log of homicide offenses known to the police per 1,000 population[i] (data: FBI)	-.139 (-1.80); -.00512 (-1.16)	.0155 (.30)	.0159 (.13)	-.107 (-3.25); .0170 (.34)	.165 (2.69); -.00171 (-2.12)		.0445 (2.29)		-.820 (-1.20)		.329	119	log-linear	2SLS	wealth maximization	All cities with 100,000 or more residents in 1960; cross-sectional
Pogue (1976): reported murders and non-negligent manslaughter per 100,000 population[j] (data: FBI)	-2.731 (-1.944)	-.775 (-1.372)	-.693 (-2.471); -.131 (-1.273)	1.107 (1.069); 1.469 (3.557)	2.840 (2.086); -6.844 (-1.937); -.015 (-.113); -.317 (-.657)		-1.260 (-2.721)				.535	66	log-linear	2SLS	ecological	SMSAs, 1968; cross-sectional
Mathieson and Passell (1976): homicide offenses per capita[a] (data: NYC police department)	-1.96 (-3.74)			-3.88 (-3.57); .098 (.34); -.0616 (-.05)				1.49 (1.57); .0338 (.05)			–	–	log-linear	2SLS	wealth maximization	New York City police precincts, 1971; cross-sectional
Ehrlich (1973; 1974): (1) homicide offenses known to the police per 100,000 (state) population[j] (data: UCR) (2)	(1) -.852 (-2.492); -.087 (-.645); -.913 (-3.062); -.018 (-1.710)			.175 (.334); 1.109 (1.984); .186 (.361); 1.152 (2.102)			.534 (8.356); .542 (8.650)			–	–	47; 47	linear; linear	2SLS; SUR	time allocation	47 states, 1960; cross-sectional
Ehrlich (1975): natural log of the number of murders known to the police per 1,000 civilian population[m] (data: UCR)	-1.553 (-1.99); -.455 (-3.58); -.039 (-1.59)		-1.336 (-1.36); .067 (2.00)	1.481 (4.23)	.630 (2.10)				-.047 (-4.60)		–	36	log-linear	non-linear three round estimation procedure of modified first differences	wealth maximization	United States, 1933–1969; time series

[a]The variables used by Quinney are as follows: education is median years of schooling; employment is percent employed in manufacturing, a measure of occupational diversity, percent females in the labor force, and percent white collar males; income is median family income; population is percent aged 50 and over, and percent change in residence; race is percent nonwhite; neighborhood is percent owner-occupied housing.

[b]Pressman and Carol use the following variables: income is percent of population with income over $10,000 and percent of population with income under $3000; population is number of people per square mile, and net migration; race is percent of population nonwhite.

[c]t-test level of significance: .01.

[d]The value shown is the multiple correlation coefficient.

[e]The independent variables used by Gylys are as follows: the deterrent variable is per capita police expenditures; education is median years of schooling; employment is percent of labor force unemployed; income is percent of families with $3000 or less and median income; population is median age of population, population density, and population size; family is percent of broken homes; race is percent of population nonwhite; neighborhood is percent of owner-occupied homes, percent of deteriorating homes, and population per housing unit; other is median temperature.

[f]The independent variables used by Hoch are as follows: (1) race is percentage of SMSA population that is black, a binary variable, South, times percent black (where South takes the value 1 if the SMSA is in the South, and 0 otherwise), percentage American Indian, and percent foreign born; other is temperature (°F in July), and a series of regional binary variables (Confederacy, South, West, North Central) which take the value 1 if the SMSA is in that region, and are 0 otherwise.

(2) employment is percent unemployment in preceding year; population is city density in 1000s, percent under 21 years of age, and percent age 65 or over; race is percent of SMSA population that is black, a binary variable, South, times percentage black (where South takes the value 1 if the SMSA is in the South, and 0 otherwise), and percent Japanese; neighborhood is percent crowded housing; other is temperature (°F in July), and two binary variables (South, West) taking the value 1 if the SMSA is in that region and 0 otherwise.

[g]The independent variables used by Brenner are as follows: employment is the total unemployment rate for ages 16 and up; income is GNP per capita in real dollars; population is the percent male population aged 15–29; other is inflation measured as the percent change in the consumer price index; not shown are the trend variables used in the regression.

[h]The following independent variables are used by Ehrlich: the deterrent variables are median time spent in state prisons by homicide offenders prior to first release, the ratio of prisoners received in state prisons to the estimated total number of homicides, and the conditional probability of execution given conviction; income is median income of families in year $t-1$, [(2) adds percentage of families with income below one-half of median income]; population is the percent of population in age group 15–24, and percent of urban population in the total state population; race is percent nonwhites in the population.

Equation (1) is weighted by the square root of urban population in 100,000s. Equation (2) is weighted by the square root of the size of population in 100,000s in UCR samples reporting homicide rates in 1951. Ehrlich uses several other equations with different weights and different variable proxies.

^{i}The independent variables used by Swimmer are as follows: deterrent variables are total expenditure on police per capita, and average time served by convicted first offenders; education is percent of 14- to 17-year-olds in school; employment is unemployment rate; income is median income in $100s, and percentage of families with incomes less than $3000 or greater than $10,000; population is population in 100,000s, and population squared; race is percent of nonwhite; other is a binary variable for South–Non-South.

^{j}The following independent variables are used by Pogue: the deterrent variable is the proportion of this particular crime category that is cleared by arrest; education is the median years of school completed by the SMSA population; employment is the percentage unemployed, and the 1968 unemployment rate divided by the 1967 rate; income is per capita income in dollars per year, and percentage of households with incomes below $3000 per year; population is percentage of population aged 12 to 17, percentage aged 18 to 24, percentage male, total population in thousands, population density in thousands per square mile, and the 1968 population divided by the 1960 population; race is percent of population that is white.

These results are derived from a 3-equation model with the other independent variables being police expenditure and clearance ratio. Pogue also runs regressions for the 1962–1967 period.

^{k}These are the results derived by Mathieson and Passell for a two equation model with the second dependent variable being the number of arrests per reported crime. The variables used in the regression are as follow: the deterrent variable is number of arrests per reported crime; income is median income in the precinct, percentage of families with income greater than $25,000, and median family income is adjacent precincts; neighborhood is a binary variable taking the value 1 for predominantly residential districts and the value 2 for predominantly business districts, and a binary variable taking the value 1 if there are no large parks or airports and the value 2 if there are large parks or airports.

^{l}Ehrlich uses the following independent variables: the deterrent variables are the number of offenders imprisoned per offenses known, and average time served by offenders in state prisons; income is median income of families, and percentage of families below one-half of median income; race is percentage of nonwhites in the population. The second equation of the two equation model is a production function of law enforcement activity. Ehrlich also runs a regression using murder and rape as the dependent variable.

^{m}Ehrlich uses the following independent variables: the deterrent variables are percent of offenses cleared, percent of those charged who were convicted of murder, and the number of executions for murder in the year t+1 as a percent of the total number of convictions in year t; employment is the fraction of the civilian population in the labor force, and the percent of the civilian labor force unemployed; income is Friedman's estimate of (real) permanent income per capita in dollars; population is the fraction of residential population in age group 14–24; other is chronological time in years. Ehrlich runs a number of other regressions with different variables and time periods.

Table 5–11. Summary of the Literature on the Effectsof Economic Factors on Juvenile Delinquency (t-ratios in parentheses)

Model: Dependent Variable	Deterrent Variables Education	Employment	Income	Population	Family	Race	Neighborhood	Other	F	R²	N	Functional Form of Model	Estimation Technique	Theoretical Base	Sample
Fleisher (1966a): number of court appearances of males aged 12 through 16 per 1,000 males aged 12 through 16ᵃ (data: State of Illinois Institute for Juvenile Research)		187 (2.3)	−.0051 (−2.8) .00038 (1.9)	160 (3.5)	22.5 (.31)	2.69 (.4)				.85	74	linear	OLS	ecological	74 census tract communities in Chicago, 1958–1961; cross-sectional
Weischer (1970): number of court appearances of males aged 12 through 16 per 1,000 males aged 12 through 16ᵇ (data: Fleisher) (1)		−46.6 (−0.5)	−.0059 (−2.3) .00016 (.5)	103 (2.4)	−5.79 (−1.3)	8.96 (.8)				.868	74	linear	OLS	wealth maximization	74 census tract communities in Chicago, 1958–1961; cross-sectional
(2)	−4.41 (−5.0)	−142 (−2.1)	−.00024 (−2) .00016 (.6)	65.5 (2.1)	−5.63 (−2.6)	−46.0 (−5.2)	.874 (4.3) .215 (3.8)			.944	74				
Singell (1967): total contacts with the Youth Bureau of the Detroit Police Department divided by the age specific populationᶜ (data: Detroit Police Department)		.824 (.066)								.77	441	linear	OLS	time allocation	census tracts in Detroit, 1960; cross-sectional

ᵃFleisher uses the following independent variables: employment is male civilian unemployment rate; income is mean income of second lowest quartile of income recipients, and mean income of highest quartile of income recipients; population is proportion of population of five-year-olds that lived in another county in 1955 (1960); family is proportion of females over 14 who are separated or divorced; race is proportion of the population that is nonwhite. Fleisher runs several additional regressions with different stratifications of the data.

ᵇThe independent variables used by Weischer are the same as those used by Fleisher, except as noted: (1) changes family variable to proportion of children living with both parents; (2) education is median years of schooling of adult population; family is proportion of children living with both parents; race is percentage of persons of foreign stock in the community; neighborhood is proportion of dwellings classified as dilapidated, and dwellings units per net residential acre. Weischer runs additional regressions using different combinations of variables.

ᶜSingell uses the following independent variable: employment is total employment as percent of labor force for each subcommunity.

Studies Using Aggregate Data

The findings of the studies using aggregate data imply that there is a positive, although generally insignificant relationship between the level of unemployment and criminal activity.[7] As would be expected from the economic model of crime, the relationship tends to be most strongly supported with respect to property crimes rather than for the violent offenses.

In interpreting the results of the income-crime relationship, the conclusion is less clear. According to the economic models of crime, the propensity for crime should vary inversely with prospects for legitimate income and directly with illegitimate income opportunities. Thus, low income would increase an individual's tendency toward criminal behavior, while high income would reduce this tendency on the part of the individual. At the same time, this high income would increase the individual's attractiveness as a target for criminal behavior on the part of others. Researchers doing aggregate studies incorporating measures of income have great difficulty obtaining adequate proxies for either legitimate income prospects or opportunities for illegal gain. Indeed, at times, the measure used as a proxy for legitimate income in one study is used as an index of illegitimate income in another. Interpretation of the results is therefore difficult. In general, the studies showed no clear cut income effect on the level of any of the specific crimes, nor on the property or violent crimes' categories.

However, the studies which incorporate a measure of low income or poverty (percentage of families with incomes below $3,000, for example, or the percentage with incomes below one-half of median income) in addition to a variable for median or average income almost always find the coefficient on the poverty measure to be positive and statistically significant and the coefficient on the income measure to be positive. The coefficient on the income measure, although positive, is statistically insignificant for violent crimes, and positive and statistically significant approximately half the time in studies analyzing property crimes.

Danziger and Wheeler [24] argue that, in addition to absolute income levels, relative income levels are also factors in the decision to commit crimes. They hypothesize that it is necessary to measure the absolute income gap, which they term the distance between an individual's income and the average income of his reference group, as well as the relative inequality across the entire income distribution. Their results show both factors to be positively related to crime, although the measure of relative inequality is insignificant for two of the three crimes they study.

In general, the findings from these studies support the existence of a relationship between economic factors and crime. They do not, however, provide any insight into the magnitudes of those effects or to the pathways through which the effects function.

Studies Using Individual Data

The studies utilizing individual data provide consistent but weak support for the expected inverse relationship between wage and crime, and weak, if any, support for the expected relationship between unemployment and crime. The strongest relationship found to date between labor market performance and crime is that between employment stability (usually interpreted as a measure of employment satisfaction) and crime.

As a whole, these results seem to indicate that it is not so much individual unemployment per se which causes crime, but rather the failure to find satisfying employment at a relatively high wage. It appears that increases in individual unemployment and the general recession in economic activity usually associated with such increases may not greatly affect the level of crime directly, but may do so indirectly by decreasing the availability of desirable employment opportunities.

A number of sociologists and radical economists have suggested that the labor markets in our economy are becoming increasingly segmented. Desirable jobs (primary sector jobs) with high wages, good benefits, employment stability, and advancement opportunities are only open to the well-trained, conforming members of our society. For the less well educated, nonconforming individuals who commit most crimes, only transitory, dead-end jobs in "secondary labor markets" are available. These jobs provide relatively low income, fail to provide skill training or advancement opportunities, and generally breed frustration and/or boredom.

The cyclical nature of economic activity during the 1970s has caused many large firms to provide fewer primary jobs than they would have in earlier periods. Fearing fluctuations in demand and the difficulties involved in terminating permanent employees, such as bad publicity or benefit payments, these firms meet increased demand in periods of prosperity by hiring temporary employees and sending work out to relatively small vendors. When demand falls back, it is quite easy to terminate temporary employees and decrease the amount of work sent out to vendors. While this type of decision making is quite rational from the point of view of the businesses involved, it means that fewer desirable jobs are generated by high levels of economic activity than would otherwise be the case. Given the research surveyed above, it may be this aspect of highly cyclical economic activity, rather than unemployment per se, which is associated with increased criminality.

The Programmatic Literature

In addition to these statistical studies, there have been several important studies of programs designed to lower criminal activity through the improvement of the individual's economic viability. The careful evaluation of programs of this type give insight into the relationship between economic viability and crime, as well as suggesting particular programs which are likely to be effective in lowering criminal activity. As a whole, the results of employment-related program evaluations provide only weak support for the simple model, "unemployment causes crime." These programs provide somewhat more support for the relationship between satisfying employment experiences and economic viability with decreased criminal activity.

Evaluations of pretrial intervention projects which provide employment oriented assistance find that such programs are more effective for adults than juveniles and that they decrease criminality in the short run, but not the long run ([95], [86]). Evaluations of vocational training and remedial education projects in prison, parole, or probation settings have almost uniformly found that such programs have insignificant effects on both labor market performance and criminality. Evaluations of work programs in prison, such as work release programs and prison industries, have had mixed results. These evaluations generally show that such programs reduce the cost of running a prison system (see [23], [62] and [63]), but there have been conflicting conclusions regarding the effect of such programs on criminal activity. On the one hand, evaluations of work release programs in California and North Carolina indicate that work releasees commit either less crime or less serious crime when released from prison than do releasees who do not participate in the program. On the other, evaluations of Massachusett's and Florida's work release programs show no beneficial effects. We could learn much from a thorough evaluation of why some work release programs appear to reduce criminal activity while others do not.

In the early 1970s, two new programs—transitional aid and supported work—aimed at improving the economic viability of released offenders in the community produced some promising results. The transitional aid program, begun in Baltimore in October 1971 by a nonprofit research organization, provided financial aid and job placement services to offenders in the period immediately following their release from prison. This program, called LIFE (Living Insurance for Ex-Prisoners), carefully selected a pool of "high risk," nonaddicted property offenders from Maryland Corrections Department releasees returning to the Baltimore area. An evaluation of the effects of the program indicated that individuals receiving only job placement services had neither better employment records nor criminal records than those who received no services, and that those receiving financial aid had no better employment records, but did have eight percent fewer arrests for property crimes. A benefit-cost analysis [52] indicated that we as a society were better off having made payments to the releasees than not having done so: the social benefits of the LIFE program exceeded its monetary cost.

The supported work program, begun in New York City in 1972 by the Vera Institute of Justice, provides subsidized employment in a "low stress" environment for ex-addicts who meet certain requirements. In the supported work program, the "treatment" is work itself in a supportive environment featuring graduated stress, peer support and close supervision. The program also features special challenges— offering cash bonuses or "psychic rewards", for example, for good performance—in an attempt to wean participants from old habits inappropriate to work life.[8] An interim evaluation of the program effects indicated that individuals who participated in the program earned more, required fewer welfare benefits, and were arrested less often than controls. Further, as was the case for transitional aid, a benefit-cost analysis indicated that the social benefits emanating from the program substantially exceeded the costs. (See [38] for additional details.)

Due partially to the favorable evaluations cited above, but probably due more to the attractiveness of economic approaches to crime to an increasingly conservative population, both the transitional aid and supported work programs were rapidly expanded. These expansions were subject to careful experimental evaluation, and, fortunately, at least partial results are currently available. Not surprisingly, the nature of both programs were substantially modified during expansion. We will discuss each expanded program in turn and the evaluation results currently available.

The transition aid program, renamed TARP (Transitional Aid Research Project), was operated in Georgia and Texas by the Departments of Corrections and Employment Security Offices, and made available to individuals released from jail and prison between January and July 1976. This program made transitional aid payments available to all Department of Corrections' releasees returning to areas with Employment Service Offices (mainly urban areas) and to selected groups of those returning to areas of the state without such offices. There are a large number of differences between LIFE and TARP; two are particularly important. First, under the LIFE program, employment and legal earnings merely deferred payments, while under the TARP program, employment and legal earning actually decreased payments. Thus, while the LIFE program gave few if any work disincentives, the TARP program provided often large incentives not to work. Second, TARP payments were given to all eligible releasees while LIFE payments were given only to nonaddicted, property offenders. Evaluation results indicate no significant differences in rearrest between individuals receiving transitional aid payments and those who did not. Further, individuals receiving transitional aid were found to work less and earn lower incomes during the follow-up year than individuals who received no aid. This latter effect is probably the result of the work disincentive in the TARP program noted above. When the work disincentive effect of transitional aid payments is controlled, evaluation results indicate that releasees in Texas and Georgia, who received transitional aid payments had significantly fewer arrests for both property and nonproperty offenses than individuals who received no such payments. In addition, consistent with job search theory, employed members of the treatment group earned higher weekly wages. (See [74] for details.)

The supported work program was expanded originally to fifteen sites and to include three target groups in addition to ex-addicts: women who had received AFDC welfare payments for substantial periods of time; prison and jail releasees; and young school drop outs. The program was administered by diverse groups in the various location ranging from governmental bodies to nonprofit community groups. While the exact program and nature of jobs available varied from location to location, the new programs were quite similar to the original. Results for the first eighteen months of the expanded program are currently available. [55] For ex-offenders, results indicate significantly improved labor market performance only during program participation, although significant welfare payment decreases continue even after ex-offenders leave the program. There is no significant decrease in reported criminal activity for ex-offenders, either while they are in the program or after termination. However, ex-addict participants do significantly decrease their criminal activity, supporting the original results. Final judgment must await results which will only be available later. Some additional support for providing supported environments comes from a recent evaluation of the job corps. [53] The evaluation found significant decreases in arrests for corpsmen after program completion.

Taken as a whole, the program evaluation literature supports conclusions similar to the more statistical literature surveyed. Unemployment, per se, appears to be only weakly related to criminal activity. Rewarding work experiences and economic viability, however, appear to be more strongly associated with decreased criminal activity.

The Underground Economy

There has been little work done to date on the relationship between the level and nature of legal economic activity and the level of production of illegal goods and services, such as gambling, prostitution, and illegal drugs, or the level of nonreporting of legal activities such as tax evasion, the size of the illegal alien population, or the size of stolen goods markets. Recently, these activities have been grouped together and analyzed as an underground or subterranean economy. (See [46], [80]). The activities comprising this portion of the economy can be divided into two broad groups: the production of illegal goods and services such as drugs, gambling, and arson; and the unreported production and trade in legal goods and services such as tax evasion, illegal aliens, and the stolen goods market.

It has been suggested by a number of people ([46], [48]) that the underground economy has grown markedly in recent years due to increased government regulation and inflation. Works by Simon and Witte [80] and the IRS [90] are not able to draw any definitive conclusions regarding trends in the entire underground economy for recent years. It appears on the basis of this research, however, that the underground economy has not grown much more rapidly than reported National Income in the mid 1970s. Government regulation undoubtedly contributes to the size of the underground economy. Indeed, it is only as a result of legal regulation that we have illegal goods and services, and illegal aliens. Other types of government regulations make "off-the-book production" more attractive and, thus, tend to increase the size of the underground economy. Perhaps, most importantly, increased levels of taxation increase the size of potential gains from such evasion and are likely to increase the overall level of evasion. A number of other regulations, however, including health and safety regulations, pollution regulations, social insurance laws, minimum wage laws, and reporting requirements, serve to make reported business activity more expensive and hence increase the relative attractiveness of "off-the-book" activity. These regulations also undoubtedly contribute to the amount of unreported economic activity. Inflation may increase the amount of unreported activity in two ways. First, and most importantly, inflation places individuals in higher tax brackets and thereby increases the potential gains from tax evasion. A recent study [37] found that "the fraction of earned income reported becomes very elastic with respect to the tax rate." In other words, as tax rates become higher and higher, the fraction of income unreported increases even more quickly. Second, if individuals see their legal income eroded as a result of inflation, they may be tempted to supplement their legal income by "off-the-books" or illegal activity.

The effect of recession on the size and structure of the underground economy has been little studied. But if property crimes increase during recessions, one would expect the size of the stolen goods market to increase as well. The effect of recession on production of illegal goods and services is more difficult to judge, but would depend mainly on the way in which demand for the goods and services respond to real income declines (the income elasticity of demand) and to stresses related to unemployment and falling real income. As we are aware of no evidence on the nature of these relationships, we can only conjecture that certain sectors such as illegal drug traffic might grow quite rapidly, while others such as prostitution might actually suffer declines.

Implications of Current Economic Trends for Crime Rates and Criminal Justice

The literature surveyed in the previous section, although flawed in a number of ways, allows us to draw at least tentative conclusions concerning the effect of likely economic trends on crime rates and the criminal justice system. First, the literature using aggregate data suggests that increased unemployment, particularly youth unemployment, will lead to moderately higher overall crime rates. Secondly, this increase is likely to occur disproportionately in property crimes. Studies which have analyzed the effect of unemployment rates on persons offenses have reached conflicting conclusions, with some studies finding that unemployment increases persons offenses (e.g., [15]) and others finding higher unemployment associated with lower levels of persons offenses (e.g., [27]).

Studies using individual data provide greater insight into the nature of the relationship between unemployment and crime. Recent work by the Vera Institute [83] and Rand [65] suggests that the nature of the relationship depends on the type of crime and type of individual involved. Sviridoff and Thompson identify four distinct types of relationships between unemployment and crime. First, some types of crime (white-collar crime, or employee theft) require jobs in order to be possible. As unemployment rises, one would expect a decrease rather than an increase in these types of crime. Second, some offenders mix employment and crime. These individuals either "moonlight" in criminal activities or use their legitimate job as a front, as do fences and drug dealers. For this group, like the first, employment and crime go hand in hand. For individuals moonlighting in crime, unemployment may increase criminal activity; for those using legitimate employment as a front, however, unemployment may make criminal activity more difficult and may lead to decreased rather than increased illegal activity. Third, some offenders, particularly younger offenders, appear to alternate between employment and crime. For these individuals, unemployment or dropping out of the labor force indicates a switch from legal to illegal income, generating employment rather than unemployment as we normally perceive it. For individuals in this group, we would expect the rise in unemployment and drop in labor force participation associated with recessionary times to lead to increased levels of property crime and increased participation in the underground economy. Finally, there appears to be a small group (5 to 10 percent of property offenders) that are firmly committed to crime as their primary means of support. For this group, unemployment or nonparticipation in the labor market is a way of life. We would expect no relationship between unemployment and crime for this group. Note that we only expect increased unemployment to be associated with increased criminal activity for individuals in the third group discussed above and some individuals in the second.

On the basis of these crime-unemployment relationships, one might well expect a stronger direct relationship between the quality of job and decreased criminal activity for some members of all of the first three groups. Unfortunately, the aggregate evidence has included only income as a measure of job quality and has not provided adequate proxies for this variable. The results from these studies have not provided any definitive interpretations of the job quality and crime relationship. Studies utilizing individual data have been able to provide more believable proxies for income (the wage an individual receives) as a measure of job quality. This work provides consistent but weak support for the expected inverse relationship between income and crime. Thus, the onset of a period of low economic growth, with inflation and the associated declines in real income from legitimate activities, may be expected to lead to at least moderate increases in overall crime rates. The limited results available seem to indicate that these crime increases will occur mainly in less serious property offenses, including larceny and other economically motivated offenses like the sale of illegal goods and services such as drugs.

Other studies [21] seem to indicate that job satisfaction as measured by work stability significantly affects criminality. Thus, a secondary effect of a declining economy may be that, in addition to producing fewer jobs, it is also likely to produce fewer desirable jobs, and the individuals employed in these jobs are likely to increase their criminality.

While there has been very little work on the effect of inflation on overall crime rates, there has been considerable interest in the relationship between inflation and the growth of the underground economy. Existing work seems to suggest that a number of sectors of this shadow economy are likely to grow rapidly in periods of sustained inflation. Given our current tax structure, inflation pushes people into ever higher marginal tax brackets, making tax evasion continually more attractive. Further, as pointed out in the previous section, levels of noncompliance appear to increase at an accelerating rate as tax rates rise. Thus, we would expect both criminal and civil offenses associated with tax evasion to rise if our present rates of inflation continue. If high inflation is accompanied by declines in real income for the middle and upper middle classes, we might expect white-collar crime such as employee theft and embezzlement to rise as well. Depressed economic activity and a continued shift of economic activity out of central cities may also make fraud arson attractive to larger number of property owners. Indeed, the shift of economic activity out of our inner cities and the increasing concentration of poor and minority groups in these cities may be great contributors to higher crime rates.

A further effect of a decline in real income would occur as a result of redistributional effects. Danziger and Wheeler ([25], [24]) have found that levels of criminal activity for both violent and property crimes increase with changes in the distribution of income which are perceived as unequal. If the declining economy tends to increase income inequality, either through increased concentration of market power due to bankruptcies or through the effects of high inflation on relatively fixed incomes, we can expect a further increase in criminal activity.

Although the effect of coming economic and social changes on the criminal justice system has been less thoroughly studied, we can draw some tentative conclusions. First, the decline in real income associated with periods of decline and inflation will continue to spawn taxpayer revolts, such as Propositions 9 and 13, as they have in the past. This means that the criminal justice system is unlikely to have substantially greater funds available to deal with an increased offender population. Further, the maturing of the baby boom population will mean that an increasing portion of the criminal justice burden will fall on the adult as opposed to the juvenile systems. Blumstein, Cohen and Miller [14] and Rutherford et al. [75] have pointed out that the maturing of the criminal sector of this population will place a particular burden on our adult prison systems. In addition, the type of offender with which the system must deal will become increasingly white-collar as the middle class responds to the pinch by increasing its level of criminal activity. The criminal justice system has had great difficulty in handling this population in the past.

The female population is also a difficult one for the largely male criminal justice system to handle. It is likely that, in response to a declining economy, females will participate increasingly in traditionally "nonfemale" crimes (those other than shoplifting or prostitution). Indeed, there is a secular trend of incrasing female crime rates, particularly for property offenses. Bartel ([5], pp. 88–89) found that between 1960 and 1974, property crimes committed by females rose at three times the rate of property crimes committed by males. The rate of increase for participation in violent crimes was approximately the same for both sexes.

Summary and Conclusions

As a whole, our survey of the literature relating economic factors to crime, provides only weak support for simple economic models of crime which see high unemployment, low incomes, and high returns to illegal activity as major factors causing crime. Most support is provided for a relationship between property crimes and these factors. However, the literature surveyed provides tantalizing clues to the nature and causes of the relationship between economic factors and crime. For example, the literature suggests that the nature of the relationship may vary with the type of property offense. Rising unemployment is likely to decrease the opportunity for employee theft, but make traditional property crimes such as shoplifting, burglary, and robbery more likely. This literature also suggests that it is not economic deprivation versus good opportunities alone which leads to higher crime rates, but rather that relative economic positions and overall satisfaction with work are also important factors in determining the level of crime. In addition, the work surveyed suggests that other economic factors such as the rate of inflation and the level of government regulation may have important effects on the level of certain offenses. Inflation, for example, by pushing people in higher and higher marginal tax brackets, is very likely to lead to increasing levels of tax evasion. Government regulations such as pollution laws, social insurance, and other reporting requirements, which increase the costs of doing business, are likely to lead to increasing amounts of "off-the-books" activity.

If current trends toward rapidly rising unemployment and moderating, although still high, inflation persist, the literature we have surveyed suggests that we will have rising rates of property crime, growing stolen goods markets, and increasing levels of tax evasion. In addition, if these trends increase income disparities and/or decrease the relative number of "good" jobs, the rises in overall crime rates may be even higher than expected.

Our survey of the literature on the relationship between economic factors and crime indicates that if we are to understand the relationship between economic factors and crime we must narrow our perspective in some ways and broaden it in others. First, we must broaden our perspective to take in the whole issue of economic viability, rather than just employment or income per se. We must consider the quality of job as well as simply whether an individual is employed, and we must consider an individual's relative income rather than simply absolute income measures. Second, we must narrow our perspective insofar as the nature of the relationship between employment and crime varies with the type of offender and type of offense under consideration. Unemployment may lead to more violent crimes simply because unemployment allows more time for interpersonal contact in nonstructured environments, lowers the opportunity cost of crime, and often causes greater family stress. Unemployment may lead to less white-collar crime and employee theft because of lack of opportunity, but to more traditional property crime such as larceny and robbery and other illegal activities (gambling, drug sales) as individuals substitute illegal for legal employment.

NOTES

1. This assumption is relaxed, and the same comparative static results are shown to hold [26].
2. Becker, Ehrlich, and Sjoquist introduce time allocation only implicitly through the effects of this allocation on wealth.
3. These results also hold if a Bernoulli distribution for the probability of apprehension and conviction is assumed.
4. Baldwin [4] provides a good discussion of ecological studies of crime. Empey ([31], [32]) provides a more thorough discussion of sociological and criminological theories of crime.
5. For example, Sjoquist assumes that the values of the parameters of the individual crime function "are the same for all individuals in a given community and that the density function between individual values and the community mean of the variable are homogeneous of degree one with respect to changes in the individual values and community means." [82], p. 441

6. For example, Ehrlich observes: "if all individuals were identical, the behavioral function . . . , except for changes in scale, could also be regarded as an aggregate supply function in a given period of time." [27], p. 534

7. A variable is judged to be significant if a two-tailed hypothesis test at the 5 percent level ($\alpha = 0.05$) would lead to a rejection of the null hypothesis that the coefficient of the variable is equal to zero.

8. This description was given by personnel of the Vera Institute of Justice who ran the original supported work program.

REFERENCES

[1] Allison, John P. 1972. "Economic Factors and the Rate of Crime," *Land Economics,* 2:48 (May): 193–196.

[2] Avio, K. L., and C. S. Clark. 1976. "Property Crime in Canada: An Econometric Study," Ontario Council of Economic Research Studies. Ontario, Canada.

[3] Baldwin, John. 1974. "Social Area Analysis and Studies of Delinquency," *Social Science Research,* 3:2 (June): 151–167.

[4] Baldwin, John. 1979. "Ecological and Areal Studies in Great Britain and the United States," in Norval Morris and Michael Tonry, eds., *Crime and Justice—An Annual Review of Research,* Vol. 1, Chicago: The University of Chicago Press, pp. 29–66.

[5] Bartel, Ann P. 1979. "Women and Crime: An Economic Analysis," *Economic Inquiry,* 17:1 (January): 29–51.

[6] Becker, G. S. 1968. "Crime and Punishment: An Economic Approach," *Journal of Political Economy,* 76:2 (March/April) 169–217.

[7] Becker, Gary S., and William M. Landes, eds. 1974. *Essays in the Economics of Crime and Punishment,* New York: Columbia University Press.

[8] Block, Michael K. 1972. "Theft: An Econometric Study," Paper to be presented at the Second Interamerican Congress of Criminology, Caracas. (Novermber)

[9] Block, M. K., and J. M. Heineke. 1973. "The Allocation of Effort Under Uncertainty: The Case of Risk Averse Behavior," *Journal of Political Economy,* 81:2 (March/April): 376–385.

[10] Block, M. K., and J. M. Heineke. 1975. "A Labor Theoretic Analysis of the Criminal Choice," *American Economic Review,* 65, 3 (June): 314–325.

[11] Block, M. K., and Robert C. Lind. 1975. "Crime and Punishment Reconsidered," *Journal of Legal Studies,* 4:1 (January): 241–247.

[12] Block, M. K., and R. Lind. 1975. "An Economic Analysis of Crimes Punishable by Imprisonment," *Journal of Legal Studies,* 4 (June): 479–492.

[13] Blumstein, Alfred, Jacqueline Cohen, and Daniel Nagin, eds. 1978. *Deterrence and Incapacitation: The Effects of Criminal Sanctions on Crime Rates.* Washington, D.C.: National Academy of Sciences, The National Research Council, Panel on Research on Deterrent and Incapacitative Effects.

[14] Blumstein, Alfred, Jacqueline Cohen, and Harold D. Miller. 1978. "Demographically Disaggregated Projections of Prison Population," Working Pa-

per, School of Urban and Public Affairs, Carnegie-Mellon University, Pittsburgh, Pa.

[15] Brenner, H. 1976. *Estimating the Social Cost of National Economic Policy: Implications for Mental and Physical Health, and Criminal Aggression.* (October) Paper No. 5 in Vol. 1: Employment, Achieving the Goals of the Employment Act of 1946, Thirteenth Anniversary Review, Joint Economic Committee.

[16] Brenner, Harvey M. 1979. "Pathology and the National Economy," statement prepared for the Task Force on Economic Disparities, Joint Economic Committee of the U.S. Congress.

[17] Brown, Malcom J., J. Wallace McCulloch, and Julie Hiscox. 1972. "Criminal Offenses in an Urban Area and Their Associated Social Variables," *British Journal of Criminology,* 12:3 (July): 250–268.

[18] Carr-Hill, R. A., and N. H. Stern. 1973. "An Econometric Model of the Supply and Control of Recorded Offense in England and Wales," *Journal of Public Economics,* 2:4 (November): 289–318.

[19] Center for Econometric Studies of the Criminal Justice System. Hoover Institute. 1978. "Property Crimes and the Returns to Legitimate and Illegitimate Activities," (March) Technical Report CERDCR-2-78, Stanford University.

[20] Center for Econometric Studies of the Justice System. Hoover Institution. 1979. "A Review of Some of the Results in Estimating the Social Cost of National Economic Policy: Implications for Mental and Physical Health, and Criminal Aggression." Mimeo.

[21] Cook, P. J. 1975. "The Correctional Carrot: Better Jobs for Parolees," *Policy Analysis,* 1 (Winter): 11–51.

[22] Cook, P. J. 1977. "Punishment and Crime: A Critique of Current Findings Concerning the Preventive Effects of Punishment," *Law and Contemporary Problems,* 41 (Winter): 164–204.

[23] Cooper, W. D. 1968. "An Economic Analysis of the Work-Release Program in North Carolina," unpublished Ph.D. dissertation, North Carolina State University, Raleigh, N.C.

[24] Danziger, S., and Wheeler, D. 1975a. "The Economics of Crime: Punishment or Income Redistribution," *Review of Social Economy,* 33:2 (October): 113–131.

[25] Danziger, Sheldon, and David Wheeler. undated 1975b. "Malevolent Interdependence Income Inequality, and Crime," Readings in Correctional Economics, Correctional Economics Center of the American Bar Association, Washington, D.C., pp. 35–66.

[26] Ehrlich, Issac. 1970. "Participation in Illegitimate Activities: An Economic Analysis," Ph.D. thesis, Columbia University, 1970.

[27] Ehrlich, Issac. 1973. "Participation in Illegitimate Activities: A Theoretical and Empirical Investigation," *Journal of Political Economy,* 81 (May/June): 521–65.

[28] Ehrlich, Issac. 1974. "Participation in Illegitimate Activities: An Economic Analysis." In *Essays in the Economics of Crime and Punishment,* Gary S. Becker and William M. Landes, eds., New York: Columbia University Press.

[29] Ehrlich, Issac. 1975. "The Deterrent Effect of Capital Punishment: A Question of Life and Death," *American Economic Review,* 65:3 (June): 397–417.

[30] Ehrlich, Issac. 1979. "Capital Punishment and Deterrence: Some Further Thoughts and Additional Evidence," in Sheldon L. Messinger and Egon Bittner, eds. *Criminology Yearbook Review,* Vol. 1, Beverly Hills, Calif.: Sage Publications.

[31] Empey, Lamar. 1978. *American Delinquency: Its Meaning and Construction.* Homewood, Ill.: Dorsey.

[32] Empey, Lamar. 1980. "Constructing Crime: Evolution and Implications of Sociological Theories," in Panel on Research on Rehabilitative Techniques, *Report II.* Washington, D.C.: National Academy of Sciences.

[33] Fleisher, B. M. 1963. "The Effects of Unemployment on Juvenile Delinquency," *Journal of Political Economy,* 71:6 (December): 543–555.

[34] Fleisher, B. M. 1966a. "The Effect of Income on Delinquency," *American Economic Review,* 56:5 (March): 118–137.

[35] Fleisher, B. M. 1966b. *The Economics of Delinquency.* Chicago: Quadrangle Books.

[36] Forst, B. 1976. "Participation in Illegitimate Activities: Further Empirical Findings," *Policy Analysis,* 2:3 (Summer): 477–492.

[37] Friedland, N., S. Maital, and A. Rutenberg. 1978. "A Simulation Study of Income Tax Evasion," *Journal of Public Economics,* 10 (August): 107–116.

[38] Friedman, L. S. 1977. "An Interim Evaluation of the Supported Work Experiment," *Policy Analysis,* 3 (Spring): 147–170.

[39] Gansemer, Duane G., and Lyle Knowles. 1974. "The Relationship Between Part I Crime and Economic Indicators," *Journal of Police Science and Administration,* 2:3 (September): 395–398.

[40] Gillespie, R. W. 1975. *Economic Factors in Crime and Delinquency: A Critical Review of the Empirical Evidence.* Final report submitted to the National Institute for Law Enforcement and Criminal Justice.

[41] Glaser, Daniel, and Kent Rice. 1959. "Crime, Age and Employment," *American Sociological Review,* 24:5 (October): 679–86.

[42] Gordon, David M. 1971. "Class and the Economics of Crime," *The Review of Radical Political Economics,* 3:3 (Summer): 51–75.

[43] Gordon, David M. 1973. "Capitalism, Class, and Crime in America," *Crime and Delinquency,* 19:2 (April): 163–186.

[44] Greenberg, David F. 1977. "The Dynamics of Oscillatory Punishment Processes," *Journal of Criminal Law and Criminology,* 68:4 (Winter): 643–651.

[45] Greenwood, Michael J., and Walter J. Wadycki. 1976. "Crime Rates and Public Expenditures for Police Protection: Their Interaction," in McPheters, Lee R., and William B. Stronge, eds. *The Economics of Crime and Law Enforcement.* Springfield, Ill.: Charles C. Thomas.

[46] Gutmann, P. M. 1977. "The Subterranean Economy," *Financial Analysts Journal,* 33 (November/December): 26–27, 34.

[47] Gylys, J. A. 1970. "The Causes of Crime and Application of Regional Analysis," *Atlanta Economic Review,* 20:9 (September): 34–37.

[48] Henry, James. 1976. "Calling in the Big Bills," *Washington Monthly*, (May): 27–33.

[49] Hoch, Irving. 1974. "Factors in Urban Crime," *Journal of Urban Economics*, 1:2 (April): 184–229.

[50] Land, K. C., and Felson, M. 1976. "A General Framework for Building Dynamic Macro Social Indicator Models: Including An Analysis of Changes in Crime Rates and Police Expenditures," *American Journal of Sociology*, 82:3 (November): 565–604.

[51] Leveson, Irving. 1976. *The Growth of Crime*. Croton-on-Hudson: Hudson Institute.

[52] Mallar, D. C., and V. D. Thornton. 1978. "Transitional Aid for Released Prisoners: Evidence From the Life Experiment," *Journal of Human Resources*, Vol. 13, pp. 208–236.

[53] Mallar, C. D. 1979. "A Comprehensive Evaluation of the Job Corps Program," *The MPR Policy Newsletter*, (Spring): 4–6.

[54] Mathieson, D., and P. Passell. 1976. "Homicide and Robbery in New York City: An Economic Model," *Journal of Legal Studies*, 6 (June): 83–98.

[55] Maynard, R., et al. 1979. *The Supported Work Demonstration: Effects During the First 18 Months After Enrollment*. Princeton, N.J.: Mathematica Policy Research, Inc.

[56] McPheters, Lee R., and William B. Stronge, eds. 1976. *The Economics of Crime and Law Enforcement*. Springfield, Ill.: Charles C. Thomas.

[57] McPheters, Lee R., and William B. Stronge, 1976. "Law Enforcement Expenditures and Urban Crime," in McPheters, Lee R., and William B. Stronge, eds. *The Economics of Crime and Law Enforcement*. Springfield, Ill.: Charles C. Thomas.

[58] Merton, Robert K. 1957. *Social Theory and Social Structure*, rev. ed. New York: Free Press.

[59] Messinger, Sheldon L., and Egon Bittner, eds. 1979. *Criminology Review Yearbook*. Vol. 1, Beverly Hills, Calif.: Sage Publications.

[60] Morris, Douglas, and Luther Tweeten. 1971. "The Costs of Controlling Crime: A Study in the Economics of City Life," *Annals of Regional Science*, 5:1 (June): 33–50.

[61] Nagin, D. 1978. "General Deterrence: A Review of the Empirical Evidence," in Alfred Blumstein, Jacqueline Cohen, and Daniel Nagin, eds. *Deterrence and Incapacitation: Estimating the Effects of Criminal Sanctions on Crime Rates*. Committee on Research on Deterrent and Incapacitative Effects, National Academy of Sciences, Washington, D.C.

[62] National Institute of Law Enforcement and Criminal Justice. 1978. *Study of the Economic and Rehabilitative Aspects of Prison Industries: Analysis of Prison Industries and Recommendations for Change*. Washington, D.C.: U.S. Government Printing Office.

[63] National Institute for Law Enforcement and Criminal Justice. 1978. *Study of the Economic and Rehabilitative Aspects of Prison Industries: Technical Tasks and Results*. Washington, D.C.: U.S. Government Printing Office.

[64] Orsagh, Thomas, and Ann Dryden Witte. 1980. *Economic Status and Crime: Implications for Offender Rehabilitation.* The University of North Carolina at Chapel Hill, mimeo.

[65] Petersilia, J., et al. 1972. *Criminal Careers of Habitual Felons.* Santa Monica, Calif.: The Rand Corporation.

[66] Peterson, Mark A., Harriet B. Braiker, and Suzanne M. Polich. 1980. *Doing Crime: A Survey of California Prison Inmates.* Santa Monica, Calif.: The Rand Corporation.

[67] Phillips, L., H. L. Votey, Jr., and D. Maxwell. 1972. "Crime, Youth and the Labor Market," *Journal of Political Economy,* 80 (May-June, Part I): 491–504.

[68] Phillips, L., and H. L. Votey, Jr. 1972. "An Economic Analysis of the Deterrent Effect of Law Enforcement on Criminal Activity," *The Journal of Criminal Law, Criminology and Police Science,* 63:6 (September): 330–342.

[69] Phillips, Llad, and Harold L. Votey, Jr. 1975. "Crime Control in California," *The Journal of Legal Studies,* 3:2 (June): 327–349.

[70] Pogue, Thomas F. 1975. "Effects of Police Expenditures on Crime Rates: Some Evidence," *Public Finance Quarterly,* 3:1 (January): 14–44.

[71] Pressman, Israel, and Arthur Carol. 1976. "Crime as a Diseconomy of Scale," in McPheters, Lee R., and William B. Stronge, eds. *The Economics of Crime and Law Enforcement.* Springfield, Ill.: Charles C. Thomas.

[72] Quinney, Richard. 1966. "Structural Characteristics, Population, Areas, and Crime Rates in the United States," *Journal of Criminal Law, Criminology and Police Science,* 57:1 (March): 45–52.

[73] Rattner, Steven. 1980. "Recession Puts Budget Plan Lower on Probability Index," *The New York Times.* (Sunday, May 4): Section 4, E4.

[74] Rossi, P. H., R. A. Berk, and K. Lenihan. 1980. *Money, Work and Crime.* New York: Academic Press.

[75] Rovner-Pieczenik, R. 1970. *Project Crossroads as Pre-Trial Intervention: A Program Evaluation.* Washington, D.C.: National Committee for Children and Youth.

[76] Rutherford, Andrew, et al. 1977. *Prison Population and Policy Choices.* 2 vols. Washington, D.C.: U.S. Department of Justice.

[77] Schmid, Calvin F. 1960. "Urban Crime Areas," *American Sociological Review,* 25, Part I (August): 527–42 and Part II (October): 655–78.

[78] Schuessler, Karl, and G. Slatin. 1964. "Sources of Variation in U.S. City Crime, 1950 and 1960," *Journal of Research in Crime and Delinquency,* 1:2 (July): 127–148.

[79] Sickles, R. C., P. Schmidt, and A. D. Witte. 1979. "An Application of the Simultaneous Tobit Model: A Study of the Determinants of Criminal Recidivism," *Journal of Economics and Business,* 31 (Spring/Summer): 166–171.

[80] Simon, Carl P., and Ann D. Witte. 1979. *The Underground Economy: Estimates of Size, Structure and Trends,* prepared for the Special Study on Economic Change conducted by the Joint Economic Committee of the U.S. Congress.

[81] Singell, L. D. 1967. "Examination of the Empirical Relationships Between Unemployment and Juvenile Delinquency," *American Journal of Economics and Sociology*, 26:4 (October): 377–386.

[82] Sjoquist, D. L. 1973. "Property Crime and Economic Behavior: Some Empirical Results," *American Economic Review*, 63:3 (June): 439–446.

[83] Sviridoff, M., and J. W. Thompson. 1979. "Linkages Between Employment and Crime: A Qualitative Study of Rikers Releasees," Working Paper, Vera Institute of Justice.

[84] Swimmer, Eugene. 1974a. "Measurement of the Effectiveness of Urban Law Enforcement—A Simultaneous Approach," *Southern Economic Journal*, 40:4 (April): 618–630.

[85] Swimmer, Eugene. 1974b. "The Relationship of Police and Crime: Some Methodological and Empirical Results," *Criminology*, 12:3 (November): 293–314.

[86] Taggert, Robert. 1973. *The Prison of Unemployment*. Baltimore: Johns Hopkins University Press.

[87] Thaler, Richard. 1975. "An Econometric Analysis of Property Crime: Interaction Between Police and Criminals," Information Paper No. 10, Graduate School of Management, University of Rochester, New York.

[88] Thaler, Richard. 1977. "An Econometric Analysis of Property Crime: Interaction Between Police and Criminals," *Journal of Public Economics*, 8 (August): 37–51.

[89] Tullock, Gordon. 1974. "Research Report: Does Punishment Deter Crime?," *Public Interest*, 36 (Summer) 103–111.

[90] U.S. Department of the Treasury, Internal Revenue Service. 1979. *Estimates of Income Unreported on Individual Income Tax Returns*. Washington, D.C.: U.S. Department of the Treasury, Publication 1104 (9–79).

[91] Votey, Harold L., Jr., and Llad Phillips. 1969. *Economic Crimes: Their Generation, Deterrence, and Control*. National Institute of Law Enforcement and Criminal Justice, Final Report.

[92] Votey, Harold L., Jr., and Llad Phillips. 1974. "The Control of Criminal Activity: An Economic Analysis," in Daniel Glaser, ed. *Handbook of Criminology*. Chicago: Rand McNally.

[93] Weicher, John C. 1970. "The Effect of Income on Delinquency: Comment," *American Economic Review*, 60:1 (March): 249–256.

[94] Weller, D. C., M. K. Block, and F. C. Nold. 1978. "Unemployment and the Allocation of Time by Criminals," Technical Report CERDCR-3-78, Center for Econometric Studies of Crime and the Criminal Justice System, Hoover Institution, Stanford University.

[95] Witte, Ann Dryden, and Peter Schmidt. 1977. "An Analysis of Recidivism, Using the Truncated Lognormal Distribution," *The Journal of the Royal Statistical Society Series C (Applied Statistics)*, 26:3, pp. 302–311.

[96] Witte, Ann Dryden, and Peter Schmidt. 1979. "An Analysis of the Type of Criminal Activity Using the Logit Model," *Journal of Research in Crime and Delinquency*, 16:1 (January): 164–179.

[97] Witte, A. D. 1979. *Theoretical Models for Some Measures of Labor Market Performance*, Working Paper 79–5, The Osprey Company, Raleigh, N.C.

[98] Witte, A. D. 1979. *Unemployment and Crime: Insights from Research on Individuals,* statement prepared for the Hearings of the Joint Economic Committee of the U.S. Congress on the "Social Costs of Unemployment."

[99] Witte, A. D. 1980. "Estimating the Economic Model of Crime with Individual Data," *Quarterly Journal of Economics,* 94 (February): 57–84.

Responses to Economic Crisis

The selections in Part II, by describing the impact of an actual economic crisis, further expand the consideration of possible effects which economic adversity might have on the criminal justice system. Specifically, the two chapters examine the effects of Proposition 13 on the agencies of the California criminal justice system.

Proposition 13 was a constitutional amendment which was passed by the California voters in June of 1978. It substantially reduced property taxes and thus produced a significant decrease in local government revenues. The state government, however, bailed local governments out and the total fiscal impact was not as substantial as originally expected. The overall reaction of local government to the crisis is noteworthy; several significant changes did take place within criminal justice agencies. The findings also suggest that the assumption that economic adversity may reduce inefficiency and waste while stimulating needed change may be false.

In the first chapter of Part II, Beatrice Hoffman chronicles the events which occurred in the San Francisco criminal justice system in the wake of Proposition 13. She describes the reaction within the city as similar to the response to a natural disaster. Interagency cooperation was not initiated on a wide basis. Furthermore, cuts which, in accordance with the amendment, were intended to reduce waste and improve efficiency, actually eroded service delivery. Due to budgetary reductions, vacated positions were not filled and salary increases were substantially reduced. Personnel shortages, programmatic reductions, and lower morale have resulted.

Findings quite similar to those of Hoffman are reported by Walker, Chaiken, Jiga, and Polin in their extensive study of the effects of Proposition 13 on the criminal justice system across the state. They describe the end result as a system which is much harsher. Both criminal and victim are now receiving less attention and are not treated as well as in the past. The attitude of criminal justice personnel toward the public is more resentful and less concerned than ever before. Walker and his associates conclude that Proposition 13 has produced a criminal justice system which is less humane and less responsive.

Chapter 6

Proposition 13 and the San Francisco Criminal Justice System—First Reactions to a Disaster

*Beatrice Hoffman**

BACKGROUND

Methodology

On June 6, 1978, the voters of California passed a constitutional amendment unprecedented in the state's history, one which became the forerunner of taxpayer revolts across the country. It reverted assessments on real property to 1975–76 values, limited property tax to one percent of valuation and annual increases to two percent, while outlawing new taxes except by the approval of two-thirds majority of the voters. Depending on one's perspective, Proposition 13 was a victory, a deliverance, a model, a trend, an omen, a warning, or a catastrophe.

At the time, this writer was in the process of studying the criminal justice system of the City and County of San Francisco. Therefore, she was in an ideal position to conduct a case study on the immediate im-

This article is a revision of a paper prepared for the 1979 meeting of the Academy of Criminal Justice Sciences in Cincinnati, Ohio. It was financed in part by Law Enforcement Assistance Administration Grant A-2926-2-78, System Improvement Project, awarded by the Mayor's Criminal Justice Council and the Office of Criminal Justice Planning to the Municipal Court of the City and County of San Francisco.

*Court Research Associates, San Francisco, California

pact of Proposition 13 on individual justice agencies and the system as a totality. Not only did she keep notes and document events as they occurred, she spent much of her time during the first thirty days of the crisis observing City Hall and Hall of Justice reaction and talking to decision makers.

Although the reductions which were called for by the mayor in his declaration of an emergency did not happen then, due to state monies being distributed to the cities from a state tax surplus, the crisis provided the opportunity to view the system in a compacted period of tension and uncertainty.

Description of the San Francisco Criminal Justice System

San Francisco enjoys a worldwide reputation as a city of beauty, marked by vistas of hills and water and noted for wide variety in its ethnic populace, citizen lifestyles, restaurants, and entertainment. There is another side, not publicized by the Chamber of Commerce. Whether compared to other cities or other counties (its city and county boundaries are coterminous), San Francisco has the highest crime rate in the state and ranks very high nationally.

To deal with the problem, the city and county funds six large executive agencies, the municipal court, and most of the cost of the superior court. Crime control and law enforcement is the responsibility of the police; the sheriff is responsible for the county jail and for providing the courts with bailiffs and the serving of legal notices and processes. The county clerk's office handles the filing for, and is responsible to, the superior court;[1] municipal court has its clerk's office within its own structure. Adult and juvenile probation are separate agencies, with each chief probation officer appointed by the superior court. The district attorney and the public defender are elected officials. The city also funds the O.R. (Own Recognizance) Project, a private nonprofit organization which provides investigation and jail release recommendations on arrestees.[2]

The city's criminal justice system suffers from a poor reputation. Improvement has come slowly in spite of numerous attempts by an active city bar association, other professionals, and interested citizens. The difficulty lies in an entrenched civil servant bureaucracy enforced by a strong civil service commission, a generally conservative law-and-order attitude by those in authority, and a multitude of well-organized and politically active ethnic, religious, and neighborhood organizations whose goals often conflict with proposed reforms.

In addition, the city operates under a complicated charter which authorizes an elected mayor, plus a board of supervisors elected on a district basis, and an appointed chief administrative officer, all of whom have limited powers. Many administrative changes must go to a vote of the people as charter revisions.

At the time Proposition 13 was being debated, there was hope that a liberal mayor, new direction in some of the agencies, and a newly elected and responsive board of supervisors might make reform attempts viable. Federal and private grants had been obtained to pay for professionals to assist agencies in working together more cooperatively than they had in the past and to improve administrative and management practices.

THE EFFECT OF PROPOSITION 13 ON SAN FRANCISCO'S BUDGET

The Budget Process

The city works on a fiscal year basis, July 1 through June 30. The process begins the previous late fall and early winter, when executive agencies start preparing their budgets for presentation to the mayor's budget office in December. Each agency is given the opportunity to discuss its budget with the mayor's budget staff and to justify requests. The judicial branch is not required to participate in this part of the process. The municipal court sends a complimentary copy of its budget to the mayor; the superior court does not.

Historically, the mayor has presented a completed executive budget to the board of supervisors by the latter part of March. In April, the finance committee of the board begins public hearings, and the supervisors' budget staff begins their analytical work. The finance committee sends a completed recommended budget to the board of supervisors by the end of the month, and a budget is passed by the first week of May and sent to the mayor for signature.[3]

Theoretically, the board cannot add, but only delete, parts of the budget, but political compromises have sometimes made additions possible, by consent of the mayor.

Pre-Proposition 13

In the winter of 1977 and the spring of 1978, the budget process proceeded in its customary manner, although many agency directors suspected it might be a useless exercise. Budgets were developed, analyzed, and accepted on the premise that revenues would remain as high as always. It was recognized that the 1978–79 budget would be discarded if Proposition 13 passed, but in the early days of budget preparation the possibility was too distant and uncertain to be fully comprehended. Even those who felt the amendment would pass did little more than speculate on what they would do should the initiative pass.

Consequently, the 1978–79 budget followed its standard route, from original agency requests, to the mayor's budget, to the budget approved by the supervisors (referred to here as the supervisors' budget). The mayor postponed signing it into law, pending the election outcome. Had Proposition 13 failed, the city would have operated under the supervisors' budget.

In late May, the mayor's office prepared what was termed a "worst-case budget," the first numerical indication of what cuts would have to be sustained if property taxes were reduced and the state gave local governments no relief. With some exceptions, the mayor's staff did not cut specific services or programs as such but merely recommended percentage cuts per department.

Proponents of Proposition 13 scoffed at the worst-case budget, calling it "scare tactics" designed to frighten the voters. They maintained that projections of 6,500 people losing their jobs, libraries closing, and the city having limited fire or police protection were empty threats that need not nor would happen.

The supervisors' budget staff presented a number of contingency budgets, dependent on various estimates of the amount of state aid that might be expected. At that time, the Governor was campaigning heavily against the amendment and would not guarantee the amount of state aid localities would receive.

As the days drew close to election day and public opinion poll results were disclosed, it appeared more and more likely that the amendment would pass. However, even as department heads expressed certainty of passage, their acts denied the reality. They were like people in a canyon, who see the cracks in the dam above them, but won't launch a boat until they see the water flowing by the door. Since there was no possibility of knowing what the state would do, contingency plans were considered a waste of time and done half-heartedly or not at all.

The First 30 Days

Consequently, when the votes were tallied and what was dreaded had become an actuality, the city government reacted as they might to any disaster. At first there was shock, tinged with bitterness. Statements made by officials elsewhere in the state, indicating resolve "to carry out the wishes of the voters" were not appropriate to San Francisco, where the measure had been defeated. After the shock, came resigned determination. With no certainty as to what amount revenues would be, a new budget had to be prepared and passed within three weeks.

The timetable in the Appendix cannot begin to convey the speculation, confusion, and dejection that pervaded city offices and halls in the month of June, immediately after voting day. Regular work either stopped entirely or was done in dispirited fashion as employees wondered whether they would have jobs after July 1.

The mayor proclaimed a state of emergency which suspended existing charter provisions and city ordinances. He announced that he would allow department heads to decide where and how to cut costs in their departments. This promoted lengthy discussion of the issue at every level, as employees argued the relative merits and disadvantages of layoffs for some versus reduced work weeks for all.

Agency supervisors assumed that the amounts in the worst-case budget would be the rule, and sought the most painless savings that would achieve the percentage allotted their department.

At the same time that department heads were seeking savings, the controller's office was searching, and finding, ways to transfer special allocation money into the general fund. As examples, $16 million in cash reserves, $6 million in surplus water and power revenue, and a $2 million surplus received for administering the Comprehensive Employee and Training Program (CETA) were moved.

The budget staffs of the mayor's office and the supervisors proceeded separately, although the mayor's plea for a moratorium of the usual adversarial and political postures met with quiet acceptance. After naming a select committee of their members, the supervisors began holding public hearings and preparing a budget, legally only as a recommendation to the mayor. He had before him the 1978–79 supervisors' budget, not yet approved by him. He had the power to blue pencil whatever portions he wished. The amended budget would then go to the board for possible overriding of his vetoes. It was clear that if there was to be a budget operative on July 1, both branches of government had to cooperate.

In a matter of days, budget after budget was prepared. As supervisory and accounting staffs conferred, calculators clicked, numbers were erased and subtracted and revised, and the data processing division worked around the clock. One department accountant estimated he eventually prepared 14 separate budgets between June 6 and time the final one passed into law. Details regarding state aid was so indefinite that, by the time the third departmental budget had been prepared a few days after June 6, the chief adult probation officer ordered a halt until he knew the final percentage figure. "I'm tired of planning against unknowns," he said.

Information was so vague that on June 20, two weeks after election day, a memorandum from the mayor's chief budget officer to the department heads contained these words: "The amount shown is still tentative. It is what we now believe we will be showing on the appropriation ordinance to be returned to the board of supervisors where it is subject to legislative scrutiny. It is also possible that major revenue items will change in the next few days. Nonetheless, we believe it is the best planning figure you are going to have to work with." In spite of the ambiguity, the memo ordered department heads to present their suggestions for meeting the reduced budget figures (in some instances raised from the first worst-case levels) within two days, or the mayor's budget office "would reluctantly have to make our own choices."

Within a period of a few short days, agency heads were forced to cope with low employee morale, make emotionally difficult decisions, prepare a rock-bottom budget for the mayor to which they might be held, and plead before the board of supervisors for increases to maintain their departments at near customary levels of service.

Since the situation was so fluid, it was the agencies who were astute enough to keep informed, and to take advantage of hourly changes in developments, who managed to get their budgets restored first. As the board began to "find" revenue, through new taxes and "nest egg" transfers, even before the state bailout had been announced, the mood of the hearings changed. The board had been listening to agency presentations of proposed reductions to the supervisors' budget. With no notice, they reversed the procedure, adopted the worst-case budget as a base, and entertained agency comments on money amounts needed. Those agencies that were present and saw the board begin to add money rather than subtract it, quickly grasped the advantage and began to ask for restoration of specific budget items. The first evening this occurred, the board was restoring funds to budgets with such abandon that one supervisor called it "playing Monopoly with real money."

Fortunately, after the announcement from the state that San Francisco would receive more than double the amount that had been expected, the mayor's office and the budget staffs took a cooler and closer look. They restored funds to some of the forgotten departments to more closely equalize those additions which had occurred in the excitement of the hearings.

Budget Changes During the Crisis

The five budgets shown in Table 6–1 represent only the most significant 1978–79 budgets discussed during the process; they do not convey the many ups and downs both in dollars and in mood that occurred as various budgets were prepared.

The original request budget represents what agency heads felt were their true needs; the mayor's budget shows severe cuts; the supervisors' budget is the one which the city would have operated under if Proposition 13 had not passed; the worst-case budget is close to the one which the city would have operated under if no state aid had been given; and the final budget is the one which the board approved June 26 as its official 1978–79 budget.[4] It should be noted that the city operates on much more than $823.9 million, with many agencies requesting and receiving supplemental appropriations throughout the year.[5] The exact amount spent is not known until the final books are closed, sometime after the end of the fiscal year.

Agency heads maintain that the first budget—their original requests—should not be considered an overstated one, and that the mayor's and supervisors' budgets were sharply reduced for politically motivated reasons, designed to show voters that the city could trim fat without the need of a constitutional amendment. They feel the percentage change from original request to final budget, as shown in Table 6–2, is much more meaningful in showing their losses than the percentage change from supervisors' budget to final, as shown in Table 6–1.

Examination of Table 6–1 shows that the mayor's budget staff, anticipating intense public scrutiny of the budget while debate mounted over the issue of "waste in government," made substantial cuts in agency requests, first in the recreation and culture category, followed by central government, and third in the justice system.[6]

Although the mayor presented it as a "bare bones" budget, the supervisors attempted to outdo him. The supervisor chairing the finance committee, rumored to be a leading candidate in the next mayoralty election, was determined to pare the budget as much as possible. Because the budget was already very trim, and because each supervisor had favorite projects and different vocal constituencies, the budget was reduced by only 4.1 percent more. Fire and emergency services, public health, and the justice system were increased slightly, while public service enterprises were reduced by an additional 14.7 percent.

The worst-case budget represents an 18.2 percent reduction overall from the supervisors' budget, a 21.5 percent reduction from the may-

Table 6–1. City and County of San Francisco, 1978–1979 Budgets

	Original Request	Mayor's Budget	Supervisors' Budget	Worst-Case Budget	Final Budget	% Difference: Super/Final
Adult Probation	3,085,166	2,679,382	2,663,202	1,882,701	2,263,772	−15.0
District Attorney	5,876,985	4,854,870	4,828,841	3,606,559	4,346,559	−10.0
Municipal Court	8,567,329	8,567,329	7,776,921	7,105,048	7,365,048	−08.5
Police Department	87,652,040	81,070,209	83,556,151	69,418,538	82,610,826	−01.1
Public Defender	4,304,088	2,473,280	2,446,070	1,988,503	2,201,463	−10.0
Sheriff	13,632,714	11,265,967	11,268,073	9,854,122	10,141,266	−10.0
Superior Court	4,661,803	4,661,803	4,612,475	4,222,992	4,222,992	−08.4
Juvenile Court Probation	4,869,418	4,589,187	4,531,283	4,056,348	4,056,348	−10.5
Juvenile Hall	3,237,254	2,735,675	2,619,359	2,371,001	2,371,001	−09.5
Log Cabin/Hidden Valley	1,617,712	1,282,822	1,285,459	747,654	709,457	−44.8
Jail Medical Services[a]	2,261,740	2,125,224	2,067,458	1,925,959	1,925,959	−06.8
Med. Clinic–Juv. Hall[a]	255,383	245,161	245,156	122,578	202,578	−17.4
County Clerk	2,398,282	2,550,761	2,309,314	1,686,137	2,086,137	−09.7
Delinquency Commission	51,861	55,849	49,929	−0−	42,440	−15.0
Justice System	142,471,775	129,157,519	130,259,691	108,988,140	124,545,846	−04.4
Fire/Emergency	70,471,028	64,691,343	66,545,504	54,561,169	65,795,445	−01.1
Recreation/Culture	62,427,184	47,436,342	46,579,160	9,972,369	35,093,354	−24.7
Public Health	135,795,473	131,870,524	132,738,771	106,166,642	119,424,701	−10.0
Social Services	167,111,980	163,171,387	160,598,050	148,995,264	158,559,148	−01.3
Central Government	138,199,377	119,935,242	119,168,005	104,961,170	121,677,847	+02.1
Public Service Enterprises[b]	268,655,567	249,804,149	212,971,727	177,429,113	198,756,122	−06.7
Total	985,132,384	906,066,506	868,860,908	711,073,867	823,852,463	−05.2

[a]Subtracted from Public Health
[b]Includes Muni RR, Airport, etc.

Table 6–2. Percentage Reductions in the 1978–79 Budgets

	Original Budget	Mayor's Budget to Original Budget	Percentage Reduction Supervisors' Budget to Original Budget	Worst-Case Budget to Original Budget	Final Budget to Original Budget
Adult Probation	3,085,166	–13.1	–13.7	–39.0	–26.6
District Attorney	5,876,985	–17.4	–17.8	–38.6	–26.0
Municipal Court	8,567,329	—	–09.2	–17.1	–14.0
Police Department	87,652,040	–07.5	–04.7	–20.8	–05.8
Public Defender	4,304,088	–42.5	–43.2	–53.8	–48.9
Sheriff	13,632,714	–17.4	–17.3	–27.7	–25.6
Superior Court	4,661,803	—	–01.1	–09.4	–08.4
Juvenile Court Probation	4,869,418	–05.8	–06.9	–16.7	–16.7
Juvenile Hall	3,237,254	–15.5	–06.5	–19.1	–19.1
Log Cabin/Hidden Valley	1,617,712	–20.7	–20.5	–53.8	–56.1
Jail Medical Services[a]	2,261,740	–06.0	–08.6	–14.8	–14.8
Med. Clinic–Juv. Hall[a]	255,383	–04.0	–04.0	–52.0	–20.7
County Clerk	2,398,282	06.4	–03.7	–29.7	–13.0
Delinquency Commission	51,861	07.7	–03.7	100.0	–18.2
Justice System	142,471,775	–09.3	–08.6	–23.5	–12.6
Fire/Emergency	70,471,028	–08.2	–05.6	–22.6	–06.6
Recreation/Culture	62,427,184	–24.0	–25.4	–84.0	–43.8
Public Health	135,795,473	–02.9	–02.3	–21.9	–12.1
Social Services	167,111,980	–02.4	–03.9	–10.8	–05.1
Central Government	138,199,377	–13.2	–13.8	–24.1	–12.0
Public Service Enterprises[b]	268,655,567	–07.0	–20.7	–34.0	–26.0
Total	985,132,384	–08.0	–11.8	–27.8	–16.3

[a]Subtracted from Public Health
[b]Includes Muni RR, Airport, etc.

or's budget, and a 27.8 percent cut in the original request budget. Recreation and culture received the most pruning, with public health next; justice was fifth out of the seven general budget classifications in order of magnitude of the reductions.

When the supervisors finished making additions to the worst-case budget, the order in the size of reductions remained substantially the same, although fire and emergency services went from third to sixth and justice moved from fifth place to fourth.

The biggest cuts sustained by the justice system were in the juvenile area, as evidenced by a 45 percent reduction in the closing of the Hidden Valley juvenile detention facility and the 17 percent reduction in juvenile hall's medical clinic, plus a 15 percent reduction in money allocated to operate the juvenile delinquency commission, a planning body.

There is little question that Hidden Valley was closed because it represented a large amount of savings with a relatively low number of involved personnel, and it had previously been considered for elimination by the budget staff and had been under pressure by various segments of the citizenry to be closed or improved.

Both the public defender and adult probation sustained heavy cuts. These agencies are customarily lowest among the criminal justice agencies in receiving operating funds.

Almost half the public defender's staff, including attorneys, were CETA employees, and the department suffered from problems of limited space, an inadequate telephone system, and no allocation for training. Funds for permanent staff had been eliminated by the mayor's staff, but the new telephone system had been allowed, and also endorsed by the supervisors. This had been a major victory for the public defender, who had been seeking funds for such a system for years. Unfortunately, a Proposition 13 result was sacrifice of the telephone system to save personnel.

Adult probation had a history of poor management and philosophy prior to the hiring of a new director, and suffered doubly from a poor reputation and no strong constituency. Although the department had been struggling with heavy caseloads and temporary staffs, the mayor's budget people had not allowed any additional personnel, even before Proposition 13.

The police department received no cuts at all, with the exception of the elimination of salary increases for its personnel (along with all city and state employees, of course). This is the reason for the 1.1 percent less in their final budget, as compared to the supervisors' budget.

The police department, accounting as it did for 66 percent of the entire justice system costs, brings the overall loss for the justice system to 4.4 percent. However, exclusive of the police department, the average decrease comes to 10.2 percent, and if the log cabin facility is deducted, the average loss for the remaining departments comes to 9.2 percent.

That puts the justice system in the posture of sustaining relatively minor cuts compared to the rest of the city systems, if the police department is included, but in a more damaged situation relative to others if the police department is considered separately. It is clear that recreation and culture, with its budget cut by almost one-fourth, took the brunt of the blow. Because social services funds were supplied by the state, the 1.3 percent less in its budget represents only the raises employees had expected to receive but did not.[7]

It is interesting to note that central government, the one system the taxpayers had hoped to reduce, not only did not sustain cuts but even increased, although admittedly only minimally. The mayor's office justified this by pointing out that central government had been reduced heavily initially.

CITY GOVERNMENT REACTION TO PROPOSITION 13

From local government's point of view, Proposition 13 fits the definition of a disaster; that is, it was thought of as a tragic situation over which the city had no control.

In most respects, the situation indeed corresponded to general theories of what occurs when natural disasters strike. The reaction pattern after a disaster typically follows a course which has been variously described,[8] but as a rule includes the following:

1. A first stage of dazed bewilderment, disbelief, sometimes refusal to accept the fact, and zombielike apathy or immobility.

2. This is followed quickly by intense activity. Even though the situation is not yet seen clearly or rationally, action is demanded as a means of asserting control. Leadership begins to function and orders are obeyed even if the purposes are not understood.

During this second phase, there is a need to "make sense" of the changed social world through exchange of communication. Collective rumors spread with ease; there are buzzing groups of people evident, plus close monitoring of media reports.

3. Whether considered as part of the second phase or as a new stage, there occurs a period of time when persons and institutions submerge their old rivalries and conflicts and work together cooperatively in a common effort.

4. As time goes on, many become frustrated with the disorganization and with the decisions made. Hostility may result; old conflicts

may be revived. A search for a scapegoat on which emotional tension can be released may begin.

5. As a result of the shared common tasks of high priority, new tasks and patterns of coordination may occur, leading to new social group formations.

Because Proposition 13 was a man-made fiscal disaster, without loss of life or physical damage to people or property, the degree of reaction was not as deep or prolonged as would be expected in the wake of a natural disaster such as a flood or tornado. Nevertheless, people in city government progressed through essentially the same stages as detailed above.

There was a very abbreviated period after June 6 when city officials and agency decision makers seemed stunned. During this time, and for the next few weeks, there was intense communication around the topic of Proposition 13. Other news was relegated to back pages of the newspaper; television dramatized personal "tear-jerker" vignettes as well as presenting straight news. Wherever people congregated within the hall of justice or city hall, it was safe to predict that they were discussing Proposition 13. Rumors primarily concerned the amount of money the state would give to "bailout" the city, the procedures other agencies were using to achieve savings, and the number of employees reputed to be laid off.

The most evident manifestation of postdisaster behavior occurred in the relationship between the mayor and the board of supervisors. While both took steps in directions that could have been in conflict, they succeeded in working together effectively. They took separate actions as means of establishing authority, which at some other less chaotic time might have led to a clash. Instead, both groups managed to compromise on amounts of individual budgets, selected programs, and methods of financing.

The mayor visited the council chambers of the board while debate ensued, and frequently asked for specific assistance. Behind the scenes, new and renewed political alliances between the mayor and some of the supervisors assured cooperation.

When the crisis was over, the alliances dissolved. After the new budget had been passed, financed heavily with state monies, the increased taxes the mayor had requested and passed by the board were revoked. Because the taxes had to be passed prior to July 1, the mayor literally begged the supervisors to keep them as a hedge against future times when the state surplus would be gone. Pressure from the business community and labor was too overwhelming for the supervisors, and the temporary coalition was renounced.

Proposition 13 provided the opportunity to make changes that had been previously proposed but defeated. For instance, some supervisors had long urged an increase in municipal railway transit fares, needed in order to qualify for transportation aid from the state.[9] The fare increase was a sensitive issue; San Francisco citizens are heavy users of public transit and had resisted fare increases for years. The loss of revenue provided the excuse of choosing increased fares over reduced services. Once the rationale had been eliminated through the extension of state aid, the increase was killed.[10]

The budget office took advantage of the crisis to urge elimination of programs of which they had previously been critical. They had tried for five years to eliminate the Hidden Valley juvenile detention facility, citing the high per diem cost of maintaining a large facility at less than total occupancy. The chief juvenile probation officer did not fight the closing, recognizing that, in any case, he might not be able to keep enough staff to maintain it.

Another instance concerned the district attorney's consumer fraud unit, a division felt by the budget analysts to be neither cost effective nor of high priority. They had tried to eliminate it prior to Proposition 13 and, having failed, marked it for extinction again in the early June cuts. The district attorney was successful, for a second time, in getting it restored.

Criminal justice agency responses to Proposition 13 followed similar postdisaster patterns, and are described in the next section.

CRIMINAL JUSTICE SYSTEM REACTIONS TO PROPOSITION 13

Intraagency Reaction

Even in crisis times, agency loyalty, territorial protection, and personal pride proved stronger than sacrifice for the common good. At first, agency heads fought less stridently than usual to save programs; it was not considered proper to ask for rescue of one's own department at the expense of others. Later, it became acceptable to appear before the board with a plea for restoration of their budget, "should funding permit."

Behavior patterns and social relationships formed prior to the crisis remained consistent. Police and sheriff uniformed personnel relied heavily on their strong unions to speak for them and to prevent both layoffs and reduced work weeks. On the other hand, the public defender's staff, a small but highly idealistic group, voted to save each other's jobs by taking two-week unpaid vacations in turn.

An interesting division evidenced itself within the sheriff's department. The newly appointed sheriff[11] asked his personnel their preference regarding the two options. The deputies, who had philosophical differences with the more social service-minded prisoner services civilian staff, voted for layoffs. They were willing to sacrifice a few in their ranks, knowing that the bulk of the layoffs would fall on the prisoner services division, whose people had shorter tenure. Prisoner services voted for a 36-hour work week for everyone.

Relations between the two groups grew strained, but later eased as both groups blamed the undersheriff for causing all their problems. This illustration of the scapegoat syndrome surfaced because the undersheriff, then departmental spokesman for financial affairs, was out of town at a long-planned training session during the days of crisis.

By June 20, when budgets were being restored, all criminal justice agency budgets, with the exception of the sheriff's department, had been raised. A personal appearance before the board would have achieved that, but the inexperienced sheriff did not realize it. Departmental hostility turned against the undersheriff who the employees felt had let them down. In the panic of the times, if the sheriff had not appealed to the mayor at the last moment, his department's budget might not have been restored along with the others.

It is evident that, after examining its various alternatives, each agency was most resistant to reducing personnel. It appeared that the reason for this was not merely the desire to keep as large an establishment as possible. The emotional reluctance to choose which employees were most expendable, and then to order their dismissal, was overwhelming. Middle-line departmental supervisors, accountants, and budget staffs made such recommendations, but agency heads directed them to continue to seek other mechanisms for saving money.

In the past, civil service bureaucracy and labor union vigilance had been blamed for the inability of agency supervisors to control inefficiency, eliminate "deadwood," and reward industrious employees. Proposition 13 might have been a vehicle whereby an agency could streamline its staff to a bare but efficient minimum. Certainly that is what the voters had in mind.

However, even if civil service had not ruled that the newly hired would be the first to be terminated, each agency would have chosen that criterion, since none of the agencies had been maintaining performance appraisals in a systematic, realistic manner. If the state had not rescued local government, preventing large numbers of layoffs, among the first to go would have been the newly trained, the minorities, and the most eager and productive.

Those agencies with a large number of employees at high rates of pay would have suffered the least. Attrition through resignations and retirements would have accounted for practically all the savings in the district attorney's office, for example, but the same situation did not apply in the public defender's office or in adult probation.

There is one interesting sidelight for those critics who feel LEAA-sponsored programs are without substance. Even in the first panic-stricken days, when all programs were being scrutinized, no locally absorbed programs in criminal justice agencies that had originated with LEAA seed money were eliminated.[12] As might be expected, existing LEAA grants, bringing in 90 percent Federal and five percent state money at a minimal local cost, were retained.

Interagency Reaction

Because this writer was studying and encouraging improvement of criminal justice from a system approach, she particularly sought evidence of the recognition of a system concept. The influx of state funds prevented the financial disaster from actually occurring as projected. It may also have turned the crisis into enough of a period of normalcy that the kind of utopian cooperation that occurs in times of disaster was aborted.

For example, in the first budget-cutting days, the communication between the municipal and the superior courts increased. The need for the two separate bodies in the judicial branch of government to support each other reinforced itself during the days of crisis, then quickly disappeared.

In spite of the increased exchange of information, each court still did not see itself acting other than unilaterally. Both courts decided to eliminate the payment of overtime by reducing the public hours their clerk's offices would remain open. This would give clerks time to finish their work during regular working hours. Independently, the superior court chose to remain open from 8:30 A.M. to 4:00 P.M., while the municipal court hours changed to 8:00 A.M. to 4:30 P.M. No attempt was made to coordinate the hours for the convenience of the public.

The entire budget process had always been predicated on examination of individual agency presentations; there had been no recognition that a major change in one part of the criminal justice process impacts on the other parts. If the budget staff or the city officials considered the probable effect of leaving the police force intact, while sharply reducing personnel in district attorney, public defender, probation, and sheriff staffs, they ignored it. The media is so strident about the crime problem, the perception of a fearful public is so strong, and the Police Association is so powerful, that few politicians will offer the police anything but support. Only the mayor dared to suggest that savings should be sought in police budgets as well as in others.

There was no evidence that agencies entertained the possibility of presenting the supervisors with a unified approach to the budget presentations. None tried to explain the possible impact such unbalanced funding might have on the criminal justice system.

The tendency to use economy as an excuse for effecting a difficult-to-implement decision made prior to Proposition 13 has been mentioned before. It surfaced in a number of different agencies.

The court management system (CMS) is a computer calendaring system supported and shared by all the criminal justice agencies. The municipal court resented its job of entering certain information it considered the responsibility of the district attorney. The court informed the CMS policy committee,[13] it could no longer afford to do the task, and it was, in fact, taken over by the district attorney.

The public defender, who had tried before, renewed his attempts to withdraw from CMS, explaining that his personnel were of higher priority. In this case, the rest of the agencies refused to cooperate and informed the public defender they would oppose his action, since their agencies would have to make up the monetary difference.

On the other hand, when the municipal court at first appeared to be in danger of losing most of their data entry clerks, the other agencies offered to assist with transfer of funds. The difference in attitude was due, in part, to the heavy reliance on municipal court information and, in part, because of good interagency relationships previously established by the municipal court.

JUDICIAL REACTION TO PROPOSITION 13

The judiciary in San Francisco and in California had long resisted a trend, discernible in other states, towards state financing of the courts. The state funds the salaries of all superior court judges, the salaries of all appellate court judges, and all expenses of appellate courts. Superior, municipal, and justice courts are almost entirely locally supported.

The governor had previously criticized the judiciary, advocating consolidation and state financing, and it was generally thought that the chief justice, as his appointee, agreed. The judicial council, the administrative office of the courts, and the California Judges Association, all of whom have responsibilities for statewide coordination of the courts, either were silent or against the issue of court reform that relied on state funding or centralized administration.

Literally overnight, judicial attitudes in San Francisco and the state did a turnabout. In the face of apparent loss of operating funds, the Judges Association and the judicial council hastily called executive meetings and voted to endorse the concept of state financing.

No prior planning had been done as to what form this might take, and no legislation was ready to be presented. Although the chief justice appeared before the legislature with a temporary plan, the issue was too complex and the need too demanding in other areas, to be undertaken in the frantic post–Proposition 13 legislative session.

Once it was apparent that the state would supply needed funding, the pressure for state funding evaporated, and the judiciary returned to its former resistant posture.[14]

Although this example of people having to recant their former dedication to local control in the face of loss of local funding is the only one readily apparent within the criminal justice field, the same type of renunciation happened within the education, welfare, and public health fields.

CONCLUSIONS

Observations of local governmental and criminal justice agency actions in San Francisco immediately following passage of Proposition 13 indicate the following:

1. Local government reactions to the crisis followed patterns that have been evidenced in communities struck with natural disasters.
2. Although there were instances of interagency cooperation, the crisis did not inspire any coordinated movement of criminal justice agencies to work together for the maintenance of the system.
3. Previously held attitudes and social relationships provided guidelines for difficult decisions. New coalitions held only during the period of extreme crisis.
4. LEAA-initiated city funded programs and LEAA-funded grants were not seen as a source of savings but were retained by criminal justice agencies.
5. Proposition 13 was used as an excuse for attempting to effect changes that had previously been advanced or contemplated.
6. When the dust had settled, the criminal justice system received about a ten percent cut, with the exception of the police department, which took a one percent cut. In general, reductions were

paid for by attrition (positions not being filled), and by the loss of a salary increase for all employees, with the exception of judges.

7. The justice system, other than the police, was hurt less than recreation and culture, but equally or more than any of the other general classifications within city government.

8. The intent of the law, as expressed by the voters, which was to cut "waste" and "fat," and improve efficiency, did not immediately succeed, at least in San Francisco city government. Civil service regulations and supervisory reluctance prevented selective dismissals. Instead, the uncertainty of local financing hastened the retirement of long-term personnel, encouraged the movement of professionals to private industry, and discouraged the entry of career-minded young people into government.

9. City government and the criminal justice system were hobbled but not severely crippled by the first year reductions. City employees took the full brunt of the cuts, essentially working at reduced wages in a period of high inflation.

10. It was the children of San Francisco who sustained the biggest first-year loss. Because the state formulas favored San Francisco city government but penalized the school district, the school system did not receive a high amount of state bailout money. The summer school program was essentially eliminated; fall classes opened to fewer schools, fewer teachers, reduced staff and reduced programs.

11. Although city officials breathed a collective sigh of relief when state monies replaced loss of local funds, there was recognition that the state had only postponed, not eliminated, Proposition 13's inevitable impact. The whole story could not begin to be told in the first thirty days nor in its first year; its effect was yet to come.

TWO YEARS LATER: UPDATE
AS OF MAY, 1980

Because wholesale firings and dramatic stoppages of service did not occur immediately after the passage of Proposition 13, the public has been largely unaware of the amendment's impact in San Francisco. There has been a slow erosion of services too gradual and disbursed to attract attention. The criminal justice agencies (with the exception of the police) are currently experiencing the effect of two successive 10 percent cuts, resulting in an approximate 32 percent reduction since 1977–78. Accounting for amounts that must go for annual employee raises and soaring inflation costs means that departments have "real" operating budgets with reductions of 40 percent or more.

Although budget savings through personnel attrition protect the employee and are hidden from the public, they are painful to the agency. Shortages are beginning to be felt; a recent large jailbreak blamed by the sheriff on the fact that his custody staff is well below minimum standards is but one example.

City government presently faces a $126.6 million deficit. Over and above the amount of last year's (1979–80) budget are the following mandatory expenses: salary standardization increases, $42 million; open space, $2.3 million; retirement rate increases, $13 million; inflation-caused costs of operating the Muni Railway, $19 million;[15] and costs of a settlement in a police minority discrimination suit, $5.4 million.[16] These, coupled with a projected $44.9 million decline in general fund revenue, and an unforeseen drop in interest payments[17] puts the city in a serious financial position.

The mayor and the board have placed four revenue-raising measures on the June 3 budget, three of which will require a two-thirds majority vote. Since the city charter requires a balanced budget, if the propositions do not pass, the extremely severe cuts threatened in 1978 may become a reality in 1980. Once again, San Francisco awaits a vote to determine if it will again be saved from a disaster.

NOTES

1. At the time, only the court filing function of the county clerk's office was subject to the jurisdiction of the superior court. A charter change on July 1, 1979, put all functions of the office under supervision of the court.
2. The organization contracts with the city to perform O.R. services. Half the funds are in the superior court budget; half in the municipal court budget.
3. Since the passage of Proposition 13, the budget process has been extended. Because the state share is uncertain until late in the fiscal year, the budget is passed close to the June 30th deadline.
4. City and County of San Francisco, *Consolidated Budget and Annual Appropriation Ordinance. Fiscal Year Ending June 30, 1979.*
5. Prior to the state bailout, the budgets presented here included some federal and state grants, but predominately were ad valorem funds. A separate city budget, consisting of federal and state funds only, was never in question.
6. Total budgets of the criminal justice agencies have been combined under the category of justice system. It was found to be impossible to separate criminal from civil expenses, which include such costs as the civil clerk's offices in the courts, mental health representation by the public defender, eviction actions by sheriff's deputies, and so forth.

7. In August 1979, in response to a California supreme court opinion that found that government had erred in not granting wage increases according to salary standardization requirements, the city returned the equivalent of seven months 1979–79 salary increases to its employees. A suit is still pending asking the city to pay employees the remaining five-month equivalencies.

8. Harry E. Moore, *Tornadoes Over Texas: A Study of Waco and San Angelo in Disaster* (Austin: University of Texas Press, 1958); James B. Taylor, Louis A. Zurcher, and William H. Key, *Tornado: A Community Responds to Disaster* (Seattle: University of Washington, 1970).

9. The Muni Railway operates the city diesel buses, electric buses, streetcars, and cable cars.

10. Supervisor Dianne Feinstein led the fight for the fare increase at that time. In 1980, as mayor, she was finally successful in getting the fare increase passed by the board.

11. Resignation of the previous sheriff to take a new position allowed the mayor to make an appointment until the upcoming 1979 election.

12. One LEAA-initiated program was terminated by the San Francisco school board. *Basic Skills,* a project which provided junior high school age youngsters with an alternative education at community sites, had been supported by school funds in 1977–78 and been continued for 1978–79. It was eliminated in the revised September 1978–79 budget.

13. The policy committee, composed of a representative from each of the criminal justice agencies, supervises the administration of the CMS system by the city data processing division.

14. In the 1978–79 session, a bill for consolidation of locally funded superior and municipal courts failed, due primarily to judicial opposition.

15. Net amount after calculating projected revenue from farebox increases.

16. In November 1978, the city signed a consent decree with the Officers for Justice, a group of black police officers, who had accused the police department of discrimination. The agreement required the city to hire 300 minority police officers over a period of two years.

17. The controller reports a decrease of $9 million in annual interest payments, due to lower cash reserves held by the city, and to a long lag period between outlays by the city and reimbursement by the state for grant projects.

APPENDIX: TIMETABLE OF PROPOSITION 13 EVENTS IN SAN FRANCISCO AND THE STATE

June 6
State voters approve Proposition 13. San Francisco is the only major city or county to defeat it, voting: 104,000 No; 93,000 Yes.

June 7
City officials and employees go into a state of shock. The mood in city offices is one of deepest gloom. There is talk of nothing else; rumors abound. $7 billion state wide tax

loss is hoped to be alleviated by $4 billion state surplus.

June 8

Lawsuits are filed challenging the constitutionality of Proposition 13. Governor orders a freeze on state hiring. Mayor says that although 5,000 city jobs may be lost, "San Francisco has risen from the ashes before."

June 9

Mayor tells department heads they have option of reducing the work week or the number of employees within their departments, asks cooperation in creating new budget in period of three weeks. Board of supervisors designates its finance committee as a special unit to implement Proposition 13, calling it the select committee. Expecting loss of accumulated sick pay, 300 city employees apply for early retirement; among them are 40 police officers, including 6 captains (one-third of the department's captains). The governor announces the state surplus is actually $5 billion.

June 12

Mayor's official declaration of a state of fiscal emergency is approved by the board of supervisors. Declaration includes: 1) repeal of salary increases; 2) authority to department heads to lay off personnel and cut back work hours; 3) deferring of vacation and sick leave payments due city employees on retirement; 4) suspension of charter sections and administrative codes that earmark portions of property tax revenues, putting them in general fund instead; and 5) raising of Muni fees. Muni Railway (public transit) announces proposed 20 percent cut in service and boost in fares.

June 13

Supervisors' select committee starts hearings. Protests begin over proposed closing of five district health centers, layoffs of city personnel and increases in Muni Railway fares. Governor suggests giving $4 billion of state surplus to local governments and schools.

June 14

All summer programs in public schools and community colleges are cancelled with exception of a few remedial classes. Select committee anticipates city will receive approximately $50 million from state in "bailout" money.

June 15

In near panic, government officials and workers beseech legislature for tax assistance. State surplus is now set at $4.5 million. The mayor and president of board of supervisors ask state to absorb $8.1 million to finance courts, plus $124.2 million for health and welfare. The state judicial council, plus contingent of 11 judges, asks state to finance trial courts, at 1978 cost of $319 million, gets little sympathy from legislative committee. Select committee votes to recommend 30.8 percent cut in adult probation, first agency to testify. After listening all day to agency heads presenting proposals for reduced budgets, committee changes procedure in mid-stream, adopting worst-case budget as a base, and letting departments request needed additions if funds become available. A doomsday mood pervades city offices as employees hear that worst-case budget has been adopted.

June 16

Civil service commission, failing to placate unions or minorities, adopts layoff rules giving special protection to employees on payroll five years or more; after those, the rule is: last hired, first fired, by job category within each department.

June 19

Board of supervisors passes ordinances expected to provide $28.4 million, by raising: 1) gross receipts and parking taxes from 15 to 25 percent; 2) employers' payroll tax from 1.1 to 1.5 percent; 3) real estate transfer tax from .5 to 1.5 percent. Select committee begins to restore previously reduced agency budgets.

June 20   Legislature promises police and fire departments will get "top priority" in state aid. Republicans want guarantee of full financing but Democrats succeed in giving local authorities flexibility to cut "fat" where it exists.

June 22   Crocker Bank full-page ad urges governments to release persons with skills easily transferrable to private industry and try to keep teachers, policemen, and firemen whose skills are unique. The state Bar Association releases report on court improvement, designed to save money. Recommendations include doubling civil filing fees, eliminating juror fees, pooling bailiffs, and having litigants pay court reporter fees.

June 23   Legislature compromises on $5 billion rescue package, $4.1 billion in direct cash relief and $900 million in short-term emergency loans. City and county employee raises are tied to percentage allowed state employees, which in bill is 2.5 percent.

June 24   Emergency aid bill signed by Governor allots relief dollars to be distributed according to each jurisdiction's losses.

June 26   Board gets news from Sacramento that San Francisco will receive an unexpected windfall: $50 million in takeover of social service costs plus an additional $50 million in relief monies. In holiday atmosphere, supervisors increase agency monies to 95 percent of former budget. Board passes $823.9 million budget, keeps Muni fare increase, kills one tax but keeps the other two while deferring collection for one year.

June 27

Board changes its mind and kills all new taxes. At mayor's request, the Muni fare hike is nullified.

June 28

Dismissal notices are sent to 77 public works employees, 45 health department workers, six in various departments. Other departments stop filling vacancies. Petition drive to recall mayor and board, because they are not carrying out intent of Proposition 13, soon fizzles.

June 30

Faced with no summer school and elimination of 11 teachers, juvenile court mobilizes volunteers from colleges and their own staff to maintain program. Judges get scheduled five percent pay increases as bill to cancel them is defeated. The president of the Judges Association says, "Bear in mind we have been living under a freeze since September, 1976. We kind of think we paid our dues to Proposition 13 in advance." The formula used by the state penalizes the San Francisco school district; its 16 percent cut is the highest in the state. The school board adopts a budget that freezes salaries, closes 11 schools, eliminates 938 jobs (primarily substitute and nonpermanent teachers). Half of central administrative staff returns to classrooms. Construction and equipment funds are cut 63 percent; administrators' salaries are down 25 percent. Hidden Valley Center, juvenile minimum security facility, closes. Six juveniles are sent to a more secure facility; 50 are released and sent home. Fees double at the Zoo and at all museums.

July 1

Proposition 13 takes effect. State legislature, still fighting over state budget, adds monies for child care programs and the deaf, cuts increases for mentally ill and retarded.

July 6

Governor signs budget but vetoes salary raise for state employees which, in effect, eliminates salary raises for local government employees; vetoes 2.5 percent cost-of-living increases for AFDC; keeps 3.7 percent increase for aged, blind, disabled because these are paid by federal funds.

Chapter 7

The Impact of Proposition 13 on Local Criminal Justice Agencies: Emerging Patterns

*Warren E. Walker, Jan Michael Chaiken,
Anthony P. Jiga, and Sandra Segal Polin**

INTRODUCTION

Proposition 13 and the State Bailout

Proposition 13 was a citizen initiative, approved by the voters in June 1978, that reduced property taxes in California by amending the state constitution. The main provisions of the amendment follow.

This chapter was prepared under Grant Number 78-NI-AX-0155 from the National Institute of Justice, U.S. Department of Justice. Points of view or opinions stated in this document are those of the authors and do not necessarily represent the official position or policies of the U.S. Department of Justice.

The authors wish to express their gratitude to a large number of people for helping them with their study. The information in the chapter is drawn in large part from over sixty interviews with persons who are closely related to California's criminal justice system, both inside government and outside. The issues covered in our study were developed with the guidance of a twelve-member advisory panel. We wish that we could thank them all individually, but space precludes this. At the National Institute of Justice, encouragement and support for this work was provided by Joseph Kochanski and W. Robert Burkhart.
*The Rand Corporation, Santa Monica, California

The value of residential, commercial, and business property for tax purposes was rolled back to 1975–76 market values, except for property that was sold, changed ownership, or was constructed after 1975.

Property values were permitted to increase at no more than 2 percent per year to reflect inflation.

The total property tax on any property was limited to 1 percent of its value, except that additions were permitted to cover indebtedness previously approved by the voters.

Imposition of new or higher taxes (other than property taxes) was made more difficult.

Since the average property tax rate was reduced by more than half (from 2.67 percent in the year before Proposition 13 to 1.2 percent in the year afterward) and property values in 1978 were substantially higher than they had been in 1975, Proposition 13 reduced property tax revenue to California's local governments by an estimated 60 percent, or $7 billion out of anticipated revenue of $11.4 billion.

If the local governments had been forced to absorb this entire revenue loss, the impact would have been substantial—about a 23 percent decrease in their expected total revenue. However, the state government bailed out the local governments with a combination of two fiscal relief mechanisms that reduced their losses by $4.1 billion. First, the state took over certain state-mandated expenses previously borne by counties. Second, it provided block grants to schools, cities, counties, and special districts.[1] The state's source of funding for the bailout was a large accumulated surplus whose existence, together with confusing and erroneous predictions of its size, had contributed to the passage of Proposition 13.

Because of the state's bailout and increases in revenues other than property taxes, total California local government revenues actually increased slightly in the year after Proposition 13, and by drawing down on reserves, local government expenditures increased even more. However, after adjustment for the high rate of inflation, the average local government experienced a real loss in revenue. Moreover, the fiscal situation after passage of Proposition 13 stood in sharp contrast to the steady increase in real revenue to which many (but not all) local governments had been accustomed.

Research Focus

Because the fiscal effects of Proposition 13 on local government were small, at least in the short term, we did not expect to find major immediate changes in government services or in the impacts of those services on ultimate performance outcomes. This was especially true of the criminal justice system—the subject of our study (and the source of examples for this chapter)—since the state bailout legislation had required a continuation in the level of police programs provided by recipients of bailout funds.[2] Instead, we anticipated finding, and did find, trends and patterns that portend changes for the future.

The study paid particular attention to the following areas of change:

Patterns of expenditures and resource allocations. The types of agencies, programs, and activities that suffered the most or survived most completely in the wake of both budgetary changes and uncertainty about the future that followed the passage of Proposition 13.

Intergovernmental relations. The extent to which control over local programs shifted to the state and federal governments, and changes in the degree of cooperation among agencies—either agencies of different types (sheriff and district attorney, for example) or agencies of the same type in different jurisdictions.

Innovation and efficiency. Enhanced or degraded climate for instituting major cost-cutting improvements.

Our detailed findings about each of these subject areas are presented elsewhere [9]. In this chapter we present general observations from our research. While the data we have brought to bear, and nearly all of our examples, are drawn from the criminal justice system, we believe that many of the emerging trends identified here apply as well to other functions of local government. We cite related studies that suggest, either empirically or theoretically, the general applicability of some of our statements. In some instances we have speculatively mentioned trends that seem likely to arise, even though no clear evidence for them has yet appeared in our work or that of others. Limitations of the study's scope and methods prevent us from asserting any more than that the trends we see are worthy of more careful attention and research.

In general, the picture is not an encouraging one. With some notable exceptions, we did not find local government grappling with resource allocation problems nor focusing expenditures on the highest priority activities. Instead we found:

Attempts to apply short-term solutions to long-term problems.
An exodus of some of the best people from local government, a lowered sense of dedication and reduced morale among those remain-

ing, and increased difficulties in attracting high quality replacements.

A growing influence of the state and federal governments over local government activities.

A growing conflict between local government autonomy and the mandates and dictates of higher level governments.

Changes in the goals and objectives of the criminal justice system.

These five general findings are discussed in the following five major sections of this chapter. Before that, however, is a brief description of the types of information we collected for this study.

Research Methods

The study was basically a reconnaissance effort, intended more to identify the major trends and consequences of fiscal limitation than to produce a comprehensive, statistically reliable portrait of changes throughout the state.

In order to develop insights into the types of changes that were likely to occur, we selected for careful examination a small number of jurisdictions that we believed would display a wide range of representative responses to property tax limitation. The jurisdictions selected for study included four primary counties (Alameda, Los Angeles, Kings, and San Joaquin) and two secondary counties (San Diego and San Francisco). Within each primary county we selected three or four cities as study sites, including the largest city, as listed in Table 7–1.[3]

In all of the study counties (whether primary or secondary), the research team tracked developments related to fiscal limitation through published sources such as newspapers, public opinion polls, and studies that were conducted locally. In the primary counties, the project team carried out the following two additional activities:

Analyzed budgetary changes in the county government, in the countywide criminal justice agencies (district attorney, public defender, sheriff, courts, county clerk, probation, and any criminal justice planning or coordinating agencies), in the selected city governments, and in the city criminal justice agencies (police and city attorney).

Interviewed over 60 key people inside and outside the system, such as criminal justice agency administrators, private providers of diversion services, union leaders. The interviews were semistructured, following a detailed list of research questions within the various subject areas (resource allocations, intergovernmental relations, personnel, and so on). Not every topic was covered in every interview, but the interviewer's notes were transcribed into a

Table 7–1. **Primary Study Sites**

County	City
Alameda	Oakland
	Fremont
	Piedmont
	San Leandro
Los Angeles	Los Angeles
	Compton
	Hawthorne
	Cerritos
Kings	Hanford
	Corcoran
	Lemoore
San Joaquin	Stockton
	Lodi
	Manteca

uniform format that facilitated comparison of comments by different people on a given topic. All the interviews were conducted during the fiscal year that followed passage of Proposition 13 (July 1978 to June 1979).

The discussion in the sections that follow draws on these budgetary analyses and interviews as well as on published data and reports that apply to other counties or the state as a whole.

SHORT-TERM SOLUTIONS TO LONG-TERM PROBLEMS

A shock to the local government system such as that provided by Proposition 13 can turn out to be either a crisis to be weathered with politically expedient changes in organization, management, and delivery of services, or an opportunity to make innovative changes in the system that would have been more difficult to implement without the shock. In fact, many people who supported Proposition 13 felt it would lead to less fat and more efficiency in government. This may yet be the long-term result, but in the short term we have seen the opposite effect: innovation and efficiency in local government have been stymied.

In the years before Proposition 13, there was no dearth of creative responses by local government to their problems. However, continued growth of the overall budget during that same period enabled local government to be innovative while avoiding hard resource allocation decisions. All services and functions could get more resources while the budget pie was expanding. Some hoped that the realities of fiscal contraction—tightened budgets, publc scrutiny, and increasing costs—might change the patterns that had prevailed during budget growth, and force local governments to face the hard choices they had previously been able to ignore. This line of reasoning suggested that local officials might rethink their priorities, reexamine the way they allocate resources, and restructure their internal organizational and operational processes.

However, research such as that by Levine [25] and Berman and McLaughlin [4] suggests that political, organizational, and systemic obstacles are likely to prevent innovative management of contraction. An important conclusion of the research is that whether fiscal contraction leads to innovation and efficiency (and whether local government services deteriorate or not) depends primarily on the way in which government bureaucrats react to their changed reality.

Based on the first year's record in California, indications are that their responses are primarily being governed by Levine's "Tooth Fairy Syndrome:"

> In the initial stages of contractions few people are willing to believe that the talk of cuts is for real or that the cuts will be permanent. The initial prevailing attitude in the organization will usually be optimistic; i.e., that the decline is temporary and the cuts will be restored soon by someone—in some cases as remote as the tooth fairy. . . . The preferred tactical response for nearly everyone is to delay taking action while waiting for someone else to volunteer cuts or for a bailout from a third party. [25, p. 181]

In California after Proposition 13, the state government played the role of tooth fairy in bailing out local government. Local government expenditures had to be reduced in real terms (adjusted for inflation), but not by very much. As a result, most local governments got through the first year by taking what seemed to be the politically expedient route, making cuts that were largely invisible to the public. These cuts generally provided short-term savings, but might lead to higher costs in the long run. They were generally the opposite of what would have been needed to promote innovation and efficiency in local government. We discuss a number of these responses below.

Equipment Purchases and Maintenance of Facilities

Deferring equipment purchases and the maintenance of facilities are prime examples of short-term savings that are likely to increase long-term costs. Because the consequences of these actions are not immediately visible, they are tempting candidates for spending cutbacks.

Although expenditures budgeted for FY 1979 by California counties increased by over 12 percent over actual FY 1978 expenditures, budgets for property management (which include custodial services, maintenance, and remodeling of facilities) declined by 0.5 percent [2]. Los Angeles County, for example, planned to delay building maintenance and alterations, and to cancel the scheduled replacement for all nonemergency county vehicles [36].

Cutbacks such as these can be carried out for a year or two without much harm. But they quickly lead to the deterioration of buildings, roads, parks, and other state property. Replacement and repair of equipment that breaks down because it was not maintained will generally cost more than what the preventive maintenance would have cost. The long-term implications of this strategy are visible in some of the older cities of this country, where the deterioration of their capital plant has been one significant factor in their loss of appeal both to business and to more affluent populations.

Planning, Research, and Innovation

Another "invisible" way in which local governments reacted to Proposition 13 was to reduce expenditures on planning and research activities, to postpone the development and implementation of management information systems, and generally to shun all innovative approaches to management that have high front-end costs. As is the case with deferred equipment purchases and facility maintenance, this approach produces short-run savings, but is more costly in the end. It is a reflection of what Levine terms "The Productivity Paradox":

> When dealing with productivity, it takes money to save money. Productivity improvement requires up front costs incurred by training and equipment expenses. Under conditions of austerity, it is very difficult to find and justify funds to invest in productivity improvement, especially if these funds can only be made available by laying off employees or failing to fill vacancies. [25, p. 181]

For example, the Los Angeles City Attorney cut his staff in the planning and research division by more than 50 percent. He explained that it was a question of weighing alternative risks. The potential costs of reducing the planning function are great, but "in the scale of priorities it is more important to prosecute than to plan programs."

In some cases, the hesitancy to implement new systems or procedures reflected reluctance to risk possible failure. However, the presiding judge of the Oakland Municipal Court predicted that even projects that would clearly result in long-term cost savings would not be adopted if there were substantial start-up costs.[4]

In addition to cuts in planning and research functions, the budgets for data processing departments and management information systems were hard hit in FY 1979 or earmarked for substantial cuts in FY 1980. The rate of attrition for data processing personnel was also higher than for most other types of personnel, since opportunities for them were plentiful in the private sector and were looked upon as being more attractive in the post–Proposition 13 world. These findings correspond to the scenario postulated by Levine:

> First, the most capable analysts are lured away by better opportunities; then freezes cripple the agency's ability to hire replacements; and finally, the remaining staff is cut in order to avoid making cuts in personnel with direct service responsibility. [25, p. 180]

An example of the type of problem encountered through loss of data processing personnel was given to us by the presiding judge of the Oakland Municipal Court. He reported that, due to the high attrition rate in Alameda County's data processing department, maintenance of the county's defendant record and court calendaring system (CORPUS) had suffered, and planned enhancements had been deferred. In addition, the system's unscheduled down time had increased, which was having a disruptive effect on the activities of the municipal courts.

In the short term, aside from some disruptions in operating systems, costs in planning, research, and information system functions are reduced with no reduction in direct services to the public. However, these reductions mean that the data needed for effective problem identification, planning, and management are not available; that new planning tools are not being developed or used; that talented personnel who could suggest long-term solutions are not being retained or kept knowledgeable; and that innovative responses to fiscal constraints are unlikely to be forthcoming.

These outcomes are likely in spite of the fact that local government officials have become aware that they need better planning and budgeting systems for dealing with the problems presented by fiscal contraction. For example, officials in the city of Los Angeles admitted that many of their workload and personnel problems in FY 1979 could have been avoided if they had had a better understanding of the process of attrition and its implications for budgeting and workload management.

Some changes in budgetary practices did take place in each of the counties studied. The changes made, however, were crisis-oriented—temporizing measures to permit rational decision making by budget officers in the face of uncertain FY 1979 and FY 1980 revenues, rather than a means of making permanent improvements in the budgeting process or the financing of local government. In Oakland, for example, the city manager for the first time ranked all programs so that he could present to the city council a set of priorities for choosing budget reductions.

In our interviews, we specifically asked about innovations and procedures to increase efficiency, but found very few. Those that we did find were generally minor and unrelated to Proposition 13, although its passage acted as a catalyst for the adoption and implementation of most of them. For example:

> The cities in Kings County, together with cities in a neighboring county, inaugurated a self-insurance program for general liability claims that should result in a significant reduction in insurance costs.
> In the Stockton Police Department, investigators began tape recording their reports rather than writing them out. The Alameda County Probation Department adopted a shortened presentence investigation form.
> The Manteca Police Department eliminated some "unnecessary" internal reports and shortened several others.

Some proponents of Proposition 13 believed that the private sector could provide services more efficiently than the public sector, and they anticipated increased reliance on contracts with private firms for provision of governmental services. We found that fiscal limitation did provide an impetus for at least experimenting with contracted services, but government officials have been very cautious about actually turning services over to the private sector. For example, the voters in Los Angeles County approved a charter amendment sponsored by the board of supervisors that permits certain types of contracts with private firms, but very few contracts have actually been awarded.

Contracts that survive the review process and are actually awarded tend to be unquestionably cost-effective. The following are typical examples of cost-cutting transfers to the private sector:

> The city of Cerritos dropped its contract with the county of Los Angeles for sewer maintenance and contracted with a private firm for the same services at a much lower price.

Two private credit collection agencies are under contract to the Los
Angeles County Department of Health Services to collect delinquent bills [6].

Numerous contracts have been awarded for maintenance of land-
scapes, parks, and recreation areas.

However, many recommendations for contracts related to the criminal
justice system were unsuccessful. For example, the Los Angeles County Contract Services Advisory Committee recommendation that the
county should contract with private firms instead of using sheriff's
deputies and county employees to provide protection for its facilities
and buildings was not adopted. Functions included in criminal system
budgets, but peripheral to the system's operations, may be more amenable to contracting. In Los Angeles County, a probation department
proposal that a private food vendor take over food services at its juvenile hall was accepted.

Some instances of budget reduction appear to bring about nearly
automatic increases in dependence on the private sector, but if they
are not cost-effective they tend to be short lived. For example, as
workloads of the public defender increase, additional cases are assigned to private counsel for defense. If the fees offered to the private attorneys are lower than the cost of the public defender (as
happened in Kings County), then the quality of indigent defense
may be unacceptably low, leading to a need to reverse the situation.
If the fees of private counsel are high, the reduced budget for the
public defender's office does not actually save costs overall, a matter
that is readily observed in the next budget cycle. After the passage
of Proposition 13, Los Angeles County cut the number of budgeted
positions in the public defender's office by 36. The next year's budget
showed a restoration of 26 of these positions, accompanied by a
statement that "the cost for these positions will be more than offset
by . . . avoidance of the need for court appointment of private counsel
at a high cost to the County."

Overall, our interviews seem to substantiate the fact that innovation and efficiency in local government have come upon hard times.
This may be a temporary phenomenon that resulted from the uncertainty surrounding continuation of the state's bailout of local government. If so, stabilization of revenue sources—permitting projection of
future revenue—could potentially reverse this situation. The political
climate does not portend such stability in the near future. California
governments may have set themselves on a path that will make future innovation more difficult.

IMPACTS ON PERSONNEL

State and local government employment mushroomed after World War II. [31] In 1949, state and local governments in the United States employed 9.5 percent of all nonagricultural civilian employees. By 1969 this figure had risen to 13.8 percent. Average real compensation for these employees grew about 13 percent faster over this same period than it did for employees in the private sector. As a result, while state and local government compensation for full-time employees was below that of the employees in the private sector in 1949, it had achieved parity with the private sector by 1969. This, coupled with better job security than offered by the private sector, made public employment increasingly attractive.

Growth in state and local government employment began to moderate in the 1970s. For example, municipal government employment, which had been growing at an average annual rate of 3.2 percent between 1962 and 1972, grew at an average rate of less than 1 percent per year between 1972 and 1976. Thus, even without Proposition 13, government was no longer a growth industry. With fiscal limitation measures like Proposition 13, forces arise to prevent compensation of state and local government employees from keeping pace with that in the private sector. Moreover, two factors specifically related to the implementation of Proposition 13 had impacts on government personnel in California. These factors were:

The elimination of cost-of-living increases in the first year's bailout legislation. (This provision was later declared unconstitutional by the state Supreme Court.)

Hiring freezes imposed by many governments.

These developments convinced many local government employees that the gains they had made over the last few decades were now being eroded. They saw uncertainty over job security; smaller increases in salaries and benefits; reduced chances for advancement; deteriorating working conditions (including an increase in workloads and a decrease in clerical support for professional staff); and a decline in the prestige of their jobs and in their job satisfaction.

If this decline in morale were to continue for a substantial period, state and local government could face serious problems in the future. For example, administrators claimed that many of the best people in government were leaving. These were primarily skilled people such as nurses, computer programmers, attorneys, and legal secretaries, who had better opportunities in the private sector. The quality of their replacements (and even those for less skilled positions) appeared to be declining. The Alameda County Administrator observed a lowered sense of dedication among county employees. The Oakland police chief claimed that declining morale had a more deleterious effect on the operations of his department than the loss of positions. There was an increased militancy among workers, including a greater tendency to participate in job actions, and less of a public service orientation.

In the following sections we examine some of these trends in more detail, using information gathered in our interviews and from newspaper articles and published reports.

Layoffs

One of the major arguments used by opponents of Proposition 13 was that its passage would force local governments to lay off massive numbers of employees. Early predictions of 500,000 firings were common. Local governments prepared "doomsday" budgets calling for large reductions in staffing levels. Los Angeles County's proposed budget for FY 1979, for example, which was presented to the Board of Supervisors just prior to passage of Proposition 13, called for a 36 percent reduction in the number of employees.

As a result of the state's bailout, local governments did not have to make massive cutbacks in personnel. The cutbacks that were required were generally made by imposing a hiring freeze and letting attrition take its course. Thus, layoffs accounted for only a small fraction of the estimated 100,000 state and local government positions lost during FY 1979. And almost all of the layoffs occurred in the first few months after the passage of Proposition 13. In Los Angeles County, the number of employees dropped by over 4000 between June and December 1978. However, there were fewer than 300 layoffs (less than 0.4 percent of its work force).

With but one exception, our interviews revealed that layoffs were based on strict seniority within a classification. In those agencies forced to lay off relatively large numbers of employees, the seniority rule was regarded as the least painful criterion, and the one most amenable to use in a crisis, when decisions had to be made quickly. It also had the widest acceptance among employees. The Alameda County District Attorney is the only agency in one of our study sites whose employees were exempted by the county charter from civil service seniority protection. Although he used this freedom, the district attorney viewed it as a mixed blessing. It was not easy to lay off or force retirement of older employees who were not as productive as employees with less seniority.

Officially, none of the agencies we surveyed reported a disproportionate impact on minorities and women resulting from the agencies'
reductions. But according to the Alameda County probation employees association, there was disproportionate impact on their ability to
serve Chicano clients, due to the layoff of Spanish-speaking
employees.

Attrition

The clearest sign of a change in the desirability of employment in
state and local government was the increased attrition of employees.
Public employment in California had been increasing by 3 to 5 percent
per year between 1973 and 1978. In the first year after Proposition 13,
public employment dropped by 7 percent—a loss of approximately
100,000 government positions. As noted above, layoffs were practically nil. Most of the reduction in filled positions was due to the combined
effects of rapid attrition and hiring freezes.

During the first few months after the passage of Proposition 13, res-
ignation-retirement rates were twice the pre–Proposition 13 level.
The reasons for attrition cited most often by the managers we interviewed were perceived job insecurity and limited prospects for future
pay increases and promotions. Increased workloads were not an important factor, although anticipation of greater workloads in the future may have contributed to the decisions of some persons to leave.

The most dramatic manifestation of increased attrition in the criminal justice system that we noted was the movement of clerical staff out
of law and justice agencies. Legal stenographers, in particular, are being sorely missed by their former employers, who are unable to compete with private law firms paying significantly higher salaries.
Replacements have been hired, but they generally lack the experience
of those who left. The impact of this loss is reflected in delays in the
preparation of briefs and other legal documents, and the "borrowing"
of senior administrative secretaries to perform line duties.

Attorneys with two or more years of experience left public law offices at higher rates than usual. For example, in June 1978, the Contra Costa District Attorney's office had 61 lawyers. Because vacancies
were not being filled, the staff of prosecutors was down to 50 by March
1980. [48] According to a number of prosecutors and defenders, attitudes are returning to those of earlier years when employment in a
public law office lacked sufficient prestige to encourage good attorneys
to make a career out of such employment. Once again they may remain with a public office only long enough to gain trial experience
before moving to the private sector. There is a concern now that the

increased attrition will result in a lack of "depth" in the offices of the public defender and district attorney. That is, there may be only a small cadre of capable senior attorneys between those recently hired and the managers at the top. It is the senior attorneys who handle most felonies and other difficult cases.

Attrition varied greatly among police and sheriff departments. The rate of attrition in the Los Angeles Police Department was much greater than anticipated by command personnel, who had estimated the size of the force after Proposition 13 by assuming normal attrition and a hiring freeze. Attrition was also very high in the San Diego Sheriff's Department and Police Department. The Piedmont Police Department, which for years has had a high turnover due to low salaries and benefits, experienced an even higher attrition rate the year after Proposition 13. The Oakland Police Department lost one-fifth of its criminal investigation staff.

In contrast, police departments in smaller cities that were not so dependent on property tax did not experience increased attrition. The department in San Leandro, a city of 70,000, which is in such an enviable state of fiscal soundness that it was able to deposit its bailout check in the bank to use as a contingency for the future, actually experienced a *decline* in attrition after the passage of Proposition 13. The police chief attributes this to a perception on the part of his employees that the city is financially well off. Employees can look forward not only to job security, but also to continued moderate salary increases, he said.

Early retirements account for a significant share of the increased police officer attrition. In Los Angeles, early retirements from the sergeant level and above were cited as the main component of the heightened attrition rate. Increased frequency of early retirements was also noted in San Diego. Now, instead of recruits being supervised and trained by senior officers, "what you've got is probationers training probationers," according to a sergeant in the San Diego Police Department [40]. The effects of inexperience remain to be seen, the sergeant added. In many jurisdictions, a burst of early retirements preceded the passage of Proposition 13. This was caused by concern among police officers that changes in their pension plans would be made if Proposition 13 were passed.

Who were the employees who resigned or retired early from local criminal justice agencies in the wake of Proposition 13, and where did they go? Many of those who resigned—including legal secretaries, attorneys, and computer programmers—had skills that were readily transferable to the private sector. However, it was the impression of the managers with whom we spoke that most of the police officers, deputy sheriffs, and probation officers went into occupations in the private sector totally unrelated to the professions they left. For example, a lieutenant in the personnel office of the San Diego Sheriff was quoted as saying "one deputy quit to become an airline pilot. Another left to operate a delicatessen. A lot of guys are just getting soured on law enforcement in general." [47] Those who retired were generally the more experienced employees in the various agencies. Thus, the attrition that followed the passage of Proposition 13 drained many criminal justice agencies of their most skilled and experienced personnel.

The above-average attrition experienced by state and local government agencies just before and just after the passage of Proposition 13 had tapered off by the end of 1978. In addition, the complete or partial hiring freezes that had been imposed were generally lifted by the end of FY 1978. As a result, many criminal justice agencies (with the notable exception of probation) ended FY 1978 with only small reductions in staff (although a larger proportion were younger and less experienced).

Recruitment and Advancement

Although one might expect that agencies whose employees were departing in abnormally large numbers might have some difficulty in attracting high quality replacements, in the short term such problems did not often occur in criminal justice agencies. Most police departments reported an ample supply of people wanting to become officers. In fact, the Manteca Police Department had so many qualified officers from other departments seeking employment that it did not anticipate hiring any inexperienced recruits in the foreseeable future. Similarly, officials in public law offices expressed little concern over their ability to attract capable young attorneys. Since the number of newly graduating attorneys exceeded the employment opportunities for them, and most of them desired trial experience, it was not difficult to fill open positions for assistant district attorneys and public defenders. The officials we interviewed expressed concern primarily with the implications of attrition for the overall quality of their staff. They anticipated that the best of the recruits would remain in public employment for the shortest period of time.

We also did not observe severe limitations on promotional opportunities in the criminal justice agencies we studied. Since attrition rates were fairly high among employees eligible for retirement, numerous supervisory or management level positions were opening. In agencies where this was not the case, management sought opportunities to reward exceptional performance by means other than promotion, for example by instituting merit increases within grades. However, despite the dearth of immediate restrictions on personnel advancement, the perception of most government employees seemed to be that promotional opportunities would definitely decrease in the future, and this was a consideration for some of them leaving their jobs.

Decline in Public Employee Working Conditions and Prestige

Since the workloads of most criminal justice agencies are externally generated (crime reports, arrestees, court cases, probationers to be supervised), reductions in staff sizes naturally resulted in increased work per employee. In the Contra Costa County District Attorney's office, mentioned above, the average lawyer handled 450 cases in the year before Proposition 13 was passed, and 550 cases in the year after. Many agencies were forced to increase the span of supervisory control, too. The number of probation officers under the control of a single supervisor increased from 7 to 9 in San Diego County, from 7 to 10 in San Mateo County, and from 6.5 to 8 in San Bernardino County [45, p. 60]

In addition to handling a larger volume of cases, employees more frequently found themselves doing work outside of their normal range of responsibilities. The employees association of the Alameda County Probation Department filed a grievance, alleging that a number of supervisors now expect the line staff to "cover for them." A chief assistant district attorney observed that his administrative responsibilities were being neglected because he had to handle trials of cases dropped by attorneys who left his office.

Other indications of deterioration in working conditions included less satisfactory support services, such as secretarial and data processing, and the necessity to reschedule or even postpone vacations in order to handle the increased amount of work. Signs of increased strain among employees were readily noticeable. The chairwoman of the Los Angeles City Council's Police, Fire and Public Safety Committee said she was receiving an increasing number of complaints from citizens about poor treatment from the police. "It probably is the fact that our officers are uptight," she said. "Many of them are discouraged" [33].

Many local government employees have perceived a loss of prestige in public service jobs. Typical of their feelings is a complaint voiced by the Alameda County Superior Court Administrator whose neighbors cannot understand what he does or why he is needed. Those people who do acknowledge the necessity of his position fail to see it in equivalent private sector management terms; they think he should be paid significantly less than his current salary. But the administrator believes he could readily get a job in the private sector at a salary 50 percent higher than he now receives. Others expressed similar complaints: "It's embarrassing to say in social circles that one works for the government," a budget analyst in Los Angeles County told us. And other researchers have concluded: "Not too many workers or job seekers are likely to feel overly enthusiastic about employment that so often is associated in the public mind with waste, inefficiency, and ineffectiveness." [45, p. 62]

Some jurisdictions have reacted to Proposition 13 by cutting back on training and limiting attendance at conferences. However, one yardstick of the professionalism of an agency that is informally used by employees is the agency's commitment to training and support for participation in professional conferences. Training and conferences give an employee a heightened sense of self worth that is often underestimated.

Labor-Management Relations

Immediately after the passage of Proposition 13, labor-management relations were temporarily but strongly influenced by the provision in the bailout legislation that prohibited cost-of-living increases for employees of local governments accepting bailout funds. Until this provision was overturned by the California Supreme Court, personnel morale plummeted and attrition skyrocketed, but labor was very docile in contract negotiations. "Apparently government workers were so intimidated then by the threat of massive layoffs that they curbed any inclination to protest the ban on pay raises" [5]. Instead, they concentrated their efforts on legal challenges to the ban, which proved successful in February 1979.

Once the court permitted local governments to award pay raises, labor organizations became much more militant and demanding. Negotiations in the summer of 1979 over contracts for fiscal year 1980 were marked by labor unrest unprecedented in recent California government experience. This development had been foreseen in the news media at the time of the court's decision [29], and was described in July 1979 as "an unprecedented number of strikes in local governments throughout the state, almost all triggered by the pent-up frustrations of Proposition 13 limitations on local government budgets" [5]. During this period, the California Highway Patrol and numerous police departments experienced sickouts, and large numbers of state and local government workers went on strike.

In Los Angeles County, sickouts encompassing 60 to 90 percent of employees were carried out by sheriff's deputies, prosecutors, and public defenders, among others. As a result, more than 400 prisoners held for minor offenses were released from county jails [23], citizens were asked to go to sheriff's stations to file certain crime reports [23], and criminal proceedings involving suspects in custody were almost all postponed [35]

Although the period of maximum labor unrest has passed, the sources of employee frustrations and militancy have not abated. As long as inflation exceeds the rate of increase in government revenues, the average employee will not be able to return to the level of compensation in real dollars that he or she received prior to the passage of Proposition 13. Under such circumstances, negotiations over salaries and benefits will necessarily be strained.

INTERGOVERNMENTAL RELATIONS

One of the most visible and immediate consequences of the passage of Proposition 13 was a change in the relative importance of the various sources of funds available to local governments. The role played by property taxes—the primary local source—became less important; revenue from state government (and, to a lesser extent, the federal government) began to play a larger role. (For example, state and federal sources accounted for 51 percent of Alameda County's budgeted revenues in FY 1978 and 70 percent in FY 1979.) Local officials are worried about the threats to local autonomy and home rule posed by this trend.[5] Below we discuss general financial and operational relationships between the state and local governments, and between the federal government and local governments. The more specific issue of federal and state mandates is treated in a later section.

Relationships among local governments, and among different agencies within them, have also been affected by Proposition 13. In many cases, interaction and cooperation have decreased. Debates and discussions about the consolidation of similar services being provided by different jurisdictions, and about the consolidation of agencies within a jurisdiction, have intensified. These relationships are treated later in this section.

Local-State Relations

Increasing State Influence. Although local government revenues showed very little change in the year after Proposition 13 was

Table 7-2. **City and County Revenues by Source**

(Millions of dollars)

Revenue Source by Recipient	Actual FY '78	Percent of Total	Budgeted FY '79	Percent of Total	Percent Change in Percentage
State					
Cities	514	9.8	815	16.0	63.3
Counties[a]	1,756	19.1	3,417	37.2	94.8
Total	2,270	15.7	4,232	29.6	88.5
Federal					
Cities	1,118	21.3	1,087	21.3	—
Counties[a]	2,273	24.8	2,416	26.3	6.0
Total	3,391	23.5	3,503	24.5	4.3
Property Taxes					
Cities	1,177	22.4	526	10.3	−54.0
Counties[a]	3,358	36.6	1,467	16.0	−56.3
Total	4,535	31.4	1,993	14.0	−55.4
State + Federal + Property Tax	10,196	70.6	9,728	68.1	−3.5
Other Sources	4,238	29.4	4,555	31.9	8.5
Total Revenue	14,434	100.0	14,283	100.0	—

Source: [2], pp. 9, 10, 18.
[a]Includes San Francisco.

passed, the relative contributions of the various sources changed dramatically. Table 7-2 compares actual revenues received by city and county governments in FY 1978 to budgeted revenues (after the state's bailout) for FY 1979. Total revenues were expected to decline by about 1 percent. Property taxes, however, which had constituted over 31 percent of the revenues in FY 1978, were expected to contribute only 14 percent in FY 1979, a decline of over 55 percent in its share. The federal government's share was expected to increase modestly, while the state share was expected to practically double, from just over 15 percent to just under 30 percent.

Most of the local officials with whom we spoke believed that it would be very difficult for the state to resist greater involvement in local affairs following its increased role in financing local government. They held this opinion despite the fact that the actual interference in local programs during the first year following the passage of Proposition 13 was slight. All of the bailout funds were given to local governments in the form of "buyouts"[6] and block grants. A provision in the bailout legislation that was most restrictive on local officials—the elimination of cost-of-living raises for local government employees—was stricken by the Supreme Court.

The state increased its role in local criminal justice affairs only slightly. The major post–Proposition 13 state decisions that affected local criminal justice agencies were: (1) to give priority to funding public safety services; (2) not to "buy out" the courts; and (3) not to provide targeted funds for district attorneys, public defenders, or correctional programs. The requirement of the bailout legislation that public safety services be maintained at FY 1978 levels appears to have had little effect. The legislation provided no definition of "service level" and no enforcement mechanism, so we found reductions in both patrol and nonpatrol activities in police and sheriff departments.

The *possibility* of greater state control of agency operations in *future* years was of more concern to the people we interviewed than the degree of additional control that actually occurred in the first year following the passage of Proposition 13. The concern of those who feared greater state control in the future was based on what to them seemed two compelling arguments: First, they believed that it is unrealistic to expect the state—or any organization—to provide all or most of the funding for a particular purpose without exerting significant control over their expenditure. In short, experience shows that power follows money. In the words of William Oakland, "local control or home rule may become a thing of the past in California" [28, p. 403].

The second argument is that, even if the state sincerely tries to minimize the amount of interference in local program decisions, it cannot avoid dealing with the question of how to make an "equitable" allocation of state funds to local agencies throughout the state. The allocations it might decide upon would invariably affect program inputs, which would in turn determine the latter's capabilities and achievements. So far, the state has avoided equity considerations by returning money to each local government in direct proportion to its lost revenues. As a result, since local governments had been providing sharply different service levels prior to Proposition 13, the state is now subsidizing these different levels of service. There are even those who claim that the legislature has "rewarded the profligate and penalized the penurious" [14, p. 36].

Carried to its logical conclusion, the push for equality would result in less variation of types and levels of services across jurisdictions. In the law enforcement and prosecutorial functions, for example, citizens of some counties might request a larger share of state funds to give them an equal degree of protection against criminal victimization. The argument by persons who foresee this result is that residents who previously received a level of service that matched their property tax rate (ranging from below 1 percent of market value to above 4 percent) are unlikely to accept a uniform tax rate unrelated to the level of service they receive.

In fact, some expect that the state's new relationship to local governments will lead to increased consideration of the equity issue that was raised with respect to school finance in the *Serrano* v. *Priest* court case;[7] that is, the inequity of spending differences between poor and wealthy jurisdictions. As Reischauer has said, "What Californians are beginning to call the 'Serranization' of education will occur in all services" [39, p. 19]. He points out that signs of "Serranization" appeared in the first year bailout legislation, which relieved counties of all financial responsibility for welfare payments (benefiting counties with depressed inner cities and impoverished rural areas most) and took the spending rates of school districts into account in distributing funds for education (providing high-spending districts with 85 percent of their budgeted FY 1979 expenditures, and low-spending districts 91 percent of their planned outlays). He concludes, "Thus Proposition 13 will help equalize local spending as well as local tax rates and will provide a more equitable distribution of welfare and school services" [39, p. 20]. The California Department of Finance has observed, "Political bodies may be pressured to provide equal services or lower taxes for low service level areas" [43, p. 25].

In addition to the possibility of greater direct state involvement in local government affairs, Proposition 13 has had an indirect "spillover" effect. Although it contained no provisions that would limit the state's revenues, its passage sent a clear message to the governor and the legislature that the public wanted to reduce the size and scope of government—state as well as local. As a result, cuts were made in the state's budget, which have already affected the relationships between state agencies and local criminal justice agencies.

Some activities that had been performed by the state were reduced or dropped. In some cases, the slack was picked up by local agencies, increasing their workload, and in other cases the activities were not replaced. For example, the California Highway Patrol (CHP) reduced its patrol of county roads and lesser-traveled state highways. One sheriff asked rhetorically in an interview whether he shouldn't be able to increase his patrol of the affected unincorporated areas in his county by the same amount of the CHP reduction (20 officers). The sheriff believes that the loss of the CHP units will be noticed not only in the lessened enforcement of traffic laws, but also in the reduced deterrence to other types of crime due to there being fewer "black-and-white" cars on patrol.

Another impact of the state's retrenchment was that state agencies were not able to assist local government agencies as much as they had in the past. For example, one district attorney told us that because the state attorney general was "strapped" for funds, he was less able to provide assistance in investigating official corruption and organized crime at the local level. This district attorney said his office had knowledge of a potentially "very large" case of fraud that it was unable to act on without assistance from the attorney general's office.

Concerns of Local Officials. Local officials with whom we spoke were practically unanimous in fearing greater control of their operations by the state. Some believed it was possible to have increased state financial assistance of their agencies' functions without overbearing control, but these officials were in the minority. Pressure from local officials who feared increasing state control was a factor in the passage of long-term local government financing legislation (Assembly Bill 8) in 1979 that had even fewer restrictions on local programs than did the first year bailout.

Even those who benefited from the restrictions in the first year bailout were concerned about a possible reduction in local control. For example, police chiefs did not overwhelmingly endorse the provision of the bailout legislation calling for the preservation of public safety services at FY 1978 levels. Sentiment favoring home rule was at least as strong as the desire of the chiefs to protect their budgets. A chief of police whom we interviewed stated this most colorfully: It is part of his job, he said, to convince the city council of the need for a certain level of police services. But if the council believes it is in the best interests of the city to fund the city museum, for example, at the expense of the police, that is the way it should be, even if the people then "have to shoot their way in and out of the museum."

Another worry of the local officials we spoke to was that the state government would be unable to take into account the wide diversity of local needs and desires when it enacts legislation providing financial assistance to local governments. The bailout legislation itself illustrates this problem. It attempted to take local need into account by reducing the allocation to cities and counties whose reserves exceeded 5 percent of their total 1977–78 revenues. One city in our sample, which had a policy of setting aside revenues for capital outlay in its general fund reserve rather than in a separate capital fund, was seriously affected by the allocation formula. Other cities and counties may likewise have received less than their fair share of the state aid, due to local accounting anomalies.

Another example provided by the same legislation is that its allocation formula and its special provisions failed to account for differences in local growth rates. One police chief in a rapidly growing city told us that if the provision of the law relating to maintenance of public safety service levels were the sole means used to determine the size of his budget, the needs of the city would not be met because the growing population required *more* police services than the previous year's budget provided.

District attorneys, who are elected officials, are concerned that increased state funding will make it harder for them to offer the voters policies for fighting crime that are tailored to the local conditions. In the past, candidates for the office would lay out their policies during the campaign—each one placing different emphases on the various types of crime. As a result, district attorneys throughout the state exhibit a variety of prosecutorial policies which reflect the varying concerns of their constituencies. In addition, there are different crime rates and different mixes of crimes among counties. Would the state attempt to develop a payment formula that would take account of these differences? Would it attempt to standardize policies? Or would it base the amount of the buyout on the size of past budgets, thereby avoiding direct consideration of policies and caseloads?

According to Lowell Jensen, Alameda County District Attorney, unintended consequences might result if the state were to directly fund one or more criminal justice functions that are now locally funded. He suggests, for example, that local legislative bodies may tend to view requests from agency heads for supplemental local funding as being for nonmandated functions, and hence totally discretionary. This could have the effect of interfering with district attorneys' responsibilities to initiate their own investigations of matters not brought to them by the police (particularly white-collar crime, official corruption, and consumer fraud).

Several persons we interviewed were concerned that, since the state government is not knowledgeable enough about local criminal justice systems and there is no unified voice representing these systems, state financing and control decisions were likely to be made on an ad hoc basis, with no appreciation for their systemwide implications.

The FY 1979 state bailout provides an illustration of this problem. A survey by California's Department of Finance found that local government officials were concerned about the spillover effects of the maintenance-of-effort provision for fire and police services:

> If the police activities had to be maintained, then so did those programs where workloads are determined in large part by the level of police activity...courts, public defender, district attorney, probation, and detention and corrections facilities. In the aggregate, such programs constitute a large portion of noncategorically restricted funds available to counties, and should county revenues fall, any prohibition on spending reductions will necessarily result in even larger reductions in other

areas of county government supported by general fund dollars. [44, p. 66]

Since the state will be making important decisions affecting local governments with increasing frequency, local government officials will be paying more attention to state political affairs, and there will be more interaction between state and local officials. Many of the local criminal justice officials we interviewed had spent considerable amounts of time in the state capitol prior to the adoption of the first year bailout legislation. Professional associations, as well as local criminal justice officials, offered testimony on the anticipated consequences of various forms of aid to local government. Most were arrayed on the same side of the issue—trying to get as much state money as possible in the form of block grants for local governments. This led one public defender, whose testimony before a state committee agreed with that of the district attorney of his county, to comment that the response by local officials to post–Proposition 13 legislative proposals led to the association of "strange bedfellows."

State Responses Desired by Local Officials. While opposing greater control over local decisionmaking, most officials with whom we spoke nevertheless acknowledged the need for additional "permanent" revenue to replace the loss of property tax revenue. Coming up with an annual bailout was viewed as both unlikely and unacceptable, because of the great uncertainty imposed on local governments. Among those who expressed an opinion, most favored redistribution of the remaining property tax and changing the allocation of the state sales tax in such a way as to guarantee local governments a predictable source of revenue. (A long-term plan for local government financing along these lines was adopted by the state legislature in July 1979.)[8]

Local government officials also hoped, but realistically did not expect, that the state would in the future pay the full costs of new mandated programs, and would provide local agencies with the full amount of assistance that current law allows. On this latter point, two public defenders noted that a section of state law currently *allows* the state to pay up to 10 percent of the annual costs that counties incur in providing indigent defense, but actual payments have been much less. (The payment to Alameda County has never been more than 3 percent.) As part of his testimony before the joint committee of the legislature that drafted the bailout legislation in June 1978, one public defender recommended that the law be changed to *require* a 10 percent subvention.

There were two avenues for enlarging the state's involvement with the criminal justice system that drew some positive responses from local government officials: state buyout of the courts; and state takeover of the public defender's responsibilities. A buyout of the courts was recommended by the state's Commission on Government Reform. Its final report stated:

> The commission recommends transfer to the state of full financial responsibility for the Superior, Municipal, and Justice courts, including judges, court administrators, court reporters, jury commissioners, court clerks, including clerks in the county clerk's office engaged in court work, and bailiffs, for the present retaining administration at the local level. [13, p. 44]

As for the public defender, indigent defense lacks a strong constituency at the local level. Unlike law enforcement, which has strong support at both the state and local level, political support for the continued viability of high-quality indigent defense is much stronger at the state level. This may partly reflect the fact that the values underlying high-quality indigent defense transcend local differences, whereas law enforcement agencies are organized to reflect the diversity in local values. It is understandable, therefore, that some public defenders with whom we spoke were not opposed to complete state takeover of their operations. One actually hoped for legislation that would authorize the state public defender's office to assume responsibility for the defense of indigents at the trial stage, while continuing to maintain its current obligation to handle appeals. As evidence of the lack of local political support for his office, he pointed to the movement toward contracting with private attorneys to perform some of his duties. Another public defender with whom we spoke stated that a properly administered local branch of the state Public Defender could do as good a job as his own office was currently doing.

A number of "good government" groups have bemoaned the fact that the state did not seek to effect comprehensive intergovernmental policy changes and structural reforms in response to the passage of Proposition 13. These groups argue that the state, like local governments, provided a short-term solution to the long-term problems of local governments in its bailout legislation. "Instead of seizing the opportunity to encourage restructuring and support the necessary planning and design work, the legislature merely provided enough replacement revenue to finance the current inefficient system" [37, p. 83].

Local-Federal Relations

There was very little direct interaction between the federal government and local governments before 1960. The federal government dealt with local governments through state agencies, if at all. However, Lyndon Johnson's "Great Society" and Richard Nixon's "New Federalism" changed this pattern. Large amounts of federal money now flow directly to local governments. There are unrestricted general revenue sharing grants; HUD provides community development block grants; HEW provides grants for the educationally disadvantaged; the Department of Labor provides funds for employment and training under the Comprehensive Employment and Training Act (CETA) program; and the Department of Justice, through LEAA, dispenses some of its grants directly to local criminal justice agencies. As a result, the passage of Proposition 13, which would have had little or no impact on local-federal relations before 1960, is likely to have important impacts now. In particular, it will affect the types of grants local governments seek, how they use them, and even the way cuts are made in local services.

Targeted Grants. Federal assistance can be provided in one of two ways: through general revenue sharing and through targeted grants. General revenue sharing funds are distributed by formula with few or no limits on the purposes for which they may be spent and few if any restrictions on how they are spent. The funds can be treated just like other general purpose revenues, such as those from property taxes and sales taxes. Targeted grants, however, must be used for more specific purposes, which are usually spelled out clearly before a local government receives such funds.

In the case of the criminal justice system, the most important targeted grants are those distributed by the Law Enforcement Assistance Administration under the Omnibus Crime Control and Safe Streets Act of 1968. We found that local criminal justice agencies have continued to apply for LEAA grants at the same rate as before the passage of Proposition 13. However, government officials felt that fewer programs would be continued after the LEAA funding ran out, and that some conditions of aid would be harder to comply with.

The executive director of one of the state's regional criminal justice planning boards said she was surprised that there was no decline in the number of applications in FY 1979 compared with the previous year. Two factors, she had thought, would affect the number of applications: 1. the inability of the Planning Board to commit funds for more than one year, due to the expiration in 1980 of LEAA's authorization, and 2. the Planning Board's intention to focus on maintaining existing programs of merit, rather than creating new programs. She believes it usually is not cost-effective to provide funding of a new program for only one year. It takes at least three months to get a program underway, and often another three months before it is operating smoothly. Nevertheless, "quite a number" of applications were received for new programs.

One deputy police chief, reflecting the general attitude of local government officials, said that his department will continue to "vigorously seek the federal buck." A chief probation officer, who believes that "most [innovative] things have been tried" and that LEAA should, instead, supply funds for regular operations, conceded that he will nevertheless continue to "sell [his] soul to the devil" in order to obtain federal funds. Part of the reason that some will continue to seek federal grant money is that grant programs represent hope of positive change, no matter how slim or how peculiar the focus of the particular grant might be. More importantly, there are political pressures to seek the federal grants, since they supply additional revenues to the city or county, even if only temporarily.

There was general agreement that fewer LEAA programs are likely to be continued when their funding runs out than have been continued in the past. This did not seem to bother local officials. They said it was standard practice, before accepting a grant, to make it clear, usually through a written clause in the contract, that the local government will not be under any obligation to continue the grant program after its expiration. We were told by several officials that only those parts of a program that meet local needs are continued, and then only to the extent local funds allow.

Nearly without exception, the criminal justice officials we interviewed have had one or more projects in their agencies that were at least partially funded by the Law Enforcement Assistance Administration. Almost without exception, these same officals also expressed dislike for certain features of the grants. Most of their objections are well known and long standing, and have nothing to do with the passage of Proposition 13. For example, many officials highlighted the gaps between the goals of federally funded grant programs and the needs of local governments. Some police officials in rural areas felt that LEAA programs tended to be much too oriented toward the needs of urban areas.

However, the heightened concern of local officials with the "hard match" requirements of LEAA grants was a direct result of Proposition 13.[9] They claimed that, because of hidden costs, the amount of local funds expended on a project always exceeded the 10 percent share assumed when the grant request was being developed. Such costs (for administering the grant and reporting on its progress, for example) had been more easily absorbed in pre–Proposition 13 days when there was more slack in the budgets of local agencies.

General Revenue Sharing. The General Revenue Sharing Act of 1972 initiated a program of unrestricted federal transfer payments to local governments. The size of the payment that a city or county receives under the program is directly related to the revenues the jurisdiction raises in local taxes. Thus, Proposition 13 could result in reduced revenue-sharing allocations to California localities. No reductions will occur until fiscal year 1981, however, since the data base used to determine the allocations lags by two years. Statewide, it is estimated that revenue-sharing grants would be reduced by $70 million in FY 1981 if the program is reauthorized by the Congress in 1980 with no changes in the formula or funding level. [36, p. 37]

As fiscal limits on local governments restrict the contributions of locally generated revenues to the general fund, the federal revenue-sharing contribution assumes a greater importance. The impact that this increased importance has on local programs depends to a large extent on how revenue-sharing funds were being used prior to fiscal limitation.

Most local governments had already been directing the bulk of their revenue-sharing funds to property tax relief; the funds were added to the general fund to pay for operating expenses. A few, including Alameda County, had earmarked significant portions of their revenue-sharing grants for the support of new or expanded human service programs. As a result of Proposition 13, these jurisdictions have switched funds over to substitute for lost property taxes, producing a serious funding problem for the human service programs.

In FY 1978, Alameda County allocated $7.3 million, or 42 percent of its general revenue-sharing funds, to human service programs. Most of this amount was spent on contracts with 115 community-based programs. Twenty-five percent of the amount spent on community programs went to those labeled "public safety." In fiscal year 1979, the county cut its funding of human service programs by 16 percent across the board, and shifted the revenue to the general fund to substiture for lost property taxes.

The use of revenue-sharing funds to support community programs was initially lauded by community groups. Revenue sharing, they thought, represented a relatively stable and very visible source of funding, one which they could claim a portion of as being "theirs."

Proposition 13 disrupted this situation by bringing to an end the policy of setting aside a large amount of revenue-sharing monies solely for such programs. Now, community programs in Alameda County and many other local jurisdictions must compete with all claims on the jurisdictions' budgets rather than competing primarily among themselves.

CETA. A major federal targeted grant program that cuts across practically all local government agencies is the Comprehensive Employment and Training Act program. Shortly after the passage of Proposition 13 the Congress enacted changes in the regulations governing CETA which compounded the difficulties local governments had to face in dealing with their reduced revenues.

The public service employment (PSE) portions of the CETA program have two primary goals:

1. To provide temporary jobs during a recession for otherwise unemployed workers.
2. To train the structurally unemployed or underemployed to make them more competitive in the marketplace.

Both goals imply short-term employment for relatively unskilled workers. However, the federal government had placed few restrictions on the use of PSE funds, which permitted local governments throughout the country to rely on CETA as a substantial and continuing supplement to local revenues. The goals of the program often had little bearing on local governments' use of the funds. The new federal regulations, which took effect on October 1, 1979, are intended to strictly limit use of CETA funds to employment of the hard-core unemployed. Although this change will hurt local governments throughout the country, its negative impact in California will exacerbate the effects of Proposition 13.

The new CETA earnings limit is $10,000 per year; salaries generally cannot be supplemented above this amount, and the average annual salary for all CETA employees cannot exceed $7800. Newly hired employees must have been unemployed for at least 15 weeks, and the maximum duration of their CETA employment is 18 months. There was no average salary limit under the old regulations, nor maximum length of employment, and an individual employee's salary could exceed $10,000 if the local government paid the excess. These regulations made it possible for some local agencies to employ professional employees for indefinite periods at salaries in excess of $20,000. Now those local agencies in California that in the past had placed inappropriate reliance on CETA funding must make adjustments to the loss of that funding at the same time that local revenues have also been greatly constrained.

The impact on some public law offices, for example, has been considerable. The Los Angeles City Attorney's office has lost, or will lose, 53 of its 89 CETA positions due to the change in federal regulations. In the district attorney's office of another county, all but one of the attorneys hired in the three years before the passage of Proposition 13 had started as CETA employees. In the spring of 1979, 8 of the 24 attorneys in the office were still being paid partially through CETA funds. In that same county, 12 of the 20 attorneys in the public defender's office were CETA employees before the new regulations went into effect. Both the district attorney and the public defender say they see now, in hindsight, that they placed too much reliance on CETA funding, and used the program for the employment of persons it was never intended for. Attorney positions must now be paid for wholly out of the general fund, or else be cut.

The new CETA regulations have not pleased local government officials. The Los Angeles City Administrative Officer (CAO) recommended to the City Council in May 1979 that the city should not accept the estimated FY 1980 allocation of $90 million. [32] The CAO had two principal objections to the new CETA regulations. First, the regulations require that city CETA employees spend a considerable amount of time in formal training programs. This reduces the amount of time they have available for carrying out their work, and also places a burden on the city to provide the training. Second, he felt it would be difficult to recruit people within the salary guidelines, since few city jobs pay less than $7800. As a result, Los Angeles and other jurisdictions have significantly curtailed their participation in the CETA program. While they have switched many ex-CETA employees to fully paid government positions (one of the goals of the CETA program), a large number have not been retained.

Relationships Among Local Government Agencies

Consolidation. One of the many creative responses to fiscal limitation envisioned by some proponents of Proposition 13 was the rethinking and revising of the structure of local government and of the systems used to provide its services. Among the changes mentioned (all of which had been proposed and considered prior to the advent of fiscal limitations) was the consolidation of agencies and activities to reduce costs and promote efficiency. (By *consolidation* we mean redefinition of organizational, political, or geographical boundaries to achieve the combination of two or more agencies.) The proposals included interjurisdictional consolidation of agencies such as police departments, intrajurisdictional consolidation of agencies such as police and fire departments, reorganization of a service provided jointly by the state and local governments, as in the consolidation of municipal courts, and consolidation of duplicative activities, such as the bailiff and process-serving functions of the county sheriffs and marshals. The assumption underlying most such proposals is articulated in a recent report of the Los Angeles County Economy and Efficiency Commission:

> The entire city-county system of services has excess capacity because of its interjurisdictional structure. This is true even when each of the individual jurisdictions is designed and operating at peak efficiency. It is a case where the aggregate efficiency of the system is much lower than the efficiency of any single part, because of the relationships among the various parts. [37, p. 17]

Ironically, the mechanism that the state legislature chose to use in the bailout legislation to allocate funds among local governments made interjurisdictional consolidation (and even informal cooperation) harder after Proposition 13 than it was before. By allocating funds to jurisdictions based on past expenditure patterns, the bailout legislation effectively froze existing service delivery structures and patterns. Prior to the passage of Proposition 13, if one or more municipalities thought it would be more cost-effective to give up a certain activity—a crime lab or the training of police officers, for example— and have the county provide the service, the budgets of the municipalities would be decreased, the county budget increased, and property tax rates adjusted to reflect these shifts. In the post–Proposition 13 world, each municipality would have to contract with the county for the service, and the county would have to bill each one for the services rendered. Similar mechanisms for transferring payments would be required for several cities to jointly provide services. The financial containment experienced by most local governments was not severe enough to push them in this direction.

A number of arguments, most of them political, were advanced to justify not carrying out consolidations. With respect to law enforcement, consolidation was said to be either infeasible for political reasons or not beneficial because no savings would result from doing it (except in Los Angeles County, where several cities already contract with the sheriff for law enforcement services, but no cities were added after Proposition 13). In Alameda County, where a reasonable argument could be made that economies of scale might be obtained by combining the jurisdictions of one or more police departments, there were no serious discussions toward this end. The city of Piedmont, for example, has an area of only 1.8 square miles, and is totally surrounded by the city of Oakland. Yet, according to Piedmont's chief of police, the socioeconomic characteristics of the two cities are so dissimilar that residents of Piedmont would never tolerate having their police department consumed by that of Oakland. He is confident that the residents would vote for a special local public safety assessment if necessary, in order to assure the continued financial viability of their police department.

Intracity consolidation was considered by a number of cities. In most cases, the cities were investigating the possibility of creating a public safety department by combining their police and fire departments. The city of Sunnyvale, which has had a public safety department since 1950, received an increased number of inquiries about their department from other California cities after the passage of Proposition 13. The Piedmont city council appointed a citizens' committee to study the issue of police-fire consolidation. The committee recommended against total consolidation. A major reason, according to the committee, was that the aptitude, duties, and training of firefighters and police officers are sufficiently unique that consolidation of these positions was neither feasible nor practical. [38] The committee did recommend, however, abolishing one executive position in the fire department (chief or assistant chief) on a one-year trial basis, and reallocating the subsequent salary savings to increase the salaries of the remaining police and fire department executives.

In nearby El Cerrito, the city council dropped the idea of combining the police and fire departments. [11] The mayor cited two reasons for this: First, the city felt it could not afford to lose any of its management staff, which would likely occur if the department head positions were combined. Second, employee morale would have been adversely affected, since the police officers did not want to be firefighters, nor the firefighters police officers.

One California city, Brisbane, did effect a consolidation of its police and fire departments as a result of Proposition 13. Although the firefighters' union is fighting the consolidation in court, the city manager reports that "the new system is working more effectively and at much lower cost than the former system did."[10]

Proposition 13 gave support to the cause of some county supervisors and administrators who previously had favored the consolidation of municipal courts. In Alameda County, where court consolidation had been discussed off and on for the past several years, the county administrator proposed during the June 1978 budget hearings that the six municipal court districts in the county be combined into one district. "The purpose of the recommendation was to increase the efficiency of the municipal court system, provide a sound flexible administrative base to meet future problems and to reduce the cost of the system."[11] The board deferred action for several months, and then requested the California Judicial Council to conduct a study of the issue. The council report suggested a limited form of consolidation. [46] Most judges strongly oppose consolidation, while the Board of Supervisors supports it. The board has yet to vote to implement consolidation.

In Los Angeles, the issue of court consolidation has been a major source of tension between municipal court judges and the county board of supervisors for a number of years. Proposition 13 did little to change the situation. The judges recently tried to get the state legislature to assume the power of assigning municipal and justice court district boundaries, in order to prevent the board of supervisors from consolidating judicial districts having only one or two judges. (The county has 26 judicial districts. Three have one judge; six have two judges.) Opponents of the bill argue against the potential loss of local control ("The Municipal Court and the Justice Court are county obligations. What sense does it make to have the legislature make decisions for Los Angeles County?"), [12] and in favor of consolidating small districts (consolidation would result in "more efficiency, more economy, and more just handling of disputes").[13] Supporters of the bill contend that "the power to set the boundaries is better exercised by the Legislature"[14] and "we might save a few dollars through consolidation, but we could lose convictions by making it necessary for witnesses and others to travel farther."[15] Although passed by the Senate Judiciary Committee, the bill died on the Senate floor.

Another proposal affecting the courts that is perennially rejected by the state legislature involves the consolidation of some of the functions of the county sheriff and marshal. In 15 counties, the sheriff provides bailiffs for the superior courts, the marshal for the municipal courts. Both the sheriff and marshal serve writs and processes issued by any court. According to the Los Angeles County Economy and Efficiency Commission, consolidation of these two duplicative activities in Los Angeles County would save an estimated $5 million annually. Ten counties in California have already consolidated these activities, but the legislature has failed to pass legislation permitting 15 other counties with the same situation to consolidate. [37, p. 78]

Cooperation. Most officials with whom we spoke reported few large changes in cooperation among local criminal justice agencies.

No major institutional changes were reported and no new compacts or agreements were reached. To the contrary, agencies have become less cooperative, less generous in providing free services to other agencies.

Proposition 13 seems to have marked the end of an era of expanding free services provided by counties to cities. This is understandable in light of the fact that Proposition 13 and the bailout legislation made such cooperation hard to justify. As discussed in the previous section, the bailout legislation effectively froze existing service delivery structures and patterns. Counties are no longer able to recoup their costs for taking over a service by raising property taxes.

We noted this development in all our study counties, but it was most clearly manifest in Alameda County. In the past, that county had generally assumed responsibility for a large number of law enforcement support services that presented opportunities for economies of scale if performed on a countywide basis (including crime laboratory work, pretrial detention, and certain telecommunication networks). We were told that in the future the county is not likely to undertake new service responsibilities to the cities unless it is reimbursed. Furthermore, reductions in the sheriff's FY 1979 budget lowered the quality of some services already being provided—for example, an increase in the turnaround time for work requests made of the sheriff's crime lab by the cities. The county also considered instituting charges for the support of some services it had been providing free. This brought an immediate storm of protest from the cities, who threatened to obtain the services elsewhere. The county's desire to maintain centralized services prevailed, and there was no further serious discussion of charging cities for services currently being provided.

The opposite problem arises when a county or other jurisdiction has overall legal responsibility for a service that it did not actually provide in the past. In that situation, the jurisdiction can be forced to expand the services it provides to a lower-level unit of government and may be unable to charge for the service. Suppose, for example, that a city agency stops performing some kinds of activities that it used to perform. (This is called "demand shedding," and is discussed further in a later section.) If there is no legal requirement for the activity to be performed, such as investigating white collar crime, or directing traffic at a busy intersection, then no county agency, or other government agency, is likely to assume responsibility for the activity. However, in some cases the dropped activity is legally required, and the responsibility falls on another agency; then the burden of performing the service is transferred without a concomitant transfer of cost.

Some cities in Los Angeles County are considering closing their jails to save money. Montebello has already done so. The sheriff is legally required to assure that arrestees not released by the court are detained, and so offenders from these cities must be housed in county facilities. The sheriff can only ask for reimbursement of costs from the city if the offender is charged with a violation of the municipal code. In less dramatic fashion, city police departments that continue to operate their own detention facilities can transfer prisoners more rapidly to county jails than they did in the past—even though the transfer may be inconvenient for purposes of interrogation. The cost of guarding and feeding the prisoners must then be assumed by the county. Similarly, should a city decide to eliminate its police department, the sheriff would be obliged to provide law enforcement services whether or not an arrangement for compensation had been made.

We also found that government agencies have reduced their participation in activities involving shared responsibilities. For example, when a career criminal program was being planned in one of our study counties, both the sheriff and the major city's police department agreed to assign one full-time officer each to assist the district attorney. Both departments now say they can no longer afford such assignments.

Many local government agencies seem to be revising downward their estimates of the service levels they can expect when dealing with other agencies. For example, judges in Alameda County appear to be more willing to accept budgetary limitations as an excuse for tardy submission of presentence reports on convicts by the Probation Department. In Los Angeles, however, judges appear to be no more tolerant now in this area than they were prior to Proposition 13.

Where there has been rivalry and duplication of effort in the past, there is evidence that Proposition 13 has stimulated some interest in improving cooperation between city and county agencies. In one county, where there are two advanced crime laboratories—one in the sheriff's department and one in the police department of the largest city— the police chief of that department would like to enter into an agreement with the sheriff that would divide responsibilities for the development of expertise in costly lab procedures.

Intercounty cooperation in the post–Proposition 13 world faces the same impediments as does intercity and city-county cooperation. Formal mechanisms for cost sharing have to be set up, but few (if any) have been so far. For example, in probation services and corrections, the two areas where the potential for intercounty cooperation would seem to be the highest, there have been few significant developments in our study counties.

We have some evidence that, where there are no impediments to consolidation and cooperation, such approaches could be expected to be increasingly attractive in the face of fiscal limitations. One approach to improving the economy and efficiency of the courts that falls somewhere between informal cooperation and formal consolidation—the San Diego Municipal Court Experiment—has been thriving in the post–Proposition 13 environment. It was begun in El Cajon with LEAA funding in September 1977 and has gradually been expanded to include other parts of San Diego County. Under the program, with the agreement of the parties in a case, municipal courts handle many matters that superior courts handle elsewhere, including civil suits involving damages up to $30,000, and certain felony cases. As a result, workloads in the superior courts have been reduced, continuity is obtained for certain felony cases, and overall system costs have been reduced. Implementation of this program has not been impeded by the bailout legislation, since funds for both the municipal and superior courts come from the county's budget.

Systemic Effects. The local government service delivery system and some of its subsystems, like the criminal justice system, are composed of groups of delicately balanced independent but interdependent agencies, with little centralized control or authority. A reduction in the budget of any one agency necessitates a rebalancing of the entire system, which often takes time. In the interim, there may be instances when behavior seems dysfunctional and operations irrational.

Our interviews turned up several cases in which programmatic changes by one criminal justice agency had an adverse impact on the programs of one or more other agencies. For example, soon after manpower reductions were made by Alameda County's public defender, the Oakland Municipal Court began to experience delays because defendants were appearing at arraignment who had yet to be interviewed by the public defender. Adjustments were quickly made in the Public Defender Department to remedy this situation. Similarly, superior courts experienced some delays in processing cases due to the late filing of documents by county clerks. The clerks' delays resulted from staff reductions.

Changes in police patrol manpower affected the municipal court and the revenues of one community. There, due to reductions in police patrols, the number of traffic citations fell. This reduced the number of filings and resulted in less revenue "generated" by the court.

Nearly every criminal justice agency in Alameda County has been affected by layoffs and increased attrition in the county's data processing department. That department maintains the system that records local criminal histories and helps manage transactions between agencies and offenders. As a result of the manpower shortage, the frequency and duration of system downtimes have increased, and scheduled new developments have been postponed.

We came across several instances where a criminal justice agency was affected by reductions in a noncriminal justice agency. For example, one police department received a greater number of calls from playgrounds and recreation fields for assistance in settling disputes and handling complaints that were previously the responsibility of recreation department employees. The chief of police there urged the city council to restore some of the recreation supervisor positions that were cut.

FEDERAL AND STATE MANDATES

Until as recently as forty years ago, the local, state, and federal governments in the United States operated relatively independently in their respective spheres of influence. Since then, state governments, and subsequently the federal government, have played larger and increasingly important roles in local affairs.

As noted above, local budgets now include large amounts of federal and state money. For example, in FY 1979, 38 percent of Alameda County's revenue came from state subventions, and 34 percent from federal subventions. The growth in such intergovernmental revenue transfers, particularly from the federal government, has been rapid. The Advisory Commission on Intergovernmental Relations, for example, reports that direct federal aid to the city of Los Angeles constituted less than 1 percent of its general revenues in 1957, 16 percent in 1976, and an estimated 28 percent in 1978 [21].

In most cases, the state and federal revenue comes with "strings" attached. These strings have many sizes, shapes, and forms, as illustrated by the classification into *requirements* and *constraints* given by Lovell et al. [27, p. 34]:

Requirements

A. Programmatic
   1. Program
   2. Program quality
   3. Program quantity
B. Procedural
   1. Reporting
   2. Performance
   3. Fiscal

4. Personnel
5. Planning/evaluation
6. Record keeping
7. Residual

Constraints

A. Revenue base
B. Revenue rate
C. Expenditure limits

Common examples of constraints associated with state and federal grants include:

Matching requirements, under which the local government must provide a specified percentage of the grant costs as a condition for receiving the assistance.

Maintenance-of-effort provisions, which require that the grantee maintain a given level of spending for the program. Some programs include provisions that prevent grantees from using the funds to supplant local funds that would have been spent for the program in the absence of the state or federal funds.

In addition to attaching strings to grants, state and federal governments require local governments to perform many other activities that implement national or state policy objectives. Some of these include mandates to protect environmental quality, ensure prevailing wages for construction workers under contract, provide equal access to services for the handicapped and disadvantaged, and provide legal defense services to the indigent.[16] Mandates pervade all functions and levels of government—from specifying the frequency with which dogs in cities must be counted, to setting minimum training standards for auxiliary police officers and earliest wake-up times for inmates in county jails.

The increase in the number of state and federal mandates on local government closely parallels the increase in state and federal funding of local governments. Lovell et al. identified over 4,000 federal and state mandates affecting local governments in five states (not including court mandates), 67 percent of which were imposed after 1970. Most federal mandates are imposed as conditions of aid, while most state mandates are direct orders. The Department of Housing and Urban Development (HUD) alone is responsible for a substantial portion of all federal mandates (over 35 percent), while the Department of Health, Education and Welfare (HEW) and the Environmental Protection Agency (EPA) account for an additional 32 percent between them.

There have been a number of recent studies dealing with the effect of state and federal mandates on local governments. [12, 27, 34, 42] Our discussion of the likely effects of mandates in a period of fiscal contraction draws heavily on the information in the excellent paper by Posner and Sorett of the U.S. General Accounting Office and the study Lovell et al. performed for the National Science Foundation.

Cost

Mandates are often costly. If a local government were already performing a mandated activity, the imposition of the mandate would not increase the government's expenditures. However, a mandate is generally imposed because, without it, many local governments would most likely not perform the activity. Lovell et al. found that in well over 50 percent of the cases, local governments were either not carrying out or only partially carrying out certain specifically mandated activities before the mandate was imposed. [27, p. 169]

Local governments are sometimes reimbursed for the cost of carrying out a mandated activity, but most are unfunded or significantly underfunded. Lovell et al. found that "over half of all mandate costs . . . are paid for by the local governments, overwhelmingly from the general fund." [27, p. 195] It is clear that mandates have contributed to the increasing cost of local government.

Each mandate placed on local government typically has a very small cost (with a few notable exceptions, such as certain provisions of the National Environmental Policy Act of 1969). However, the cumulative weight of hundreds of mandates can produce a significant financial burden. For example, the reporting requirements for most federal programs are not excessive in relation to their size, and yet the cumulative impact of all reporting requirements is very large. A study performed by the Academy for Contemporary Problems estimates the costs to state and local governments resulting from federal information requirements are $5 billion per year, of which only a small part is paid for by the federal government. [20]

Most federal mandates are imposed as conditions of aid. Although local governments are not directly required to comply with such mandates, the potential loss of federal assistance is usually punishing enough to force compliance. A local cost is mandated as a condition of aid for over 60 percent of federal assistance programs in the form of "matching" requirements, under which a share of the program's costs must be contributed by the grantee. The required nonfederal match varies from 10 percent for LEAA programs to 50 percent for outdoor recreation grants.

A hidden cost to local government is the expense of continuing federally initiated programs after federal sponsorship has terminated. This applies to federal grants that are intended to stimulate the creation of new state and local government activities by providing "seed money" for a few years. To the extent that the federal program is successful, it creates a continuing demand for public services that local governments with fiscal problems cannot easily absorb. As described by Posner and Sorett, "Federal grants that start new services create a clientele that continues to be dependent on the service regardless of the continued availability of federal funds. When federal funds do expire, local officials are faced with the dilemma of increasing the budget to accommodate the new service or alienating a public that has grown accustomed to the service." [34, p. 360]

In some cases, federal "seed money" is provided for the purpose of initiating a new mode of operation which is projected to be more efficient than past operations and perhaps even less expensive, as in the case of improved procedures for managing criminal investigations. Nonetheless, the final result often costs more. It may provide better services or more services than in the past, but nevertheless at higher costs. The local government still faces the decisions of whether and how to continue the program upon termination of federal funding.

Local government officials express considerable optimism about their ability to terminate programs. Our interviews indicated that Proposition 13 had not reduced local officials' propensity to seek federal grants, although they specifically intended not to continue many of them when the federal funding ran out. They may find it more difficult to terminate such programs than they think, since granting agencies and interest groups which stand to benefit could bring direct pressure to bear on local officials or could press for revised contractual or legislative language to forestall the terminations that the officials seek.

Within the criminal justice system, the corrections and public defender functions are the most heavily mandated, while the law enforcement function has the fewest mandates. Information from our interviews seems to indicate that the mandates in corrections are the most costly. Many such mandates result from court orders aimed at increasing the rights of inmates and improving their physical surroundings. For example, a 1977 decision by a federal court judge required the Los Angeles sheriff's department to provide inmate recreation facilities, modify the existing custody facilities, and provide inmates in outside cells with a way to "see the sun" during the day.[17] The county budgeted $3 million for these mandates in FY 1979, and will have continuing costs every year. In another example, a federal court decision in April 1979 directed Los Angeles County to improve toilet and shower accommodations and medical care for inmates in the Central Juvenile Hall. The county, which is appealing the decision, said its cost would exceed $100 million.

There is no doubt that most of the mandates on local government have worthwhile objectives. However, they are generally formulated with little regard for the cost burden they impose, and with little or no effort made to see if their benefits are likely to outweigh those costs. For example, a section of the Rehabilitation Act of 1973 providing for nonexclusion of qualified handicapped individuals in federally assisted programs was adopted by the Congress without hearings or debate. Only later, after implementing regulations had been issued, were the costs estimated: approximately $2 billion a year to meet the HEW regulations and another $2 billion to $8 billion in capital investments to meet HEW and DOT regulations. Said Representative Charles A. Vanik, the sponsor of this section of the Act, "We never had any concept that it would involve such tremendous costs."[18] The question of whether the benefits did or did not exceed the cost of this mandate had evidently not been considered in the legislative process.

Impacts on Priorities of Local Governments

Federal and state subventions and mandates have had a significant impact on the mix of services provided by local governments. Before 1960, local governments provided little more than basic services like police, fire, sanitation, education, parks, and roads. Since then, with the carrot of federal spending and the stick of mandates, they have begun to place much more emphasis on areas such as community development, social services, and health. This trend is defended by some as a legitimate expression of state and national priorities, and criticized by others as reducing the autonomy of local governments and compromising principles of local self-government.

Posner and Sorett provide some examples to support the argument that federal mandates infringe on local autonomy and distort state and local priorities:

> The Energy Policy and Conservation Act of 1975 requires local implementation of energy conservation standards certified by HUD. "The codes must be statewide, uprooting long traditions of local control over building codes in many states."
> As a condition for receiving federal juvenile justice grants, LEAA requires states to develop programs to deinstitutionalize juvenile "status" offenders.[19] In states where the local criminal justice offi-

cials and planners believe deinstitutionalization is a controversial and unproven strategy, the federal government is, in effect, dictating an unwanted policy for the state.

Local governments devote resources to areas that they claim have relatively low local priority, simply because the bulk of expenditures are covered by federal programs with low matching fund provisions. "Thus, while state and local governments may not feel that drug abuse prevention or air pollution control is of sufficient local priority to warrant a new commitment of 100 percent local funding, they would be hard pressed not to participate when the federal government offers to pay 75 to 100 percent of the costs."

While it is true that local governments can refuse federal and state aid, and therefore avoid the mandates that come as conditions of aid, it is politically difficult to do so. Local officials repeatedly express the wish that national and state priorities more closely matched their local needs. Most can cite examples of severe mismatches between state or federal priorities and particular local circumstances. Kings County in California set up a public transportation agency to provide bus service that the county supervisors felt was unnecessary. The alternative was to forfeit the $750,000 per year that is available to the county from the state for transportation purposes. One county supervisor, who voted against setting up the agency, lamented: "It bothers me to have to build a bus service when the road in front of my house is ready to go to pot" [7].

Even when federal priorities originally match state and local priorities, they may fail to respond rapidly to changing local needs. Federal spending on highway research, planning, and construction, for example, is seen as mistargeted by local officials who face increasing costs for maintenance of existing highways and a decreasing need for new highways.

In some cases, differences in opinions about the proper role of the federal government lead to perceived mismatches in priorities. An example is given by police officials who in their interviews argued for LEAA funding of police officers' compensation. The Oakland police chief told us that what his department needed more than anything was federal grants for "righteous, upfront, good old fashioned police officers." But Congress has consistently avoided authorizing LEAA to fund any programs with even the slightest taint of establishment of a federal police force.

In times of fiscal expansion, the pushes and shoves applied to local governments by federal and state mandates, which force local governments to undertake what to them seem to be low priority activities, can be accommodated with few complaints. The budget is expanding, so all agencies and client groups can get at least as much as they were getting before, and taxes can be raised to pay for the expansion of services. In times of fiscal limitation, however, mandates play a perverse role that was clearly unintended when they were imposed.

Mandated activities, whether imposed by the courts, the legislature, or an executive agency, were intended to be carried out *in addition* to traditional local government services, not instead of them. It was assumed that programs with strong local constituencies, such as police patrol, fire protection, and refuse collection, would always be able to secure sufficient funding. This is true during fiscal expansion, but not during fiscal contraction. We found that, when budget cuts are required, mandated programs and functions remain, and nonmandated programs and functions get cut.

For example, in Alameda County, after the passage of Proposition 13, all county services were categorized as follows:

1. Mandated.
2. Nonmandated, but revenues exceed costs (such as a bureau that collects bad debts).
3. Nonmandated but critical (life and limb or property would be jeopardized without the service).
4. Nonmandated, and either noncost-effective or noncritical.

Cuts were then made from the bottom up, so that services in category 4 were hit very hard. Similarly, the California Department of Finance found that after the passage of Proposition 13 "the maintenance of mandated programs—public assistance, health ..., the courts and public safety ... forced discretionary programs—libraries, parks and recreation, general administration—to absorb the sharpest reductions." [43, p. 15] It should be noted that public assistance programs, which are heavily mandated and were in large part unaffected by Proposition 13, were at the top of the list of programs that voters said should be cut if cuts were needed to implement Proposition 13.[20]

A study of New York City's budgets between FY 1961 and FY 1976 revealed a marked shift away from basic services like police, fire, and sanitation toward social services and health—areas with heavy federal funding. [18] For example, welfare accounted for 12 percent of the city's expenditures in FY 1961 and 23 percent in FY 1976; police, fire, and sanitation accounted for 20 percent of the city's expenditures in FY 1961 and 12 percent in FY 1976. The study concludes that this shift is counterproductive to New York's long-term health, and resulted from a process whereby federal categorical grants distorted the city's normal budget allocation process. During the 1960s, the city decided to invest new revenues among competing functions based in part on the federal dollar return. When a fiscal crisis hit the city, budget cuts were concentrated on services that were not eligible for federal funds.

According to Posner and Sorett, this process is likely to repeat itself in any city faced with fiscal limitations. "Because of match requirements, it makes eminently good financial sense for cities with fiscal problems to cut their budgets in areas with no federal funding in order to maximize local dollar savings while minimizing program impact and avoiding loss of external aid." [34, p. 355]

One need not look only to health and welfare agencies to observe what happens when federal and state priorities dominate local priorities. District attorneys' offices reveal an interesting pattern. We found that they had fared the best of all criminal justice agencies in the fiscal year following the passage of Proposition 13. (Although the total budget for Alameda County's criminal justice system was cut by 6.5 percent from the previous year, the district attorney's budget increased by 8.5 percent.) However, most of the increases in the budgets of district attorneys did not go to expand their prosecutorial activities, but were allocated to their "child support" function.[21] (The budget for the Alameda County District Attorney's prosecutorial activities increased by 1 percent in FY 1979, while the budget for child support activities increased by 32 percent.) The child support function is mandated by the federal government, which pays 75 percent of the cost of administering the function, and provides incentive payments equal to 15 percent of the amount collected. In addition, the State of California matches the federal incentive payment. As a result, the child support function actually generates net income for most California counties. Thus, it is not surprising that, in our study sites, 30 to 50 percent of the district attorney's budget was allocated to the child support function, and that this percentage has been steadily increasing over the last few years. (Even with an overall increase of 8.5 percent in his budget, the Alameda County District Attorney was forced to cut back on investigations and eliminate the prosecution of certain misdemeanors.)

A county's board of supervisors would probably not allocate 50 percent of the district attorney's budget to the child support function if they had their choice of what to do with the money. A survey of local government officials carried out by the Advisory Commission on Intergovernmental Relations (ACIR) found that 75 percent of officials would have made moderate or substantial changes in allocating federal funds if they were freed from categorical grant restrictions. The ACIR concludes that "clearly, as seen by the officials surveyed, federal grants tend to skew local decisionmaking." [22]

An important question is whether these views of local officials are also the views of a majority of their constituents. If so, the trends in program cuts that we have identified portend a coming imbalance between voters' wishes and the budget allocations of local government. Assuming that nonmandated activities continue to be reduced as a result of fiscal limitations, the mandated activities—including those that local officials feel are mistargeted—will be absorbing an increasing share of local government revenues. Voters who are opposed to these trends will find it difficult to hold local officials accountable, because these same officials claim they are powerless to resist the mandates. Increasingly, then, political actions on local policies will occur at state and federal levels, resulting in less local autonomy. William Oakland observed that, as a result of Proposition 13, "local control or 'home rule' may become a thing of the past in California." [28, p. 403]

When we began our project, we thought that by observing which services experienced budget cuts and which did not we would see revealed the essential priorities of local government. Instead, we have seen revealed the essential priorities of the state and federal government. Harry L. Hufford, Chief Administrative Officer of Los Angeles County, in his recommendations for the proposed 1979–1980 budget, wrote:

> The Budget recommendations vividly demonstrate that Federal and State mandated programs continue to increase while locally financed programs are decreasing. Thus, the effects of Proposition 13 are seen—increased reliance on State and Federal funds with a corresponding loss of home rule over budget priorities and level of service. [19, p. 2]

EMERGING PATTERNS IN THE CRIMINAL JUSTICE SYSTEM

Fiscal limitation implies a decrease in real expenditures of the criminal justice system. Inevitably, this leads to a change in the nature of justice and a rethinking of what the system should do and should not do. Some trends we have identified are described in this section.

Cost Considered in Court Decisions

In principle, justice should be dispensed without reference to the financial burdens placed on those who must achieve justice. Courts have rarely explicitly considered the costs imposed on the criminal justice system in their decisions or operations. However, in practice, judges are aware of the financial implications of their decisions and may take costs into account implicitly. There have recently been indications of a growing willingness to consider costs explicitly. While still a minority position, the issue has increasingly been raised and debated. In a dissenting opinion in a California supreme court civil case, for example, to decide whether due process required the appointment of counsel to represent indigent defendants in paternity suits, one of the justices wrote:

> While access to the courts is constitutionally protected, this access need not be guaranteed in the form of free counsel. . . . It is my view that the financial implications of such a decision may very well be tremendous and beyond our capacity to determine. If the civil litigant is now to be furnished free counsel, what of the expenses of extensive discovery, and can the cost of the retention of an expert witness be far behind? The majority is strangely silent on the critical question—who is going to pay for counsel?[22]

The growing conflict between the demands of justice and the ability of governments to meet those demands has profound implications. It seems likely that the issue will eventually be forced: either some individuals' rights will be compromised in the interest of government solvency or the government in question will actually be unable to comply with the court's order. Early cases of this type will no doubt be controversial and will lead to some rethinking of the values underlying our system of justice.

Revision of Functions

One way in which criminal justice agencies respond to lowered budgets is by shedding demand: they stop performing certain kinds of activities that they previously would have undertaken on their own initiative or at the request of a citizen or another criminal justice agency. Some of these changes are minor or even peripheral to the objectives of the criminal justice system. Others, however, constitute abandonment of an entire function customarily associated with the agency, reflecting a contemplation of the agency's past successes and failures and a rethinking of its goals and priorities. This section gives examples of major demand shedding in various parts of the criminal justice system.[23]

Prosecution. District attorneys have commonly reacted to fiscal limitation by reducing the categories of offenses that they will prosecute. Even before Proposition 13, case screening by prosecutors in California tended to be much more stringent than in most jurisdictions elsewhere, yet the recent trend has been toward even greater stringency.[24] Less serious types of crimes are being prosecuted less frequently, and some are not being prosecuted at all. For example, for a period of time in 1979 the San Joaquin District Attorney was refusing some nonviolent misdemeanor cases brought in by the police, and the Alameda County District Attorney stopped prosecuting infractions in traffic cases.

Some changes in case screening policies are publicly announced and understood. Other u announced or invisible reductions in investigations and prosecutions are also taking place. The Alameda County District Attorney told us that the reductions in staff that he had already experienced make it difficult for him to conduct original investigations into matters such as official corruption and consumer fraud. In general, fiscal limitation is likely to reduce self-initiated efforts and focus the time of prosecutors on reacting to demands placed on them by other parts of the system. In so doing, some types of crimes inevitably become deemphasized even if no explicit decisions are made about them. The recent growing concern with white-collar crime, for example, is unlikely to be sustained in the face of fiscal limitation.

Law Enforcement. Police departments are also forced to concentrate resources on high priority crimes, and reduce their efforts elsewhere. An official in a small rural city told us that although the police currently follow up on all calls, they would begin to ignore certain offenses—the "minor stuff." The police might not respond to take traffic accident reports or to investigate suspicious circumstances or burglaries. "In the future, the people will have to come into the station to report something like a stolen television." Detectives in the city of Los Angeles, where a long-standing tradition of investigating all reported felonies was surviving in the face of national trends toward case screening, were recently instructed to concentrate their resources on crimes that have a high probability of being solved, screening out those that are unlikely to be solved. The department publicly attributed this decision to budgetary pressures after Proposition 13.

While some observers may welcome the increased efficiency implied by these efforts to focus police resources where they will do the most good, others will discern a disturbing philosophical shift in the role of the police. Under fiscal pressure, basic service functions of the police are being sacrificed in favor of the crime control functions. Ironically, this trend runs counter to the thrust of much recent research on police effectiveness. In particular, the research casts doubt on the ability of the police to bring about any substantial reduction in crime rates, especially if trends in society and in the remainder of the criminal justice system push toward greater amounts of crime.

One reason for the weak link between police resources and crime rates is that the police spend most of their time on functions unrelated to crime—order maintenance and provision of services to the public. Far from criticizing the police for allocating their time in this way, modern reform-minded researchers and practitioners have called for devoting more talent and attention to the service functions, so that they can be performed more effectively. They point out that the general climate of trust and cooperation between the police and the citizenry, which arises out of a multitude of minor interactions, has a greater ultimate influence on crime rates than how the police handle a particular crime [15].

Whether a police chief or sheriff agrees or disagrees with this view of the role of police in society, fiscal restrictions inexorably press toward sacrifice of the service functions. The link between such functions and police effectiveness is too subtle, too unproved, and—most importantly—too long-term to hold sway in the budgeting process. In contrast, cutbacks in crime fighting functions can have immediate and easily understood consequences. They are made generally only with great reluctance and concern by all of the government officials who are involved.

Probation. In probation departments, the demand-shedding behavior has been very different from that in police departments. Budgetary constraints have brought about a serious rethinking of the role of probation in the criminal justice system and a movement away from previously central crime prevention activities. The probation function has traditionally been oriented toward rehabilitation of offenders. But the method used by probation officers pursuing this goal, namely intensive personal supervision, is very expensive. Moreover, recent research suggests that expensive efforts at rehabilitation are not more effective than inexpensive ones. Kenneth Fare, acting head of the Los Angeles County Probation Department, speculated that probation will undergo major changes in the future, mostly because of anticipated budget cuts: "We are going to have to look at the role of probation and what the expectations of the community are, then we will have to adjust the resources we have to what is needed. . . . The expectation that probation will have the resources to change criminal behavior will be removed" [1].

In California, probation departments have carried out a wide range of activities, so a movement away from supervision implies a relative increase in emphasis on less well-known functions. Probation is likely to center its activities around investigations of offenders' backgrounds that are required by courts for sentencing purposes, and monitoring and surveillance of offenders in bail release programs. Probation officers, relieved of case supervision work, may be able to do a better job at these functions than they are currently doing, and still reduce overall costs.

Courts and Corrections. Courts and corrections agencies have little discretion to control their workload by dropping or ignoring some of the demands placed on them. If the prosecutor chooses to prosecute a case, the courts are obliged to handle it in some way, whatever backlog or financial limitations may exist. Similarly, when a person is sentenced to jail or prison for a specified term, the corrections agencies cannot refuse to receive him or release him early on their own volition.

We did not find any major instances of demand shedding in these agencies after Proposition 13. In an effort to reduce backlogs of civil cases by eliminating the necessity for court trials in some of them, arbitration was made mandatory in California for certain civil cases involving $15,000 or less in damages.

Corrections agencies have undertaken efforts to locate alternatives to traditional secure facilities for housing persons in their custody. However, the movement toward such alternatives is propelled less by a desire to reduce expenditures than by a need to accommodate a rapid increase in the incarcerated population. Trends toward greater incarceration and longer sentences in California, which are quite independent of fiscal limitation, have been leading toward a serious problem of prison overcrowding. During 1978, the felon population in prison increased 12 percent. Even if adequate funding for new or expanded facilities were readily available, which it is not, the time delays involved in selection of sites and construction of facilities would necessitate the same interim adjustments that are now under consideration.

Privatization

Privatization occurs when a governmental unit stops supplying a service, and private firms provide some kind of substitute for the previously public service. Such firms are compensated directly by the public. Thus, privatization differs from the process of contracting out public services to private firms discussed above, since the contractual arrangement leaves the service under the control of a public agency.[25] An example of privatization in California after Proposition

13 involved summer schooling. Most school districts eliminated nearly all of their summer classes, and a variety of private sector organizations picked up the business, including private schools, voluntary service groups, recreational facilities, summer camps, and travel organizations.

The criminal justice system offers few opportunities for the recipients of services to pay for the level of services they desire, because criminal offenders handled by the system are—to say the least—reluctant recipients of its services. However, there are some opportunities for privatization, and we find hints or indications that it may be occurring. Businesses that are not satisfied with their level of police protection can hire their own security guards or invest in security equipment. Neighborhood groups concerned with a reduction in police patrol activities can organize their own patrol teams or contract with private security services. Residents can also purchase home security systems. While the growth in sales of the private security industry indicates that these trends are occurring, the relationship between private investment and fiscal limitation in government is unclear. (The industry's growth began several years before Proposition 13 in California and has not shown any dramatic change since.)

Quality of Justice

The overall impact of fiscal containment has been capsulized by Pascal and Menchik as follows: "a leaner and smaller public sector may also turn out to be meaner and harsher" [31, p. 10]. The impressions we gained from our interviews and analyses suggest that this is true for the criminal justice system in California. (Our impressions are necessarily tentative, however, because we did not collect or analyze data about system performance.) In focusing its energies on serious crimes, the system appears to be losing some aspects of the humaneness it previously showed toward arrestees, defendants, convicts, complainants, victims of crimes, and citizens needing various kinds of assistance or reassurance, and toward the system's own employees.

Earlier sections of this chapter have contained examples of harsher treatment in all components of the criminal justice system. Consider what has happened to individuals convicted of crimes after Proposition 13. They have fewer opportunities for meaningful probation supervision or treatment in a community correctional facility, but much larger numbers of them are being sent to prison. The prison facilities themselves, experiencing overcrowding and its attendant problems of increased violence, are harsher forms of punishment than they previously were.

Consider people who are victims of crimes that the system considers minor, or who experience some form of unusual or suspicious behavior. They may find the situations traumatic, frightening, or extremely annoying, even while recognizing that they are not dealing with a serious crime. Since Proposition 13, they are less likely to be able to get the police to respond at all. If the police do respond, they are less likely to take anyone into custody. If someone is arrested, the district attorney is less likely to prosecute.

Employees of the system have had some of the more interesting and rewarding aspects of their jobs eliminated. They feel the public does not hold their occupation or performance in high regard. And the prospects for future enhancements in their salaries and benefits do not look nearly as favorable as they did a few years earlier.

Litigants in routine civil cases may wait several years in some jurisdictions before they reach trial and adjudication. While they understand that the courts must concentrate attention first on serious criminal cases, their frustrations with an unresponsive system are real nonetheless.

These examples of movement toward a less humane and less responsive criminal justice system, and other examples that could be offered, may be viewed by some proponents of Proposition 13 as just what they wanted to happen when they voted for its passage. Other people may find them dismaying. With the passage of time, voters will be able to judge whether they value their tax savings more or less highly than any disadvantages they experience from changes in government services. Their collective judgment will determine whether fiscal limitations on government become more stringent or are relaxed in the future.

NOTES

1. The details of the state bailout, and its political history, are presented in [26].
2. The legislation also protected fire departments with the same provisions that applied to police and sheriffs programs.
3. The full report of this study [9] shows the locations of the study sites and gives information about their characterictics.
4. He had recently submitted a proposal for a computerized jury selection system. Although significant savings were demonstrated, he felt the Board of Supervisors would alter the existing "bad system rather than spend more initially."
5. This trend began long before the passage of Proposition 13, but it has been accelerated and intensified by its passage.
6. A state *buyout* of a service means that the state assumes the financial responsibility for the service while the local government maintains administrative and operational responsibility.

7. *Serrano* v. *Priest* (5 Cal. 3d 584 (1971)) declared that the existing system for financing education in California was unfair to low wealth school districts, and ordered the implementation of a new system that would result in a more equal distribution of revenues per pupil.
8. Assembly Bill 8, Chapter 282. See [26, Chapter VII] for a description of the legislation.
9. LEAA grant programs require 10 percent of the project costs to be contributed by the grantee as a condition for receiving the grant.
10. News item in *Public Management*, February 1979, p. 19.
11. Letter dated September 18, 1978, from the County Administrator to the Alameda County Board of Supervisors.
12. Alan Sumner, legislative advisor to Governor Brown. This and the following three quotes are cited in [3].
13. Steve Birdlebough, California Judicial Council.
14. Roy Norman, Presiding Judge, Los Angeles County Municipal Court.
15. Frank Vicencia, California State Assemblyman.
16. For a detailed description of the generally applicable national policy requirements for grant programs, see [8, Chap. VII].
17. *Rutherford* v. *Pitchess, 57 F. Supp. 104 (1977)*.
18. Quotation and cost estimates from [10].
19. A *juvenile status offense* is an act that is unlawful when done by a juvenile and not unlawful when done by an adult (e.g., running away from home).
20. From a press release of election day poll conducted by CBS news for its Los Angeles station and the *Los Angeles Times*.
21. Pursuant to federal and state laws, district attorneys are responsible for investigating, processing, and prosecuting complaints against absent fathers for failure to provide support for their children. For further information about this function, see [24].
22. *Salas* v. *Cortez*, 24 Cal. 3d 22 (1979).
23. Examples in which demands that are shed by one criminal justice agency must be picked up by another agency are discussed in the section on intergovernmental relations.
24. A nationwide survey of police departments [16] showed that in 1973, less than 15 percent of departments experienced a felony rejection rate over 20 percent. During the same year, the typical California felony arrest had a 29 percent chance of not being prosecuted at all and only a 33 percent chance of being prosecuted as a felony. (The remaining 38 percent were prosecuted as misdemeanors.) Source: California Offender Based Transaction Statistics, 1973.
25. For more details and other examples, see [30].

REFERENCES

1. Adler, Lisa, "Juvenile Justice: Will Money Decide Its Path," *Beverly Hills Independent*, 31 January 1980.
2. *An Analysis of the Effect of Proposition 13 on Local Governments*, Legislative Analyst, State of California, Sacramento, October 1979.
3. "Ban Sought on Consolidation of Local Courts," *Los Angeles Daily Journal*, 7 June 1979.

4. Berman, Paul, and Milbrey W. McLaughlin, *The Management of Decline: Problems, Opportunities, and Research Questions*, The Rand Corporation, Santa Monica, Calif., P–5984, August 1977.
5. Bernstein, Harry, and Bruce Keppel, "Thousands of Public Employees Threaten Statewide Job Actions," *Los Angeles Times*, 17 July 1979.
6. Bernstein, Sid, "County Going Slow on Private Contracts," *Los Angeles Times*, 28 April 1980.
7. "Board Approves Transportation Agency," *Hanford Sentinel* (Calif.), 23 May 1979.
8. *Categorical Grants: Their Role and Design*, Report A–52, Advisory Commission on Intergovernmental Relations, Washington, D.C., 1977.
9. Chaiken, J. M., W. E. Walker, A. P. Jiga, and S. S. Polin, *The Impact of Fiscal Limitation on California's Criminal Justice System*, The Rand Corporation, Santa Monica, Calif., Publication No. R-2675-NIJ/RC, 1981.
10. Clark, Timothy B., "Access for the Handicapped—A Test of Carter's War on Inflation," *National Journal*, 21 October 1978, pp. 1672–1675.
11. "Council Drops Police, Fire Consolidation," *The Oakland Tribune*, 11 June 1979.
12. Cuciti, Peggy, *Federal Constraints on State and Local Government Actions* (Paper prepared for the Office of Intergovernmental Relations, Congressional Budget Office, Washington, D.C., January 1979).
13. *Final Report*, Commission on Government Reform, State of California, January 1979.
14. Fitzgerald, Maureen, "Jarvis II," *California Journal*, January 1980, pp. 35–36.
15. Goldstein, Herman, *Policing a Free Society* (Cambridge, Mass.: Ballinger, 1977).
16. Greenwood, P. W., et al., *The Criminal Investigation Process* (Lexington Books, Lexington, Mass., 1977).
17. Grimm, Eric, "Gates Calls for New Crime Laws," *Westchester-Ladera Observer*, 29 November 1978.
18. *An Historical and Comparative Analysis of Expenditures in the City of New York*, Temporary Commission on City Finances, New York, 1976.
19. Hufford, Harry L., *Recommendations for the Proposed 1979–1980 Budget*, Los Angeles, California, 24 April 1979.
20. *Impact of Federal Paperwork on State and Local Governments: An Assessment by the Academy for Contemporary Problems*, Commission on Federal Paperwork, Washington, D.C., 1977.
21. *The Intergovernmental Grant System: An Assessment and Proposed Policies*, Advisory Commission on Intergovernmental Relations, Washington, D.C., 1978.
22. *The Intergovernmental Grant System as Seen by Local, State, and Federal Officials*, Report A–54, Advisory Commission on Intergovernmental Relations, Washington, D.C., 1977.
23. Johnston, David, "Return To Work, Court Orders Striking Deputies," *Los Angeles Times*, 14 July 1979.

24. Lee, Timothy J., "District Attorney Collection of Child Support: The Need for Reform," *California State Bar Journal* (April 1980): 156–161.
25. Levine, Charles H., "More on Cutback Management: Hard Questions for Hard Times," *Public Administration Review,* Vol. 39, No. 2 (March-April 1979): 179–183.
26. Lipson, Albert J., with Marvin Lavin, *Political and Legal Responses to Proposition 13 in California,* The Rand Corporation, Santa Monica, Calif., R–2483–DOJ, January 1980.
27. Lovell, Catherine H., Robert Kneisel, Max Neuman, Adam Z. Rose, and Charles A. Tobin, *Federal and State Mandating on Local Governments: An Exploration of Issues and Impacts* (Riverside, Graduate School of Administration, University of California), June 1979.
28. Oakland, William H., "Proposition 13: Genesis and Consequence," *National Tax Journal,* Vol. XXXII, No. 2 (June 1979).
29. Orlov, Rick, "Pay Ruling May Spur Labor Woes," *Valley News* (Los Angeles), 17 February 1979.
30. Pascal, Anthony H., *User Charges, Contracting Out, and Privatization in an Era of Fiscal Retrenchment,* The Rand Corporation, Santa Monica, Calif., P–6471, April 1980.
31. Pascal, Anthony H., and Mark David Menchik, *Fiscal Containment: Who Gains? Who Loses?,* The Rand Corporation, Santa Monica, Calif., R–2494/1–FF/RC, September 1979.
32. "Piper Pushes for L.A. to End CETA Program," *Valley News* (Los Angeles), 4 May 1979.
33. "Police Staff Near 'Breaking Point'," *Valley News* (Los Angeles), 22 December 1978.
34. Posner, Paul L., and Stephen M. Sorett, "A Crisis in the Fiscal Commons: The Impact of Federal Expenditures on State and Local Governments," *Public Contract Law Journal* (1978): 341–378.
35. Pressman, Steven, and Gail Diane Cox, "Job Protests by Bailiffs, Clerks Disrupts Courtroom Dockets," *Daily Journal,* 13 July 1979.
36. *Proposition 13: How California Government Coped with a $6 Billion Revenue Loss,* Comptroller General of the United States, Report GGD–79–88, Washington, D.C., 23 September 1979.
37. *Proposition 13 in Los Angeles County Government: Before and After,* Los Angeles County Economy and Efficiency Commission, 5 February 1980.
38. "Public Safety Study Committee Final Report," a report submitted to the Piedmont City Council, 17 May 1979.
39. Reischauer, Robert D., "Intergovernmental Responsibility for Meeting the Equity Considerations of Proposition 13: The Federal Role," in *Proposition 13 and Its Consequences for Public Management* (Cambridge, Mass., Abt Books, 1979), pp. 13–21.
40. "San Diego Withstanding Prop. 13 Cutbacks Well," *Valley News* (Los Angeles), 27 February 1979.
41. Sklarewitz, Norman, "Citizen Cops," *American Way,* March 1979, pp. 30–35.

42. *State Mandating of Local Expenditures*, Report A–67, Advisory Commission on Intergovernmental Relations, Washington, D.C., July 1978.
43. *A Study of the Local Government Impacts of Proposition 13–Vol. I (Summaries)*, Department of Finance, State of California, Sacramento, January 1979.
44. *A Study of the Local Government Impacts of Proposition 13–Vol. II (Counties)*, State of California, Department of Finance, Sacramento, January 1979.
45. Stumpf, Jack, and Paul Terrell, *Proposition 13 and California Human Services: First Year Impacts on Budgets, Personnel, and Clients*, National Association of Social Workers, Inc., California Chapter, Millbrae, Calif., February 1979.
46. "Survey of Alameda County Judicial Districts," no author, no date.
47. Welkos, Robert, "Six More Sheriff's Deputies Quit Force," *Los Angeles Times*, 7 December 1978.
48. "What Passage of Jarvis II is Likely to Do," *The Oakland Tribune*, 9 March 1980.

A Social Analysis of the Economic Future of the Criminal Justice System

Parts I and II examined the relationship between economic decline and crime and criminal justice from an overall systemic perspective. The four chapters in Part III take a somewhat narrower focus by examining the possible effects of economic adversity on specific components of the criminal justice system. The first three chapters examine the effects on the traditional components—the police, courts, and corrections. They examine the possibility of success or failure which each component can expect in its adaptation to economic crisis. Changes which might occur in goals and functions, as well as in structure, are also posited. In contrast, the fourth chapter considers the possibility of the development of an alternative justice model in response to the inadequacies of the existing system to respond in an economic crisis.

Jack Greene, in Chapter 8, notes that the traditional concept of the police function has been that of crime control. This function is rooted in criminal law and has been pursued through a law enforcement orientation aimed at deterrence and incapacitation. However, as the municipal economy has worsened, there has been an increased demand for accountability; consequently, all public agencies are expected to be able to prove their effectiveness. Since police organizations have been unable to stem the rise in crime, much less, significantly control it, they have been forced to reexamine their purported crime control function. Greene argues that the services police agencies provide have always gone beyond simple law enforcement, and that the number of services is continuing to expand. The recent pressure to reconsider their function, however, has forced the agencies to incorporate these additional services into their self-definition. Police work is now being defined in terms of collective goods rather than crime control. Greene forecasts continued structural and process change within police agencies as municipal resources become more and more scarce.

Focusing on the courts, David Saari argues that neither the court system nor public defender office is immune from economic adversity. His thesis is supported by empirical analysis which indicates a recent reduction in resources. Given this fact, Saari describes the effect of fiscal resource reductions as creating a situation in which justice must be rationed. The quality of defense may suffer as a consequence, or the length of pretrial confinement may be inordinately long. Ultimately, a trial could become discriminatory or due process could be denied.

Saari argues that certain court and public defender offices will be more susceptible to the effects of economic adversity than others. Those with exceptional management, lowest reasonable cost per case, no unusual delays, and sufficient capacity to accept more clients or hear more cases will be less likely to suffer severely in a declining economy—and hence less likely to have to ration justice.

In Chapter 10, David Duffee suggests that changes in the national economy are likely to have impact on the goals and structure of penal organizations. The form and extent of impact depends upon the shape of the political economy of penal systems. Mandating groups are likely to attempt to alter penal resources in accordance with the value of processing offenders relative to the value of dealing with other social problems. In contrast, penal agencies are likely to attempt to maintain a level of resources that will preserve the internal social system. Changes in penal domain, particularly the shift toward offender needs, deterrence, and services to nonoffender groups, may be seen as attempts by the organization to maintain resources as the social value of the offender declines.

Dennis Longmire takes a contrasting approach, arguing that dissatisfaction with service provision by bureaucratic criminal justice agencies, in combination with the fiscal cutbacks currently being imposed on many agencies, creates a climate in which alternative forms of justice delivery may develop. We may see a move from formally constituted and recognized bureaucratic justice organizations to popular justice organizations—the latter operating to resolve interpersonal disputes, but totally from outside the boundaries of the formal justice system. Longmire provides several examples of popular justice efforts which exhibit the diversity of function within this area. The current economic crisis, he argues, may serve a stimulus for furthering such developments.

Chapter 8

Changes in the Conception of Police Work: Crime Control Versus Collective Goods

Jack R. Greene*

In the 1960s, the public increasingly began to view the police as a social and political institution. Since that time, law enforcement has emerged as a major public bureaucracy, experiencing what is perhaps the greatest rate of growth of any civic agency. A number of issues have contributed to the political, social, and economic growth of the police. Such factors as the absolute growth in population, the relative changes in population characteristics (particularly age distribution), the increase in reported crime, the social turmoil of the 1960s, and the expansion of the public sector economy during the era of the Great Society have all greatly influenced the development and expansion of law enforcement services. Implicit in many of the factors associated with the growth of the law enforcement enterprise are a number of assumptions regarding the relationship between the nature of police work and crime control expenditures, police expenditures and the rate of crime, and the model of organization most appropriate to achieve law enforcement goals.

These assumptions have been challenged in recent years, and empirical evidence suggests that many may in fact be erroneous. Moreover, as the municipal economy continues to worsen, the public has abandoned crime as a major issue and focused instead on govern-

*School of Criminal Justice, Michigan State University

ment accountability. All public bureaucracies, including the police, are being pressured at least to appear efficient and effective. Such pressure for organizational accountability in law enforcement calls into question previous assumptions about what services the police actually provide, as well as the manner in which such services are provided. Furthermore, pressure is growing from within the police bureaucracy to reconsider the nature of policing itself. The cumulative effects of both externally induced economic pressure for police effectiveness, and internal organizational pressure focused on the utilization of police resources, are likely to affect profoundly the structure of law enforcement in the future.

Until recently, the crime control model of law enforcement has been the dominant conception of policing. The traditional assumptions inherent in the crime control model include the idea that law enforcement is rooted solely in the criminal law, that law enforcement is essentially a process aimed at controlling and deterring deviant social behavior, and that a control-centered bureaucracy is the most appropriate organizational form to oversee the police function. As such, the crime control model of law enforcement defines a rather narrow range of police outcomes, most of which are related to the occurrence of crime. It excludes the service clientele from access and input into the decision-making process, thus being police-centered in policy making, and centralizes decision making and authority within the bureaucracy, further limiting police officer access to the organizational policy making process.

In the past few years, an alternative model of law enforcement—the collective goods model—has emerged in the operations of the police, as well as in the research literature on law enforcement. While no single police department has embraced a truly collective orientation, there is evidence to suggest that internal police personnel pressure and external economic conditions are confronting and modifying the assumptions held under the crime control orientation. Specifically, the collective goods model of policing expands the rather narrow concept of crime control by broadening the quasi-legal and administrative functions of the police, focuses on problem resolution and the substance of policing rather than the application of law enforcement, expands the range of policy outputs and effects, includes the service clientele in both the definition and development of law enforcement policy, and incorporates a shared authority and decision-making model of organization designed to facilitate organizational goal attainment.

In this chapter, I examine the growth of American municipal policing from the perspective of the underlying model of police organization—the crime control model—which has dominated police organizations.[1] I also have attempted to assess the impact of the emerging collective goods model of law enforcement in terms of the economic and social conditions supporting the development of such a model, and its implications for the future of law enforcement.

MUNICIPAL POLICING AND THE CRIME CONTROL MODEL

The importance to the public of municipal policing during the 1960s was affected by numerous factors. First, the rate of reported crime rose dramatically from those levels reported in the 1950s. During the period 1960 to 1965, the President's Crime Commission reported that violent crime had increased by 25 percent and that property crime had increased by 36 percent.[2] Furthermore, long-term crime trends for particular crime types were rising at an alarming rate. These dramatic increases in crime rates were related to such factors as the change in the age composition of the general population, increased affluence, increased expectation, and changes in police reporting practices.[3] Nevertheless, increases in the level of reported crime were noted by the Commission as affecting the overall level of police expenditure and the "costs" of crime prevention.

In addition to the increase in reported crime, law enforcement was confronted with massive social and political unrest. Public demonstrations, civil disobedience, and urban riots focused attention on the role of the civil police in maintaining the social order. At the height of the political and social turmoil, Congress passed the Safe Streets and Omnibus Crime Control Act of 1968, authorizing the expenditure of federal resources for local police efforts. The federal "war on crime," coupled with the acknowledged need for maintenance of civil order, supported a large increase in expenditures for law enforcement. Undergoing unprecedented technological and social change, the federal government thus turned to local law enforcement to bring the country through the turmoil.

A third factor affecting policing in the last 20 years was the emergence of government as a major employer. The service economy burgeoned during this period, as government expanded its role in providing public goods. The police were not immune from this trend, and they acquired substantial support for additional growth of service, duties, and personnel. For the period from 1973 to 1977, the average expenditure for police protection across all levels of government rose by 105 percent, with the largest increases occurring at the county and state levels (123.2 percent and 110.7 percent respectively); there was a 78.6 percent increase at the municipal level of government.[4]

Prior to the emergence of the police as a national issue, expenditures for public law enforcement kept pace with inflation, population increases, and the rate of urbanization. In a study of police expenditures between 1902 and 1960, Bordua and Haurek concluded that while certain large urban areas were spending proportionally more for police protection in 1960 as compared to 1902, the police had made few financial gains independent of other factors—demographic factors (population, urbanization, motor vehicles), and inflation—which were generally beyond their control.[5]

Extending the analysis of Bordua and Haurek, Odoni found that the average police expenditure more than tripled from 1959 to 1973 in the 33 major police agencies he examined.[6] This increase represented a 40 percent increase in police personnel and accounted for a substantial increase in police officer salaries. With respect to the effect of rising crime rates on the rate of growth of police agencies, Odoni concluded:

> Thus, the incidence of crime kept pace with the growth in city police expenditures, which . . . also more than tripled during the same period. If, then, the frequency of incidents of serious crime is used as an indicator of police workload, it is easy to understand city police department employment for 1959-73.[7]

Odoni infers a workload relationship in which police employment is somehow directly related to crime levels. This assumption has permeated police work force arguments for many years, and stems in some measure from Peel's criterion of police effectiveness—that is, the absence of crime.[8]

In addition to the absolute growth experienced by police agencies in recent years, law enforcement agencies have increased their relative share of the public dollar vis-à-vis other public service agencies. A review of statistics collected by the Bureau of Census regarding the distribution of public expenditures for various governmental functions indicates that in 1950 the police consumed about 0.9 percent of total governmental expenditures, while by 1977, law enforcement's share of the expenditure had increased to 11.7 percent.[9] In contrast, expenditures for fire protection rose from 0.5 percent in 1950 to 4.3 percent in 1977; health expenditures rose from 0.7 percent to 9.1 percent; expenditures for sanitation increased from 0.8 percent to 8.9 percent; and expenditures for parks and recreation rose from 3 percent to 3.9 percent of total governmental expenditures. These data clearly indicate that public expenditures for law enforcement have increased more rapidly than other public service agencies.

Since Sir Robert Peel suggested that the criterion of police efficiency was the absence of crime, law enforcement agencies have accepted the crime indicator as the measure of organizational success. To that end, the division of labor in police agencies has been devoted to crime deterrence and criminal apprehension. According to the President's Crime Commission, over 80 percent of the police workforce is devoted to basic patrol, a primary function of which is provision of a general deterrent force in the community.[10] The remainder of police personnel are usually assigned to the investigation function, which is focused on deterrence at the individual level through follow-up investigations and criminal apprehension.

The assumptions which have guided the crime control model of policing have gone unchallenged in the past. Myth, folklore, and subcultural definitions of police work have in fact guided the acquisition and use of police protective services.

These unchallenged assumptions have led to the development of what Manning calls "police presentational strategies," or the methods by which the police manipulate public expectations and understandings about crime and the police response.[11] Among these strategies are the reliance on bureaucratic organization, secrecy, technology, the manipulation of crime statistics, and styles of policing.[12] Each of these presentational strategies affects public understanding of the police role and the crime relatedness of the police function. Each attempts to create the image of policing as a profession with all the attributes inherent in that concept. For example, bureaucratic rationalism is believed to enhance public perception of the police as an efficient and well-organized bureaucracy.

Manipulation and presentation of crime statistics, styles of policing, and technology are all factors which shape public expectation regarding police response and methods of crime control. Since the police are responsible for the collection of crime statistics, they exercise great control on the definitions of incidents included in crime reports, as well as the actual quantities of incidents reported. For years, the rise of crime, as described in official statistics, has indicated an urgent need for increased police presence.[13]

Technology has also entered into the police realm as a method for creating the aura of efficiency and effectiveness. Advances in information technology, vehicle monitoring systems, and radio equipment have been used by the police to attempt to demonstrate a greater capacity to react to crime.[14] By styles of police, I refer to the method by which police interact with their community. Wilson's distinction between legalistic, watchman, and service styles of policing suggests that the police can, and do, manage their style of presentation according to perceptions of community needs.[15] Each of these presentational strategies ostensibly increases the professionalism of law enforcement by creating a public image of a crime-fighting organization, efficiently managed, and using rational science and technology to intercede in crime problems.

In periods of rapid economic expansion, these assumptions were of little concern. As long as the service economy could absorb the "cost" of crime prevention, underlying premises were ignored. The current fiscal crises faced by many municipal governments, and the economic forecasts for the 1980s, have raised questions about how service delivery in all government sectors—including the police—will be accomplished. The police themselves have become more willing to assess their role in light of research findings, and are beginning to reconsider the methods of police work previously defined.[16] As police self-awareness grows, and municipalities reconsider the questions of service delivery, we can expect the assumptions underlying police work to be critically reappraised.

POLICE EXPENDITURE, POLICE WORK AND CRIME CONTROL

A major assumption underlying police expenditures in the crime control model concerns the presumed relationship between police expenditures and the incidence of crime. As crime escalated in the 1960s and 1970s, police executives throughout the country exhorted the citizenry about the need to increase police protection—despite the fact that the relationship between police expenditure and crime levels was unclear. In fact, numerous studies concluded that no such relationship exists between overall police expenditure and the rate of crime; other studies found a positive relationship, where the more resources were expended, the more likely that crime rates would increase.

In a study of the 21 largest urban areas in the country, Wellford examined the relationship between crime rates, various socioeconomic characteristics of the population, and certain measures of official crime control efforts, including the per capita police budget.[17] Analyzing crime statistics for 1960 and 1970, he concluded that the crime control variables accounted for only approximately 7 percent of the variation in crime rate, while the socioeconomic variables such as population characteristics accounted for 42 percent of crime rate variation. Wellford further examined the relationship between police expenditure and clearance rates, and found that, in the cities studied, the level of police effort expended (measured by budget) had little effect on police clearance rates. Wellford's findings regarding clearance rates are consistent with those reported by Ehrlich[18] and Sjoquist,[19] each of whom found no significant relationship between per capita police expenditures and the probability of arrest and conviction.

Pressman and Carol, in a cross-sectional study of 95 Standard Metropolitan Statistical Areas (SMSAs), found a positive correlation between the number of police per capita and crime rates.[20] They interpreted this finding to mean that areas with higher crime rates employed more police personnel; but they also concluded "that more police may not be the answer to high crime rates and that larger expenditures on police protection are not cost effective in combating crime."[21]

In a study conducted by Greenwood and Wadycki, the relationships between police expenditure and crime rates for 199 SMSAs were examined for the year 1960.[22] The researchers in this study were concerned with the problem of simultaneity presented by the interaction between police expenditures and crime rates: "not only are measured crime rates a function of the number of police employed, but the number of police employed are a function of measured crime rates, via the impact that crime rates have on (police) expenditures."[23] Using a simultaneous equations model of crime rates and public expenditures, the authors concluded that 1. the police are more efficient at detecting crime rather than deterring crime, and 2. that a rise in the number of police (increase in police expenditure) will ultimately result in a rise in the number of detected crimes and, hence, a higher crime rate. Such a positive relationship between police expenditure and crime rates raises serious questions about the reliability of assumptions that expenditure for crime control has a deterrent effect.

Studying the deterrent effect of law enforcement using cross-sectional data on crime rates in 113 southern cities, Cloninger found little support for the deterrence hypothesis between aggregate level crime rates and police expenditures.[24] In another examination of law enforcement expenditure and urban crime, conducted by McPheters and Stronge, data for the year 1970 were analyzed for the 43 largest central cities in the United States.[25] Per capita police expenditures were found to be positively related to crime rates. These authors concluded that, given the relatively weak impact police expenditures have on crime, such expenditures might better be regarded as expenditures "to clean up after crime rather than specifically to deter future crime."[26] Lastly, a study examining crime and employment data, collected for 252 northern and northeastern suburbs for the years 1970 to 1972, concluded that police employment was responsive to crime rates in that communities with high crime rates expended higher amounts of resources for police protection.[27] The authors noted, however, that these expenditures were presumably made under the assumption that increases in police protection would ultimately deter crime. A positive effect of police employment on violent crime was found instead, suggesting that the police capacity to process rather than deter crime had increased for violent crime. The authors found no relationship between police expenditures and property crime.

The collective evidence to date suggests that, in the aggregate, expenditures for police protection rarely affect the rate of crime and, when they do, the relationship is often positive. As police resource expenditures are increased, it is not unusual to find that the police have increased their capacity to detect rather than deter crime. Hence, arguments for increases in per capita police expenditure rarely yield the desired results—lower crime. The relationships between aggregate-level police expenditures and the incidence of crime suggest that, in the future, police executives will find it increasingly more difficult to persuade municipal decisionmakers that crime will be reduced by merely increasing police expenditures. More importantly, such an inability to demonstrate the crime deterrent relationship suggests that the conception of police work as predominantly crime-related is also subject to municipal review.

In the latter half of this century, the police role has become synonymous with crime fighting. As police reformers have stressed the "professional" norm, the crime-related aspects of the police role have become the sine qua non of the occupation.[28] Consequently, the crime-related aspects of the police occupation have dominated the method of service delivery as well as the organizational structure of law enforcement in ways which affect the overall quality of policing.

In one of the first challenges to the nature of police work, Wilson argued that while the police are called to provide numerous services, their work essentially revolves around a concept of order maintenance.[29] In a study of police patrol supporting Wilson's study, Albert Reiss concluded that much of law enforcement activity is citizen-directed and reactive to crime rather than proactive; hence, it is oriented toward crime prevention.[30] More recent police workload studies have generally rebuffed the idea that a great share of police work is oriented to law enforcement. These studies have been grouped by Cordner according to the methods used to collect information about what the patrol officer does; the results of such workload analyses are reported for studies using dispatch records, patrol officer self-reporting surveys, and observational studies.[31] Although the completeness of these studies has been debated, their general thrust indicates that some large proportion of the patrol officer's daily routine is not directly concerned with law enforcement activities.

Studies employing police dispatch records generally focus on the distribution of calls for service over various types of police activity—for example, law enforcement versus service-related. Cumming, Cumming, and Edell, using dispatch records for 82 selected hours from a metropolitan police department, concluded that about one-half of the calls to the police complaint desk involved calls for help "and some form of support for personal and interpersonal problems."[32]

A study conducted by Wilson in Syracuse, New York, involved the classification of a sample of radio calls during a week in June, 1966.[33] Wilson classified 10 percent of the calls as law enforcement, 22 percent as information-gathering, 30 percent as order maintenance, and 38 percent as service-related. Wilson concluded from this analysis that much of what the police do is related to "handling people" rather than enforcing the law. Analyzing dispatch records for the cities of Detroit and St. Louis, Bercal found that of the calls received by the police in both cities, only about 16 percent could be classifed as crime-related.[34]

Examining both dispatch records and officer activity reports, Webster concluded that only about 16 percent of the duties performed by the patrol officers could be classified as crime-related.[35] In terms of the crime relatedness of patrol officer activity while on patrol, Webster concluded that about 18 percent of patrol activity was crime-related, while approximately 14 percent of patrol officer time was social service-related, and about one-half was devoted to administrative functions. Reiss, using Chicago Police Department dispatch records for April, 1966, found that 83 percent of patrol calls were classified as involving noncriminal matters, and that calls for service accounted for approximately only 14 percent of total patrol, while 85 percent of patrol officer time was used for routine patrol.[36]

The findings of the dispatch studies generally suggest that the police workload is not predominated by law enforcement activities. Yet some doubt remains because these studies do not account for at least 50 percent of the patrol officer's time—time which is generally devoted to uncommitted patrol. Studies using both officer-reported information and direct observation attempt to expand on the earlier dispatch record examinations.

Using the self-reported method to examine patrol officer activity, O'Neill and Bloom, in a study of 18 California cities, found that about 5 percent of patrol time was reported to be involved in crime-related activities.[37] This study also concluded that about 73 percent of the patrol officer's reported time was spent in patrolling, and that such activities as traffic, nonduty activities, and administrative and secondary activities each accounted for from 10 to 20 percent of the patrol officer's time.

An analysis of the data collected through the Kansas City Preventive Patrol Experiment, which used observers to document officer activities, revealed that 60 percent of patrol time was uncommitted, that 25 percent of this time was spent on nonpolice-related activity, and that officers spent only 25 percent of their free patrol time on mobile police-related activities, spending another 25 percent of their time traveling to and from the station, going to court or headquarters, or servicing vehicles.[38]

A recent study conducted by Cordner, examined the patrol officer's time utilization in a midwestern city during July and August 1977.[39] Using both the observational and survey method, the study concluded that 55 percent of the observed patrol time was uncommitted, and that of this uncommitted time, 39 percent was spent taking breaks and 39 percent was spent engaged in various types of patrol. Cordner concluded that, in the aggregate, 44 percent of the patrol officer's time was considered "down time" (spent performing administrative tasks or taking breaks), 39 percent involved ambiguous activities which were neither solely crime- nor noncrime-related, and that the remaining 13 percent was spent in clearly crime-related activities.

We can conclude from these police workload studies that, of the roughly 50 percent of patrol time which is committed through radio dispatches, some sizeable proportion is not directly law enforcement-related. Of the remaining 50 percent, at least one-half is accounted for by administrative duties and breaks. These results suggest that a large proportion of the patrol officer's time is not committed to law enforcement activities and that the model of police organization which views the crime-fighting role of the police as paramount is not supportable.

Despite such evidence, the crime control model of police operations is still very appealing to the police and the public alike. For example, when the general public was asked for ways their local police department could improve, the selected sample from 13 American cities called for more police to be deployed at certain times or in certain areas, the total number of police to be increased, the police to be more prompt in responding, and that they patrol or investigate more.[40] Each of these responses is conditioned on the assumption that the police have an impact on the level of crime.

The crime control model of police organization devotes most of the resource in police agencies toward crime prevention and criminal apprehension. As we have seen, however, neither the aggregate expenditure for police personnel nor the per capita ratio of police to citizenry seems to be related to crime levels. Moreover, the documented activities undertaken by the patrol workforce appear to be only partially related to crime outcomes. Part of the reason for this lack of evidence of a relationship between expenditures for crime control and crime rates has to do with the level of aggregation used in the expenditure studies. Wilson and Boland, for example, find only a moderate correlation between the number of total police officers and the number of patrol units on the street at any given time, suggesting that such factors as whether patrol officers are assigned one or two to a patrol unit or whether the department has an aggressive or passive patrol strategy are likely to reduce or mask the effects of increased police expenditures on the level of crime.[41] This suggests that what the police do with the resource expended, rather than the proportionate increase in that resource, will be more likely to affect crime—assuming of course, that the crime control model of policing is accepted.

THE POLICE RESPONSE AND CRIME CONTROL

Studies which examine the strategy of the police in affecting the rate of crime generally focus on the two major aspects of the police function—patrol and investigations—each of which is expected to contribute to the police capacity to deter crime. In the case of patrol, both preventive patrol and response time have been assumed to affect crime deterrence by increasing police presence and, hence, the probability of crime detection and apprehension. This in turn is expected to lead to lower crime and increased citizen feelings of safety and satisfaction with police service. Criminal investigation, in contrast, has focused on the follow-up investigation process as a method to increase the likelihood of individual apprehension, thus affecting both general and special (individual) deterrence. A recent examination of these police strategies suggests that police service delivery as presently constructed does little to affect crime, citizen perceptions of safety, or citizen satisfaction.

A major project challenging the presumed effects of police preventive patrol was conducted in Kansas City, Missouri, by the Police Foundation in 1972.[42] The Kansas City experiment sought to manipulate the level of preventive patrol occurring within fifteen matched patrol beats. Researchers created three patrol conditions (reactive patrol, normal patrol, and proactive patrol), and measured such crime control police outcomes as reported crime levels, victimization rates, levels and types of arrest, citizen fear of crime, and citizen satisfaction with the police. The study concluded that no statistically significant differences could be found between the experimental conditions, indicating that preventive patrol efforts were not associated with their presumed effects.[43]

Another patrol-oriented crime control strategy is concerned with police response time. It is argued that by reducing the patrol officer's response to a citizen request for police service, arrest rates will increase, the deterrent presence of the police will be enhanced, and citizen perception of safety and satisfaction with the police will be increased. A number of studies have examined response time and, in general, conclude that patrol response time has little effect on the arrest rate, citizen satisfaction with police services, or citizen perceptions of safety.[44]

Bertram and Vargo concluded that, in the case of robbery, an inordinate amount of time elapsed between the time of victimization and the time the police were called.[45] This lag in citizen activation of the police by far overshadowed the time involved to either dispatch the call to a patrol unit or the time required for the patrol unit to respond to the call. Response time studies have also concluded that it is the citizen's expectation which guides evaluations regarding both the speed at which the police services are delivered and the individual citizen's assessment of the quality of those services. These studies also raise a serious question about police ability to prioritize the vast number of citizen calls for service which they receive.

While detective novels and television crime shows have created a folk hero out of the police investigator, a number of studies seriously question whether detectives do anything at all.[46] A series of studies examining the investigative function find that the vast number of cases reported to the police are unsolvable. That is, in a majority of cases, there is generally no evidence, no witness, and no suspects. In such cases, the likelihood of a successful investigation is severely reduced. There is further evidence to suggest that most minor crimes go uninvestigated and that a large number of serious felonies receive little, if any, investigative effort. The evidence also suggests that the police rarely provide feedback to the citizen regarding the status of the investigation, and that crime victims know little about the resolution of their case, thus negating the detectives' symbolic role.

These findings seriously challenge the current organization of patrol and investigative services in most American police departments. Despite such findings, however, the organizational structure of policing continues to orient police service delivery in the manner suggested by the crime control model—increased deterrence, rapid response, and follow-up investigations.

THE CRIME CONTROL BUREAUCRACY

A number of themes have emerged in the reformation of law enforcement throughout the last half century. Each has in some way been related to a concern with controlling the police. In the early 1900s, concern with law enforcement centered on ridding police departments of corruption and political interference in the management and operation of law enforcement. In recent times, while corruption and political neutrality are continuing themes, the focus of concern has shifted to professionalization of the police. Due in large measure to external pressure to reform, law enforcement embraced a strict model of bureaucracy, relying heavily on models of organization used in the military. Now, the paramilitary crime control bureaucracy of law enforcement has emerged as the organizational structure of the police.[47] Such a model of law enforcement organization has been influenced tremendously by the assumptions of policing discussed earlier. In particular, the crime focus of law enforcement has led to an organizational model which attempts to rigidly control and guide the behavior of the individual police officer.

The paramilitary organization of law enforcement, emphasizing control, includes such features as a strictly interpreted hierarchy of authority and centralized decision making, formalized role relationships including legalistic distinctions of superior/subordinate relationships, a downward-directed communications process, overreliance on formalized procedures, rules and regulations, and a harsh disciplinary and sanction system designed to gain individual compliance. Some of the reasons the paramilitary model of organization has been (and continues to be) attractive to policing include the general analogy between the military and war, and the police and the war on crime; the desire to control the exercise of deadly force in society; the belief that the police should be a well-disciplined, tactical response arm of the civil government; and the more generalized American disdain for state intervention into private affairs. Each of these factors has an underlying theme—the need to restrain the force of the state as it is exercised in a democratic society.

The need for this control has served to enhance the application of the military organizational structure because the model presumes that control is exercised through such an institutional arrangement. The nature of police work, however, does much to repudiate the belief that the police are in fact a paramilitary organization; rather, it suggests that the control assumed to derive from this form of organization is illusory.[48] Due to the entrepreneurial nature of policing—characterized by individual police officers acting in roles largely independent of the police organization, generally unsupervised, and developing and maintaining essentially secret information which is not shared with other organizational members—the police agency is reduced in practice to a "mock bureaucracy," arbitrary and capricious in its use of sanction and with little control over the work of organizational incumbents. Such a characterization of the police bureaucracy does not obviate the fact that much of what is done in police management is done under the assumed control implied in the paramilitary model of organization.

The conflict which emerges from this description of police work and police organization is obvious. The social organization of policing suggests that internalization of rules and norms of behavior may be most efficient in assisting individual police officers in the performance of their duties, which are highly ambiguous in nature and require the exercise of a great amount of discretion. Formal police organization, in contrast, assumes that individual police officer discretion is minimal, due in large measure to the proliferation of rules and regulations by the bureaucracy, and that the police response has been routinized and thus made unambiguous through organizational edict. Such contradictions place great strain on individual organizational members as well as the entire system of police management. An alternative model of policing has recently emerged; its implementation portends a substantial alteration of police organizational thinking.

THE EMERGENCE OF A COLLECTIVE GOODS MODEL OF POLICING

In recent years, economic conditions faced by most municipal governments have seriously challenged the assumptions inherent in the crime control model of policing and the style of police service delivery. As crime continued to rise in the 1970s and the police were unable to demonstrate a capacity to affect the level of crime, the sacrosanct nature of the police as a municipal agency came under question. The first major layoff of police officers occurred in New York City in 1975, with approximately 3,000 police officers being discharged. Similar economic conditions in other cities (Detroit, for example), have called into question the traditional methods of providing police services and the outcomes of those services provided.

As municipal resources become increasingly scarce, at least two related economic concerns confront policing. The first has to do with alternative means of providing policing services, or the efficiency of service provision. The second concern is with the particular outcomes of policing as currently defined, or the effectiveness of policing. These two issues have given rise to an alternative model of law enforcement—the collective goods model.

A primary issue in the emergence of the collective goods model of policing is the recognition that the police are a multipurpose public bureaucracy responsible for numerous functions, some of which are crime-related and some of which are not. As Herman Goldstein indicates:

> Viewing the police—first and foremost—simply as an agency of municipal government, elementary as this concept may seem, serves a number of important purposes. It puts to rest the argument that police functioning should be viewed solely within the context of the criminal justice system. It rids us of the notion that the police are a legal institution created with a function strictly defined by statute, and it substitutes in its place a more flexible concept of the police as an administrative unit of local government. And it contributes toward challenging the widely held belief that dealing with crime is the sole function of the police; that all other tasks are peripheral or ancillary.[49]

Viewing the police as a multipurpose civic agency broadens the crime control definition of policing to include the larger public regulatory function, only a portion of which is crime-focused. Such a view of public law enforcement also includes such equally important police functions as order maintenance, crime prevention, crime identification, public safety, conflict management and conflict resolution, the protection of constitutional liberties, and a host of social services which are not provided regularly by other municipal agencies.

Such a redefinition of the police role, recognizing the multiple objectives of law enforcement, obviously entails consideration of the ways in which these various police services are provided, the types of police personnel performing these various roles, and the administrative structures most appropriate to oversee such a diverse set of functions. It is also immediately apparent that the focus of attention shifts from mere consideration of the quantity and speed at which crime control services are delivered, to considerations of the quality of police output and the efficiencies of various service delivery methods.

The quality of police output has been an illusive concept, particularly when the output criterion was the absence of crime. But the police provide numerous services which can be measured on both quantitative and qualitative dimensions. Reductions in vehicular and pedestrian accidents, increases in citizen understanding of crime prevention and the role of the public in law enforcement and order maintenance, increasing citizen satisfaction with services provided, and providing equity in the law enforcement services delivered are outcomes which have qualitative dimensions. Increasing the quality of citizen/police interaction over the entire range of police functions can also be made a central focus for police efforts. To some degree, the social institution of law enforcement is moving toward such outcome specification and measurement. What is not always recognized, however, is the change in the institution of policing which will be necessary for the attainment of such outcomes.

One of the most demonstrative changes in law enforcement, induced in part by external concerns for productivity and effectiveness, is that of patrol officer deployment. As previously indicated, both the preventive patrol and response time analyses of patrol operations indicate that current patrol deployment practices are less than optimal.

Various new patrol strategies have recently been implemented in a number of cities. Initial results suggest that 1. directed patrol at night may contain certain crimes, most notably burglary; 2. crime analysis information disseminated to patrol officers can increase the probability of arrest; 3. the extended use of field interrogations in cities where such practices have been established can affect suppressible crime; and 4. investigative efficiency can be increased by including patrol officers in investigative decision making.[50] Furthermore, there is evidence to suggest that community relations can be maintained without loss of arrest productivity by ensuring that patrol officers learn about the social and economic characteristics of their patrol areas.[51] These studies forcefully illustrate that a major restructuring of the patrol function can be undertaken and that such a restructuring can contribute to the quality of police output.

The consolidation of police service is becoming increasingly appealing, despite local control objections. While reserach has indicated that the fragmentation of law enforcement is not synonymous with duplication of police services, current and projected economic restriction have focused public concern on police service delivery.[52] Efforts at coordinated or consolidated law enforcement include the contracting of police services, the partial coordination of selected police services and the complete consolidation of contiguous police jurisdictions. The contracting of police services, usually undertaken through sheriff's departments or countywide police agencies, is gaining in popularity.[53] The coordination of selected police services has occurred for many years in certain technological areas (notably police crime labs and centralized dispatch services[54]) and has recently broadened to include specialized investigation services, including narcotics and organized crime detective units.[55] The consolidation of public services has occurred in such places as Dade County and Jacksonville, Florida, and

Multnomha County, Oregon. The projects represent an alternative to the traditional local police agency.[56]

One of the most distinctive alternatives to the traditional crime-centered police bureaucracy is the practice of team policing. While numerous projects of varying structure have been included under the concept of team policing, it generally refers to a model of organization focused on joint decision making, the decentralization of authority, the broadening of job definitions, and the increasing of interaction between the police and the public. Early team policing efforts were implemented in such cities as Los Angeles, New York, Dayton, Syracuse, Detroit, Holyoke (Massachusetts), and Richmond (California). More recent efforts were undertaken in Cincinnati, Ohio. While each project experienced differing social, economic, and political environments, the evaluators of these projects concluded that there were consistent factors across each program which negatively affected success.[57]

First, and perhaps most important, is the threat which team policing poses for traditional styles of law enforcement. Such team policing attributes as decentralized authority and decision making, reduced distinctions between functional and operational organizational status, mutual problem resolution, and the inclusion of the service clientele in the decision-making process are anathema to traditional practice in the police bureaucracy. Such tremendous vested interest in the maintenance of the traditional police organizational structure cannot be easily dismissed. In general, studies of team policing and police organizational reform have identified a substantial amount of resistance to change from within the police bureaucracy itself, including, most notably, individuals occupying middle management levels of authority and the organized efforts of unions.[58] This internal organizational resistance has greatly affected the adoption of the alternative team model of policing.

A second impediment which is believed to affect the success of the team model is police technology itself. Information systems, command and control systems, dispatch procedures and the like have been designed to increase centralized control over the patrol officer. Such systems directly interfere with team policing efforts to the extent that team members are diverted from team assignments by central dispatch, or officers not included in the team are directed to calls for service within team areas. Information and technological systems also affect the team approach insofar as officers have been traditionally expected to expend a minimal amount of time in the resolution of any particular citizen call.[59] Under the team concept, increased interaction with the citizenry is a primary goal; such an individually centered approach to policing is obviously in conflict with the assembly line production model of the crime control response.

Lastly, team efforts have generally not been inclusive of the jurisdiction in which they operate. They have been designed as demonstration projects, never really affecting the centralized nature of the police bureaucracy. Attempted for limited time periods and over limited geographic areas, team efforts have not changed the institution of policing in a major way. While the team policing model of law enforcement has had only marginal impact on the structure of police organizations, the results of recent team approaches are encouraging, nevertheless, in that such improvements as increases in patrol officer job satisfaction, increases in patrol officer involvement in preliminary investigations, reductions in the frequency of certain types of crime, greater patrol officer awareness of community characteristics and needs, and improved or sustained levels of police community relations are now associated with a number of team policing efforts.[60]

Beyond the structural changes in law enforcement such as consolidation, contracting, patrol redesign and team-centered models, internal pressures relating to the climate of the police bureaucracy and the nature of the worker to the organization are growing and are likely to improve law enforcement structure and process in the future. For example, police agencies throughout the country are expanding the role of civilians and parapolice in public law enforcement. Economic considerations for a number of years have challenged the idea that sworn police personnel had to perform most, if not all, of the police organization's functions. The President's Crime Commission, as early as 1967, suggested the development of levels of policing differentiated by task.[61] The proposal is becoming increasingly acceptable as police agencies consider the costs of various delivery methods. In a similar fashion, police agencies are employing more and more nonsworn or civilian personnel to perform many organizational functions. In 1950, civilian employees in police departments accounted for about 7.5 percent of total police agency employment; by 1970, that figure had risen to 13.2 percent and was projected to double over 1970 levels by 1990.[62] The reasons for the increase in the use of civilian employees in law enforcement agencies includes, in addition to the obvious cost savings, the recognition of a differentiation of tasks and specialties within the agency, as well as the community input which such "civilianization" implies. Although there is currently substantial resistance to civilianization in police agencies, economic considerations and the issues of equal opportunity and affirmative action create pressure for increased use of nonsworn police personnel.

Another major factor affecting the internal restructuring of American police agencies is related to increases in police education and training. The expansion of police training curricula, the development of standards and training commissions, and the increase in college attendance among the police contribute to the changing organizational climate of policing. Training in such areas as conflict management and resolution, neighborhood justice teams, and police community relations have affected the structure of law enforcement in less obvious ways. In addition to the training which police officers receive, college coursework, with its social science and liberal arts perspectives, has begun to raise the expectation of the police themselves with respect to the quantity and quality of services they provide. Such subtle changes, it is hoped, will lessen organizational resistance to future change efforts.

A critical internal change affecting the organizational climate of law enforcement is unionism. Police unions are greatly affecting budgetary considerations in law enforcement. Collective bargaining activities have focused traditionally on such issues as salaries and overtime and special duty pay, but now, in addition to these economic concerns, police unions have begun to affect such personnel issues as employment entrance requirements, promotions, discipline, and individual efficiency evaluations. Moreover, collective bargaining in law enforcement has extended beyond personnel process matters to include concerns for the quality of the work environment. Union agreements in law enforcement now include issues that were traditionally viewed administrative prerogatives such as work assignment, manpower allocation, and equipment-manpower configurations.[63]

Currently, the policy-making process in law enforcement is being directly affected by collective bargaining arrangements. The role of police unions is likely to increase in the future. But the present conflict between police bureaucratic interests and police union interests neglects, in large measure, to include the public interest in the policy-making process. Unionism, thus, as currently defined, may inhibit public input into law enforcement matters.

PROCESS AND SUBSTANCE IN LAW ENFORCEMENT

Organizational modifications in law enforcement—as evidenced by increasing civilianization and collective bargaining, the use of team-centered policing strategies and other modifications to service delivery, the inclusion of community concerns in operational police decision making, and the impact of police training and education on organizational climate—suggest that the crime control model of law enforcement may be less intractable than was previously thought. Despite these obvious changes in the character of the law enforcement organization, numerous other situational and structural aspects of policing need to be considered before a truly public goods policing model can emerge.

A major problem confronting the conversion of the crime control model of policing is what Herman Goldstein calls the problem of "means over ends," or process over substance.[64] The means-over-ends problem relates to organizational goal displacement. During the past 10 years, the police, as a social institution, have been subject to much experimentation and review, a sizeable portion of which was designed to enhance the administrative process in police departments. Goldstein states, "The police seem to have reached a plateau at which the highest objectives to which they aspire is administrative competence. And, with some scattered exceptions, they seem reluctant to move beyond this plateau toward creating a more systematic concern for the end product of their efforts."[65]

Such a conclusion suggests that the police need to reconsider their relationship with the broader municipal government and the ways in which law enforcement and public safety concerns can be built into the public policy-making process, rather than being only tangentially related to that process. Law enforcement is a process concern, a means to a broader end; problem resolution, in contrast, is a substantive end, toward which law enforcement means can be devoted.

The emergence of the collective goods model of law enforcement is predicated on the assumption that both the quantity and quality of police-citizen exchanges can, and do, have an effect on the quality of life with regard to public safety issues. This model of law enforcement is gaining the attention of researchers and practitioners alike, as its linking of police and public issues has an intuitive appeal. The future development of the model, however, will require continued public pressure and law enforcement effort to improve the outcome of municipal police service. To the extent that economic pressures increase for the police to become more accountable for the expenditure of public resources, the police must strengthen community ties by creating realistic expectations for both the police and the public about the law enforcement role in American society.

NOTES

1. Discussion has been limited to municipal policing, as it represents approximately 75 percent of police employment and accounts for about 17,000 police agencies. See, *The National Manpower Survey of the Criminal Justice System, Volume Two, Law Enforcement* (Washington, D.C.: U.S. Government Printing Office, 1978): p. 5.

2. President's Commission on Law Enforcement and Administration of Justice, *Task Force Report: Crime and Its Impact—An Assessment* (Washington, D.C.: U.S. Government Printing Office, 1967), pp. 19–21.
3. Ibid., pp. 22–24. It was acknowledged by the Commission that changes in police reporting practices had a tremendous impact on initial increases in the crime rate. Certain of these changes were related to the general professionalization of crime reporting systems and the increased police use of centralized dispatch services.
4. U.S. Department of Justice, Law Enforcement Assistance Administration and U.S. Bureau of the Census, *Trends in Expenditure and Employment Data for the Criminal Justice System: 1971–1977* (Washington, D.C.: U.S. Government Printing Office, 1978), p. 65.
5. David J. Bordua and Edward W. Haurek, "The Police Budget's Lot: Components of the Increase in Local Police Expenditures, 1902–1960," *American Behavioral Scientist*, 13(May/June, 1970): 667–680.
6. Amedeo R. Odoni, "Recent Employment and Expenditure Trends in City Police Departments in the United States," *Journal of Criminal Justice*, 5(1977): 119–147.
7. Ibid., p. 142.
8. For a review of police reform and Sir Robert Peel, see: T. A. Critchley, *A History of Police in England and Wales,* rev. ed. (London: Constable and Co., Ltd., 1968), pp. 47–50; and, T. A. Critchley, "Peel, Rowan, and Mayne," in Philip John Stead (ed.), *Pioneers in Policing* (Montclair, N.J.: Patterson Smith, 1977), pp. 82–95.
9. U.S. Bureau of the Census, *Statistical Abstracts of the United States,* 100th ed. (Washington, D.C.: U.S. Government Printing Office, 1979), p. 284.
10. President's Commission on Law Enforcement and Administration of Justice, *Task Force Report: The Police* (Washington, D.C.: U.S. Government Printing Office, 1967), p.13
11. Peter K. Manning, *Police Work: The Social Organization of Policing* (Cambridge, Mass.: The MIT Press, 1977), Chapter 5, pp. 127–138.
12. Ibid.
13. The manipulation of crime statistics has been particularly attributed to the Federal Bureau of Investigation, to whom local police report crime information. The most noted criticism of this approach appears in Ramsey Clark, *Crime in America* (New York: Simon and Schuster, 1970), particularly chapter 3, pp. 44–55. See also Manning, *Police Work*, pp. 130–132.
14. For an excellent critique of the impact of technology on crime control efforts including those of the police, see Peter K. Manning, "Crime and Technology: The Role of Scientific Research and Technology in Crime Control," paper prepared for the National Science Foundation in connection with the "Five Year Outlook" for Science and Technology Project (May 1979).
15. James Q. Wilson, *Variety of Police Behavior* (Cambridge, Mass.: Harvard University Press, 1968).
16. See Peter K. Manning, "The Reflexivity and Facticity of Knowledge—Criminal Justice Research in the 1970s," *American Behavioral Scientist,* 22, 6(July–August 1979): 697–732.
17. Charles R. Wellford. "Crime and the Police: A Multivariate Analysis," *Criminology,* 12(August 1974): 195–213.
18. Isaac Ehrlich, "Participation in Illegitimate Activities: A Theoretical and Empirical Investigation." *Journal of Political Economy* (May–June 1973): 521–565.
19. David Lawrence Sjoquist, "Property Crime and Economic Behavior: Some Empirical Results," *American Economy Review,* 63(June, 1973): 439–446.
20. Israel Pressman and Arthur Carol, "Crime as a Diseconomy of Scale," *Review of Social Economy,* 29(September 1971): 227–236.

21. Ibid., p. 229.
22. Michael J. Greenwood and Walter J. Wadycki, "Crime Rates and Public Expenditures for Police Protection: Their Interaction," *Review of Social Economy*, 30(October 1973): 138–151.
23. Ibid., p. 149
24. Dale O. Cloninger, "The Deterrent Effect of Law Enforcement: An Evaluation of Recent Findings and Some New Evidence," *American Journal of Economics and Sociology*, 34(July, 1975): 323–335.
25. Lee R. McPheters and William B. Stronge, "Law Enforcement Expenditures and Urban Crime," *National Tax Journal*, 27(December 1973): 633–644.
26. Ibid., p. 641.
27. John Stahura and C. Ronald Huff, "Crime and Police Employment—A Structural Model," in David M. Peterson (ed.), *Police Work: Strategies and Outcomes in Law Enforcement* (Beverly Hills, Calif.: Sage Publications, 1979), pp. 73–95.
28. For an excellent review of the professionalization of law enforcement, see Samuel Walker, *A Critical History of Police Reform* (Lexington, Mass.: Lexington Books, D. C. Heath and Company, 1977), particularly chapter 3; and Robert M. Fogelson, *Big-City Police* (Cambridge, Mass.; Harvard University Press, 1977), particularly chapters 1–4.
29. Wilson, *Varieties of Police Behavior*, p. 18.
30. Albert J. Reiss, *The Police and the Public* (New Haven, Conn.: Yale University Press, 1979).
31. Gary W. Cordner, "Police Patrol Work Load Studies: A Review and Critique," *Police Studies*, 2(Summer 1979): 50–60.
32. Elaine Cumming, Ian Cumming, and Laura Edell. "Policeman as Philosopher, Guide and Friend," *Social Problems*, 12(1965): 285.
33. Wilson, *Varieties of Police Behavior*, p. 18.
34. Thomas Bercal, "Calls for Police Assistance," *American Behavioral Scientist*, 13(1970): 681–691.
35. John A. Webster, "Police Task and Time Study," *Journal of Criminal Law, Criminology and Police Science*, 61(1970): 94–100.
36. Reiss, *The Police and the Public*.
37. Michael O'Neill and Carlton J. Bloom, "The Field Officer: Is He Really Fighting Crime?" *The Police Chief*, 39(February 1972): 30–32.
38. George Kelling, et al. *The Kansas City Preventive Patrol Experiment: A Summary Report* (Washington, D.C.: Police Foundation, 1974), pp. 40–43.
39. Gary W. Cordner, "While on Routine Patrol. . . : A Study of Police Use of Uncommitted Patrol Time," unpublished master's thesis, Michigan State University, 1978.
40. Nicolette Parisi, et al. (eds.), *Sourcebook of Criminal Justice Statistics—1978* (Washington D.C.: U.S. Government Printing Office, 1979), p. 301.
41. James Q. Wilson and Barbara Boland, "The Effect of the Police on Crime," *Law and Society*, 12(Spring 1978): 367–390.
42. Kelling, et al., *The Kansas City Preventive Patrol Experiment*.
43. For an excellent review of police-related research and the "presumed effects of policing," see: George Kelling, "Police Field Services and Crime: The Presumed Effects of a Capacity," *Crime and Delinquency* (April 1978): 173–184.
44. For example see: Tony Pate, et al., *Police Response Time: Its Determinants and Effects* (Washington, D.C.: Police Foundation, 1976); Deborah Bertram and Alexander Vargo, "Response Time Analysis Study: Preliminary Findings on Robbery in Kansas City," *The Police Chief*, 53, 5(1976): 74–77; and, National Institute of Law Enforcement and Criminal Justice, *Executive Summary—Response Time Analysis* (Washington, D.C.: U.S. Government Printing Office, 1977).
45. Bertram and Vargo, "Response Time Analysis."

46. See: Peter W. Greenwood, Jan Chaiken, and Joan Petersilia, *The Criminal Investigation Process* (Lexington, Mass.: D.C. Heath and Company, 1977); Peter Bloch and James Bell, *Managing Investigations: The Rochester System* (Washington, D.C.: The Urban Institute, Police Foundation, 1976); and, Bernard Greenberg, et al., *Enhancement of the Investigative Function, Volume I* and *Analysis and Conclusions, Volume III* (Menlo Park, Calif.: Stanford Research Institute, 1972).
47. Walker, *A Critical History of Police Reform* and Fogelson, *Big-City Police.*
48. Manning, *Police Work,* pp. 102—116. See also: Arthur Niederhoffer, *Behind the Shield* (Garden City, N.Y.: Doubleday, 1967); Jonathan Rubenstein, *City Police* (New York: Farrar, Straus and Giroux, 1973); Jerome Skolnick, *Justice Without Trial: Law Enforcement in Democratic Society* (New York: John Wiley and Sons, 1966); John P. Clark and Richard Sykes, "Some Determinants Of Police Organization and Practice in a Modern Industrial Democracy," in Daniel Glaser (ed.), *Handbook of Criminology* (Chicago: Rand McNally, 1974), pp. 455–494.
49. Herman Goldstein, *Policing a Free Society* (Cambridge, Mass.: Ballinger Publishing Company, 1977), p. 33.
50. For an excellent review of changing patrol strategies and future developments, see: George L. Kelling and David Fogel, "Police Patrol—Some Future Directions," in Alvin W. Cohn (ed.), *The Future of Policing* (Beverly Hills, Calif.: Sage Publications, 1978), pp. 153–181.
51. John E. Boydstun and Michael E. Sherry. *San Diego Community Profile—Final Report* (Washington, D.C.: Police Foundation, 1975).
52. Elinor Ostrom, Roger B. Parks, and Gordon P. Whitaker, *Patterns of Metropolitan Policing* (Cambridge, Mass.: Ballinger Publishing Company, 1978).
53. The most notable efforts in contracting have occurred in California, undertaken by the Los Angeles County Sheriff's Department.
54. See: John J. McDonnell, *Central Police Dispatch—An Exemplary Project* (Washington, D.C.: Office of Technology Transfer, National Institute of Law Enforcement and Criminal Justice, 1976).
55. Manuel R. Garza, *Multi-Agency Narcotics Unit Manual* (Washington, D.C.: Office of Technology Transfer, National Institute of Law Enforcement and Criminal Justice, 1976).
56. Illustrative of these projects are the project reports of Multnomah County, Oregon. See: Oregon Law Enforcement Council, *Police Consolidation Project—Concept Papers* (Portland: Oregon Law Enforcement Council, 1975); *Police Consolidation Project—Executive Summary of the Staff Report* (Portland: Oregon Law Enforcement Council, 1974).
57. Lawrence W. Sherman, et al., *Team Policing: Seven Case Studies* (Washington, D.C.: Police Foundation, 1973). Also see: William G. Gay, et al., *Neighborhood Team Policing, National Evaluation Program, Phase I, Summary Report* (Washington, D.C.: U.S. Government Printing Office, 1977); Peter B. Bloch and David Specht, *Neighborhood Team Policing* (Washington, D.C.: U.S. Government Printing Office, 1973); and for an overview of the team policing concept, Alfred I. Schwartz and Sumner N. Clarren, *The Cincinnati Team Policing Experiment—A Summary Report* (Washington, D.C.: The Urban Institute, Police Foundation, 1977).
58. Sherman, et al., *Team Policing.* Also see: Mary Ann Wycoff and George Kelling, *The Dallas Experience: Organizational Reform, Volume I* (Washington, D.C.: Police Foundation, 1978)
59. Kelling, "Police Field Services and Crime."
60. Boydstun and Sherry, *San Diego Community Profile;* Gay, et al., *Neighborhood Team Policing; National Evaluation;* Bloch and Specht, *Neighborhood Team Policing;* and Schwartz and Clarren, *Cincinnati Experiment.*
61. President's Crime Commission, *Task Force Report: Police,* pp. 120–143.

62. Alfred I. Schwartz, et al., *Employing Civilians for Police Work* (Washington, D.C.: U.S. Government Printing Office, 1975), p. 2.

63. See: Harvey A. Juris and Peter Feuille, *Police Unionism* (Lexington, Mass.: Lexington Books, D.C. Heath and Company, 1973); Paul Lawson, "Police Militancy and Collective Bargaining," *Crime and Social Justice* (Fall–Winter, 1977): 64–67; and Stephen Halpren, *Police-Associations and Department Leaders* (Lexington, Mass.: Lexington Books, 1974).

64. Herman Goldstein, "Improving Policing: A Problem-Oriented Approach," *Crime and Delinquency* (April 1979): 236–258.

65. Ibid., p. 239.

Chapter 9

On Rationing Justice and Liberty in a Declining Economy

*David J. Saari**

In the United States in 1980, the problems of a declining economy are compounded by extraordinarily high and persistent inflation. Under these circumstances, scarce resources for private and public sectors are allocated—rationed, one could say—in different ways across the economy. The rationing process for public funds for courts and public defender systems, which are the focal point of this chapter, is examined here with an eye upon the possibly detrimental effects of such rationing in humanitarian terms. The questions of justice and liberty involve life or death sentences, liberty or prison and jail sentences, equality or discriminatory treatment and due process or unfair, capricious and arbitrary governmental and private action. The rationing process gives rise to several additional questions: What is the meaning of a declining economy for these two public systems? Are courts and public defenders affected by economic trouble, and, if so, what are the effects? Has anything happened to court systems and public defender systems to enhance their planning and operating capacity, so that harm to these public services in a declining economy would be minimized?

These questions reflect the wisdom of one of America's most widely respected judges, Judge Learned Hand, who said: "If we are to keep

*School of Justice, The American University

our democracy, there must be one commandment: Thou shalt not ration justice."[1] Yet some rationing of justice is inevitable due to unequal distribution of scarce resources. Some inequalities are blatant: the lack of defense counsel for poor people; pretrial incarceration of the poor while the rich are released; or the failure to provide transcripts of trials to the poor, whose appeal to correct trial error is thereby effectively blocked. These instances of rationing are correctable by social action and taxation. But Justice Hand's commandment has been overlooked so far in many budget meetings.

A common assumption about both courts and public defenders is that they are highly resistant to economic swings, impervious to the ups and downs of business and government spending. The assumption for courts is based on several factors: constitutional provisions against diminishment of salaries; lifetime or long-term judicial tenure; constrained judicial removal systems; the independence borne of separation of powers; and inherent powers to finance the branch. Few reductions in force are ever experienced in the judiciary. The courts represent a very small part of total government expenditures, and the budgets are largely composed of the salaries of professional personnel as opposed to price-sensitive product inventories and capital expenditures. The assumption of invincibility for defense of the indigent is based solidly upon the Sixth Amendment to the U.S. Constitution. It applies to the states since 1963 through *Gideon* v. *Wainwright*; is constitutionally mandated expense for states, cities, and the federal government; and is directed by increasing numbers of professionals, usually young attorneys, with semiautonomous status in the communities. As we shall see, these assumptions of imperturbable constancy are open to question.

Some evidence to challenge these assumptions for courts is seen in the comments of the director of the National Center for State Courts, Edward C. McConnell, who stated: "Cutbacks at both the federal and state levels have limited the availability of funds to support state court improvement efforts."[2] When the Indiana judicial center faced a possible 60 percent cut in its 1980–1981 budget, it cut a planned major educational judicial conference. Oregon's legislature recently decreased judicial education funding. The District of Columbia superior court asserted a $300,000 shortage of funds and announced plans to halt all civil jury trials for two months in the summer of 1980. Congress was confronted with a supplemental appropriation request at the same time it was planning to cut the entire federal budget for 1981 by about $15 billion. In California, the home of the Jarvis property tax limit amendments, judicial expenditures sagged from $315 million to $314 million in 1976–77. The District of Columbia dropped from $25 million to $22 million in allocations for the judiciary, and New York judicial expenditures dropped from $281 million to $252 million in the 1976 and 1977 fiscal years.[3] More recently, in January 1980, the U.S. Bureau of Census reported 1978 federal intergovernmental data showing a 14.8 percent or $115 million decline in LEAA block grants to state and local government. States show a 13.9 percent or $66 million decline in LEAA block grants from states to local governments. In 1980, both Congress and the President plan further cuts or outright elimination of revenue-sharing programs in the criminal justice field. The gradual slowing of growth in criminal justice expenditures at all levels of government in the 1970s is showing itself more sharply nov·, at the onset of the 1980s. Yet total criminal justice expenditures in all governments rose from $10 billion to $24 billion in the years from 1971 to 1978—a 129 percent growth deflated by about 90 percent inflation from 1970 to 1979. The federal intergovernmental expenditure of $712,000,000 for criminal justice in 1978 joined the $6,688,713,000 spent by states and $14,307,806,000 spent by local governments for the same function that year. While important for certain expenditures, $712 million in federal money is small in comparison to the $20.9 billion annual state and local expenditure for criminal justice. With trends toward sharp decreases or the elimination of federal funding, the nation is returning to a fiscal posture similar to that of 1964 when the federal government did not share revenue.

Increases in public defender expenditures in 1978 were ahead of all other expenditure categories for courts, police, and corrections, with a 29.8 percent increase over the prior year. There is yet no evidence of decline in that data. From 1971, when $67 million was spent nationally on public defense, to 1978, when $315 million was spent in all 50 states and 3,000 counties, the public defender offices of the nation have grown steadily—by 370 percent in expenditure—in the decade. (Later in this chapter, I will analyze the growth figure in more depth, because alone it is misleading.) The effect of economic decline is not readily evident in the data for public defense. Some extrapolation from more refined data is needed.

For both courts and public defenders, the current funding prospects are reflected in an ominous, anxiety-provoking fiscal mood described by strange words: freeze, cutback, squeeze, crunch, pinch. None of these terms describe economic decline in terms of growth reduction or inflation. Some additional criminal justice data and inflationary data gives more meaning to this analysis. See Table 9–1 for results of the latest trend data.

The growth rates are a function of the base. Since the base of public defense was extraordinarily low for a nation of 200 million people, its growth rate seems large; yet if one reorganizes the data slightly, a different perspective emerges. This perspective clarifies the separation of powers in the criminal justice system and the relative resources devoted to checks and balances of the executive branch by the judicial branch.

Executive Branch	FY 1971	FY 1978
Police	5,400	11,150
Corrections	2,200	5,200
Prosecution and Legal Services	400	1,250
	8,000	17,600
Judicial Branch and Defense		
Judicial	1,200	2,700
Public Defense	67	315
	1,267	3,015

In FY 1971, the executive branch/judicial branch expenditure ratio was 8:1.2 in actual dollars, or reduced, 6.6:1. In FY 1978, this same actual dollar ratio was 17.6:3, reduced to a ratio of 5.8:1. The forces of the executive branch, checked and balanced by the public defender/courts complex, is represented by a significant ratio of fiscal balancing potential in this expenditure data. The consistency of this ratio means that little or nothing was done in 1971–78 to alter the role of the state in either the executive or judicial branches. Total growth has left unaltered the 90 percent plea bargaining and mass justice situation of many courts and defender offices in America. The 6:1 ratio in favor of executive over judicial/defense spending would not be significant except that other balances might move to 6, 7, 8, or 9:1, to assure more convictions, or to 5, 4, 3, or 2:1, to reduce the convictions and state pressure on the accused citizen. Nothing on the horizon appears to require a change in this fiscal balance between parts of the state in their relationship to the individual.

Another significant force is inflation. Its impact must be considered a serious concomitant with economic decline and increased unemployment. What would inflationary pressure do to the 6:1 ratio in a time of expanding population? Inflated resources, now more costly than ever, would be spread among a large and growing user base; but inflation reduces the ability of organizations to compete for talent to serve the larger user base. With fewer dollars to hire persons at ever higher

Table 9-1   State/Local Expenditures for Criminal Justice (Millions)

Function	FY 1971	FY 1978	% Increase 1971–1978
Police	5,400	11,150	106
Corrections	2,200	5,200	136
Judicial	1,200	2,700	125
Prosecutor and legal services	400	1,250	212
Public defense	67	315	370

salaries, the numbers of positions would not rise and may even be reduced; and further, if resignations result from failure to keep salaries in line with inflation, then increased workload per attorney or judge would tend to make the work both unbearable and unprofessional. Inflation thus has an undermining, long-term impact for public defenders and courts. Inflation certainly affects their capacity to attract and retain quality professional talent.

The nature of current inflation deserves particular mention. The consumer price index for the years 1967 to 1978 is shown in Table 9-2. In 1979, the CPI rose drastically, as shown in Table 9-3.

So severe is inflation in 1980 interest rates, credit controls, and other economic indicators are now at emergency levels. Under these circumstances, there is no escape for any public office; the quality of the public defense function and the quality of the courts will inevitably decline, if inflation continues at its present rate. Politically, a "Proposition 13 mentality" took part of the toll in the form of property tax limits; economically, inflation did the rest to establish conditions under which justice may have to be rationed extensively in the 1980s. The 1980s are looking much like the 1960s, when Francis M. Bator stated in *The Question of Government Spending*:

> Our postwar political history reflects an intense preoccupation with government spending, a pervasive sense that expenditure by government has been perilously high. Periodically, it is true, this sense of excess has been dulled by dramatic reminders of national crises; the threat of a Communist Europe, a Communist-conquered Korea, and the Sputniks— these diverted us from our budgetary anxieties. But not for long. Reaction soon set in, leading, if not to less government spending, at least to firmer resistance against more.[4]

Now, in 1980, those pent-up feelings have exploded into a world of dangerous inflation and energy crises.

Table 9–2 Annual National Consumer Price Index

Year	CPI	Year	CPI	Year	CPI
1967	100.0	1972	125.3	1977	181.5
1968	104.2	1973	133.1	1978	195.4
1969	109.8	1974	147.7		
1970	116.3	1975	161.2		
1971	121.3	1976	170.5		

Source: U.S. Department of Commerce, Bureau of Census, *Statistical Abstract of The United States*, 100th ed. (1979):483.

Table 9–3 Consumer Price Index, June 1979 to January 1980

June 1979	216.6
July	218.9
Aug.	221.1
Sept.	223.4
Oct.	225.4
Nov.	227.5
Dec.	229.9
Jan. 1980	233.2

Source: U.S. Department of Labor, *Monthly Labor Review* (April 1980):89

We should interpret economic decline in the context of courts and public defenders to be a loss of resources and an inabilility to attract more resources. Decline is related to past expenditure patterns, to inflation, and to a host of other forces. The whole environment shapes courts and defender agencies in a fundamental way.

Given this interpretation of economic decline in its application to courts and defender agencies, it is possible now to provide a social analysis of the political and economic aspects of the problem. The problem can also be analyzed from an organizational perspective. These two levels of analysis offer different perspectives of the problems of rationing justice, just as the 6:1 systemic ratio mentioned above casts a different light on the state versus individual balance in funding criminal justice agencies.

SOCIAL ANALYSIS

Some groups deny that social harm results from excessive rationing of justice and liberty in American society. Advocates of reduced property taxes through Proposition 13 in California also reduced the resources available to courts and public defender agencies, which are dependent on such taxes. The advocates implicit message is denial that rationing justice harms society. On the other hand, those who see serious harm in rationing justice's resources can foresee that certain social classes—namely, the poor and minorities, who are the principal clients of public defender agencies across the nation—will have less support available for their defense. The promise of the right to counsel will fall short of the ideal of representation embodied in the Sixth Amendement. Yet an inability to defend well will inevitably increase the potential for social control through more convictions by police and prosecutor. The ability to obtain and retain quality legal counsel in defenders' offices is also likely to be severely constrained by rationing.

Courts

More specifically, courts are likely to suffer primary impacts through rationing. Improvements in the quality of the judicial branch, carefully constructed in the last 15 years, are now falling apart. Education for the judiciary is about to disappear from public budgets, and with it, the benefits. Pending lawsuits by federal judges which challenge a Presidential reduction in a planned pay raise left judges wondering whether they were in fact part of the executive branch. The morale of federal judges cannot be improved by such unseemly wrangling over salaries. This is more evidence of federal fiscal trouble.

The lower courts, handling justice on a mass scale—traffic, misdemeanors, small claims, and housing—are likely to be hit the hardest. Implied pressure to raise more revenue through traffic fines lurks in the background, since traffic fines are the largest source of revenue generated by court systems across the nation. More to the point is the overwhelming property tax dependency of lower trial courts which face advocates of property tax limits. The consequences of stifling judicial service in a big city housing court are readily understood in the context of having—or not having—a roof over one's head. The picture of the future nationwide is not very pleasing to the courts.

While it is difficult to classify severity of impacts, there are a number of probable secondary impacts on the courts which flow from declining resources. Some of these are rather complex. For example, the fostering state-funded court systems is a result of the Proposition 13 syndrome, but states are reluctant to take on such new burdens. North Dakota and Oregon turned away recently from such efforts to relieve local government expenditure burdens.[5] A lid on witness and juror fees is likely, making the fees, once again, unresponsive to a real world of inflation. National court and defender service organizations are likely to expire or at least have a difficult time surviving. New programs for restitution for victims and witnesses, jury management, alternative programs for minor offenses—these and many others will have to struggle for survival. Pretrial liberty may be jeopardized if ROR, bail, or pretrial release programs are cut. The fear of federal control of local courts can now disappear with the planned loss of LEAA revenue sharing resources. And unequal resources for courts in states will remain unequal without at least a state-based, revenue sharing effort. When jobs are scarce, public positions will very likely come under the intense political scrutiny of patronage systems.[6] Court unions are likely to find willing members in a declining economy. As elaborated above and later on in this chapter increasing mass production of justice is a logical outcome of rationing: These are some of the more obvious consequences at a secondary level of impact.

Public Defender Systems

Property crimes are at a high level in the United States because there is so much property to steal and so little private security. Shoplifting, already rampant in a society of open-shelf marketing of goods, is coupled with a whole range of crimes such as bad check writing, petty theft, fraud and embezzlement, and credit card fraud; the list of these crimes is tedious and long. At an equally serious level of social harm, burglary and robbery are common crimes for some of the "havenots." This vast sea of recorded and unrecorded property crime means that there will be a lot of heavy pressure on public defender offices. A real test of the meaning of the Sixth Amendment right to counsel is coming in the 1980s. More property cases with less defender resources spells mass justice—if it could be called justice. Since defender organizations in most states draw heavily from the local property tax base— which is now being constrained—the actual time that a professional lawyer spends on each case should drop steadily in the 1980s. If correctional facilities are crammed beyond capacity (which is their current condition) and not available for sentences of prison, the probation and parole options may be quite attractive for some classes of property offenders. The state's sanction would be weakened in a obvious way if penalties in property crimes were less stringent and so would the concept of private property. If correctional facilities were to be available, they would probably be filled. Under these circumstances, the rise of the public defender in America is likely to be short and sweet—or perhaps sour. Things are not so sweet when a defender is so harried that he fails to raise a constitutional issue to suppress evidence seized in violation of the Fourth Amendment of the U.S. Constitution. But the public is just as soured when the penal sanction loses its real bite. Many believe that public defenders give a lower quality of defense than retained private counsel. In a declining economy, reduced resources to the defender in the face of increasing case loads is likely to make that opinion of lower quality come true. It may be a self-fulfilling prophecy that defender services are doomed to marginal effectiveness in American society, in the same way that correctional services are the first to be cut by a cut-minded budget director of the state or county. However, nothing is inevitable; only thinking makes it so. Perhaps reality will be more gentle to public defender agencies in the 1980s.

To summarize the argument up to this point, court and public defender systems are affected in the same way and in some different ways by virtue of their basic charter and responsibility in our society; clearly, neither is immune from inflation. The fiscal squeeze is much more evident in the courts. The cutback for public defenders is more a matter of a decline in the rate of expenditure increase in some jurisdictions.

It is not easy to assess the potential degree of harm to society by rationing resources to courts and public defender agencies. No one can catalogue the daily insults to our sense of justice, or the days of liberty taken by the state in pretrial confinement, which, at the very least, reduces one's enjoyment of living while waiting for a decision from a prosecutor or a court. The consumer price index shows the devastating affects of inflation on our market basket. We probably need a "justice consumer pretrial liberty index" to quantify the harm done to our daily freedom to pursue life and happiness. Such an index could periodically be consulted during times of "economic stagflation"—as confused economists are dubbing the current period of uncertainty. The index could record "persons wasted per year," a dramatic figure for mortal man in his six or so decades of stumbling on this planet. One person wasted would be equal to 365 days of pretrial confinement. (Daniel Freed has suggested that more time is spent by Americans in pretrial confinement before conviction than after conviction under prison or jail sentence. He calls this paradox The Imbalance Ratio.[7]

ORGANIZATIONAL ANALYSIS

What has happened to the management of court systems and public defender systems? This question moves away from broad social analysis of political and economic questions to thinking about specific organizations in each of the 3,000 counties, some 250 or more of which are in metropolitan areas. If the environment is hostile—that is if economic decline makes it difficult to obtain resources—then the amount of time and the type of management talent needed will be different than that of an era of plenty. In organizational terms, the management of the organization becomes more important in times of stress. Both court systems and defender organizations have attempted to improve the management of their resources in a variety of ways. Courts have adopted court management programs, and defender offices, particularly large offices in the metropolitan areas, are staffed with management specialist. This employment of management specialists is a very recent development—in the last ten years for both types of organizations. Both types have always received some form of management, but much of it was informal and some of it ineffectual, particularly in times of stress.

Issues of domain in organizations are much more important in the turbulent environment of an economy headed downward.[8] Each specific public defender's office was established to serve defendants exclusively in a jurisdiction, or to share that service with the private bar on assignment in specific criminal cases. Often the latter case prevails, which allows judges to appoint proportionately more private attorneys and sign more orders for payment of fees, a court-mandated cost supported by statute and constitutional command that is to be obeyed by county and state executive officials. Budget and spending levels can therefore be compromised to protect the constitutional provision of counsel. If the exclusive domain option exists for a defender office, then the courts may be mandating service in the public defense function. In both cases, the responsibility of courts to provide effective assistance of counsel for the indigent accused is not being met when the prosecutor faces a dismissal of the information or indictment because assistance of counsel is not available for monetary reasons. Political blame can be heaped on state or local officials for failing to provide sufficient resources for indigent accused to obtain a constitutional defense, or for causing dismissal of valid cases because of lack of counsel. In either event, executive branch officials would be denying their own oath of office to uphold the Constitution. This systemic joint interaction of public defense and court systems suggests a very powerful weapon to protect the domain of public defender organizations from difficulty in a period of economic decline. The efficiency of defender organizations can be addressed by better management, so that difficulties can be foreseen. Tests of efficiency can be developed well in advance of a crisis, thereby reducing some of the uncertainty inherent in a declining economy. By having more managerial savvy, public defenders will be better able to compete for scarce shares of public funds in a direct and powerful manner. Some of this managerial logic also applies to the courts.

Confronted with a tougher resource picture, what will managers do to assist elected or appointed presiding judges and elected or appointed public defenders? The first reaction is to cut out the fat, until it is believed muscle, not fat, is about to be cut. However, there is another logic at work. Criminal cases now dominate the daily agenda of lower courts and an increasing share of the time of trial courts of general jurisdiction. A significant cause of this domination stems from widespread adoption in the 1970s of speedy trial court rules and statutes, and from constitutional decisions by the U.S. Supreme Court, starting in 1967 with *Klopfer v. North Carolina*.[9] Just as the right to counsel for indigent accused is a relatively new national standard, so is the national standard of a speedy trial in criminal cases. This being so, criminal cases receive top priority in courts with mixed civil and criminal cases. Civil cases wait. In some jurisdictions across the nation, this is a very common event on the daily litigation calendar. Human rights are being elevated over property rights—a result greatly desired by many, and achieved through a fortunate confluence of right to counsel and speedy trial standards. Decisions in civil cases may be delayed even further to accomodate criminal case priorities, under those economic conditions when civil and criminal demand for judicial services exceeds supply and when resources for the judiciary are being held constant or declining. This logic will not escape courts and public defenders. Nor will it escape civil litigants and others who hope to obtain judicial decisions in a private lawsuit.

Reflection on this systemic interplay reveals a number of new factors which will impinge on the decision to hold constant, decrease, or increase financial resources to courts and public defender agencies. Many of these factors point toward substantial political power in courts and defender agencies. First, the constitutional order of the 1980s is different in terms of criminal case priority. It is clear that local expenditure by states and cities is driven by federal demand for counsel and speedy trial as well as by state constitutional, legislative, and judicial standards that are much more clearly articulated in the current decade than in any past decade in the history of the nation. Given clearly articulated goals, managers can function more effectively in the highly competitive public resource scramble which results from a declining economy. The gradual absorption of the Bill of Rights into the Fourteenth Amendment, in the context of criminal cases, has significant political and monetary implications for states, counties, and cities. These implications are dimly perceived in times of plenty, but starkly vivid in times of economic decline. Defenders and courts are on the strong side of political battle, assuming they manage their resources wisely and in the public interest. Another factor rests in having both national and local bar associations committed to support of professional standards for better management in courts and defender offices. With clearer standards of bar support, changing economic conditions can trigger courts and defenders to seek almost automatic official bar support. Surviving national service, technical assistance, research, and other support is another new factor. All of these new factors combine to make the threat of economic decline somewhat less serious for those public defenders and court systems which are already defensibly managed from efficiency and effectiveness viewpoints. The probability of maintaining a favorable political climate for courts and public defenders, appears stronger than twenty years ago.

CONCLUSIONS

What coherent strategy can be used to face the uncertainties and contingencies posed by a declining economy? Much of the argument so far suggests that the best strategy is to keep a well-managed house and then protect against the squeeze by presenting a wide range of basic political decisions mandating professional process in constitutional, statutory, and court rule terms. There are three possible options—the worst, best, and probable outcomes for courts and defender agencies. Let us consider what these different outcomes would include in terms of cost, delay, accessibility and management—four significant factors in each case.

For the defender agency, the worst outcome is an agency which has a combination of sloppy, uninformed management, poor performance, excessive costs, and unusually long delays. That combination suggests that the defender agency is limiting the access of accused indigents through professional incompetence. This outcome has some political reality.

The defender agency with the best outcome has exceptional management, lowest reasonable cost per case, no unusual delays, and sufficient capacity to accept more clients. If the excess or slack capacity is not too large, then this defender agency would attract support from every side. But the ideal office is rare.

The defender agency with the most probable outcome has a reasonably competent management and average or mixed and variable costs per case, suffers no unusual delay but is continually uncomfortable and pushed, and now finds perpetual difficulty in providing wide accessibility to indigent accused and adequate professional time per case. This outcome for a public defender agency is probably the most typical.

The court system with the worst outcome manages resources thoughtlessly, is ignorant about cost data, suffers extensive delays in criminal and civil litigation, and is, therefore, cut off from the world of current events, dealing with past and outdated conflict. Access is very low, as is political support. Incompetence on a professional level is a public shame for the worst court.

The court system with the best outcome manages well, has a full array of cost data, is current in all phases of its litigation, and deals with community conflict on a fresh and current basis. Access is assured because of slight slack in capacity. The political implications are obvious and favorable for this type of court system.

The probable case for a court system is a mixed situation of some meaningful cost data, management performing satisfactorily but not outstanding, little criminal case delay but some needless civil delay, and access readily assured. Political leverage to obtain resources is fairly strong with an outcome such as this in a court system.

In these six hypothetical outcomes, the declining economy can be a disastrous experience for the worst agency outcomes, and it may drag down operating capability of the probable outcome agencies and systems. The best-run organizations are quite strong in the short run. Economic downturns will hardly faze the court systems and public defender agencies with the best possible outcomes. The key strategy is related to conscious development of slack capacity, especially in times of greater environmental turbulence, economic decline, and challenges to domain. Given the deck of cards already dealt to courts and defenders, their talent for playing them will reduce the level of anxiety provoked by a declining economy. Contingency planning to develop organizational alternatives when conditions change around the court or defender may reduce the impact of some minor (perhaps inevitable) rationing of justice and liberty in a declining economy, when everyone takes cuts for the good of all.

There is one special and important situation for defenders which involves the southern states. Here conditions in the 1970s were favorable, but severe economic decline could create fundamental problems. Southern states from 1971 to 1978 outstandingly met the challenge of providing greater resources to provide defense services for indigent accused. In Table 9–4 a near five-fold increase is tabulated which is the best constitutional civil rights news this nation has received since the end of the Civil War.

The level of continuous and growing support is an expression of a new South and evidence that the South has changed in important ways with significance to constitutionally acceptable order.[10] Economic conditions in the sunbelt will not be so bleak, because of continual population migration from the North and a more robust regional economy. this favorable regional variation is especially interesting, because the South was poor and racial relations were bad, as reflected by *Brown* v. *Mississippi* and *Powell* v. *Alabama* (the Scottsboro case).[11] The probability of such days returning is reasonably low because of new legal and professional standards, new public standards, and long-term commitment an policy to adequate defense for the indigent. But probabilities are based on chance, and in the roll of the dice, the wrong number may come out for defense.

The unique meaning of a declining economy to courts and public defender agencies has been described. It is true that courts and public defenders are affected by economic decline in the community they serve. But there has been a basic shift in the last twenty years. The shift in constitutional right to counsel and speedy trial places financial priority on these activities—a priority which supercedes public demands for almost every other public service. This basic constitutional change has been accompanied by an adoption of management innovations which makes it more probable that resources for courts and defenders in a declining economy will be directly and forcefully addressed by managers within these agencies. In times of economic decline in the past, the local and state government managers had a much stronger hand when dealing with courts and defenders. The battle over scarce resources has been significantly altered in terms of constitutional order.

Limited government in American constitutional order means limited police and limited prosecutors. The checks and balances of courts and public defenders are just as important as a Presidential veto of congressional bills. The basic design of our constitutional democracy posits goals of liberty and justice for all. A cultural postulate of Western civilization, good for the Magna Carta in 1215 and for us in 1980 is: "To no one will we sell, to none will we deny or delay, right or justice."[12] Embedded in our social norms, this historical prescription drives public policy in eras of economic decline. Courts and public defenders ought to remember this clear voice of social reason and compelling logic. The legitimacy of the Republic depends on it.

Table 9 -4   Southern States—Expenditure for Public Defense FY 1971–78, Ranked by Order of Percent Increase in Expenditure (in thousands of dollars)

State	FY 1971	Fiscal Years-$ 1976	1977	1978	% Increase
Kentucky	$ 37	1,281	1,358	2,039	5,410
Alabama	34	1,122	1,819	1,816	5,241
Virginia	122	4,822	5,273	5,669	4,546
Mississippi	41	774	912	876	2,036
Arkansas	38	572	614	552	1,352
Maryland	790	6,847	6,708	7,074	795
Tennessee	514	2,246	2,523	3,183	519
Georgia	481	3,300	2,316	2,274	372
Florida	3,641	11,161	14,120	16,458	- 352
South Carolina	430	1,158	1,162	1,483	244
Louisiana	497	1,581	1,690	1,631	228
North Carolina	1,619	4,840	4,755	5,101	215
Total	$8,244	39,704	43,250	48,156	484

Source: LEAA, Bureau of Census, Expenditure and Employment Reports, 1971–1977 and 1978 annual data.

NOTES

1. Arnold S. Trebach, *The Rationing of Justice*, (New Brunswick, N.J.: Rutgers University Press, 1964).
2. *1979 Annual Report 4*, National Center for State Courts, Williamsburg, Virginia.
3. U.S. Bureau of Census, *Trends in Expenditure and Employment Data for the Criminal Justice System 1971–1977*, January 1980, pp. 79–82.
4. Francis M. Bator, *The Question of Government Spending* (New York: Collier Publishers, 1962), p. 4.
5. Harry O. Lawson, *State Funding of Court Systems* (Washington, D.C.: American University Law Institute, June 1979), p. 23.
6. See *Branti v. Finkel* 48 U.S. Law Week 4331, March 31, 1980, for U.S. Supreme Court decision holding that the First and Fourteenth amendments protected two Republican assistant public defenders in Rockland, New York, from discharge by a Democratic public defender solely because of their political beliefs.
7. See Malcolm Feeley, *The Process is the Punishment* (New York: Russell Sage, 1979), p. 235.
8. James F. Thompson, *Organizations in Action* (New York: McGraw-Hill Book Co., 1967).
9. *Klopfer v. North Carolina* 386 U.S. 213 (1967); Barker v. Wingo 407 U.S. 514 (1972).
10. David J. Saari, "*The Financial Impacts of the Right to Counsel for Criminal Defense of the Poor*," unpublished paper presented May 10, 1979, at the Law and Society Conference, San Francisco.

11. Brown v. Mississippi 297 U.S. 278 (1936) and Powell v. Alabama 287 U.S. 45 (1932).
12. A. E. Dick, Howard, *Magna Carta, Text and Commentary* (Charlottesville: University Press of Virginia, 1964).

Chapter 10

Changes in Penal Goals
and Structure In
a Downward Economy

*David E. Duffee**

Will penal systems reorganize themselves in line with public judgments that the administration of criminal punishment is less important to the public welfare than administrations that deal with energy and inflation? What rearrangement of organized punishment will be made? As the room temperature in the chambers of state legislatures steadily declines in the coming winters, how cold will those lawmakers allow cellblocks to become? As health care costs for average voters become exorbitant, what standards of health care will these people be willing to support for prisoners? What will happen to capital and maintenance budgets for departments of correction if mortgage interest rates become prohibitively high for private family housing?

A number of social forecasters have argued that a fundamental change is taking place in the American economy, and consequently in American social structure. In the language of the forecasters, we are moving from an industrial to a postindustrial economy; from a period when the dominant organizing principle was one of "economizing," or

An earlier draft of this paper was presented at the American Society of Criminology Conference in Philadelphia, November 1979.

The author wishes to express his gratitude to Dennis Sullivan and Michael Gottfredson for their helpful comments.

*School of Criminal Justice, State University of New York at Albany

efficiency, to a period when the dominant organizing principle will be one of "sociologizing" or effectiveness; from a concentration on the creation and amassing of private goods to a concentration on deliberation about social goods.[1]

Bell, Vickers, and others examining this trend have focused on the broad changes which these shifts may entail for private corporations and government. They have concentrated on the generic shift from secondary to tertiary industry, from a thing-based technology to a service-based technology. We are told that there will be fundamental differences in our understanding of freedom and in the challenges of social responsibility.

Among the most important changes confronting us today are the alteration in scope of our accounting systems, and an alteration in the location of power and authority. Examining the first problem, Bell points out that the best things in life are no longer free. Industrial capitalism has squandered important and nonrenewable resources, which heretofore had not been considered production costs. This squandering has reached a point where the interdependence of people can no longer be ignored. It will soon be impossible to play win-lose games because winners will, in one way or another have to pay not only for their own victories but for the maintenance of those they defeat as well. In relation to the second problem—alteration in the location of power and authority—most commentators agree that the nature of politics will shift from a system that supports and maintains an economy of goods to a system which actively controls what social values will be pursued. That is, we are reaching a stage of history where political power will be used to determine what social problems are the most crucial relative to other social problems. Governments and their diverse and conflicting constitutencies, still burdened by the unpaid costs of our previous economy, will be making deliberate choices about which social goods must come before others. There will no longer be room for all.

In determining the ranking of social values, elites of various sorts will play important political roles. One elite which will have particular influence on how public resources are distributed are the executives of our large public bureaucracies. While they may not hold the balance of political power, they do hold positions which give them access to information less available to others. They also have experience and some credibility in arranging the resources and services on which many other groups depend. As the political forum concerning selection of social ends becomes more open and more deliberate, executives face severe challenges as well as great opportunities. The threat stems from their dependence on political decision for organizational re-

sources. The opportunity lies in their ability to influence those deliberations or at least to benefit from their outcomes. They may be able
to influence the decision process by convincing important groups that
their own particular organizations are better able to contribute to the
public welfare (social goods) than other specific organizations. They
may be able to benefit from the outcomes—from a public choice among
social ends—by manipulating their own organizations to meet that
new public choice.

The executives of penal systems will play a part, albeit modest, in
such deliberations. It would be safe to assume that they will not simply sit back and wait for a change in their public mandate. The risk of
waiting is too great in terms of potential resource loss and organizational instability. But it would also seem likely that penal executives
may have to make significant shifts in the representation of penal
goals, significant shifts in the structures of their organizations, or
both, in order to maintain an adequate level of resources. In the remainder of this chapter, I examine some of the constraints which penal organizations and their managements are likely to feel in the
course of the shifting political economy, and attempt to forecast some
of the adjustments which penal organizations are likely to make. My
hypothesis is that most of these adjustments will be geared to reducing strain on the organizations as social systems, independent of the
organizations' value as contributors to the special good.

From the period of early Quaker reform until the present day, penal
organizations have usually emphasized their ability to manipulate the
body and mind of the offender. This technical ability was their major
justification in the process of obtaining public resources.[2] For the most
part, the extent to which penal organizations could capture public resources has depended upon the fluctuating image of the offender in
public debate about priorities in public welfare. In periods when individual offenders were seen as particularly dangerous or peculiarily in
need of help, penal organizations have been able to draw upon those
images to justify new goals, new personnel, new facilities, and new
programs. Will penal organizations continue to emphasize some form
of offender processing as the principle means of defining their niche in
the public domain?[3]

If so, they are likely to face large cuts in financial and human resources in years ahead, for two related reasons. First, regardless of
how frequent or how heinous crimes may become in the future, the
relative public damage attributable to criminals is likely to decline
because the extent and diversity of other social problems are likely to
increase. This spread in the sources of disorder should reduce the effectiveness the issue of dangerousness of offenders to marshal support

for penal organizations. Second, regardless of how needful offenders can be, the needs of other groups will be at least as frequent and just as severe. But these other groups in need of service will not have their images smeared by the moral undeservedness implied by the *mens rea* concept of criminal law and in the just deserts aspect of criminal punishment. Therefore, reliance on the reclamatory aspect of the offender image is also likely to be ineffective as a mobilizing symbol in the search for resources. Face-to-face with the probability of triage in the determination of public expenditures, and organizations mandated to process them may be in for hard times.

Another possibility is that penal organizations will abandon justifications based on the offender and seek a new niche by claiming to be the logical purveyors of other services, outcomes, and functions not directly associated with the processing of convicted offenders. Should penal organizations do this, they may escape at least the severest effects of resource reductions that might otherwise be forthcoming. Penal organizations following either course may have to make significant internal adjustments. Should the penal system cling to the offender as its principal justification, it will have to find ways to do less with fewer resources. Such a contraction would mean significant losses for many organizational members, but it might enable the system to retain its core technology for keeping and guarding offenders.[4] The second alternative—that of claming new social functions—may allow the system to reduce resource losses, but would also entail a vast overhaul of organizational goals and structure.

In the section that follows, I examine some of the factors which are important in structuring the domain claims of penal organizations. There is a special emphasis upon some internal organizational dynamics which reduce the organization's potential to act in accordance with changes in the political and economic priorities of society. I argue that even when powerful external groups seek to limit the functions of penal systems and devalue those functions relative to other societal needs, the organization can counter those impositions with surprising effectiveness. The ability of public organizations to alter the mandates and directives of policy makers raises some important issues concerning the ways such organizations can be controlled.

THE POLITICAL ECONOMY OF PUBLIC ORGANIZATIONS

The interplay of political and economic forces in the determination of organizational behavior is most complex in organizations in which resources are mainly human rather than material and most objectives are the reinforcement of social norms or cultural symbols rather than standards of proficiency.[5] The political economy of organizations can be briefly defined as "the interrelationship between structure of rule (polity) and a system for producing and exchanging goods and services (economy)."[6] All types of organizations are clearly influenced by both political and economic factors. But object-processing organizations, particularly private ones, seem to be less constrained by political negotiation concerning social ends. These organizations arrange people indirectly in the course of doing other work.[7] In organizations such as penal systems, however, the technology of work concerns the management of people directly, and technical statements concerning means and ends remain political statements.[8] The political economy of penal organizations is all the more turbulent and uncertain because implementation of programs by these organizations are direct reflections of what is seen as right and valuable in society. Since the connection between social values and organizational technology is relatively direct, the relationship between changes in the environment of these organizations and alterations in internal organizational structure remains a key organizational problem.[9]

The External Political Economy

Wamsley and Zald suggest that the political economy of public organizations has two aspects, the internal and the external.[10] The external political economy concerns the interactions and deliberations of outside groups who have some stake in the operations of the organization in question. Warren, Rose, and Bergunder emphasize the importance of a particular segment of this external environment in the determination of organizational domain and access to resources. This segment they call the input constituency.[11] Input constituencies determine the value of the public organization and the extent and kinds of resources it should receive; they provide legitimacy for organizational operations. Output constituencies, in contrast, are often the groups influenced directly by organizational technology.[12] The input constituencies for penal systems include legislative bodies, lobbying groups, the state executive office, and various ad hoc or continuing professional groups which determine standards for personnel or practice. Output constituencies include offenders and those in immediate contact with the offenders who are processed through the system.

The term "input constituency" is broad enough to connote groups whose inputs are insignificant to the actual determination of a public organization's social value. Therefore, in order to refer to those groups which play a significant role in determining the niche of penal organizations, I will use the term "mandating constituency." The mandating constituency is not necessarily a coherent group acting in concert. In fact, there are often many conflicts and disagreements within mandating groups, and the mandate or mandates to penal organizations are never firmly settled or logically consistent—although there may be at any one time within the mandating groups a coalition which has more weight than other group members in determining what penal organizations are good for and how much public support they should receive. For present purposes, the most important aspect of the mandating constituency is its tendency to relate to penal organizations as social utilities, or abstract instruments of public welfare, rather than as distinct social systems which strive to endure. In other words, mandating groups tend to treat penal organizations as machines constructed or abandoned in relation to social purpose. Penal systems, however, are likely to adopt or abandon certain purposes in order to survive.[13]

The Internal Political Economy

The internal political economy of public organizations includes decisions about division of labor, distribution of resources to various divisions, arrangement of internal organizational power among various groups, and the elaboration of the internal social system in accordance with these factors.[14] The internal aspect is organizationally specific, and includes the history and ethos of each specific organization as an ongoing coherent social system. Externally, the mandating constituencies might weigh the value of punishment against health maintenance, education, transportation, fuel shortages, and so forth. But internally, the political economy of penal organization concerns the arrangement of groups, functions, and persons for the accomplishment of specific tasks and for the maintenance of the organization for itself and its members. While a mandating constituency can constrain or limit the range of internal organizational behavior, other important constraints will have exclusively internal sources.[15] Whether the internal and external constraints are congruent is an empirical, not a logical, question.[16] While deliberations about the nature and value of punishment may be salient to mandating constituencies, inside the organization such deliberations are likely to be seen as abstract philosophizing, important only to the extent that they influence resource supply. The salient concerns inside the organization are the administration of programs, the maintenance of resources, and the arrangement of personnel and offenders.[17]

TYPES OF ENVIRONMENTAL DISORDER

To what types of external change must the internal organizational order adjust? Organizational environments are in constant change, becoming increasingly more turbulent. Preservation of internal order depends more and more upon the ability of organizations to span their own boundaries and actively engage the environment.[18] But external turbulence can take several different forms, each of which might have a different impact on internal organizational structure. The concern here is with expansion and contraction of the national economy, the impact of these changes on the priorities of mandating constituencies, and the result of these changes on the administration of penal systems.

From the point of view of the internal political economy, both national economic expansion and contraction represent forms of environmental disorder. Organizational innovation is required in either case. The types of internal change required will vary depending on the direction of external change. In periods of economic expansion, the public organization must find ways to take advantage of slack public resources before its competitors can claim the available slack. In such periods, the organizational resources can be increased, personnel added, facilities expanded, and programs enlarged or diversified. But if the organization does not move quickly, it may be bypassed. The mandating constituency may find the claims of more opportunistic organizations to be more compelling. The organization may thus lose ground and be less well able to compete for resources in the future.[19]

In periods of economic contraction, the organization will often seek to maintain a steady flow of resources from a diminishing pool. It may try to make its capacities for achieving public good seem more valuable than the capacities of other organizations. If it cannot make the claim effectively, the organization must contract and find ways to deal with resulting conflicts in the internal political economy. As is the case in penology, if the organization has recently taken advantage of a growth spurt, the disruption caused by sudden contraction can be particularly acute because there is an even larger social system to maintain than would otherwise be the case.[20]

Finally, the impact of contraction and expansion on the mandating constituency is likely to have significant effect upon the types of claims to organizational domain that will be effective. When mandating constituencies have slack resources, their calculation of the value of supporting one social instrumentality rather than another will be imprecise. The mandating constituency will want to invest in organizations that are expected to have returns, to be sure, but it will not necessarily base its investment decisions on the comparative validity of organizational claims. In this situation, duplication is generally not a problem, and development of technical proficiencies in a variety of specialized social areas seems not only possible but desirable. To take the penal example, even if there are not many offenders to be processed, relative to the numbers of school children to be processed, some form of punishment will be acknowledged as a valuable social function; therefore, penal claims of becoming more proficient in punishing are likely to be well received. However, in periods of economic contraction, mandating constituencies are less likely to be concerned with the abstract benefit of investing in increased technical competence. They will be more concerned with reducing duplication and waste, and with maintaining core functions and operations. In such a period, the mandating constituency can call back its previous growth period investments in the form of a loan, asking "what have you done for us?," and "is what you are doing more valuable than what organization X can do?" An organization's access to resources is then determined not so much by its claim to progress through time on one function, but by the extent that it can claim a range of functions that are more attractive than those of its competitors.[21]

Ten or fifteen years ago, for example, schools may have been effective in making domain claims centered on numbers of children to be processed and advances in the way that that processing could be done. But now, as the number of school children goes down, and as the mandating constituency considers other severe problems in relation to education, schools are beginning to emphasize their ability to deliver in other areas such as adult education and community service. There is some evidence that the domain of penal organizations in also undergoing considerable change. New populations are being sought for processing, and claims of new competencies are being made.

Changes in Penal Domain Over Time

In the past, penal functions did not change significantly. The core penal technology has always been the structures and procedures for processing offenders. Whether this technology has been politically effective for obtaining resources has therefore depended upon whether the mandating constituency was willing to bank on the offender as a human resource. Such periods have been infrequent but predictably observable in the aftermath of major wars. American penology was out to save sinners after the American Revolution,[22] out to resocialize children of immigrants after the Civil War,[23] out to cure warped psyches after World War II,[24] and out to integrate conflicting social groups after the Vietnam War.[25] In such periods, penal organizations claimed not only to be able to hold captive and to supervise offenders but, with sufficient new resources, to change offenders into rehabilitated, usable persons. Perhaps the very image of investing in a human reclamation process was seen as a resource to the mandating constituency because it reflected well on the moral beneficence of the expanding economy.

During periods of economic contraction, the value of processing offenders declines, and claims that it can be done so as to reclaim the person processed become downright threatening to some members of the mandating constituency. Immediately prior to the Civil War, the utopian energy of Auburn and Cherry Hill was sapped. Sing Sing was advertised by its warden as a place of harsh punishment for persons who deserved no better.[26] As the Great Depression hit, Attica Prison, which was originally designed as a new industrial showplace, opened instead as a Spartanesque holding cage.[27]

Now that the Kennedy-Johnson social enterprise has given way to austerity, we are again facing reduction in the legitimate images of the offender and the resulting simplification of penal mandates.

Alternatives for Prison Structure

If penal organizations were mere instruments for obtaining public good, they might respond passively to these external changes. But correctional management has grown quite sophisticated in the last ten years; the strength of personnel unions has also added to the complexity of organizational structure.[28] Because of more sophisticated management, the penal system is better able to shape its own domain by raising its own claims about social function which blunt the impact of changes by the mandating constituency. Because members of penal organizations are more entrenched, there will be greater internal pressures to maintain the internal political economy to the benefit of members, and therefore greater pressure than in the past to use the new organizational capacities for manipulating its environment.[29]

If penal organizations were mere instruments of the mandating constituency, internal structural changes would be relatively straightforward. Offenders would be treated more superficially, and with more equality among them, under the mandate of just deserts. Staff divisions unessential to the meeting of basic human needs would be abandoned, and staff prestige and power differentials based upon professional competencies would be simplified. However, many staff groups will not want to lose the internal niche they secured during economic expansion. The organization will be pressured from within to preserve the current internal social system, despite external economic changes, because of the present political and economic value of that social system to the organizational members.

These pressures to maintain the internal political economy of the organizations will lead to four separate domain claims which are rather new to penology.

1. There will be attempts to professionalize and specialize in meeting basic offender needs. Emphasis on behavioral objectives[30] or the "normative needs" of offenders will increase.[31] By expanding and elaborating the technology for meeting basic offender needs, penal treatment staff will seek to preserve the niche that separates them from custodial status. However, the importance of greater professionalism to meet basic offender needs is unlikely to be sufficient to justify a claim for adequate resources. Penal organizations may therefore be expected to expand in areas that are not directly associated with offender processing.

2. One of these new areas will be an emphasis on the symbolic value of penal organization. For example, penal organization may start to make claims in the area of general deterrence, stressing their contribution to the reinforcement of norms among nonoffenders. The recently publicized film, Scared Straight is one example of this kind of activity. Determinate sentencing may be another.

3. Penal organizations are also likely to seek new populations for supervision. Such expansion may bring penal claims into questionable legal ground, because these new populations will not be convicted and thus, strictly speaking, not punishable. Nevertheless, penal organizations will stress the similarity in social characteristics between these new groups and convicted offenders and thereby make a claim for the expertise in their supervision. Persons under preadjudication probation and other forms of preconviction supervision are the most likely target groups. The community based programs in Des Moines are perhaps the best known examples.[32] Evidence of this trend can also be seen in data suggesting that diversion programs are in fact bringing under penal authority groups that had not been processed previously.[33]

4. Finally, penal organizations may claim expertise in rendering services to persons who have been involved with the offender but who are seen as more deserving. Victims and even witnesses of crimes will be seen as fair game by penal officials.[34]

ISSUES IN THE CONTROL OF
PENAL SYSTEMS

This chapter began with certain assumptions about imminent changes in the external political economy of penal organizations. I argued that the new mandate would not be received passively by penal organizations. Rather, in order to preserve their internal political economy, penal organizations will try to find new ways to justify external support for their complex division of labor and differential reward system. The organization will claim that meeting basic offender needs is more than a custodial task and therefore requires support for professional growth and development. The organization will also seek to expand its domain in directions that the mandating constituency will regard as having higher priority than simply the processing of offenders. Should these predictions be borne out, it would not be the first time that penal organizations found the means to prosper at the expense of the original objectives of external mandating groups. Lerman has made a similar argument about the behavior of California penal agencies in the 1960s.[35]

These possibilities raise some questions, however, about the ways in which external groups seek to constrain the activities of penal organizations. First, there is the question of the welfare of offenders in the future. The time when it is politically most unpopular to care for offender well being may be precisely the time when penal agencies should be most careful to do it. Instead, perhaps to maintain political favor, many penal organizations have already given in to the policies of restraint and just deserts. This may leave the welfare of offenders in the hands of external groups which are not in the best position to effect change. Second, this analysis would suggest that external groups seeking to reform penal organizations need to be acutely aware of the tendency of those organizations to place system maintenance needs above the social functions which mandating groups might favor. External groups, if they wish to attain their goals, must find ways to accommodate this tendency in their planning and in the phrasing of their mandate. Third and finally, although many of the new claims that penal organizations may raise will sound reasonable and valuable, these claims should be evaluated in terms of their covert organizational functions as well as their stated purposes.

As a closing note, I wish to highlight one implication of this analysis. While a detailed treatment is beyond the scope of this chapter, momentary reflection upon the more general forecasts of social change may be appropriate in light of these predictions about penal organization. As I stated at the beginning of this chapter, social forecasters have suggested that the "externalities," or the production costs not paid for in the industrial age, have finally caught up with us. Political decisions about the social good must now take priority over economic decisions about private goods.

According to Bell and Dahrendorf, this new condition also raises a new social conflict. We have entered an age where conflict among social groups over distribution of resources is overshadowed by the conflict between groups in power and those without. In other words, class conflict has changed from one based on property and ownership to one based on the authority to manage.[36] It can be argued that in organizations, whether public or private, "ownership" of decision-making positions is more influential than strict legal ownership.

To the extent that this is true, it would mean that the determining constraints on organizational decisions are increasingly internally generated. Decisions are taken and policy made based primarily on criteria about the social system *of* the organization rather than criteria about the social system *around* the organization. This shift in the balance of power (or the indicators of class) poses a particularly important dilemma under conditions of economic crisis. While society may have reached a point where communal decisions about the public good are prerequisites to survival, our postindustrial society is not structured for communal decision making. Each organization, in effect, operates as a separate community, and the definitions of collective good that are meaningful to them spread no further than the boundaries of the organizations.

Much of our political analysis focuses on the problems of achieving a consensus among the many diverse interest groups in society. The problem is certainly a large one, perhaps insurmountable. But as those interest groups grapple with their differences, it may behoove them to consider another problem: that our organizations are structured to preserve themselves, whatever the public good.

NOTES

1. Daniel Bell, *The Coming of Postindustrial Society* (New York: Basic Books, 1976); Geoffrey Vickers, *Making Institutions Work* (New York: Halsted Press, 1973); Ralf Dahrendorf, *Class and Class Conflict in Industrial Society* (Stanford: Stanford University Press, 1959).
2. David Rothman, *The Discovery of the Asylum* (Boston: Little, Brown, 1971); Andrew T. Scull, *Decarceration, Community Treatment and the Deviant: A Radical View* (Englewood Cliffs, N.J.: Prentice-Hall, 1977); Michel Foucault, *Discipline and Punishment* (New York: Vintage, 1978).
3. Gary Wamsley and Mayer Zald, "The Political Economy of Public Organizations," *Public Administration Review* 33 (January/February 1973): 64.

4. Charles Perrow, *Organizational Analysis: A Sociological View* (Belmont, Calif.: Brooks/Cole, 1979), pp. 80–81.
5. Daniel Katz and Robert Kahn, *The Social Psychology of Organizations* (New York: Wiley, 1973), p. 117.
6. Wamsley and Zald, "Political Economy," p. 64.
7. Bell, *Postindustrial Society*, pp. 276–278.
8. Donald Cressey, "Contradictory Directives in Complex Organizations, The Case of the Prison," *Administrative Science Quarterly*, 4 (June 1959):1–19.
9. J. Meyer and B. Rowan, "Institutionalized Organizations: Formal Structures as Myth and Ceremony," *American Journal of Sociology* 83 (September 1977): 340–363.
10. Wamsley and Zald, "Political Economy," pp. 64–65.
11. Roland Warren, Stephen Rose, and Anne Bergunder, *The Structure of Urban Reform* (Lexington, Mass.: Lexington Books, 1974), p. 108.
12. Ibid.
13. Ephraim Yuchtman and Stanley E. Seashore, "A System Approach to Organizational Effectiveness," *American Sociological Review* 32, 6 (December 1967): 891–903.
14. Wamsley and Zald, "Political Economy," p. 67.
15. Philip Selznick, "An Approach to a Theory of Bureaucracy," *American Sociological Review* VIII (February 1943): 47–56.
16. Herbert Simon, "On the Concept of Organizational Goal," *Administrative Science Quarterly* 9 (June 1964): 19.
17. Kenneth Benson, "The Interorganizational Network as a Political Economy," *Administrative Science Quarterly* 20 (June 1975): 231–232.
18. Fred Emery and Eric Trist, "The Causal Texture of Organizational Environments," in F. Emery (ed.), *Systems Thinking* (Baltimore: Penguin, 1970): 241–258; Shirley Terreberry, "The Evolution of Organizational Environments," *Administrative Science Quarterly* 12 (March 1968): 590–613.
19. Marshall Meyer, "Organizational Domains," *American Sociological Review* 40 (October 1975): 599–615.
20. Leslie T. Wilkins, "Crime and Criminal Justice at the Turn of the Century," *Annals of the American Academy of Political and Social Science* 408 (July 1973): 13–20.
21. Marshall Meyer, "Organizational Domains," p. 608; Wamsley and Zald, "Political Economy," p. 66.
22. Rothman, *Discovery of the Asylum.*
23. Anthony Platt, "The Rise of the Child Saving Movement: A Study in Social Policy and Correctional Reform," *The Annals of the American Academy of Political and Social Science* 381 (January 1969): 21–38.
24. Foucault, *Discipline and Punishment.*
25. Vincent O'Leary and David Duffee, "Correctional Policy—A Classification of Goals Designed for Change," *Crime and Delinquency* 17, 4 (October 1971): 373–386.
26. Rothman, *Discovery of the Asylum*, p. 103.
27. New York Special Commission on Attica, *Attica* (New York: Bantam, 1972), p. 15.
28. James Jacobs and Norma Crotty, *Guard Unions and the Future of Prisons* (Ithaca: Cornell University Institute of Public Employment, Monograph 9, August 1978).
29. Katz and Kahn, *Social Psychology*, pp. 90–94.
30. Todd Clear, "The Specification of Behavioral Objectives in Probation Supervision," unpublished doctoral dissertation, University at New York, May 1977.
31. Frank Dell'Apa, W. Tom Adams, James D. Jorgensen, and Gerbert R. Sigurdson, "Advocacy, Brokerage, Community: The ABC's of Probation and Parole," *Federal Probation* XXXX, 4 (December 1976): 37–45.

32. D. Boorkman, E. Fazio, N. Day, and D. Weinstein, *An Exemplary Project, Community Based Correction in Des Moines* (Washington, D.C.: Government Printing Office, November 1976).
33. Thomas Blumberg, "Diversion, A Strategy of Family Control in the Juvenile Court Process," Florida State University School of Criminology, 1975.
34. Alan Harlan, "Restitution and Service by Offenders: A Summary of Previous Research," paper presented at the annual meetings of the American Society of Criminology, Dallas (November 1978); D. Helbush and D. Mandel, "Aids to Victims and Witnesses," *Federal Probation* 41 (December 1977): 3–6.
35. Paul Lerman, *Community Treatment and Social Control* (Chicago: University of Chicago Press, 1975).
36. Bell, *Postindustrial Society,* pp. 341–367; Dahrendorf, *Class and Class Conflict,* pp. 280–319.

Chapter 11

Community Justice Centers: The Citizenry Responds to Diminishing Public Services

*Dennis R. Longmire**

Worth County, Missouri, received nationwide publicity recently when it was reported that county voters had refused to support a move to increase property taxes. Media attention was not focused upon the rationale behind the citizen's tax rebellion, but instead upon how public service agencies within that jurisdiction were learning to cope with reduced fiscal resources. County officials had long been threatening that if taxes were not increased, some necessary and sacred agencies such as the county courthouse and the county jail might have to shut down. This threat was transformed into a promise following the election in which the citizenry failed to increase the tax base. The county courthouse was indeed closed as was the small jail facility, but much to the dismay of local government officials, the citizens now appear to be more satisfied with the services being provided by ad hoc agencies. The fact that trials are being conducted in the basement of the circuit judge's home was not overly problematic from the perspective of some of the citizens. In fact, one merchant was reported as saying that "It's easier to get to the county clerk's office now. You don't have to walk up all those stairs."[1] The clerk, incidentally, had relocated his office to a toolshed behind his farmhouse!

*Department of Sociology, The Ohio State University

One lesson to be learned from the Worth County experience is that when a citizenry becomes disenchanted with the continuous growth of the bureaucratic agencies supported by its tax dollars, there is a strong probability that the services being provided by those agencies will be reevaluated by the voters. If those services are deemed unsatisfactory or unnecessary, then the long-held assumption that bureaucracies, once entrenched, cannot be blocked, will be proven false.

Citizenries throughout the United States are committing themselves again to the colonial spirit which provided the social underpinnings for the American Revolution. This new revolutionary mentality contributed to the overwhelming support of the antitax proposition on the 1978 California ballot, Proposition 13. A survey conducted by the National Conference of State Legislatures reported that in 1979, 22 states had reduced income taxes and eight had voted to support tighter spending limits.[2] Alaska recently announced that it was totally eliminating its state income tax, an action not based on disdain for bureaucracy but resulting instead from the state's windfall profits from its natural oil resources. The total picture throughout the United States, however, is more accurately characterized by the California experience. Apparently the citizens are willing to gamble on the philosophy that, when it comes to the government, less is more.

The specific impact the California tax revolution has had on criminal justice services has been discussed elsewhere.[3] But the entire experience illustrates the trends facing all public service agencies in the future. The philosophy advocated by the new tax rebels is that declining taxes necessarily lead to declining bureaucracies; the supporting argument is that declining bureaucracies contribute to better more efficient services. The veracity of this argument is still unclear. It is quite possible, though, that such logic may be applicable to criminal justice agencies operating in the throes of budgetary crises. As it will be argued below, fewer tax dollars available to criminal justice agencies might serve as a catalyst to encourage greater citizen involvement in the social response to law violators. This argument is based on the belief that citizen involvement in crime control is not only going to provide the most efficient response to the social phenomenon of crime, but will also provide the most just response.

The concept of justice has received relatively little scholarly attention in recent years, especially as it relates to the distribution of legal rights and responsibilities. The most recent discussions of justice have been more attentive to social justice rather than criminal justice, focusing upon the philosophical question of how social goods (economic resources) ought to be distributed.[4] This question was recently discussed in terms of the distribution of legal goods and services (rewards and punishments).[5] The essence of this inquiry centers around the question, "What is criminal justice?" As I have argued elsewhere, there are basically three possible responses to this question.[6] Justice can be defined from the philosophical perspectives of classical theory as "deserts," from legal theory as "rights," or from positive theory as "needs."

The distribution of rewards and punishments from a needs-based system of justice provides the best support for citizen involvement in the criminal justice system; it therefore serves as the philosophical foundation upon which this chapter is based. An effort to acquire the greatest amount of criminal justice possible requires that the system of justice must move beyond positivism's limited definition of needs. Justice must reflect a more communal interpretation of the needs of society.[7] Although the tenets of positivism tell us that the scientist will best determine who needs what, it is my belief that the citizenry can best answer the question. The concept of justice from this perspective is best characterized by the term "popular justice," as it reflects the sentiments of the populace rather than bureaucratic agency administrators.

Much like the roots of the tax rebellion discussed earlier, the origins of a popular definition of justice can be traced to colonial America. As others have demonstrated, the administration of justice in the early history of America involved considerable community participation.[8] This system of justice has been termed "vigilantism" because of the relative absence of any centralized authority structure. Such a system existed through the middle of the eighteenth century.[9] Increased population size, urbanization, and industrialization all contributed to a decline in communal justice and a rise in bureaucratic justice.[10] In the complex society of today, justice becomes more concerned with matters of efficiency rather than communal sentiments, and the system of justice becomes bent on self-preservation rather than change.[11] Such tendencies have proliferated throughout the nineteenth and twentieth centuries. It is possible, however, that the growing discontent with government bureaucracies will be generalized to justice-serving agencies, and thus result in a reemergence of popular justice efforts.

Recent studies have demonstrated that the general population of the United States is significantly concerned with the problem of crime.[12] It was reported in 1975 that almost 50 percent of the population had limited or changed their activities because of a fear of crime.[13] The number of people admitting to being afraid to walk in certain areas near their homes because of possible criminal victimization rose from 34 percent in 1965 to 45 percent in 1974.[14] Such figures are not surprising in light of the rise in officially recorded crime rates during those same time periods.

The public's concern for safety is certainly not new, but there have been some new developments in their perceptions of how effectively government agencies are providing this safety. For example, 84 percent of the respondents in a 1965 nationwide survey rated the F.B.I. as "highly favorable." In 1975, only 37 percent of the respondents had such a favorable image of the agency.[15] Although there was general consensus that local police agencies were doing a better job than their federal colleagues, only 40 percent of the respondents said that the job was being performed well. The remaining 60 percent rated local police performance as either "fair" (41 percent), "poor" (12 percent), or had no opinion (7 percent).[16] When asked how their local police departments could improve, only 14 percent of those questioned in the 1975 Crime Panel Survey reported that "no improvements were necessary,"[17]

It appears that the public's concern for safety is not being addressed to their general satisfaction. Those agencies which have been given the primary authority and budget to provide a safe living environment for America's citizenry are not fulfilling their responsibilities. We need only look at the Worth County experience as an example of what can happen when a dissatisfied public begins closely to scrutinize its public officials. Perhaps the seeds of popular justice are being sowed by the leaders of the new antitax movement. These seeds may take time to grow, however; as one can see by examining the studies cited above, from the citizenry's perspective, the general dissatisfaction with local police agencies can only be resolved by an increase in the number of police officers.[18] Such increases are not likely to occur in the era of new tax militancy. It is thus argued here that an alternative system of policing must provide the citizenry with its sense of public safety. This alternative popular system can already be seen in different forms throughout the United States, paralleled by popular "adjudicative" and "corrective" approaches. Several examples of these newly emerging popular justice alternatives are described below.

Before discussing specific popular justice efforts, a brief note is warranted on what is perhaps the most significant event to stimulate this movement. Increased community involvement in the entire criminal justice process received popular attention in the middle-1960s when President Johnson established the Commission on Law Enforcement and Administration of Justice. This commission was given the charge to study the crime control strategies underway in the United States and to offer recommendations for improvement. Although the recommendations offered by the commission in its final reports are voluminous, one overriding theme emerged: citizens and authorities have to work *together* to combat the problem of crime.[19] The commission specifically stated that:

> ... controlling crime depends to a great degree on interaction between the community and the criminal justice system. ... [E]ffective policing of slums and ghettos requires programs designed to improve relations between the police and the residents of such neighborhoods and enable them to work together. Community-based correctional programs require that organizations of many kinds, and individuals as well, involve themselves actively in the job of reintegrating offenders into the life of the community. Programs designed to reduce juvenile delinquency require the same kind of public involvement.[20]

In the late 1960s, then, the stage was set for changes in the criminal justice system which would enable citizens to become more actively involved in the process of crime prevention and control. As we shall see, the exact nature of this involvement varies, depending in part on the ideological commitments of those initiating the involvement. When citizens themselves ask for a more active role in the crime control process, their requests are often seen as counterproductive by those already involved in crime control, specifically, the police. Such a reaction against citizen-initiated programs may contribute to the establishment of more radical efforts by community members to regain some control over their lives.[21] Citizen involvement in crime control efforts is discussed in the following review of two programs undertaken with the initiation by the police—team policing and citizen auxiliary police forces. These two movements are then contrasted with a more radical effort by citizen groups to police their neighborhoods—vigilante groups.

TEAM POLICING

Team policing per se is not necessarily a direct step toward popular justice; however, the attempt to form stronger bonds between police and community by assigning small teams of police officers to work in specific neighborhoods on a permanent basis reflects a step toward community involvement.[22] One of the earliest and most extensive team policing efforts was undertaken in Cincinnati in 1973. There, a program now known as COMSEC (Community Sector Team Policing) was initiated under the sponsorship of the Police Foundation. The essence of the COMSEC program involved a modification in the responsibilities and duties of police officers assigned to one of the districts in Cincinnati. Under the new approach, small teams of officers were assigned to act as generalists in the law enforcement capacity. Instead of relying on specialized units such as the narcotics or juvenile divisions, the COMSEC units were advised to handle all of the problems which arose in their community.

The intention of this team policing approach was to foster increased community awareness of the actual members of police teams. Ideally, such awareness would lead to increased familiarity and thus, to cooperation with police teams. Studies evaluating the COMSEC program suggest that such hopes were unfounded. Wilson, for example, reports that although crime prevention seemed to have been improved by the approach, citizen's attitudes toward the police were not.[23] Explanations vary about why changes in citizen attitudes did not occur. Kirkham and Wollan suggest that a "boomerang effect" may have occurred, where increased visibility of the police teams created a feeling of uneasiness among community members— a fear that crime was increasing in their area.[24] Similar arguments have been made to explain the negative results of the Kansas City patrol study.[25]

CITIZEN'S AUXILIARY FORCES

The movement toward citizen auxiliary police units reflects a much more obvious and direct move toward popular justice. Recently, there have been efforts to distinguish between various different types of auxiliary police units. Dow, for example, distinguishes between civil defense officers, auxiliary officers, and reserve peace officers.[26] The primary variables distinguishing these types are the amount of training and authority each receives. Civil defense officers receive the least amount of training and have little or no authority, while reserve peace officers are the most highly trained and have the greatest amount of legitimate authority. These variations in styles of citizen police efforts are interesting, but for the present discussion we will use the term citizen auxiliary police unit to mean something more general than Dow's usage. Any efforts to engage private citizens in the policing of their neighborhood will constitute a citizen auxiliary movement.[27]

The following list of "results sought" is offered to describe the focus of the Office of Community Anti-Crime Programs, part of L.E.A.A.[28]

1. The mobilization of community and neighborhood residents into effective self-help organizations which can develop and conduct anticrime programs within their communities and neighborhoods.
2. Neighborhood anticrime efforts that promote a greater sense of community and foster social controls over crime occurrence.
3. Improved cooperation among community and neighborhood residents and criminal justice agencies concerning the crime problems of communities and neighborhoods.
4. Increased awareness and involvement of criminal justice agencies in resident-sponsored neighborhood crime prevention activities and increased opportunities for citizen input into the criminal justice system.
5. Integration of community and neighborhood-based anticrime programs with other community improvement and neighborhood revitalization programs. . . .
6. The broad scale transfer of information about successful community and neighborhood-based anticrime programs to other groups throughout the nation.
7. A reduction in the fear of crime among community and neighborhood residents.
8. A reduction in the victimization of community and neighborhood residents.

The emphasis is clearly upon popular justice efforts. While L.E.A.A.'s intentions reflect concern for citizen involvement in crime prevention, the major thrust seems to be toward increased cooperation between the citizenry and formal criminal justice agencies such as the police. Items three and four on the above list most strongly suggest this emphasis.

Recent movements toward citizen's auxiliary police efforts have been undertaken as cooperative efforts between citizens and police. These auxiliary tactics can simply involve community awareness campaigns such as the Citizen's Alert Program sponsored by the Sacramento, California, sheriff's department. They attempt to involve citizens in such anticrime efforts as increased reporting of crimes to the police and increased awareness of mechanical crime prevention techniques (dead-bolt locks, increased lighting, and so forth). A more intense form of citizen involvement in police-related activities, however, is in the emergence of neighborhood watch programs. In these programs, citizen groups establish street patrol units and/or neighborhood associations which take an active anticrime approach much like the preventive patrol activities of the formal law enforcement officer.

In the suburbs of Los Angeles, there are numerous citizens' auxiliary units operating in neighborhood patrol capacities.[29] In response to the alarming growth in burglary rates in a neighborhood, one such group called Nosey Neighbors outfitted 50 private automobiles with citizen band radios and used these cars to patrol the neighborhood. The Nosey Neighbors would apprehend burglars in the act of committing crimes, and would also relay information about suspicious occurrences to the local authorities. While the exact impact that this movement will have upon the burglary rate is unclear, the motivation is obvious.[30] Faced with an increased threat of victimization combined with a decreased satisfaction with local police effectiveness, citizens decided to play a more aggressive role in the crime control process.

VIGILANTISM

Perhaps the most forceful movement toward popular justice efforts at the law enforcement level can be found in the recent surge of vigilante groups. Fogelson recently cited the widespread enthusiasm for self-defensive, vigilante activity as one indicator of the general discontent with big-city police in America.[31] Another extreme indicator of this discontent can be found in the widespread popularity of fictional depictions of violent vigilantism, such as *Dirty Harry* and *Magnum Force*.[32]

In the real world, the vigilante movement has also been characterized by brutality and excessive force. In Chicago's west side, a group called The Black Hand publically acknowledged responsibility for the abduction and beating of a suspected drug peddler in its community.[33]

One of the best known vigilante groups received the attention of the television news magazine *60 Minutes*. The North Ward Citizens Committee was formed in Newark, New Jersey, in response to that community's growing discontent with the local law enforcement community. Under the leadership of a former police sergeant, Anthony Imperial, the local citizens banded together to engage in a literal war against criminals.[34] There has been extensive criticism levied at Imperial's army based on reports of extreme brutality and racism.[35] The veracity of these reports has received little challenge, yet the efforts of the North Ward Citizens Committee have been met with considerable neighborhood support. Whether or not this means that popular justice is likely to include violent, racist movements similar to those depicted in the movies is a source for considerable debate.[36] For present purposes, the vigilante movement is offered as an example of possible reaction to declining public services.

In the area of criminal and civil adjudication, there are numerous examples of efforts to resolve interpersonal disputes outside the formal jurisdiction of the justice system.[37] While the overriding concern of those in support of such alternatives seems to be increased system efficiency, the potential for popular involvement in the justice process is very real at this level. There have been several Neighborhood Justice Centers, reported on elsewhere, which were created with L.E.A.A. funds.[38] For the present, we will focus on several recent examples of popular justice efforts which relate specifically to the adjudicatory phase of the criminal justice system. Two of these efforts, the Boston Urban Court Program and the Los Angeles Hearing Officer Program, function in direct cooperation with the formal adjudicative agencies of the criminal justice system. A third program, the Christian Conciliation Service, is engaged in dispute resolution practices totally outside of the formal criminal and civil justice systems.

THE BOSTON URBAN COURT PROGRAM

The Boston Urban Court Program has been operational since November 1975. The program is predicated on a desire to involve community members in the distribution of justice withn their geopolitical boundaries. Although the program has limited jurisdiction (it only operates in one county in Massachusetts), it has provided the model upon which several other programs in the U.S. are based.

In practice, the program operates in three distinct capacities: mediation, disposition, and victim services. The services offered within each of these components of the program are described as follows:

A *Mediation* Program uses trained citizens to assist in resolving interpersonal disputes in lieu of formal judicial intervention;

A *Disposition* Program also uses community volunteers who hear more serious cases after conviction; develop service plans based on presentence assessments, and prepare sentencing recommendations for consideration by the bench;

A *Victim Service* Component, operated jointly by the Urban Court Program and the District Attorney, provides a range of orientation and social assistance services to victims and witnesses.[39]

As one can see, both the mediation and victim services components of the Boston Urban Court Program entail community involvement in the adjudicative phase of the criminal justice system. If mediation efforts are successful, formal adjudication does not ensue. The cases disposed of through this informal process include crimes of assault as well as public order offenses such as disturbing the peace. While the bulk of the cases have been relatively minor offenses, the structure of the program has been established; it could be expanded to include many more serious actions. The program has limited its focus thus far to cases where the individuals involved in the disputes have to continually interact. Such cases seem to be especially amenable to informal mediation. Perhaps, as the economic crisis worsens, citizens will be faced with restricted access to traditional methods of formal case disposition—methods which, in effect, expel one or more of the disputants from the community (and into jail, for example). Such changes may result in a wider acceptance of mediation techniques.

The victim service component of the Boston Urban Court Program represents an effort to involve the actual victim of a crime in the criminal justice process. Services offered to victims include counseling to reduce the trauma associated with victimization, and transportation to and from court. Furthermore, victims are often encouraged to participate in the program's disposition component.

The disposition phase of the program reflects recent efforts to involve citizens in the corrective role of the formal criminal justice system. This component of the program involves the use of community volunteers to promote innovative sentencing alternatives in cases which have been formally adjudicated. The program relies on community members, including victims or victim representatives, to suggest sentencing plans to the official sentencing authority involved in a particular case. The intent here seems to be a desire to develop a disposition that will satisfy the needs of the victim, the perpetrator, and the community at large.

The general philosophy behind the Boston Urban Court Program is best summarized in the mandate offered by the program's administrator:

> The offender [will] have a sense of the impact of his actions on the victim and the community, and the system might fashion more appropriate sentences through the involvement of more people with a vested interest in the welfare of the community. Both the mediation and disposition components ... emphasize actual and symbolic restitution agreements as a means of further influencing both offenders' and victims' perceptions of justice.[40]

THE LOS ANGELES HEARING
OFFICER PROGRAM

Another experimental venture into the use of informal adjudication techniques was initiated by the Los Angeles District Attorney in 1976. The impetus for the creation of this experiment, now known as the Hearing Officer Program, was two-fold.[41] First, the district attorney recognized that the criminal courts were suffering from extreme overcrowding and congestion. It was believed that this problem could be resolved, at least partially, by diverting certain cases from the formal criminal justice system. A second, more relevant concern of the district attorney had to do with the quality of justice being delivered in the formal courts. While the formal dispositions were procedurally sound, the disputants in many cases were unhappy with the outcome of the proceedings. It was argued that the Hearing Officer Program would promote greater efficiency in case management, and would also enable the citizens to participate actively in the settlement of their own problems.

This program operates in a preprosecution dispute resolution capacity, avoiding the use of formal adjudication techniques—the criminal charges, convictions, and punishments which follow formal adjudication procedures. The program focuses attention on the following categories of cases:

> *Domestic or Neighborhood Disputes* (Battery may be alleged by both parties, mutual assault is sometimes evident, or a wife, while not wanting her husband arrested, may want him to stop his abusive behavior.);
>
> *Misdemeanors* (Incidents of shoplifting, vandalism, and disturbing the peace constitute the majority of cases referred to the program.);
>
> *Code Violations* (These cases usually involve violations of vehicle code, such as driving without a license, or health and safety code violations such as owning an unlicensed or uninoculated dog.); and
>
> *Truancy* (Although juveniles are not eligible to participate in the hearing officer program, their parents can be cited for failure to make a child attend school.)[42]

In these cases, the district attorney's office refers cases to hearing officers who have been trained in the use of mediation techniques. The hearing officer is responsible for arranging a meeting between disputing parties so that each can present his or her version of the incident in question. The mediator (hearing officer) then resolves the dispute, making written recommendations to each party involved. While the disputants are not legally bound by the hearing officer's recommendations, voluntary cooperation, in lieu of formal prosecution, has proven to be the most frequent response. According to the first year's statistics, only 6.9 percent of the cases heard by a hearing officer had to be formally addressed in criminal court.[43]

CHRISTIAN CONCILIATION SERVICE

Unlike the previous two examples, the Christian Conciliation Service has taken steps toward popular justice that are completely outside the control of the formal criminal justice system.[44] Operating under the general auspices of the Christian Legal Society, the Conciliation Service attempts to resolve cases by invoking moral and spiritual authority rather than legal authority.[45] Although the principals employed in the resolution of cases involve the same basic mediation and arbitration techniques used by the citizens in the Boston Urban Court Program, the Christian Conciliation Service conducts its activities within the church. The goal is the same—involvement of individuals in the resolution of their personal problems—but the ultimate authority in the Christian Conciliation Service is God, not mortal judges.

It is reported that the Christian Legal Society is operating in most states in the U.S. Similar practices have long been in existence in the Quaker and Mennonite faiths. Cases mediated this way have not received widespread public attention and have been limited to domestic matters and disputes involving other civil affairs, such as child custody, unresolved business debts, and so on. These limitations are not necessary, however. As one can see by examining the basic steps in the process, it would be totally feasible to invoke such practices in criminal as well as in civil matters.

The basic steps in the mediation process advanced by the Christian Conciliation Service were outlined for the conciliators by Jesus, as reported in the Gospel of Matthew (Chapter 18, verses 15, 16, and 17):

> If your brother sins against you, go and tell him his fault, between you and him alone. If he listens to you, you have gained a brother. If he does not listen, take one or two others along with you, that every word may be confirmed by the evidence of two or three witnesses.
>
> If he refuses to listen to them, tell it to the church, and if he refuses to listen even to the church, let him be to you as a pagan or an outcast.

In its operation, the Christian Conciliation Service follows these steps exactly. Although the common practice is to encourage lawyers who are members of the Christian Legal Society to speak on behalf of the disputants, the overriding objective is the arbitration rather than the adjudication of cases.

The typical conciliation process can be seen in a case resolved by the Christian Conciliation Service, as was recently reported in the *Los Angeles Times*:

> In a recent adoption case, the natural mother of a 10-month-old baby had the right to go back to court to get her daughter back six months after giving her up for adoption.
>
> Instead, the mother submitted the matter to a panel of three Christian Legal Society Attorneys.
>
> "It was the most satisfying and exciting legal issue I've ever been in," said Sam Ericsson, the lawyer who arranged the settlement. "At the end of the hearing, before they even knew the decision, the natural mother and the adoptive mother got up and embraced."
>
> A few days later, the decision was rendered and the baby was left with the adoptive parents. . . .[46]

CONCLUSION

While the services provided by the Christian Conciliation Service are quite different from the actions attributed to the urban vigilante groups discussed earlier, these two movements share one characteristic that distinguishes them from other community justice efforts—they operate totally outside the domain of the formal justice system. These two movements demonstrate that popular justice efforts of a relatively anarchistic nature do not necessarily result in violent reactions. Provided that there exists some overriding authority to guide man's actions, the bureaucratic authority of the law seems to be unnecessary.

As the citizenry becomes more and more dissatisfied with the formal, bureaucratic system of justice, perhaps a more traditionally based system, such as the Christian Conciliation Service, will emerge to help resolve interpersonal disputes. If such a system does not emerge, popular justice efforts can still make inroads into the formal criminal justice system in the form of community justice centers such as the Boston Urban Court Program and the Los Angeles

Hearing Officer Program. All of the efforts discussed above have two characteristics in common: 1. they encourage citizen involvement in crime control and criminal justice matters, and 2. the current economic crisis facing America's public service agencies was a catalyst for their development. Although the immediate reaction to an economic crisis is generally one of dismay, it is possible that such a crisis may be just the shock needed to stimulate movement toward true justice—popular justice.

NOTES

1. Barry Siegel, "Denied a Tax Increase, County Learns to Survive," *Los Angeles Times*, 13 April 1980, pp. 1, 6.
2. Cited in Pearl S. West, "The Taxpayer's Revolt: Budgetary Crisis in Corrections," *Youth Authority Quarterly* 32 (1979): 5–8.
3. See Warren E. Walker, et al. (Chapter 7 in this volume). See also, West, "Taxpayer's Revolt," for a discussion of how Proposition 13 has impacted upon the correctional services available in California.
4. See for example, W. Alves and P. Rossi, "Who Should Get What? Fairness Judgments of the Distribution of Earnings," *American Journal of Sociology* 84 (1978): 541–564; Sidney Hook, "Human Rights and Social Justice," in the William D. Charmichael Jr. Lecture Series, *Social Justice and the Problems of the Twentieth Century* (Raleigh, N.C.: Raleigh School of Liberal Arts, 1968), pp. 7–23; David Miller, *Social Justice* (Oxford: Clarendon Press, 1976); David Miller, "Democracy and Social Justice," *British Journal of Political Science* 8 (1978): 1–19.
5. Nils Christie, "Conflicts as Property," *British Journal of Criminology* 17 (January 1977): 1–15. See also V. L. Hamilton and Steve Rytina, "Social Consensus on Norms of Justice: Should the Punishment Fit the Crime?" *American Journal of Sociology* 85 (1980): 1117–1144.
6. Dennis R. Longmire, "A Popular Justice System: A Radical Alternative to the Traditional Criminal Justice System," *Contemporary Crisis*, forthcoming.
7. Ibid.
8. See Samuel Walker, *Popular Justice A History of American Criminal Justice* (New York: Oxford University Press, 1980), especially pp. 9–35.
9. Ibid., p. 12.
10. Gregg Barak, *In Defense of Whom? A Critique of Criminal Justice Reform* (Cincinnati: Anderson Publishing Co., 1980).
11. See Philippe Nonet and Philip Selznick, *Law and Society in Transition: Toward Responsive Law* (New York: Harper & Row, 1978). Also see Jeffrey Reiman, *The Rich Get Richer and the Poor Get Prison* (New York: John Wiley & Sons, 1979).
12. The majority of the statistics cited in this section were drawn from the *Sourcebook of Criminal Justice Statistics, 1976*, compiled by Michael J. Hindelang et al. for the U.S. Department of Justice, L.E.A.A. (Washington, D.C.: U.S. Government Printing Office, 1977).
13. Ibid., p. 310.
14. Ibid., p. 305.
15. Ibid., p. 321.
16. Ibid., p. 322.

17. Ibid.
18. Ibid.
19. President's Commission on Law Enforcement and Administration of Justice, *The Challenge of Crime in a Free Society* (Washington, D.C.: U.S. Government Printing Office, 1967).
20. Ibid., pp. 13–14.
21. For a more detailed discussion of this official response to citizen initiated justice movements see Center for Research on Criminal Justice, *The Iron Fist and the Velvet Glove* (expanded and revised edition) (Berkeley, Calif.: Center for Research on Criminal Justice, 1972), especially pp. 125–131.
22. See Center for Research on Criminal Justice, *The Iron Fist,* pp. 135–148, for a critique of this movement.
23. James Q. Wilson, *Thinking About Crime* (New York: Vantage Books, 1977), pp. 103–105.
24. George L. Kirkham, and Laurin A. Wollan, *Introduction to Law Enforcement* (New York: Harper & Row, 1980), p. 67.
25. For a review of this program see, George L. Kelling, Tony Pate, Duane Dieckman, and Charles E. Brown, *The Kansas City Preventive Patrol Experiment: A Summary Report* (Washington, D.C.: The Police Foundation, 1974).
26. Ronald E. Dow, *Volunteer Police: Community Asset or Professional Liability* (New York: New York Conference of Mayors, 1977).
27. See Norman Sklarewitz, "Citizen Cops," *American Way* (March 1979). Reprinted in Annual Editions, *Readings in Criminal Justice 79/80* (Guilford, Conn.: Dushkin Publishing Group, Inc., 1979), pp. 86–88.
28. Extracted from a memorandum circulated to employees of the Office of Community Anti-Crime Programs (21 December 1977).
29. Tim Grobaty, "They're Partners in Crime Prevention," *Long Beach Independent Press-Telegram* (15 August 1979), Section N, p. 1.
30. For the results of recent evaluation of a similar program see Edward J. Latessa and Harry E. Allen, "Using Citizens to Prevent Crime: An Example of Deterrence and Community Involvement," *Journal of Police Science and Administration* 8 (1980): 69–74.
31. Robert M. Fogelson, *Big-City Police* (Cambridge, Mass.: Harvard University Press, 1977), p. 277.
32. See Fogelson, *Big-City Police,* pp. 276–278, for a similar discussion.
33. "A Policeman in the Ghetto," *The Washington Post* (11 August 1978).
34. For a discussion of this movement see Paul Goldberger, "Tony Imperial Stands Vigilant for Law and Order," in Marx, Gary (ed.), *Racial Conflict* (Boston: Little, Brown, 1977), pp. 397–399.
35. See James P. Brady, "Towards A Popular Justice in the United States: The Dialectics of Community Action," *Contemporary Crisis,* forthcoming.
36. For a debate on this question see James P. Brady, "Sorting Out the Exile's Confusion: Or Dialogue on Popular Justice," *Contemporary Crisis,* forthcoming; and Dennis R. Longmire, "Cutting the Gordian Knot: Continuing the Dialogue on Popular Justice," *Contemporary Crisis,* forthcoming.
37. For an excellent summary of these models, see Daniel McGillis and Joan Mullen, *Neighborhood Justice Centers: An Analysis of Potential Models* (Washington, D.C.: U.S. Government Printing Office, 1977).
38. See Sally Engle Merry, "Anthropological Models of Mediation: A Critique of Neighborhood Justice Centers," paper presented at the 31st Annual Meeting of the American Society of Criminology, Philadelphia, PA, 1979. Also see Sally Engle Merry,

"Going to Court: Strategies of Dispute Management in an American Urban Neighborhood," *Law & Society Review* 13 (1979): 891–925.

39. McGillis and Mullen, *Neighborhood Justice Centers,* p. 90.
40. Ibid., p. 91.
41. County of Los Angeles, Office of the District Attorney, (no date), "Hearing Officer Program," mimeographed program description.
42. "Hearing Officers Relieve Courts in L.A.," *Target* 6 (1977).
43. These statistics were compiled from data included in an office memorandum from Bill Martin, Assistant Director, Bureau of Prosecution Support Operations, to John Van De Kamp, District Attorney, Los Angeles, dated July 12, 1977.
44. The information about the Christian Conciliation Service was reported by Chandler, Russell, "Legal Fights Ending Up in Church Halls," *Los Angeles Times* (11 April 1980), Part I, pp. 1, 26, 27.
45. According to figures cited by Chandler in "Legal Fights," p. 26, there are not more than 30 chapters of the Christian Legal Society operating throughout the United States.
46. Chandler, "Legal Fights," p. 27.

PART IV

An Economic Model of Crime in a Changing Economy

The final chapter of this volume examines the effects of economic fluctuations on crime and its control utilizing a formal economic model. Chris Eskridge presents a very structured, systematic approach to the policy decision process, and offers some pragmatic suggestions for policy determination. He advances the notion that the future challenge in crime control will be for the United States to improve its economy at all levels. While a continuously improving economy will by no means eradicate illegal behavior, it will serve to minimize the optimal net cost of crime to society. Such techniques as increased justice system efficiency and restitution programs are shown to be cost-beneficial. Eskridge argues, however, that these efforts will not overcome the threatened increase in the net cost of crime which will accompany the impending depressed economy.

Chapter 12

The Futures of Crime
in America: An
Economic Perspective

Chris W. Eskridge*

The reduction of deviant behavior has been a volatile issue among academicians, scholars, bureaucrats, and politicians for centuries. In recent years, there has been much public unrest concerning the apparently rising rate of criminal activity in the United States. It is the purpose of this chapter to review the economic implications of crime and crime reduction, and to offer some predictions about future behavior patterns of the individual and society.

THE DILEMMA OF JUSTICE ADMINISTRATION

The criminal justice system in the United States has long recognized and operated under a painful dilemma. Banfield enunciated the principle quite clearly when he observed: "If some people's freedom is not abridged by law enforcement agencies, that of others will be abridged by law breakers. The question, therefore, is not whether abridging the freedom of those who commit serious crimes is an evil—

An earlier version of this article appeared in *Chitty's Law Journal*, January 1978, pp. 9–16.
*Department of Criminal Justice, University of Nebraska

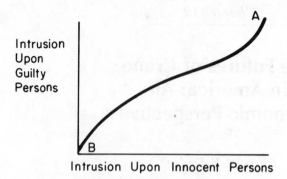

Figure 12-1. Law Enforcement Costs.

it is—but whether it is a lesser or greater one than the alternative."[1] There is a definite cost in freedom involved in the administration of social justice. Let us consider the loss of physical freedom through intrusion and/or incarceration, and the loss of economic freedom through taxation to finance enforcement. Figure 12-1 illustrates the cost of law enforcement in terms of physical freedom. The level of physical freedom lost to innocent persons as a cost of crime suppression is measured along the horizontal axis; the level of physical freedom lost to persons legally defined as guilty is measured along the vertical axis. The curve illustrates the dilemma: any level of enforcement above zero will result in an abridgement of freedom upon some number of innocent persons. The precise shape of this curve or relationship is not a matter of primary concern in this chapter, but rather the concept it attempts to portray; every level of enforcement has a cost in terms of physical freedom upon the innocent. As Stigler has emphasized, all guilty persons can be, in reality, charged and convicted, but only at the cost of convicting all innocent persons (represented by point A in Figure 12-1).[2] On the other hand, no innocent persons would be charged and convicted if no legally defined guilty persons were convicted (represented by point B in Figure 12-1). While it is reasonable to hypothesize that neither extreme is desirable, society must decide what price it is willing to accept.

The dilemma becomes more vivid when costs in economic freedom are added to the model. A review of the derived economic freedom function will render a similar conclusion: there are costs involved in any level of criminal activity desired. Figure 12-2 has been adapted from a graph originally prepared by Monzingo.[3] The level of crime is measured along the horizontal axis; costs are measured along the vertical axis. The curve which slopes down from left to right represents the cost of suppressing crime. This would include the cost of such ac-

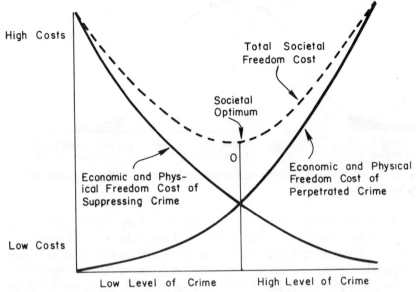

Figure 12–2. Costs of Crime.

tivities as detection, apprehension, incarceration, adjudication, institutionalization, rehabilitation and/or reintegration, plus intrusion costs. Its structure suggests that the lower the level of crime desired, the greater the cost in suppressing the crime. The curve which slopes upward from left to right represents the net social costs of crime perpetration. This would include the cost to society of such activities as murder, rape, white-collar crime, drug abuse, prostitution—anything that is defined as criminal by the legal or moral code. Its structure indicates that the greater the number of offenses, the greater the net social costs. The U-shaped dotted curve represents the sum of the two lower curves; it indicates the total loss to society due to perpetrated crime and the allocation of resources to suppress crime. While it is apparent that a societal cost is involved in any given level of enforcement, society generally seeks to minimize such costs.

It should be noted here that this optimal cost-of-crime figure is exceedingly difficult to measure quantitatively. Both the 1931 Wickersham Commission[4] and the 1967 President's Crime Commission[5] attempted to measure the cost of crime in terms of dollars. But as Hann has pointed out, these studies were based on vague and tenuous definitions of what they were trying to measure.[6] Hann further stated, "There is much work yet to be done in developing the necessary theoretical basis and operational tools for estimating any cost of crime."[7]

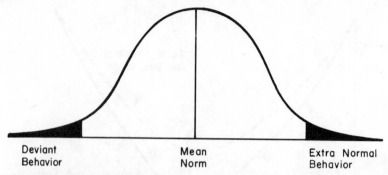

Figure 12–3. Normal distribution curve of behavior within a group or society.

Theoretically, net crime costs can be optimized by allocating enough resources to achieve a level of crime that coincides with the point of social optimum on the total loss curve. This will be at the point where the marginal costs and gains from crime suppression and crime perpetration are equal; that point is denoted by line 0 in Figure 12–2. In essence, to minimize total societal loss, society must recognize and accept some optimal, nonzero level of illegal behavior.

Let us consider this prospective within a sociological framework. Durkheim stated, "Crime is present not only in the majority of societies of one particular species, but in all societies of all types."[8] Consider Figure 12–3. Those whose activities are perceived as falling to the far right of the mean are those who have the greatest probability of serving as the leaders—academic, athletic, moral, political, or religious—in any given group or society. Those whose activities are perceived as falling to the far left are those most likely to receive negative sanctions from society. The eradication of the deviant population within a society will not serve to eradicate deviants, but only to shift the behavioral distribution curve further to the right, and thus to define the former marginal deviants as total deviants. This will be the case regardless of the moral nature of the group. The establishment of a society of extranormals will still result in a behavioral distribution, with some defined as deviants. Deviant behavior will always exist, in internal groups or society as a whole, though as in the case of the society of extranormals, it may not be judged as such by an external group.

In reviewing Figure 12–4, recall the existence of two so-called extranormal societies—the Puritan community of the 1600s and the Mormon community of the 1800s, both of which defined and punished behavior they determined was deviant. There were, in those societies, persons who did in fact represent a threat to the societal environment.

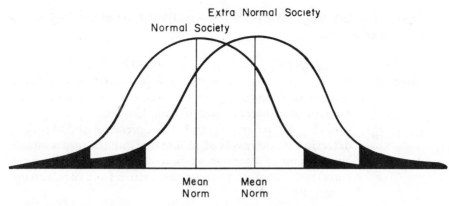

Figure 12–4. Distribution of Behavior Within Two Societies.

However, a majority of the negatively sanctioned behavior in the Mormon and Puritan societies would fall well within the behavioral tolerance of 1978 America.

The sociological perspective is thus complimentary to the economists' position. Deviant behavior will always exist and is theoretically impossible to eradicate. Society must accept, but seek to optimize, some nonzero level of illegal activity on the part of its members.

BEHAVIOR AND EXPECTED VALUE

As has been previously inferred, obedience to social law is not a matter of uniform adherence, and while resources are spent to minimize violations, a certain level of violations and enforcement exists with respect to societal loss. In the mid-1960s Becker advanced the notion of an economically based model as a useful tool in ascertaining the best way to further minimize societal loss due to illegal behavior.[9] Becker's original work suggested the existence of an optimal crime suppression cost, subject to a given legal framework. Harris' work subsequently demonstrated that the legal framework need not be taken as a constant, but is itself subject to and part of an economically modeled policy choice.[10] The economists' generalization of human behavior serves as the foundation of these analyses—namely, that the individual, as a rational being, will participate in the activity which will yield the greatest expected utility. Society must therefore support policy which tends to minimize the individual's expected utility from illegal behavior and maximize the individual's expected utility from legal behavior. Let us consider such hypotheses in an empirically modeled form, adapted from the works of Becker[11] and Sjoquist.[12] The expected utility from involvement in an illegal activity i may be expressed as follows:

$$EU_i = S_i [P_i U(Y_i - e_i - f_i) + (1 - P_i)U(Y_i - e_i)]$$

where $S_i = 1 - (1 - s)^n$ where s equals the perceived probability of success in completing activity i and where n equals the number of attempts made to complete activity i.

$P_i = 1 - (1 - p)^n$ *where* p equals the perceived probability of detection while involved in activity i and where n equals the number of attempts made to complete activity i.

Y_i = perceived monetary plus psychic return from involvement in activity i.

e_i = perceived monetary plus psychic cost on involvement in activity i.

f_i = perceived monetary plus psychic sanctions for detection of involvement in activity i.

U = personal utility factor.

The expected utility from involvement in a legal activity li may be expressed as follows:

$$EU_{li} = S_{li}U(Y_{li} - e_{li}) - (1 - S_{li})U(e_{li})$$

where $S_{li} = 1 - (1 - s)^n$ *where* s equals the perceived probability of success in completing activity li and where n equals the number of attempts made to complete activity li.

Y_{li} = perceived monetary plus psychic return from involvement in activity li.

e_{li} = perceived monetary plus psychic cost of involvement in activity li.

Ehrlich[13] and Sjoquist[14] have both empirically demonstrated that an individual will seek to allocate his time between legal and illegal activities so as to maximize expected utility. Thus, if a society desires its citizens to continually participate in legal behavior, it must maintain a higher expected value for legal behavior than for illegal behavior. To force a movement from illegal behavior to legal behavior, society must increase the relative expected value of legal behavior and decrease the relative expe~ted value of illegal behavior. Note that there is no absolute expectancy scale, but only a relative scale of the expected value of legal behavior compared to the expected value of illegal behavior. In other words, both may increase or both may decrease, but as long as the expected value of legal behavior is larger than the expected value of illegal behavior, the former activity will be undertaken. This may be accomplished within the context of the above model in any of the following ways:

1. increase the monetary plus psychic returns from involvement in legal activities
2. increase the probability of success in completing legal activities
3. increase the probability of detection while involved in illegal activities
4. increase the monetary plus psychic costs of involvement in illegal activities
5. increase the monetary plus psychic sanctions for detection of involvement in illegal activities
6. decrease the monetary plus psychic costs of involvement in legal activities
7. decrease the probability of success in completing illegal activities
8. decrease the monetary plus psychic returns from involvement in illegal activities

With reference to the empirical model presented above, these eight methods of increasing the relative expected value from involvement in legal activities would increase the value of variables Y_{li}, S_{li}, P_i, e_i, and f_i, and would decrease the value of variables Y_i, S_i, and e_{li}. Movement in the opposite direction on any one of these variables will tend to increase the relative expected value of involvement in illegal behavior. Combinations of adjustments which tend to increase both the expected value of involvement in illegal and legal activity must be subjected to analysis within the context of the empirical formula.

It must be emphasized at this point that this thesis is dependent upon the concept of individual perception of values of these eight variables, combined with the individual's utility value. Expected utility is perceived by the individual and need not conform to reality. Rather, it is a function of reality, perception of reality, and personal utility values. For example, society could increase the probability of detection while involved in an illegal activity to 100 percent. If the individual does not perceive the increase, but rather perceives the previous value of 10 percent, the individual's activity will not adjust, despite the change in reality. While the true values of the eight variables presented in this model can be socially adjusted, adjustments of the individual's perceptions and utility values are not so malleable. This is not to suggest that society is unable to affect its members' perceptions of utility functions. It can, especially through the use of America's vast communication networks. But the point here is to distinguish between adjustments in reality and adjustments in individuals' perception and individuals' utility. The three are correlated, but to a degree that is significantly less than one.

In sum, this model advances the theory that economic factors are directly related to the rate of crime. This theory is not without empirical foundation. For example, a study conducted by Allison in 1972 found a strong relationship between the rate of crime and the rate of unemployment in a community.[15] A study conducted by Greenwood and Wadycki in 1973 found the rate of crime and the poverty level highly correlated.[16] Fleisher's 1963 study among juveniles found delinquent behavior positively correlated with unemployment.[17] From this theoretical basis, it can be argued that movements must be made to improve the economic well being of the country; otherwise, the United States will be forced to accept the impingement of an increasing cost of crime upon its economic and physical freedoms. This is not to suggest an increase in the well being of the lower class alone. Rather, I suggest that all classes of people will engage in illegal activity if the perceived expected value from illegal activity is greater than the perceived expected value from legal activity. While the nature of the illegal acts may differ from class to class, the economic loss and severity of the crimes to society may be equally distributed from class to class. Thus, not only must the economy as the whole improve, but all classes within that economy must be able to improve their economic position. Even within an expanding economy, social conditions must allow all classes to be able to improve their economic position. Post–World War II America is a case in point. The economy experienced colossal growth in this period, yet not all classes were permitted to participate to the extent they desired. Merton has noted that American culture teaches us to live high and to accumulate, but does not offer the legal opportunities to do such.[18] It appears that many saw a reduction in their expected value from participation in legal behavior to a level below their perceived expected value from participation in illegal behavior, and acted accordingly. Whether crime actually increased at the rate reported is not the issue here; reported crime rates do not necessarily reflect actual crime.[19] The two may be correlated, but at a rate significantly less than one. Reported crime rate is a function of a variety of variables including the amount of resources available to police officers, education level and quality of the police officers, education and income level of the community, rapport between the community and the police department, as well as crime itself. The point is that while the economy as a whole may improve, all classes within that economy must also be able to improve their economic position for there to be a decreased cost of crime to society.

THE DILEMMA OF JUSTICE AGGRAVATED

In considering the implications of crime and prevention within the context of the economic model, two factors must be considered. Demographic trends in America continue to point toward further urbanization of the population. Dale and Schachter have noted that with urbanization comes a decreased probability of detection of involvement in illegal behavior.[20] The President's Crime Commission of 1967 noted that urbanization has caused a massive increase in the cost of police services.[21] Review of the yearly Uniform Crime Reports issued by the FBI reveals that urbanization is also highly correlated with an increase in the rate of crime perpetrated upon the community. In terms of the economic model, the urbanization movement promises to:

1. decrease the probability of detection while involved in illegal activities
2. increase the probability of success in completing illegal activities
3. force an increase in the expected value from involvement in illegal behavior with respect to the expected value from involvement in legal behavior

With reference to the empirical model presented previously, these events would increase the values of P_i, S_i, and EU_i.

In addition to the trauma of urbanization, American society may be beginning to face an even greater challenge. The United States has perhaps reached its peak as an economic power. A limited-growth economic environment now seems to be impending, not from the standpoint of a decreased number of markets, as some economic theorists advance, but rather in terms of a finite supply of resources.[22] The American economy is not resource-independent. On the contrary, it is extremely resource-dependent. Technology has and will continue to increase efficiency by supplying substitutes which facilitate adaptation to periodic resource shortages. But the development of substitutes costs in resources, and with a declining supply of resources available, the cost of substitute development will increase at a rate that is indirectly proportional to the availability of resources. As resources become more and more scarce, economic deprivation will spread to more and more citizens.

The U.S. economy will not be the only economic system to suffer. Lack of resources will restrict any economic system. However, inasmuch as the American economy is one of the most, if not the most resource-dependent economy, it will feel the shortage most severely. In terms of the economic model, the future of the American economy promises to:

1. decrease the monetary plus psychic return from involvement in legal activities
2. decrease the probability of success in completing legal activities
3. increase the monetary plus psychic cost of involvement in legal activities

With reference to the empirical model presented previously, these events would decrease the value of Y_{li} and S_{li}, and increase the value of e_{li}.

The urbanization of America and the impending economic stagnation both tend to decrease the expected value from involvement in legal activity and increase the expected value from involvement in illegal activity. What can be done to offset this trend? Three variables remain that can be manipulated. In terms of the economic model, these variables are:

1. the monetary plus psychic returns from involvement in illegal activities
2. the monetary plus psychic costs of involvement in illegal activities
3. the monetary plus psychic sanctions for detection of involvement in illegal activities

With reference to the empirical model presented previously, these events would manipulate the values of Y_i, e_i, and f_i.

In order to decrease the expected value from involvement in illegal activity, the monetary plus psychic returns from involvement in illegal activity must be decreased, while the monetary plus psychic costs of involvement in illegal activities and the monetary plus psychic sanctions for detection of involvement in illegal activities must be increased. Such decisions translate into hardening of the target techniques and increasing the severity of the sanctions meted out upon the detected and convicted.

Let us consider these proposed alternatives of crime control. A 1976 study by McPheters, reported that hardening of the target techniques may not serve to decrease the number of reported crimes committed, but may in fact serve to *increase* the number of reported crimes. McPheters further found that the critical factor in reducing crimes was the probability of arrest and conviction, not hardening of the target techniques.[23]

Much has been written over the centuries concerning the relative merits of severity of sanctions as a deterrent. Sanctions certainly are relative; different individuals tend to perceive personal utility of the same sanction differently. Sanctions may work as a deterrent for individuals who possess a low negative utility. But for a society as a whole, one could question the ability of sanctions—even a universal application of the ultimate sanction—to impact a movement towards (and an adherence to) societally defined normative behavior.

It can be seen in the model that when the perceived probability of detection and conviction for involvement in illegal behavior approximates one, and the perceived severity of the sanction is near zero, the expected value from involvement in illegal activities will remain large; it may become even larger as the perceived monetary plus psychic costs of involvement and sanctions for detection of involvement in illegal activities become smaller and smaller. Likewise, when the perceived probability of detection and conviction of involvement in illegal behavior is near zero and the perceived severity of the sanction approximates one, the expected value from involvement in illegal activities will remain large—and perhaps become larger as the perceived probability of success in completing illegal activities and the perceived probability of detection while involved in illegal activities becomes smaller and smaller. In sum, it seems that increasing sanction severity, unaccompanied by an increase in the probability of detection and conviction for involvement in illegal activity (or vice versa), will not decrease the expected value from involvement in illegal behavior, and may in reality increase its value with respect to expected value from involvement in legal activities. This conclusion complements that reached by McPheters. Given that a set of sanctions now currently exists, the critical element in reducing the expected value from involvement in illegal behavior seems to be an increase in the probability of detection and conviction. This may translate into more funds for law enforcement agencies, removal of the behavioral restrictions which have been imposed upon police investigation and arrest procedure, and an adjustment in court rules and proceedings to the benefit of the prosecutor. Such propositions, as previously noted, are prohibitively costly in terms of infringement upon the economic and physical freedoms of society. Within the context of our model, the answer to crime control does not seem to lie in decreasing the expected value from involvement in illegal activity through increasing the probability of detection and conviction through increased law enforcement power, but rather in increasing the expected value from involvement in legal behavior. Recall that criminal activity can be reduced not only by decreasing the expected value from involvement in illegal activity, but also by increasing the relative expected value from involvement in legal activity.

CONCLUSION

The dilemma now becomes clear. As previously presented, re-duction in illegal activities necessitates a relative reduction in the ex-pected value from involvement in illegal behavior with respect to the expected value from involvement in legal behavior. It could be argued that the reduction of the expected value from involvement in illegal activities is cost-prohibitive, and that an increase in the expected value from involvement in legal behavior is unlikely due to the im-pending depressed state of the economy. Is there a resolution to this dilemma? To delay expected societal unrest, federal and state govern-ments have undertaken the temporary appeasement policy of social welfare. Markets for American goods and services have been expand-ed, and recently America has opened its labor force to foreign manu-facturers as a means of temporarily improving the economy. In an attempt to improve the economy on a long-term basis, an immense amount of human energy and resources have been extended to locate new natural resource reservoirs and to develop new substitutes. Fu-ture efforts must be coordinated between government and business to achieve greater success in this endeavor. Efforts made within the criminal justice system to increase its input—output efficiency has served to reduce the cost of crime suppression, and thus has further minimized the net cost of crime to society. Continued efforts in this area will serve to further minimize the net cost of crime to society. For example, a type of cost–benefit analysis in the resource allocation of police tasks would serve to identify the nature and extent of those ac-tivities most desirable to undertake from the standpoint of benefit and cost to society. Consider a manipulation of Figure 12–2 presented pre-viously as represented in Figure 12–5.

Figure 12–5 demonstrates that involvement in activity B would yield the greatest cost/benefit to society, with its ratio of ten units spent to forty units of savings ($40/10 = 4$), versus activity A's five units spent to ten units of savings ($10/5 = 2$). A readjustment of police activities toward those with the highest return ratio seems to be the most desirable venture. However, care must be given not to saturate, and thus suboptimize, the activity. Consider another manipulation of Figure 12–2 as represented by Figure 12–6. Figure 12–6 demon-strates that the maximum resource involvement in the activity should be ten units. This results in a cost/benefit ratio of $40/10$ or 4. Addition-al units of resources expended will serve to decrease that ratio. Figure 12–6 shows that fifteen units of expenditure in the activity would re-sult in a savings of forty-five units, but the resulting ratio is only $45/15$ or 3. Additional units of resources spent beyond the optimal point will not yield a cost–beneficial return and would, therefore, be

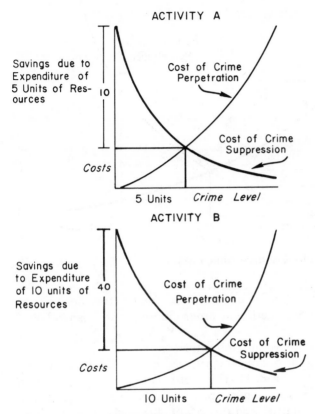

Figure 12–5. Resource Allocation Analysis.

best used elsewhere. It can be seen that an overall optimum state of resource involvement should be sought where each individual task and the sum total of all tasks are undertaken in a maximized cost-beneficial manner, given the existing resource limitations. Consider the following:

Table 12–1.

(j) Activity	(X) Monetary Plus Psychic Costs to Society for Crime Suppression	(Y) Monetary Plus Psychic Savings to Society from the Reduced Crime Due to Resources Spent in Crime Suppression	(Y/X) Ratio
1. Traffic			
2. Robbery			
3. Murder			
j. Etc.			

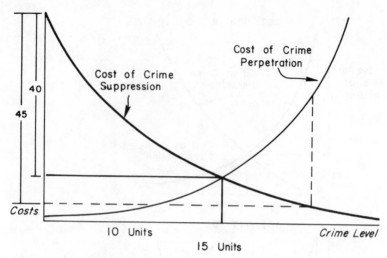

Figure 12–6. Optimum Resource Allocation.

Once values are given to each activity and ratios derived, the figures can be analyzed in a linear programming context as follows:[24]

$$\text{Maximize } Y_1/X_1 + Y_2/X_2 + Y_3/X_3 + Y_j/X_j$$

Subject to: resource limitations

While not all activities can be optimized due to the limited availability of resources, adherence to this cost/benefit linear programming model will maximize returns per input. It can be seen that this model can identify both the nature and the extent of the activities which will lead to the most efficient distribution of police resources. However, it should be noted that criminal justice efficiency will not totally neutralize the cost of crime suppression; it seems to be bounded by some nonzero maximum efficiency level. Figure 12–7 suggests that as the criminal justice system approaches a maximum efficiency level, the cost of crime suppression decreases at an ever-slower rate. In other words, there is a limit to the ability of the criminal justice efficiency factor to reduce the cost of crime suppression to society. It does appear that continued effort on the part of the justice system to increase and maintain a high efficiency level can minimize total societal crime costs, but only to a limited extent. Another alternative that has gained considerable recognition within the past few years is restitution.[25] A brief consideration of two aspects of the restitution principle is in order—defendant-financed victim compensation and defendant-financed court reimbursements. These forms of restitution are presented here as means of simultaneously reducing both the cost of suppressing crime and the cost of perpetrated crime, and thus as a means

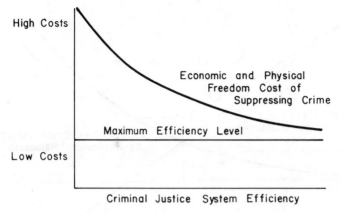

Figure 12–7. Impact of Maximum Efficiency Upon Crime Costs.

of minimizing total societal costs. A restitution orientation decreases the cost of suppressing crime two-fold: through a decreased incarceration rate, and through the financial payments or fines paid to the courts by the defendants. A decrease in the net cost of crime perpetrated is achieved through defendant reimbursement to victims for damages wrought during the course of the crime. However, as the number of defendants released on a restitution sentence who would normally have been incarcerated increases, the cost to society of new crimes perpetrated by those defendants increases. It seems, therefore, that within the restitution concept, some optimal level of application would be the most desirable. Consider the following:

let x = societal costs of suppressing crime
let y = restitution paid to the courts and to the victims by the defendants
let z = the costs of new crimes perpetrated by restitution releasees while on restitution release

The net cost of a restitution orientation can be defined as $(x - y) + z$. This is illustrated in Figure 12–8. The percentage of the defendant population released on restitution is measured along the horizontal axis; the costs of crime to society are measured along the vertical axis. The curve sloping down from left to right represents the gross cost of a restitution orientation. Its structure suggests that the greater the number of defendants released, the smaller the cost. The function suggests that at some point restitution can actually effect a gross negative cost—or in other words, a gross benefit upon the society. The

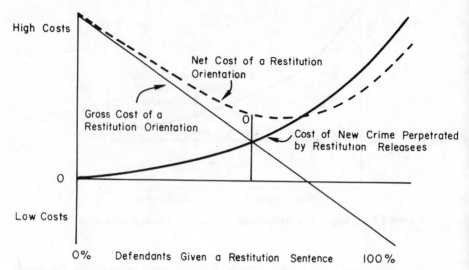

Figure 12–8. Costs of a Restitution Orientation.

curve sloping upward from left to right represents the costs of new crimes perpetrated by restitution releasees. Its structure suggests that the greater the number of defendants given a restitution sentence, the greater the cost of crime committed. The function also suggests that at some point, release of defendants on restitution sentences may cost society more in terms of new crimes perpetrated than it would to incarcerate after the initial incident. The U-shaped dotted curve represents the sum of the two lower curves and thus represents the net cost of a restitution orientation to society. The optimal level will be at the point where the marginal costs and gains from such an operation are equal, as denoted by line 0 in Figure 12–8. While it is apparent that a restitution orientation cannot totally neutralize the cost of crime, this relatively simplistic model has shown that society can minimize its crime costs by moving toward some optimal, nonzero level of sanctions oriented toward restitution.

SUMMARY

The challenge for tomorrow will be for the United States to improve its economy at all levels. While a continuously improving economy will by no means eradicate illegal behavior, it will minimize the optimal cost of crime. This is not to recommend a deemphasis on law enforcement. On the contrary, a reduction in law enforcement po-

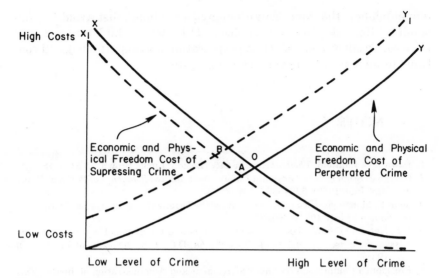

Figure 12–9. Summary of Potential Impacts Upon Crime Costs.

tency would only serve to increase the costs in physical and economic freedom of crimes perpetrated by increasing the expected value from involvement in illegal behavior. The role of law enforcement and the criminal justice system in reducing the net cost of crime to society is to increase its input–output efficiency. Among the means of optimizing crime costs are defendant-financed victim compensation and court reimbursement. However, these efforts to reduce the cost of crime suppression will not overcome the increase in the cost of crime perpetration due to the impending depressed state of the American economy. Figure 12–9 reveals that manipulations of the economic and physical freedom costs of suppressing crime (movement from line x to line x_1), through such techniques as increased justice system efficiency in resource allocations and the development and implementation of restitution programs, will reduce the societal optimum cost of crime and therefore should be undertaken. (Note the decrease of the optimum point from point 0 to point A.) The major problem the United States faces, in this context, however, is the threatened increase in the economic and physical freedom cost of perpetrated crime (movement from line Y to line Y_1) which will accompany the impending depressed state of the economy. This will increase the societal optimum cost of crime, despite the manipulations in line X. (Note the increase of the optimum from point A to point B.)

In summary, despite efforts to reduce the cost of crime through such methods as restitution programs and increased criminal justice system efficiency, the American economy as a whole must avoid the impending limited growth roadblock. Otherwise, the economic and physical freedom costs of crime perpetration and suppression will continue to increase at an ever-increasing rate.

NOTES

1. Edward C. Banfield, *The Unheavenly City* (Boston: Little, Brown, 1970) p. 184.
2. George J. Stigler, "The Optimum Enforcement of Laws," *Journal of Political Economy* (May/June 1970): 526–536.
3. John E. Monzingo, "Economic Analysis of the Criminal Justice System," *Crime and Delinquency* (July 1977): 260–271.
4. U.S. National Commission on Law Observance and Enforcement, *Wickersham Commission Reports, Volumes 1–14* (Washington, D.C.: U.S. Government Printing Office, 1931).
5. President's Commission on Law Enforcement and Administration of Justice, *Task Force Report on Corrections* (Washington, D.C.: U.S. Government Printing Office, 1967).
6. Robert G. Hann, "Crime and the Cost of Crime: An Economic Approach," *Journal of Research in Crime and Delinquency* (January 1972): 12–30.
7. Ibid., p. 24.
8. Emile Durkheim, *Rules of Sociological Method,* edited by George E. Cutlin, translated by S. A. Solovoy and J. H. Mueller, Beverly Hills, Calif. (Glencoe, Ill.: The Free Press, 1958) p. 65.
9. Gary S. Becker, "Crime and Punishment: An Economic Approach," *Journal of Political Economy* (March/April 1968): 169–217.
10. J. R. Harris, "On the Economics of Law and Order," *Journal of Political Economy* (Jan/Feb 1970): 165–174.
11. Becker, "Crime and Punishment."
12. David D. Sjoquist, "Property Crime and Economic Behavior: Some Empirical Results," *American Economic Review* (June 1973).
13. Issac Ehrlich, "Participation in Illegitimate Activities: A Theoretical and Empirical Investigation," *Journal of Political Economy* (May/June 1973).
14. Sjoquist, "Property Crime and Economic Behavior."
15. John P. Allison, "Economic Factors and the Rate of Crime," *Land Economics* (May 1972): 193–196.
16. Michael J. Greenwood, and Walter J. Wadycki, "Crime Rates and Public Expenditures for Police Protection: Their Interaction," *Review of Social Economy* (October 1973): 138–151.
17. Belton M. Fleisher, "The Effect of Unemployment on Juvenile Delinquency," *Journal of Political Economy* (Mar/Apr 1963): 543–555.
18. Robert K. Merton, *Social Theory and Social Structure* (New York: The Free Press, 1957).
19. See: Nigel Walker, *Crimes, Courts and Figures: An Introduction To Criminal Statistics* (Harmondsworth, England: Penguin Books Ltd., 1971).
20. Edwin L. Dale and Gustav Schachter, *The Economist Looks at Society* (Lexington, Mass.: Xerox, 1973) pp. 153–163.
21. President's Commission, *Task Force Report on Corrections.*

22. See Paul R. Ehrlich and Anne H. Ehrlich, *The End of Affluence* (New York: Ballantine Books, 1974); Paul R. Ehrlich and Anne H. Ehrlich, *Population, Resources, Environment* (San Francisco: W. H. Freeman & Co., 1972).

23. Lee R. McPheters, "Criminal Behavior and the Gains From Crime," *Criminology* (May 1976): 137–152.

24. For a more complete discussion of linear programming, see Robert L. Childress, *Sets, Matrices and Linear Programming* (Englewood Cliffs, N.J.: Prentice-Hall, Inc., 1974). For examples of similar computer-assisted manpower deployment models, see Ernst J. Eck, "Burglary Investigation Decision Model Replication: A Multi-Site Evaluation," paper presented at the Second National Workshop on Criminal Justice Evaluation, Washington, D.C., November 1978; Chris W. Eskridge, "Predicting Burglary Offender Characteristics: Enhancing Investigation Efficiency Through the Deployment of Probability Models," *Review of Applied Urban Research* (November 1979): 1–4; Nelson B. Heller, *What Law Enforcement Can Gain From Computer Designed Work Schedules* (Washington, D.C.: U.S. Department of Justice, 1974).

25. See John Kaplan, *Criminal Justice: Introductory Cases and Materials* (Mineola, N.Y.: The Foundation Press, Inc., 1978), pp. 466–467.

Index

About the Editor

Kevin N. Wright is an assistant professor at the State University of New York at Binghamton where he holds joint appointments in general studies and political science. He is also a research associate at the Center for Social Analysis at the university. Wright's speciality is criminal justice, and his current research interests include the relationship between crime and economic adversity, community-based institutional corrections, and crime-control models.

After receiving his Ph.D. in Community Systems Planning and Development from the Pennsylvania State University, Wright taught at Lamar University and the University of Tennessee at Chattanooga. He is the author of *An Organizational Approach to Correctional Effectiveness* as well as of numerous articles and government reports.